Foundations for Software Project Management in Classic and Agile Environments

Andreas Johannsen · Anne Kramer ·
Daniela Stokar von Neuforn

Foundations for Software Project Management in Classic and Agile Environments

 Springer

Andreas Johannsen [ID]
Fachbereich Wirtschaft
Technische Hochschule Brandenburg
Brandenburg a.d.H., Germany

Anne Kramer
Smartesting Solutions & Services
Erlangen, Germany

Daniela Stokar von Neuforn
TTM Training & Transfer Management
Berlin, Germany

ISBN 978-3-032-16796-5   ISBN 978-3-032-16797-2   (eBook)
https://doi.org/10.1007/978-3-032-16797-2

Foreword by Stephan Goericke

Managing projects successfully on schedule, on budget and on quality is becoming more and more of a challenge. The demands placed on project managers are high: production cycles are becoming shorter and competitive conditions are becoming tougher. They control the budget, keep an eye on the current project status, lead and coordinate the team. They make a decisive contribution to securing the project. But how can employers be sure to select the suitable and qualified employee for this task?

Qualified project managers are in high demand in general and in software project management in particular. Those who have comprehensive project management skills are clearly at an advantage. Those who can prove these with a certificate are even more so. To ensure comparability, the business community repeatedly calls for a standard. The importance of proof of performance in the form of examinations and certificates from independent bodies has risen sharply in recent years and will continue to do so.

There is a high number of training courses, but they have different levels. It is difficult for employers to assess what they can or cannot expect from a particular certificate. So it is very important, especially for prospective project managers, that a standard is available that continuously follows a uniform concept with all important contents. It is also easier for personnel planning if the employer can rely on employees with an established project management certificate.

The International Software Quality Institute (iSQI®) is the world-wide contact point for such software quality standards. The iSQI® certification program includes, among others, the ASQF® Certified Professional for Project Management. In 2026, this certification exam will appear in a modernized and future-proof new edition of the established scheme. The continuous maintenance of the content is intended to ensure that the training meets the requirements for employees and the needs of the industry. And will continue to do so in the future. The new curriculum for ASQF® Certified Professional for Project Management is based on standards and current international norms. iSQI® independently tests and certifies according to these standards. Likewise, iSQI® works with international partners to establish the standards in numerous countries on all continents. As a result, certifications are created that are internationally recognized symbols of excellence.

The present edition of this book refers to the ever-growing importance and the continuous establishment of standards and certifications in the field of project management. The authors have further developed the standards for project management based on their previous work and have once again reviewed and recorded the fundamentals for us. I would like to thank them for their commitment and for sharing their expertise with us.

Finally, I wish all (future) project managers and interested parties a lot of fun while working through the book, good luck for the later certification exam and good success for all following projects!

Stephan Goericke
Chairman of the Supervisory Board
iSQI Inc.
Boston, MA, USA

Preface

When we came together in 2015 to fundamentally revise the ASQF® Certified Professional for Project Management curriculum, we quickly realized that a new course would also require a new textbook. No sooner said than done—and that's how the German version of this book came to life in 2017. Soon thereafter, we observed an increasing interest in an English version of the course. Moreover, the clock keeps ticking. Agile project management frameworks have not only become established—they have also changed the formerly "classical" world. Therefore, we decided to update and translate both the syllabus and the book in 2025. You hold the result in your hands.

But does the world really need another book on project management? We thought so. Although there are already many books on this topic, we wanted to set new priorities. A book that combines both sequential and agile approaches in a practice-oriented way and deals with social skills in an appropriate way is missing on the market. We wanted to write an entertaining book for all those who are more or less explicitly entrusted with software project management tasks.

"Software project management tasks"—a term with an effect like a sleeping pill. However, this is exactly what we wanted to avoid. We find software project management fascinating day after day and hope to pass this passion on to our readers.

This book owes its creation to two parties. On the one hand to the ASQF® with regard to the curriculum and content. On the other hand to the authors with regard to the form and the text. We would therefore like to take this opportunity to express our sincere thanks. In particular, we would like to mention Ewa Sadowicz and Horst Kostal, co-authors of the German version. One of the disadvantages of project management is that you are not always free to dispose of your own time. The translation of this book was not feasible for either of them. However, they deserve due credit for the content of Chaps. 5 and 6 (Horst), 10 (Ewa), and 11 (Horst).

We would also like to thank Norbert Kastner and Klaus Overbeck for their valuable assistance in the completion of the book, Robert Maurer for his editorial assistance, and Stephan Goericke for his foreword.

Anyone who has ever been involved in the creation of a book knows only too well what strain it can be for those closest to us. Without the support of our partners, without the understanding and consideration of our children, this book would not exist in its present form. Therefore, our very special thanks go to our families.

One Last Word on Diversity

We are aware that the world is colorful like a rainbow and that there are multiple forms of gender. Nevertheless, we decided to keep the text as simple as possible. Please bear with us when we speak "his tasks" instead of "his or her tasks". Of course, this includes female and diverse project managers as well. Anyway, you will discover in the book that women may have an advantage regarding the required soft skills and especially regarding communication... (signed by the female authors).

Berlin/Erlangen, Germany   Andreas Johannsen
2026   Anne Kramer
                                                          Daniela Stokar von Neuforn

Competing Interests The authors have no competing interests to declare that are relevant to the content of this manuscript.

Background

Motivation

It is frustrating: In 1972, Edsger W. Dijkstra wrote about the "software crisis" for the first time (Dijkstra 1972). In 1996, the first Chaos Report by the Standish Group appeared and showed us how few software projects can be considered successful (Standish 1996). Today, more than 50 years later, there are countless books on software development, and yet many software projects continue to run off the rails. Software is either significantly more expensive than planned, not finished on time, or still contains unacceptable errors (i.e., bugs) when delivered.

Why is that? Haven't we learned anything since 1972? Yes, we have. In the meantime, industry adopted the process idea (initially from manufacturing) also for software development. The basic idea is to clearly define each and every work step so that they are controlled and reproducible. Thus, software with a uniform, ideally high quality can be demonstrably produced.

However, software is different from hardware. For software, development and production are not largely separated as is the case with hardware. Therefore, we need processes for software development. Software engineering is now a subject of study at universities and technical colleges.

Still, spectacular failures in software projects occur repeatedly. At the end of March 2016, the Japanese space agency JAXA[1] lost its US\$ 286 million Hitomi X-ray telescope (Japanese: eye, pupil) due to an impressive chain of hardware and software errors. During a reorientation of the space telescope, the position data were incorrectly determined, leading to the erroneous report that the satellite was rotating. To stop the non-existent rotation, the reaction wheel was activated. The telescope now actually started to spin. The 10-year mission ended abruptly after three days when the solar panels broke off.

A more recent example is the CrowdStrike outage in 2024. The cybersecurity company CrowdStrike deployed a new configuration file for their cybersecurity

---

[1] Japan Aerospace Exploration Agency.

software. Unfortunately, a wrong value in this file triggered an out-of-bounds memory access, causing Windows systems worldwide to crash or enter boot loops. Over 8.5 million Windows systems were affected across all domains, causing a financial damage of US$10 billion.

These examples are of course particularly spectacular, but they illustrate one of the typical difficulties that all software projects face: Software is usually extremely complex and the interaction of different functions or systems is difficult to keep track of. In itself, programming software functions is easy, often even far too easy. This tempts to "just change something." As a rule, however, it is precisely these changes that lead to unexpected interactions with already programmed functions.

Changes are the rule rather than the exception in our fast-moving times. This evidence has led to a revolution in software development. Since 2000, the so-called "agile" project management frameworks, in which software is developed iteratively in the shortest possible cycles, have become increasingly prevalent. Knowledge of these frameworks and their influence on project management is now part of the toolbox of a modern software project manager.

Modern Software Project Management

Which brings us to the topic. This book is aimed at all employees in software projects who are directly or indirectly entrusted with project management tasks. These can be "full-time" project managers with authority to issue directives, as well as software developers who preside over their colleagues as primus inter pares for the duration of the project. In agile project management frameworks, the boundaries to the classic project manager become even more blurred, as the project team partially assumes project management tasks. When we talk about "project manager" in this book, we therefore always mean the role and not necessarily a specific person.

This book provides fundamentals that every project manager should know and understand in order to be successful. The content of the book corresponds to the curriculum of the "ASQF® Certified Professional for Project Management" (short: CPPM).

Both the "classic" sequential and the agile approach are systematically presented in this book. In each chapter, we address how the activities are implemented in both approaches. In addition, the terminology of the syllabus (and thus also of this book) is based on the "Guidance on Project Management", the international standard ISO 21502:2020.

The increased focus on "soft skills" is closely related to the target group of the course. Software project managers often have a rather technical background. But technical knowledge is only one side of the coin. Human aspects are much more important and, in case of doubt, more decisive for the success of the project. Especially software developers with lateral management responsibility must get used to the idea that their profound knowledge (e.g., of the programming language) is less decisive for success than their soft skills. They who have been trained to design software architectures and algorithms are suddenly expected to act as facilitators, negotiators, arbitrators, and motivators. Therefore, in each chapter, we also address the "soft skills" required for each role.

The ASQF® CPPM

The first version of the "Certified Professional for Project Management" (CPPM) course was published by the international Software Quality Institute (in short: iSQI®). Previously, a working group of the Arbeitskreis Software-Qualität und Fortbildung e. V. (ASQF®) had been formed to create a streamlined curriculum specifically geared to software project management. The current revision from 2025 is also due to an ASQF working group in which the authors of this book participated. The current German and English curriculum can be found at the website of ASQF:

- https://www.asqf.de/fortbildungen/ (in German)
- https://www.asqf.de/en/further-training/certified-professional-for-project-man
agement/ (in English)

In contrast to the well-known project management training courses of the International Project Management Association (IPMA®)[2] and the American Project Management Institute (PMI®), the ASQF® CPPM focuses exclusively on the basic knowledge required for software projects. Advanced topics such as multi-project management are explicitly left out in order not to burden the course. This book also follows the same logic, but provides additional hints whenever useful.

When talking about project management courses, a reference to PRINCE2® should not be missing. PRINCE stands for "Projects in Controlled Environments." It is a British project management method that has been updated to PRINCE2® around 2004 (PRINCE2 2004), and is widely used in the UK, Australia, and Europe (O'Regan 2025, p. 90). In the meantime, there is also "PRINCE2® Agile", a supplementary module that adds the most important agile principles to the PRINCE2® manual, which is based more on sequential project management frameworks.

The Project Management Professional (PMP®) certification, developed already in 1984 by the PMI®, provides international guidelines for managing projects and the project lifecycle. The exam is based on the PMBOK® guide, first published in 1996, with its 6th edition supporting agile practices. PMP holders must maintain their certification through professional development every three years, reflecting its global relevance and continuous practical application.

---

[2] The IPMA® is represented in Germany by the German Association for Project Management (GPM).

Table 1 Comparison of the three schemes PRINCE2®, ASQF® CPPM and PMP®

	PRINCE2® (incl. Agile)	**ASQF® CPPM**	**PMP® (PMI®)**
Origin	UK government and military	ASQF®/iSQI®, ISO 21502:2020(E)[3]	PMI®, USA
Flexibility	Sequential, agile, hybrid	Sequential, agile, hybrid	Sequential, agile, hybrid
Focus	Governance, control, structured processes; Agile variant adds Scrum/Kanban	People and competencies, practical guidance, essential software project management elements	Project lifecycle, processes, guidelines
Certification and maintenance	Foundation: 2–3 days, multiple choice (MC) exam; Practitioner: 2 days, MC exam; no mandatory recertification	~3 days course, 90 min MC exam; no mandatory recertification	35 h training + 180 questions, 230 min exam; recertification every three years

By now, the attentive reader may have noticed that several highly recognized project management standards provide distinct approaches for different contexts. PRINCE2®, developed for the UK government and military, emphasizes governance, control, and structured processes, with its Agile variant extending applicability to classical, agile, and hybrid projects. The ASQF® CPPM, developed in Germany and offered by ASQF®/iSQI® in German and English, is based on ISO 21502:2020 (and the German version on DIN ISO21502:2024-12). It is a lightweight, flexible framework covering essential software project management elements while emphasizing people and competencies, making it accessible for classical, agile, or hybrid projects.

The following table compares these three schemes—PRINCE2® (including its Agile variant), ASQF® CPPM, and PMP®—highlighting their origin, adaptability, focus areas, and certification requirements (Table 1).

As a summary, the ASQF® CPPM neither contradicts the other schemes mentioned nor aspires to the same level of completeness.

A Few Words About the Book

This book is divided into 12 chapters, thus following the outline of the ASQF® CPPM (2025) curriculum almost 1 to 1.

---

[3] From now on, for the sake of better readability, we will omit the addition "(E)" and refer only to ISO 21502:2020. This always refers to the English version.

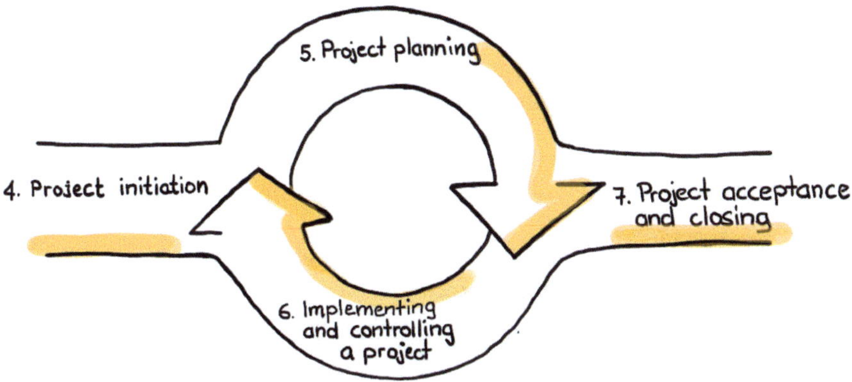

Fig. 1 Interaction of Chaps. 4–7

Chapter 1 provides an overview of the subject of software project management and contains definitions of important terms. The chapter is closely based on the ISO 21502:2020 standard with the aim of creating a uniform terminology that is also used throughout the book.

Chapter 2 deals with possible forms of project organization, distinguishing between organizational structure and process organization.

Chapter 3 describes various project management frameworks. We distinguish in principle between sequential and agile processes with their exemplary representatives "V-model" and "Scrum."

Chapters 4–7 describe the course of a project, starting with project initiation (Chap. 4), through project planning (Chap. 5), project implementation and controlling (Chap. 6), to project acceptance and closing (Chap. 7).

Figure 1 shows the interaction of these four chapters. Planning as well as implementing and controlling are usually run through several times during a project, while initiating naturally takes place only once at the beginning and acceptance and closing once at the end of the project.

Chapter 8 is dedicated to quality assurance. Here, we focus on the importance of quality assurance in projects. After all, this is not a textbook for software testers. The issue of quality assurance for processes is dealt with in somewhat more detail, since these affect the project manager at least indirectly.

Chapter 9 deals with risk management. Here, too, the basic idea of the risk management process is discussed before the individual activities of risk identification, assessment, control, and monitoring are described. A short excursus deals with risk management in safety-critical areas.

Chapter 10 is a particularly important chapter in this book because it deals with human resource management. In addition to phases and activities of human resource management, topics such as team support, social competence and employee motivation are addressed. The reader gets an insight into the importance of the human aspects in project management, which is all too often underestimated.

Chapter 11 provides an overview of maturity models and how they can be used to evaluate processes on the one hand and to improve them on the other.

Chapter 12 is the only chapter that does not have a direct equivalent in the CPPM curriculum. It contains a summary of the book.

All Chapters

The topic of "soft skills" runs like a thread through the entire book. Whenever appropriate, we address which non-technical skills a project manager needs to successfully master the tasks described in each case.

The Case Study Used Throughout This Textbook

Example As Johann Wolfgang von Goethe so beautifully said: "All theory, dear friend, is gray." Not with us! We have used a case study throughout this book, which could not be more realistic, as it is based on actual experiences of the authors.

Our case is an in-house project for the development of a platform. In other words, there was no external customer. The graphics platform to be developed was intended to be used by application and customer projects. Specifically, we are talking about graphics functions that are used, for example, to implement instrument panels for machines or vehicles.

There were two project teams in total. Seven employees developed the graphics engine, five others the graphics library. They were headed by a project manager, who was also the team leader in organizational terms. This project manager bundled all information and was the only stakeholder known to the teams.

As it happens, the project faced several challenges that could have been avoided through targeted project management. For example, up to a certain point, the project was run without documented requirements. The project manager had all the information in his head and was directing staff individually. In general, communication in the project left much to be desired. There was no discernible coordination with dependent projects. Team members knew little to nothing about the work of their colleagues, making the project extremely unattractive to them. To make matters worse, there were virtually no project management activities in terms of planning, controlling, quality assurance, and risk management.

Anyone who has worked in software projects will be able to imagine the set-up. We use this case throughout the book to show which project management activity could have helped at which point of the project.

References

(ASQF CPPM 2025): Project Management Foundations, Syllabus (EN), ASQF® Certified Professional for Project Management (2025) - Foundation Level, Version 3.0, 2025.

(Dijkstra 1972): Dijkstra, E. W. The Humble Programmer [Turing Award Lecture]. In EWD 340. Available at: https://www.cs.utexas.edu/~EWD/transcriptions/EWD03xx/EWD340.html

(ISO 21502:2020): International Organization for Standardization (ISO), ISO 21502:2020(E) – Project, programme and portfolio management — Guidance on project management. Geneva: ISO.

(O'Regan 2025): G. O'Regan: Guide to Software Project Management. Undergraduate Topics in Computer Science. Cham: Springer Nature. https://doi.org/10.1007/978-3-031-80578-3

(PRINCE2 2004): Office of Government Commerce, Managing Successful Projects with PRINCE2, (2004).

(Standish 1996): Standish Group International, CHAOS: A Recipe for Success. West Yarmouth, MA: Standish Group International.

Contents

About the Authors

Prof. Dr. Andreas Johannsen holds the professorship "System Development and Integration" since 2006 and is the scientific director of the BID research group at the Brandenburg University of Applied Sciences. In addition, he is the owner of Johannsen Management Consulting (JMC) in Berlin and has been a trainer of project management certificate courses for many years.

Dr. Anne Kramer started her career as a project manager in Paris for Schlumberger Systems. From 2001 to 2022, she worked for sepp.med GmbH as project manager and process consultant. Today, she is Global CSM and Head of Training at Smartesting Solutions & Services, a French provider of testing tools. Anne is also a passionate speaker at conferences, a trainer and author of several books.

Dr. Daniela Stokar von Neuforn has been working as an independent trainer, coach, and project manager since 1992, with a focus on HR development, communication, demographics, customer and service orientation, and train-the-trainer methodologies. Drawing on her extensive expertise in both strategic and operational project management, she has also been the owner of TTM Training & Transfer management since 2011. In addition, she contributed a substantial portion of the illustrations in this book, endowing it with its distinctive artistic character.

Acronyms and Abbreviations

AC	Actual Costs
AD	Anno Domini
AI	Artificial Intelligence
ALM	Application Lifecycle Management
ART	Agile Release Train
ASQF	Arbeitskreis Software-Qualität und Fortbildung
BC	Before Christ
BDD	Behavior-Driven Development
BGB	Bürgerliches Gesetzbuch (German Civil Code)
BP	Base practice
CAPA	Corrective Actions/Preventive Actions
CCB	Change Control Board
CI/CD	Continuous Integration and Continuous Delivery
CIP	Continuous Improvement Process
CL	Capability Level
CMM	Capability Maturity Model
CMMI	Capability Maturity Model Integration
COCOMO	Constructive Cost Model
CPPM	Certified Professional for Project Management
CPRE	Certified Professional for Requirements Engineering
CR	Change Request
CRA	Cyber Resilience Act
CV	Cost variance
CW	Calendar week
DAD	Disciplined Agile Delivery
DevOps	Development and Operations
DevSecOps	Development, Security, Operations
DIN	Deutsches Institut für Normung (German institute for standardization)
DoD	Definition of Done
DORA	Digital Operational Resilience Act
EV	Earned value

EVA	Earned Value Analysis
FMEA	Failure mode and effects analysis
FTA	Fault tree analysis
GPM	German Association for Project Management
GPU	Graphical processing unit
GRC	Governance, Risk, and Compliance
GUI	Graphical user interface
HR	Human resource
ID	Identifier
IEC	International Electrotechnical Commission
IEEE	Institute of Electrical and Electronics Engineers
IPMA	International Project Management Association
IREB	International Requirements Engineering Board
ISACA	Information Systems Audit and Control Association
ISO	International Organization for Standardization
iSQI	International Software Quality Institute
ISTQB	International Software Testing Qualifications Board
IT	Information technology
LeSS	Large-Scale Scrum
LOC	Lines Of Code
MBT	Mode-Based Testing
MC	Multiple choice
MTA	Milestone Trend Analysis
OPM3	Organizational Project Management Maturity Model
PA	Process area
PAM	Process Assessment Model
PDCA	Plan—Do—Check—Act
PI	Product Increment
PMBOK	Project Management Body of Knowledge
PMI	Project Management Institute
PMP	Project Management Professional
PO	Product Owner
PRINCE	Projects in Controlled Environments
PRM	Process Reference Model
PV	Planned value
QA	Quality assurance
QM	Quality management
RPN	Risk priority number
SAFe	Scaled Agile Framework
SDLC	Software Development Lifecycle
SFIA	Skills Framework for the Information Age
SIL	Safety Integrity Levels
SoS	Scrum-of-Scrums
SPI	Software Process Improvement
SPICE	Software Process Improvement and Capability dEtermination

SV	Schedule variance
SW	Software
TDD	Test-Driven Development
UK	United Kingdom
US	United States (of America)
UX	User eXperience
WBS	Work Breakdown Structure
Whiscy	Why isn't Sam coding yet?
XP	EXtreme Programming

Introduction

1

1.1   What Are the Reasons for Project Failure?—Criteria for Project Success and Failure

> **Stop!** Have you read the previous chapter? If not, please catch up now, because it is important for further understanding of the book and contains content that is required for certification.

As already described in the introduction, software development projects rarely run smoothly—see, for example Yin et al. (2021) for an empirical study. Often, deadlines cannot be met, costs are getting out of hand, or the supposedly "finished" software is not as advanced as expected. Upon delivery, it becomes apparent that functionality is missing or still faulty, leading to unpleasant discussions, complaints, and additional deliveries.

However, the fact that so many software projects fail also has a (questionable) advantage: It is quite possible to evaluate statistically what the cause was. A closer look reveals that many problems can be traced back to one of the following three causes:

1. Deficiencies in the process
2. Lack of technical skills
3. Communication problems and weak leadership

Deficiencies in the process occur, among other things, when it is not or only inadequately defined how work is to be done. This leads to employees doing their work to the best of their ability, but possibly skipping important steps in the process. A very typical example is the definition of a software architecture. Naturally, developers think about the architecture.

© The Author(s), under exclusive license to Springer Nature Switzerland AG 2026

A. Johannsen et al., *Foundations for Software Project Management in Classic and Agile Environments*, https://doi.org/10.1007/978-3-032-16797-2_1

> **Example** This was also the case in our case study. Unfortunately, there was no requirement that the architecture had to be documented and kept up to date. All new team members who had not participated in the initial workshop were therefore at a severe disadvantage, and the other teams lacked a binding definition of the interfaces.

Unclear interfaces are a common deficiency in the process, same as unclear requirements, insufficient coordination, or a lack of binding agreements regarding the course of action in the process or the technical implementation in the product.

Lack of Technical Skills is relatively easy to fix. If a developer does not know the programming language, you must send him to a training course and teach him. Unfortunately, it is not always obvious that there is a need for training. Those who are not familiar with requirements management or quality assurance are not necessarily aware of it. After all, you do not know what you do not know. Therefore, it is important that the project manager knows at least the basics, which we provide in this book.

Communication Problems and Weak Leadership

While the first two main causes can be avoided through technical competence, dealing with communication problems requires soft skills. A good example is dealing with conflicts. We will see in the chapter "Human resource management" that those conflicts are completely normal, especially in the team building process. Project managers should therefore know how to manage them skillfully.

It gets even trickier when we consider the topic of leadership. Here, a project manager can unconsciously do an alarming number of mistakes. Therefore, we would like to counter a widespread misconception right at the beginning: In our eyes, leading employees does not mean telling them what to do and how to do it, but rather guiding and directing them. This also includes delegating tasks.

> **Example** In our case study, the project manager acted as a "mega brain," i.e., all decisions were made by him. At the same time, however, he was regularly annoyed that team members questioned him about every little thing. Here, the decision-making competencies were completely unclear.

Figure 1.1 shows an overview of the main causes for software project failures. Often, several causes coincide, but human weaknesses are almost always involved.

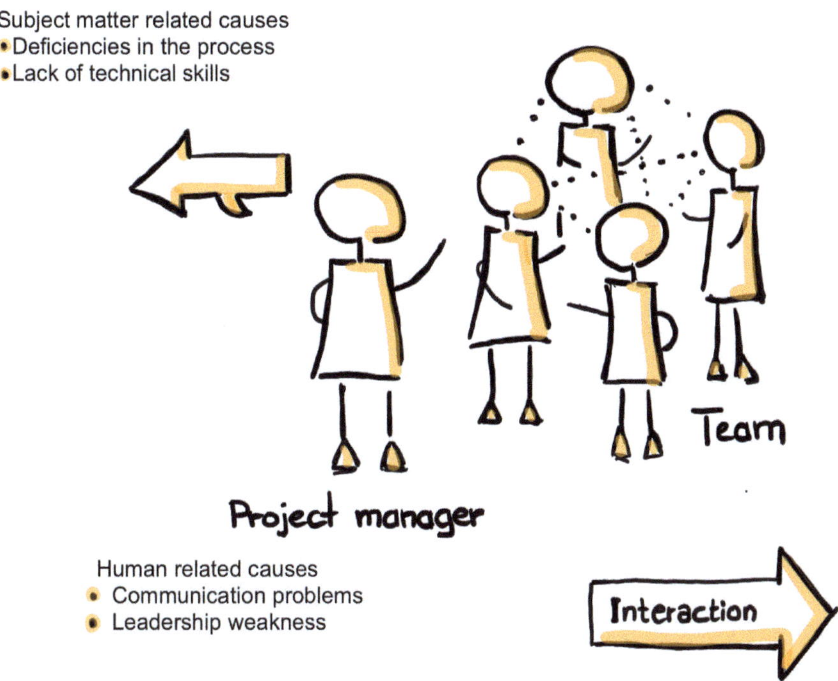

Fig. 1.1 Main causes for software project failures

1.2   Important Terms in Project Management

Since we are already in the process of clarifying terms such as "leadership," let's expand a bit further and briefly address the most important terms in project management. After all, it is a declared goal of the ASQF® CPPM to establish a uniform terminology. It is possible to discuss things at cross-purposes, for instance if everyone has a different understanding of the term "project." In the best case, you only lose time unnecessarily. However, different interpretations can also lead to annoying misunderstandings or even mistakes.

The curriculum does not reinvent the wheel, but builds on the international standard ISO 21502:2020. Some terms are important for the certification for the ASQF® CPPM. We have highlighted these in the text and compiled them again in the glossary at the end of the book for a better overview.

So, what do we mean by the term "project"?

Definition Project
ISO 21502:2020: A project is a temporary endeavor to achieve one or more defined objectives.

> It consists of a unique set of processes consisting of coordinated and controlled activities with start and end dates, performed to achieve project objectives. Achievement of the project objectives requires the provision of deliverables conforming to specific requirements (ISO 21500:2012).

As you can see, standards are not necessarily suitable bedtime reading, unless you want to fall asleep immediately. The second sentence in the box above is from the old ISO 21500 version from 2012. Translated, it means: a project consists of processes, has a beginning and an end, and is intended to achieve a predefined goal. We will talk about processes in a moment. Another part of the definition of a project is that it is coordinated and controlled. At the end, delivery objects are provided that fulfill specific requirements.

> **Hint** Many organizations use the term "project" for reoccurring product version development. Each version is seen as a temporary endeavor to add value to an existing product.

At this point, we would like to emphasize that agile project management frameworks should not be viewed purely as "project management frameworks." Rather, they arose from the idea of regulating integrated, continuous (software) product development. Agile frameworks, as we will refer to them from now on, shift the focus from a one-time, optimized project execution model to continuous, incremental value delivery (Pichler 2010; Kersten 2018). To integrate the development and operation phases of software products, the term "DevOps" has become a standard in digital product management, the potential of which for modern (software-defined) business is well summarized in (Alt et al. 2021).

> **Definition** Project management framework.
> Project management frameworks compile methods and elements of software development including project management into processes and project phases of a standardized project flow in order to achieve the often-challenging project goals as efficiently and effectively as possible (ASQF CPPM 2025).

No two projects are alike. Figure 1.2 shows a possible classification of different project types. The project management framework (sequential or agile) and other, project-specific characteristics also influence the way a project is handled. As a rule, projects are subject to several boundary conditions at once, such as:

- Fixed closing dates
- Limited budget
- Resource availability

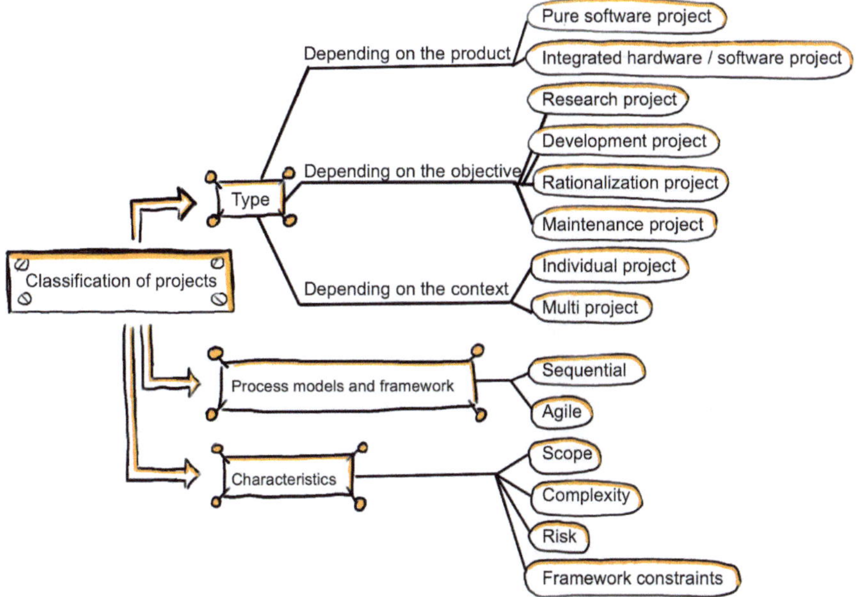

Fig. 1.2 Project classification

- Compliance to standards and laws
- Internal guidelines of the organization
- And many more

Having explained projects with processes, we also need to define the term "process."

> **Definition** Process.
>   ISO 21500:2012: A process consists of a series of interrelated procedures.
>   Software development process refers to the set of activities performed to create a software system. Input data are stakeholder requirements, output data are the created software system as well as further achievements of the project team. Project management processes determine how the activities selected for the project are managed and controlled.

By "procedures," we mean the work packages planned in the project. In this book, we are particularly interested in the software development process, i.e., the sequence of work packages that lead to the creation of a software. Each process has an input and an output. The input data of a software development process are the (more or less formalized) stakeholder requirements. The output data is the software itself, the documentation created and any other work performed by the project team.

Of course, processes must also be defined for project management. Depending on whether a sequential or agile approach is chosen, the processes or procedures that are used to manage and control the project differ. The project management processes to be applied are usually defined in the project management plan, unless they are already specified throughout the organization.

> **Definition** Project phase
>
> ISO 21502:2020: Projects can be divided into project phases. The number and names of a project's phases depend upon the type of project being undertaken, desired governance, and the anticipated risk. The phases can reflect the delivery approach or project management framework being taken, and should have a defined start and end, as well as specific milestones that relate to the decisions, key deliverables, outputs, or outcomes.

Each project should be divided into at least three phases: project initiation, project implementation, and project closing. Each of these phases comprises a number of work packages that are logically and temporally interrelated and linked accordingly in the project plan (more on this in Chap. 5). During project initiation, the foundations for implementation are laid. During the implementing phase, among other things, the software is created, and during the project closing phase, all tasks that have remained open up to that point are completed.

Longer projects should have several implementing phases so that each individual phase does not become too long. Crucial is the transition from one phase to the next, the milestone. Milestones mark the temporal, but also the factual separation of the project phases. They are a moment to pause and check whether the project is still going in the right direction or needs a change of course. The longer the phase, the greater the danger of straying far from the path.

All project phases together make up the project life cycle:

> **Definition** Project life cycle
>
> ISO 21502:2020: A project life cycle is a defined set of phases from the start to the end of a project.

Figure 1.3 shows a schematic representation of the project life cycle with project phases and milestones (M1–M5), as found in many organization-wide process descriptions.[1]

---

[1] Incidentally, the "Project implementing and controlling" phase is not subdivided in the figure, as this is intended to establish the reference to Chap. 6 in this book. On closer inspection, however, you can see from the milestones that there are subphases.

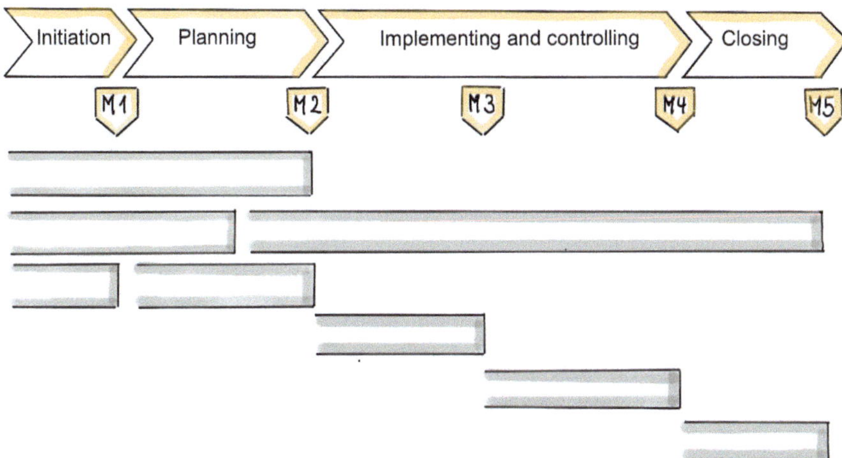

Fig. 1.3 Schematic representation of the project life cycle

> **Definition** Project management
>   ISO 21502:2020: Project Management can be defined as "coordinated activities to direct and control the accomplishment of agreed objectives. [...] Project management integrates practices to direct, initiate, plan, monitor, control and close the project, manage the resources assigned to the project, and motivate those individuals involved in the project to achieve the project's objectives.

Project management is implemented through processes that are selected and coordinated depending on the project. It makes little sense to capture requirements after the software has already been developed. However, how the requirements are captured depends, among other things, on the project management framework (sequential or agile).

In Fig. 1.3 the processes are shown schematically as half-open boxes in the lower part. A process can extend over several phases. This is typically the case for risk management. However, to be able to control the project, specific delivery objects should be assigned to the phases (e.g., the requirements specification or the risk analysis). At milestone delivery, these can then be checked at the latest and be compared with the requirements of the project sponsors, customers, and other stakeholders.

By the way, the term "stakeholder" is defined very generally in project management.

> **Definition** Stakeholder
>
> ISO 21502:2020: Person, group, or organization that has interests in, or can affect, be affected by, or perceive itself to be affected by, any aspect of a project.

Stakeholders are therefore not only people who have requirements regarding the product, but also those who may interfere because they feel threatened by the project. Consequently, it is extremely important to identify all stakeholders, to know their requirements and goals, and to manage them appropriately.

Project management is not necessarily assigned to a single person. Larger or more complex projects often have "sub-project managers" and/or project managers for specific topics. The exact division of responsibility depends on the needs of the project phases and the organizational form. The project management framework also plays a role. In an agile environment, the team members take on at least one project management task: They plan their iterations themselves. Throughout this book, we will refer to the project manager, as we use it to describe the role that is responsible for the respective subtask. This role can be shared by several people.

1.3   Software Project Management at a Glance

1.3.1   Management Practices for a Project (ISO 21502:2020)

A key challenge for the project manager is that he or she can do literally nothing without interactions with other activities. Every scope-relevant change requires replanning, involves new risks, and must be communicated.

The authors of ISO 21502 have attempted to clarify these interactions and have classified the activities of the project manager according to two perspectives.

- The so-called "management practices" summarize processes that belong to a content-related topic. There are a total of seventeen (!) management practices: planning, benefits, scope, resources, schedule, cost, risk, issues, change control, quality, stakeholders, communications, organizational and societal change, reporting, information, procurement, and lessons learned.
- The so-called "integrated project management practices" stem from the ISO 21500:2012 "process groups" and summarize processes according to the logical focus of their activities.

Table 1.1 provides an overview of the management practices according to ISO 21502:2020.

Table 1.1 Management practices according to ISO 21502:2020

Management practice	Includes all processes that are required to…	Tasks
Planning	Align planning processes and develop, maintain and monitor the projectplan and its deliverables, outputs, outcomes and constraints	• Identify and define, requirements, deliverables, outputs, outcomes and constraints in a plan
Benefits	Assist the sponsoring organization and the customer in realizing the desired benefits of a project	• Identifying and analyzing benefits, monitoring and maintaining benefits
Scope	Perform the work correctly and create the correct delivery objects (and only these, i.e., no unnecessary work or delivery objects that are not required)	• Determine and manage work and delivery • Objects
Resources	Create the environment so that the project can be successfully completed	• Determine and manage people, facilities, equipment, material, infrastructure, and tools
Schedule	Set and keep deadlines	• Schedule project activities • Monitor progress against plan
Cost	Ensure the financing of the project and keep the costs within the planned limits	• Plan and manage budget • Monitor costs
Risk	Avoid unpleasant surprises and be prepared in case of emergency	• Determine and evaluate threats and opportunities • Initiate and direct measures
Issues	Resolve issues such that there is no negative impact on the achievement of the project's objectives	• Identify issues • Resolve issues • Escalate non-resolvable issues
Change control	Control changes to the project and deliverables and formalize acceptance or rejection of these changes	• Establish a change control framework • Identify and assess change requests • Plan, implement and close changes
Quality	Create error-free, high-quality delivery objects	• Plan and perform quality assurance and control
Stakeholders	Involve stakeholders appropriately	• Identify, analyze, document and engage stakeholders

(continued)

Table 1.1 (continued)

Management practice	Includes all processes that are required to…	Tasks
Communications	Ensure that all parties involved in the project have all the information they need so that the project can run as smoothly as possible	• Plan and manage information relevant to the project • Disseminate information
Organizational and societal change	Enable the project's desired outcomes to be delivered	• Identify the need for organizational change • Plan and implement the activities needed to undertake the changes
Reporting	Provide the current status, forecast, and analysis of the project	• Plan reporting • Manage reporting • Deliver reports
Information and documentation	Enable relevant and reliable information to be available to those undertaking work and making decisions	• Identify relevant information • Store and retrieve information
Procurement	Purchase components or services, if necessary, and manage the supplier	• Plan and acquire products, services • Manage and direct supplier relationships
Lessons learned	Benefit from experience, avoid repeating mistakes and disseminate improved practices to benefit current and future projects teams	• Identify lessons • Disseminate lessons

1.3.2 Integrated Project Management Practices (ISO 21502:2020)

Table 1.2 shows an overview of the eight integrated project management practices. Although the rows in Table 1.2 are strongly reminiscent of the project phases already mentioned, they are not intended to be in a chronological order. For example, the processes from the "Closing or terminating" practice are performed at each milestone.

In general, each activity in project management can be assigned to one of the management practices. For example, determining the required project team belongs to the "Resources" practice. However, we will leave it at that and will turn to another view on project management tasks.

Table 1.2 Integrated projectmanagement practices according to ISO 21502:2020

Integrated project Management practice	Includes all processes that are required to…	Tasks
Pre-project activities	Verify the project is worth starting, and that enable a decision to initiate a project	• Obtain organizational commitment • Determine funding, authorize investment
Overseeing	Satisfy the sponsoring organization that the project team remains able to achieve the objectives, and fulfill the organization's needs with an acceptable risk level	• Involve the sponsoring organization in key decisions • Deliver periodic reporting, reviews, audits • Involve in escalations and interventions
Directing	Enable the project to continue to be relevant and justifiable	• Project sponsor confirms that organizational need is being addressed and project keeps being justified
Initiating	Start the project (among other things, the project manager is assigned to the project)	• Define project objective • Identify stakeholders • Assemble project team
Controlling	Monitor the projectimplementation and control it in such a way that the projectplans are adhered to	• Monitor compliance with content, deadlines and costs • Managing changes and risks • Monitor quality • Outsource project team and suppliers • Ensure communication
Managing delivery	Define the required outputs and outcomes, plan and implement their delivery	• Work package leader monitors, measures and controls the assigned work against the project's approved plan using the management practices
Closing or terminating a project	Complete or terminate a projectphase and in the end the whole project Initiate future improvements	• Formally establish the completion of a phase or the project • Note those activities not completed in the case of termination • Determine lesson learned
Post-project activities	Verify that the outcomes are sustainable, and the expected benefits are being realized	• Undertake review to determine the degree of the project's success • Capture lessons learned

1.3.3   Project Management Tasks

The essential task of project management is to successfully complete the project. Mind you: We deliberately speak of "project management" and not of the "project manager" because, as already mentioned, this can involve several people, each of whom assumes part of the responsibility for project activities and results. In addition, project management also acts externally. It forms the interface to the customer and is responsible for contract negotiations.

Project management takes place on two levels. On the one hand, we have the process-related tasks. Here we are talking about methods, interfaces and results. On the other hand, there are also the role-based tasks. This refers to all tasks where soft skills are important.

Typical Process-Related Project Management Tasks include:

- Maintain contact and conduct negotiations with the customer
- Define project organization
- Plan work packages and milestones
- Create project plan
- Define and monitor reporting activities
- Lead project team
- Continuously communicate, e.g., through meetings
- Select methods and tools for the project
- Monitor compliance with plans (deadlines, costs, and processes)
- Monitor costs
- Perform risk management
- And many more

In addition, project management (or the project manager and all those who assist him or her) assumes various roles, which in turn also entail certain tasks (cf. Table 1.3).

Table 1.3 Role-based projectmanagementtasks

Role	Tasks
Relationship manager (representative, leader, contact manager, motivator)	• Represent the project externally • Lead and motivate the project team • Maintain contact with stakeholders
Information provider (observer, informant, speaker)	• Observe project processes and environment • Disseminate information • Act as spokesperson for the project
Decision-maker (entrepreneur, problem solver, resource allocator, negotiator)	• Make entrepreneurial decisions • Address and solve problems • Procure and allocate resources • Negotiate contracts

Required hard skills:
- Expertise
- Methodological competence

Required soft skills:
- Social competence
- Personality
- Organizational competence

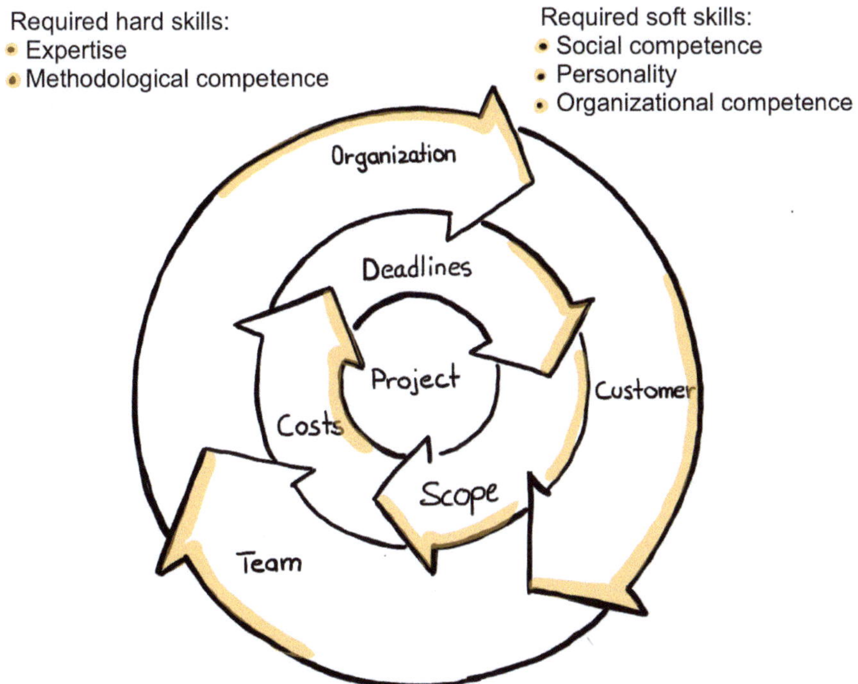

Fig. 1.4 Areas of tension in project management

It is important that the software project manager is aware of the importance of role-related tasks.[2]

1.3.4   Competence Requirements for Project Managers

Project management is a demanding task. The project manager is constantly exposed to the sometimes conflicting priorities of costs, deadlines, and quality or content/scope, which is illustrated in Fig. 1.4. If you want to deliver faster, you either have to accept higher costs, reduce the scope, or make concessions in terms of quality.

In addition, customers, the project team, and the organization also often pursue different, in the worst case even contradictory interests. The project manager must therefore constantly weigh options and make decisions. Even though it is often suggested: the customer is not always right, and for example, accepting unrealistic project goals is not doing the customer any favors.

---

[2] Table 1.3 is far from complete. The aim here is not to list all tasks in detail, but to make the reader aware of the topic.

Project managers therefore require a range of different competencies. In addition to the classic hard skills such as specialist knowledge and methodological competence, soft skills are particularly needed. These include social competence, personality, and organizational competence (see Fig. 1.4). To fulfill the role-based tasks described in Table 1.3, the manager must also be able to lead, communicate, negotiate, and to solve problems. These general management skills form the basis of successful project management. Since this topic is so important, we have devoted a separate chapter to it in this book (Chap. 10 "Human Resource Management").

The required competencies of a project manager can be divided into five areas of responsibility[3] (SFIA8 2021):

1. Autonomy
2. Influence
3. Complexity
4. Business skills
5. Knowledge

Autonomy

Good project managers have great autonomy and are not afraid to take responsibility. For team members with project management responsibilities, this means that they dare to make decisions and then stand by their actions. For superior project managers who delegate work, this means that they stand behind the decisions of their employees to whom they have assigned tasks.

Influence

Influence means that the project manager, on the one hand, influences the team in terms of the project goals, but also influences the customer and the company. Every employee in the project influences the project and the company when he or she enforces that processes are simplified, new methods or modern technologies are used. As a customer contact, the project manager can help to build stable, long-term business relationships.

Complexity

Experienced project managers are able to overlook complex problems and make strategic decisions that are consistent with the organization's goals. They understand the impact of their actions on the project, but also on stakeholders like customers or suppliers.

---

[3] The areas of responsibility are taken from the international standard SFIA8, which describes necessary competencies in the IT sector. SFIA stands for "Skills Framework for the Information Age." We recommend this standard to anyone who would like to take a closer look at the topic of competencies.

Business Skills
To a certain extent, project managers also take on entrepreneurial tasks, e.g., when they negotiate contracts with suppliers. The risk management practiced in the project also limits the organization's entrepreneurial risks.

Knowledge
The project manager should have in-depth knowledge of the industry, the technologies used and the project environment in general. In addition, the project manager should have methodological knowledge of requirements and risk management, project planning and controlling methods, and quality assurance. All this knowledge together forms a mental toolbox that helps him to master the ever-increasing complexity of software projects in terms of technology, deadlines, and quality.

The interaction of these five areas of responsibility forms the basis for successful project management. The extent to which these areas of competence are required depends in detail on the task assigned, the organization and the project environment. In large companies, a central purchasing department usually negotiates with suppliers. Here, the project manager must exert more internal influence.

1.4   Summary

This chapter provides an overview of the topic "Project management" and defines some terms necessary for understanding. The "key takeaways" include:

- Most projects fail due to deficiencies in the process (e.g., unclear requirements), lack of technical skills, and/or communication problems and leadership weakness.
- Project management is often distributed among different people.
- The international standard ISO 21502:2020 divides project management processes thematically into 17 management practices and eight integrated management practices.
- Project management consists of process-related and role-related tasks.
- Individuals who are entrusted with project management tasks require a variety of non-technical skills in addition to technical ones.

1.5   Exercises

1. Explain what factors usually cause projects to fail.
2. Name and describe three key terms defined by ISO 21502:2020.
3. Name the seventeen management practices according to ISO 21502:2020.
4. Describe the relationship that exists between the integrated project management practices "Managing Delivery" and "Controlling."
5. Name five core project management tasks.
6. Explain why a project manager should have entrepreneurial skills.

References

(Alt et al. 2021): R. Alt, G. Auth, und C. Kögler, Continuous innovation with DevOps: IT management in the age of digitalization and software-defined business, SpringerBriefs in Information Systems, Cham, Switzerland, 2021. https://doi.org/10.1007/978-3-030-72705-5.

(ASQF CPPM 2025): Project Management Foundations, Syllabus (EN), ASQF® Certified Professional for Project Management (2025) - Foundation Level, Version 3.0, 2025.

(Dijkstra 1972): Dijkstra, E. W. The Humble Programmer [Turing Award Lecture]. In EWD 340. Available at: https://www.cs.utexas.edu/~EWD/transcriptions/EWD03xx/EWD340.html

(ISO 21500:2012): International Organization for Standardization (ISO), ISO 21500:2012(E) – Guidance on project management. Geneva: ISO.

(ISO 21502:2020): International Organization for Standardization (ISO), ISO 21502:2020(E) – Project, programme and portfolio management — Guidance on project management. Geneva: ISO.

(Kersten 2018): Mik Kersten: Project to Product: How to Survive and Thrive in the Age of Digital Disruption with the Flow Framework, IT Revolution, 2018, ISBN: 978-1942788393.

(Pichler 2010): Pichler, R., Agile Product Management with Scrum: Creating Products that Customers Love. Upper Saddle River, NJ: Addison-Wesley.

(SFIA8 2021): SFIA 8 Framework Reference, Skills Framework for the Information Age, Version 8, 2021. Available at: https://sfia-online.org/en/sfia-8

(Standish 1996): Standish Group International, CHAOS: A Recipe for Success. West Yarmouth, MA: Standish Group International.

(Yin et al. 2021): Likang Yin, Zhuangzhi Chen, Qi Xuan, and Vladimir Filkov: Sustainability Forecasting for Apache Incubator Projects, In: Proceedings of the 29th ACM Joint European Software Engineering Conference and Symposium on the Foundations of Software Engineering (ESEC/FSE '21), ACM, New York, USA, https://doi.org/10.1145/3468264.3468563

Project Organization

2

2.1 Goals and Tasks of Project Organization

> **Definition** Project organization
>
> ISO 21502:2020: The project organization is a temporary structure that defines roles, responsibilities, and authorities in the project. Individuals are assigned by names to specific roles in the project organization.

Project organization enables cooperation within a project by providing a set of rules with regard to responsibilities, tasks, and rights of the persons involved. The project organization shall regulate both the static aspects (organizational structure) and the dynamic aspects (process organization) of the project. A good project organization ensures short decision-making paths and clear responsibilities.

The core task of project organization lies in governing collaboration of all project participants and partners. Everybody should know what to expect from all others, what scope and range of actions he or she has, and what he or she is responsible for. We distinguish between organizational structure and process organization. As indicated by its name, organizational structure relates to the organizational chart and the static roles, rights, and obligations of its elements, whereas process organization prescribes work and communication processes within the project and its surroundings.

Defining Responsibilities

Concerning responsibilities, project organization particularly defines:

- Which tasks and rights the individual project members possess.
- Which competencies are necessary to perform those tasks.

© The Author(s), under exclusive license to Springer Nature Switzerland AG 2026
A. Johannsen et al., *Foundations for Software Project Management in Classic and Agile Environments*, https://doi.org/10.1007/978-3-032-16797-2_2

- To what extent internal and external interfaces (e.g., sub-teams/subcontractors) are integrated.
- Which escalation paths and levels are provided.

An efficient organizational set-up of a project enables lean decision paths and transparent responsibilities.

2.2   Organizational Structure

2.2.1   Purpose and Goals of Organizational Structure

Ideally, the responsibilities and their relationships within the project are officially defined as part of the organizational set-up of the project. Basically, we are talking about defining an organizational chart, sometimes referred to as organigram. The organigram displays the responsibility and rights of the individuals and organizational entities that are involved in the project, as well as their relationships.

The specific structural organization of a project should not be confused with the structural organization of a company or institution, which we call "parent organization" to keep it simple. (Another synonym for "parent organization" is called "line organization"). Usually, new projects require the definition of a suitable structural organization that integrates into the existing parent organization of that company or institution. After all, each project is a unique endeavor, with a defined span of time, which does not necessarily fit into the "normal" structures and processes of a company.

An individually designed structural project organization enables us to perform projects effectively and in an efficient way, especially in the case of medium and large-scale projects. It enables us to reach three essential goals:

1. Establish organizational entities that are in charge of project delivery and that have been designed in an optimal way to accomplish their task.
2. Integrate these organizational entities into the line organization of the company to clarify who may or must decide what.
3. Manage cooperation (and collaboration) between project organization and line organization.

In practice, this means that several project teams report to a project manager who is neither the line manager nor the hierarchical superior of the team members—and still, it is clear who is responsible for approving their leave requests.

Which roles have to be considered by a structural project organization? Of course, the client of the project (who may be an internal or external customer for the project), the project team itself and the project management are of great importance. This applies for sequential as well as (in an adapted way) for agile project management frameworks. For the different project approaches please refer to Chap. 3.

2.2.2   Typical Forms of Project Organization in Practice

In practice, four basic models for defining structural project organizations dominate. You can read more on these four typical models in Bauer (2024), Dittmann and Dirbanis (2024), Olson (2024), or Ulusoy and Hazir (2021). Of course, it is also possible to deploy combinations or variants of the following four forms.

Project Execution Within the Parent Organization

In this case, basically nothing changes. Project execution within the parent organization refrains from defining organizational entities specifically for projects. Those departments that are relevant for the project and that are necessary will be involved. This has the advantage, that the organizational structure of the company does not need to be altered just because a project is initiated (Fig. 2.1).

However, this approach is associated with the danger of project work being neglected due to the pressure of daily business activities (or vice versa). In addition, interdisciplinary communication across departmental boundaries often suffers.

Organizing projects within the parent organization brings a set of advantages:

- No changes in the structural organization of the company are necessary ("transfers", etc.).
- Short communication paths.
- The management of the project has direct reach to the team.

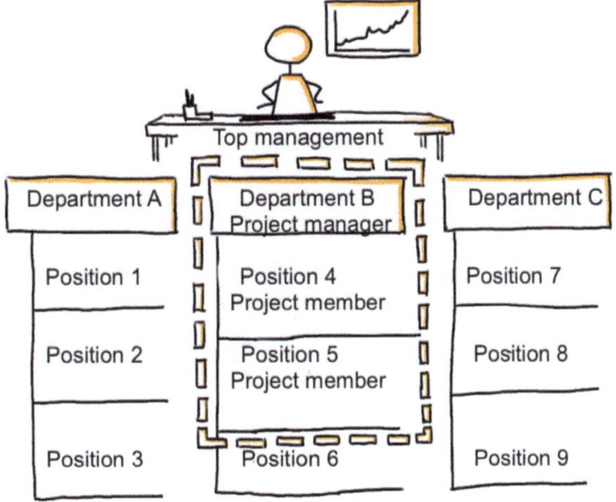

Fig. 2.1 Project execution within the parent organization

On the other hand, the disadvantages of organizing projects within the parent organization are:

- Daily business often revels "top priority."
- Subject-specific qualifications are not always existent among staff.

This form of organization is usually applied for small projects or project phases with a smaller scope. In later phases, however, it often turns out that this form is inappropriate (as happened in our example project in this book).

Staff Project Organization (Influence Project Organization)

In the case of a staff project organization—sometimes also called influence project organization—a project manager or the role of project management is existing. However, this person or role is part of an organizational staff that has no power to direct the project members. This power remains with the individual superiors ("bosses") of each employee in the parent organization. The project team members are subject to the project manager's technical authority only in the context of project work. Also, the project team members remain in their original departments or organizational entities during the time span of the project. In most cases, the project manager is located in a separate staff unit or policy unit, and coordinates the team members from this unit.

Again, in this organizational model, there is no deep intervention into the existing parent organization—except of the establishment of the staff role "project management" (see Fig. 2.2).

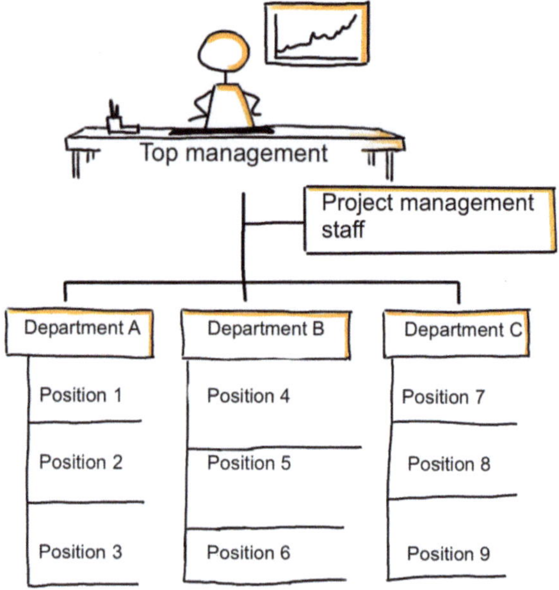

Fig. 2.2 Staff project organization

Although the project manager receives a separate staff position, or even a staff department, this organizational model can be classified as relatively effort-saving, since there are no needs for change in all other involved organizational entities.

In this staff project organization, the project manager merely has a coordinating and consulting role. The power to direct the project members still stays with the parent organization, especially for the tasks and working times outside the project, but sometimes even completely. This provides potential for conflicts from two perspectives. Firstly, the project manager depends on the cooperation of the parent organization's departments, because otherwise the project work suffers from the daily business tasks. Secondly, the project manager has to rely on the willingness of the project members to collaborate, as he has no authority to issue instructions, which could lead to a lack of acceptance.

Roughly summarized, the advantages of the staff project organization are as follows:

- Cooperation of separate organizational entities can be developed and intensified within this model.
- Only marginal changes in the structural organization of the company are necessary (project management position).

Typical disadvantages of the staff project organization are:

- Project management has no or only minor power to direct the project team.
- Often, unclear responsibilities prevail.
- There is a high coordination effort required between the departments.

Matrix Project Organization

In contrast to the staff project organization, there is no missing power to direct the project members for project management. While the project team members remain in the "chain of command" of their line organization, i.e., they still have their boss in their original department, they are under the control and command of the project manager for their specific tasks in the project. This means that general personnel responsibility stays with the department manager, whereas the specific power to direct the contents and subject matters of the project is located at the project manager. The difference between the staff project organization and matrix project organization is displayed in Fig. 2.3.

Matrix project organization hides a trap. It officially enables project team members to work in several projects under different project managers at the same time. This should be avoided, even if key personnel and key competences are rare in most companies, and thus it is tempting to allocate them to more than one project. In this situation, key personnel has to work and take over responsibility in different project settings and contexts, and has to switch contexts regularly, which requires constant and time-confusing efforts to be and stay "updated" in each project (this phenomenon is called "context switch").

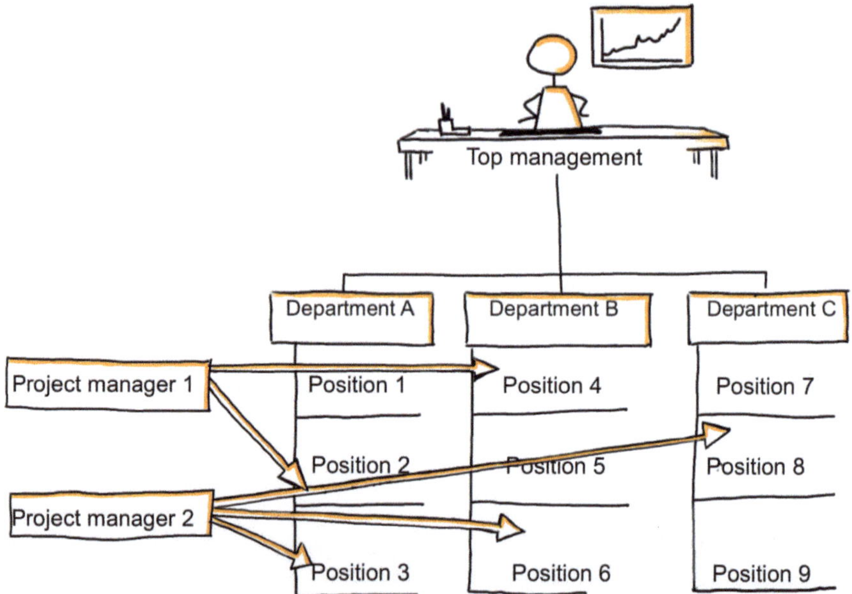

Fig. 2.3 Matrix project organization

Moreover, conflicts between projects can arise, that sometimes can only be solved by escalation to an upper level. In the worst case, the key players of the projects wear themselves out until they experience a burn-out or other problems in the medium- or long term.

In the matrix project organization, the individual project team members remain in their departments from a structural organizational point of view. Yet it is possible to form interdisciplinary teams from different departments for projects in a relatively quick manner.

Nevertheless, matrix project organization is associated with a relatively high level of communication and coordination on the side of the team members, since they have to communicate with colleagues of their own and other departments, their department heads, as well as with the different project managers in order to inform them about updates and requirements. To ease this problem, the project team members should be located together in specific rooms to enable lean communication and improve cooperation.

By the way: the potential for conflicts just described above is also prevalent if the project team member is only assigned to one project and thus one project manager, but keeps solving tasks in his department (e.g., maintenance of servers, which is a typical task in the software area that is not delegated and handed over to another person).

In situations where the project manager as well as the head of department urgently need the employee for indispensable tasks, it is hard to determine which task the employee has to perform first.

The advantages of the matrix project organization are:

- Interdisciplinary groups can be formed relatively quickly.
- Only marginal changes in the structural organization of the company are necessary (e.g., no transfer).

The disadvantages of project organization as a matrix can be summarized as follows:

- Project team members have at least two superiors.
- A high potential for conflicts exists between project and line.

Pure/Autonomous Project Organization
In the context of an autonomous project organization, all project team members are supervised by a project manager or a project management entity with single and exclusive power of direction (see Fig. 2.4). This allows to entirely focus all resources to project delivery. The project manager has the opportunity of exerting both, full personnel responsibility, and technical responsibility on the project team. This way, all project resources can be ideally aligned to realize project objectives.

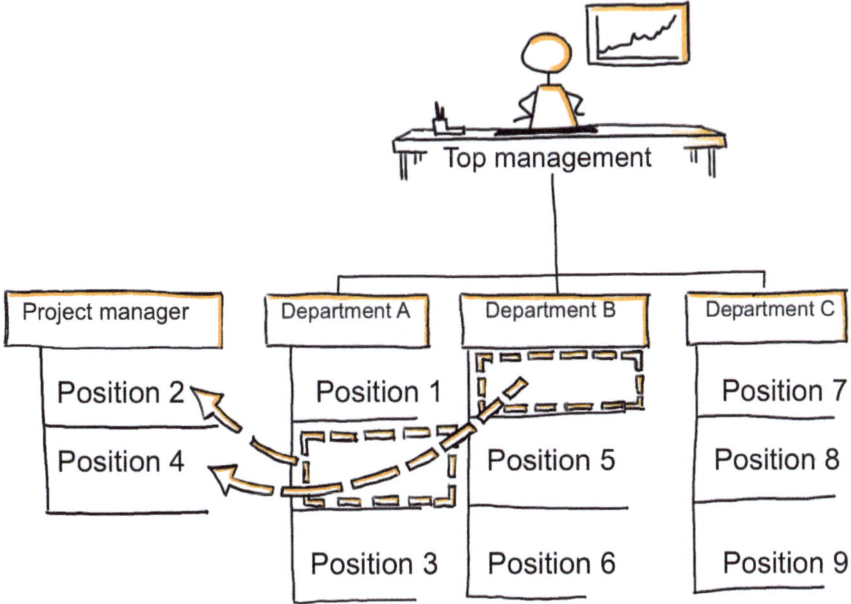

Fig. 2.4 Autonomous project organization

However, this model again entails some potential for conflict. To begin with, conflicts can arise between project management and the departments due to the fact that their employees are withdrawn entirely for the duration of the project. Moreover, employees have to be re-integrated into their departments after project closing, which sometimes triggers friction. Not everybody deals equally well with uncertainty resulting from the transfers back and forth. This could lead to increased fluctuation.

The advantages of the autonomous project organization can be summarized as follows:

- The project manager has the entire power to direct his project team.
- Within the project, short communication paths prevail.
- An optimal alignment toward project objectives is possible.

Disadvantages of autonomous project organization are:

- Disbanding of the team after project closing generates some efforts and even resistance, since structures are broken up, transfers are necessary, and loss of know-how is feared.
- A danger and tendency for duplication of work exists between project and line organization, if both are not properly coordinated.

2.2.3   Selecting the Right Organizational Model

As stated initially, for each project a suitable organizational model should be identified and selected, including the proper definition of tasks, positions, and roles. Furthermore, this project organization has to be embedded with suitable and efficient interfaces into the surrounding parent organization. Of course, the question of how to find the "ideal" organizational model arises, and which peculiar manifestation it should exhibit. Apart from the listed advantages and disadvantages of the four basic models, the following two criteria play an important role:

- Project size, as well as
- The level of interdisciplinarity, especially the number of different involved departments (and, in addition, the number of external project partners).

As shown in Fig. 2.5, the execution of projects within the parent organization is especially suitable for small projects with a low level of interdisciplinarity, while the staff project organization is rather suitable for small projects with a high level of interdisciplinarity. For projects of medium size with low (or rather low) level of interdisciplinarity, the matrix project organization fits best, while for big projects, the autonomous project organization is generally best suited.

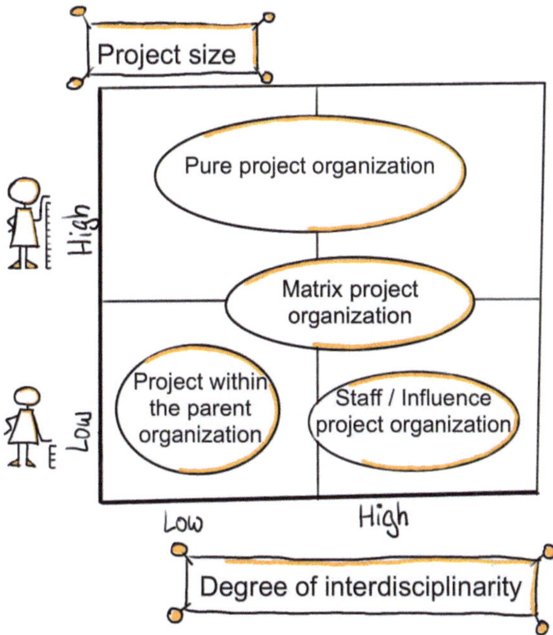

Fig. 2.5 Selection of suitable organizational models for projects

Example Let us look at our example project. The organizational model at the beginning of the project was the execution within the parent organization. With 13 project team members working over a total period of one and a half years and an average intensity of 20% of their total working time, the project had a total effort of roughly 4 person years. Thus, we classify it as a project of medium size.

The level of interdisciplinarity was low to medium, since the graphics platform played a relatively central role in internal as well as customer application projects for this IT-company.

In the course of the project, the organizational model was (among other things) changed towards a matrix due to suboptimal progression of work. The project management approach was changed to "Scrum" (see Chap. 3), and the project management role was handed over from the former superior of the team in their parent organization to a product owner and a Scrum master. Those two roles (product owner and Scrum master) received power to direct the project team.

Interestingly, the selection of a project approach (as introduced in Chap. 3 of this book) plays a rather minor role for the decision of a suitable organizational model for a given project. All of the four models above can be a suitable basis both for projects executed in a sequential approach as well as for agile projects. By the way, it is also possible (and common) to change the organizational model in the course of a project, in order to adapt to different conditions during the different project phases.

For big projects, the autonomous project organization is most commonly chosen (despite the rather large effort for establishing it). In addition, it is advisable to reflect upon the topic of governance for big projects. This makes especially sense if the outcome of the project is associated with large risks for the companies involved. The organizational structure of the project should include governance and decision committees or entities, that ensure quick and transparent information flows and decisions in the case of threatening project failure. To be precise, we speak of metrics, management dashboards, and a steering board. These elements and aspects are also part of the design of suitable project organizations.

2.3   Process Organization

2.3.1   Relevance and Goals of Process Organization

The main task of process organization within projects is to define a software development process that is best suited for a given software project, and, in turn, to properly apply this development process to the project.

Insofar, process organization within projects is also heavily determined by the software engineering approach chosen for the project at hand. We will present and discuss software engineering approaches in detail in the next chapter. In this chapter, we want to introduce the basics of process organization within projects.

While structural project organization focuses on the various tasks and executing units in projects, process organization in projects focuses on the design of workflows between the various players and departments (also known as "process design"). Here, the "grey areas" between the departments—technically speaking, we see them as "interfaces" between the positions and their tasks—must be defined and established.

For sequential as well as agile projects, the following aspects should be clarified:

- Define project interfaces to external stakeholders, e.g., subcontractors, service providers, etc.
  The interfaces become especially important during project initiation, since possible contracts, responsibilities, and communication paths are constituted.
- Organize the project infrastructure, e.g., reserve rooms, or provide of workstations.
  The organization of the project infrastructure should be planned based on the size of the team in order to enable optimal project planning. Be careful: even if your team consists only of three people, you should not hold meetings in an open-space office as you could disturb others.
- Specify a reporting system that encompasses all relevant stakeholders and has defined interfaces (to pass information in an efficient way).

Communication in projects takes place from the very beginning. Thus, this essential task should also be accomplished during project initiation.

- Define communication standards for the project and with potential external stakeholders inside and outside the company.
  This point is also important during project initiation. The HR department should be involved, as their communication tools and methods can and should be used.

The above list of tasks shows that we should definitely define the general process organization of the project before the project starts and continuously adapt it. Communication channels are established within the team and with key stakeholders, and communication channels and media are defined to ensure lean work processes without unnecessary coordination efforts or possible misunderstandings.

The persons and groups that are in any way relevant for our project (stakeholder) typically come together in different project meetings. For performing these meetings, several committees have to be installed. Project management should pay particular attention to defining and structuring these committees appropriately and keeping an eye on how they work. Project meetings are central elements of a project in which the various roles coordinate their specific tasks and have the opportunity to discuss them with each other. We introduce these project roles and committees in the following section.

2.3.2 Project Roles

Structuring tasks and positions as well as considering the required roles for a project is part of the structural project organization and has already been described. In the process organization, we need to clearly assign roles to the persons involved in the project and to consider the required coordination between the roles in detail.

Once the detailed planning of the project starts[1] a role concept for every project team must be defined. Each required role and its related tasks, rights and duties must be associated with at least one project team member. Possible roles that could be defined in the context of software projects are for example: project manager, software architect, developer, tester, quality, change and configuration manager, as well as system administrator. Of course, it is possible that the project team members take over more than one role. In small projects, this is even inevitable.

Table 2.1 shows a role concept as it is typically documented in a project plan.

In practice, the allocation of required roles to project team members is not without problems. There are roles that are difficult for one person to take on at the same time.

---

[1] In the initiation phase, at latest in the planning phase.

Table 2.1 Role concept in the projectplan (example)

Roles	Project member			
	Abel	Brown	Smith	Miller
Project management	x			
Software architecture			x	
Development		x	x	x
Test management		x		
...				

> **Example** If the same person is project manager and also (the only) software architect, as in our example project in this book, this person may be unable to cope, as each of both roles usually represents a "full-time job" in software projects.

2.3.3   Project Committees

Short and effective communication and decision paths can prevail verbally or in writing in a project. Typically, both forms exist: a regulated written report system and specified project committees, that cover specific aspects.

These committees typically exist on different levels of the hierarchy. In ascending order (from lower to higher organizational levels), we typically find the following project management committees:

- Project meetings/team meetings (daily to weekly)

  These meetings are held by the project manager and his/her team. Technical topics, (partial) project risks and the progress of the project within the hierarchical level are discussed.
- Project manager meeting (weekly)

  These meetings are necessary when several sub-project managers need to coordinate their workflows. The focus of project manager meetings is on technical and organizational issues within the hierarchical level. Project resources are coordinated and risks as well as progress are reflected.
- Steering committee (monthly)

  Project management and internal as well as external upper management hold these meetings. Possible topics are strategic decisions, financial or serious organizational problems, or risks.

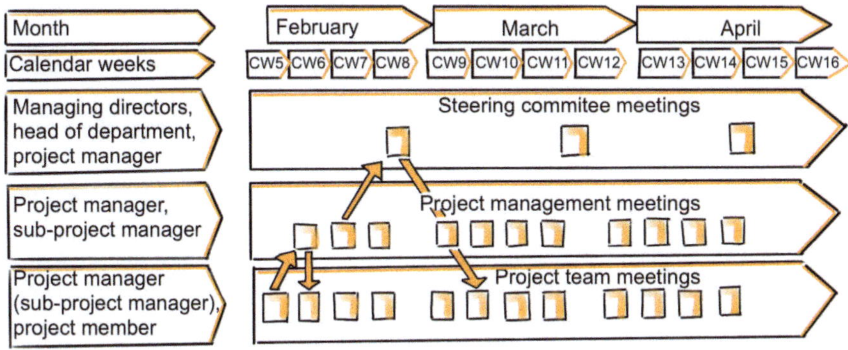

Fig. 2.6 Organization of the project process regarding committees

The frequency of the meetings indicated in the brackets are—of course—only guidelines. We wish our readers that they never manage projects where the steering committee meets several times a week.

Figure 2.6 shows a typical course of committee meetings in a project.

2.4   Summary

The structural project organization describes the distribution of tasks and established positions in a project.

Process organization of a project describes the software development processes and, in addition, the flow of information between the project team members and the project committees. As such, it is strongly dependent on the general business processes of the company, the chosen project management framework, and other project-specific aspects.[2]

Depending on the information and decision-making needs of the various stakeholders and hierarchical levels, appropriate committees are set up as part of the project organization.

2.5   Exercises

1. Please explain the difference between structural and process organization within projects.
2. Please describe, which organizational model is nearest to the example project in this book—at the beginning of the project.
3. Is the structural project organization chosen in the example project suitable for the project? What advantages and disadvantages do you see?

---

[2] We will discuss the concept of "process tailoring" later in the book.

4. Which structural project organization would you choose for the further course of the project? Please explain your choice!
5. Please explain two of the essential tasks of process organization within a project.
6. Why is it reasonable to define communication standards as part of the process organization within projects?
7. Please name three important project committees, and describe the typical information and decision paths, using two events of your choice. In these scenarios, the project manager picks up information in one committee, presents it in another committee, and the decision made there on the topic is communicated back to the first committee.

References

(Bauer 2024): Bauer, P. A Comprehensive Project Management Guide: Quality Management, Integrated Six-Sigma and Change Management Compilation. Management for Professionals series. Cham: Springer. https://doi.org/10.1007/978-3-031-68252-0

(Dittmann & Dirbanis 2024): Dittmann, K. & Dirbanis, K. Project Management (IPMA®): Study Guide for Level D and Basic Certificate (GPM), 2nd edn. Haufe München. https://doi.org/10.34157/978-3-648-16629-1

(ISO 21502:2020): International Organization for Standardization (ISO), ISO 21502:2020(E) – Project, programme and portfolio management — Guidance on project management. Geneva: ISO.

(Olson 2024): Olson, D. L. Project Management Tools. AI for Risks series. Singapore: Springer. https://doi.org/10.1007/978-981-97-1720-0

(Ulusoy & Hazir 2021): Ulusoy, G. & Hazır, Ö. (2021). An Introduction to Project Modeling and Planning. Springer Nature. https://doi.org/10.1007/978-3-030-61423-2

Project Management Frameworks in SW Development

3

3.1   Overview of Project Management Frameworks

The way in which a software product is created—that is, how it is developed—has a decisive influence on its quality. For this reason, there is a whole series of so-called process models and project management frameworks that deal with precisely these creation processes.

Note, that there is a slight distinction between "process models" and "project management frameworks". A process model provides clear instructions, e.g., on sequences of actions. The waterfall model explained below is clearly a process model. Project management frameworks focus more on structure and guidelines. Scrum is considered to be a project management framework (see Sect. 3.3). However, this distinction is somehow academic. Therefore, and for the sake of readability, we will henceforth use the term "project management framework" or simply "framework" in this book.

> **Reminder** Project management frameworks.
>
> Project management frameworks compile methods and elements of software development including project management into processes and project phases of a standardized project flow in order to achieve the often-challenging project goals as efficiently and effectively as possible (ASQF CPPM 2025).

A project management framework aims at regulating the organization of project-related processes over the entire project life cycle. Probably the best-known project management frameworks are the waterfall model, the V-model and Scrum.

Project management frameworks provide the basis and can be seen as a starting point for organizing all project processes. Using known, well-defined project management frameworks in the project has several advantages:

© The Author(s), under exclusive license to Springer Nature Switzerland AG 2026

A. Johannsen et al., *Foundations for Software Project Management in Classic and Agile Environments*, https://doi.org/10.1007/978-3-032-16797-2_3

1. They structure the multitude of necessary tasks, thus providing a guideline for daily project work, and give a certain security to do the right thing at the right time.
2. They form the organizational framework for project execution and—similar to a planned route in a street map—allow you to determine where you are within the project at any given time.
3. They have already proven themselves in other projects.

Today, there are numerous project management frameworks. The choice is therefore huge. If you take a closer look, however, you can see that there are two fundamentally different categories of project management frameworks: sequential and agile project management frameworks.

In this chapter, we will merely present the basic principles and focus on the project management frameworks most frequently used in practice: the **waterfall model** and the **V-model** as representatives of sequential project management frameworks and **Scrum** as a representative of agile software development.

The waterfall model is a model composed of sequential phases. However, it has lost importance in the meantime, which is why it is only briefly explained here. Scrum is very popular right now and is by far the most widespread agile project management framework today. Scrum is so important that we have given it its own section in which we explain the roles, processes, and work results of Scrum.

However, this chapter offers even more. As a rule, project management frameworks are not simply used "out of the box," but are adapted to the specific company and project context. This is referred to as process tailoring. As we will see in Sect. 3.4, the project management frameworks encountered in practice today are, strictly speaking, often mixtures of sequential and agile elements, so that one would usually have to speak of "hybrid frameworks."

3.1.1   Sequential Project Management Frameworks

Sequential project management frameworks divide the activities required in the project into phases which are processed sequentially, i.e., basically strictly one after the other.

Sequential project management frameworks have some general characteristics:

1. They try to reduce the complexity that often prevails in the development of large software systems to a minimum. This is done through massive "upfront" planning (advance planning of the entire project) according to the motto: "Everything that can be planned in any way is planned and therefore already determined." The goal is to have almost all open points clarified before the start of implementation.
2. User feedback often occurs only in late project phases—typically in the test phase, when parts or the entire system have already been implemented. This

carries the risk that some requirements and specifications may have been implemented inadequately, at least from the user's point of view. As it is often too late to make any major corrections, the product is nevertheless released, but user acceptance will be poor.

3. Sequential project management frameworks typically produce comprehensive planning documents and specifications during the initial phases, rather than deliverable software and other delivery objects. This is inherent to their nature. In other words, we have a document-oriented approach (in contrast to the product-driven approach of agile frameworks).

The waterfall model is a sequential, linear project management framework that is organized into several phases (e.g., requirements analysis, system design, implementation etc.). It is the "classic" among the project management frameworks, and was already published in 1970 by Royce (1970). Each phase has predefined start and end points with clearly defined results. Thereby, the phase results enter the next phase as binding specifications. The name "waterfall" comes from the frequently chosen graphical representation of the five to six phases arranged as a cascade (see Fig. 3.1).

Each phase has defined start and end points with corresponding milestones (for the term "milestone" see Sect. 5.3), that are marking the phase transitions. In newer versions of the model, feedback to the previous phase is permitted, but no jumps over several phases, for example from integration testing back to requirements analysis.

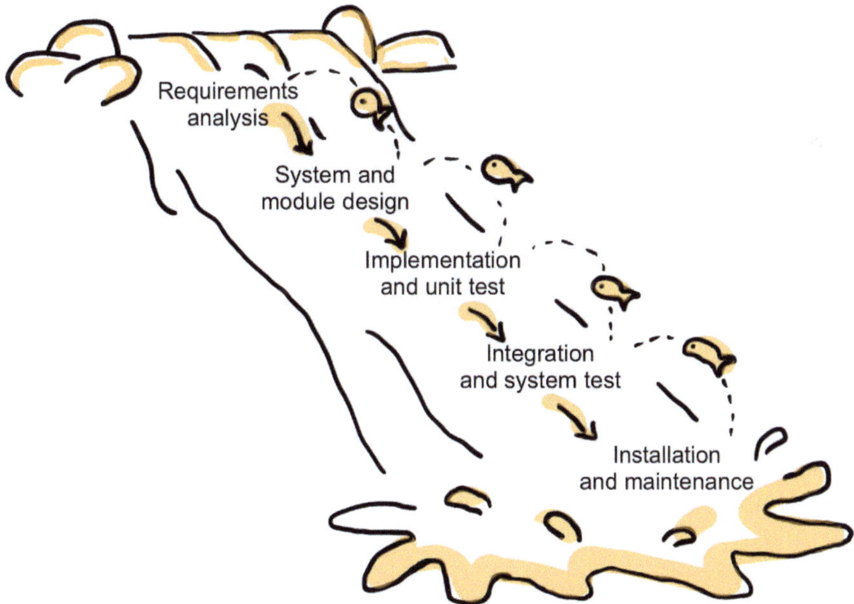

Fig. 3.1 Phases of the waterfall model

The V-model is an enhancement of the waterfall model, and was popularized and formalized by Boehm (1979), among others. In addition to the development phases, the V-model also structures the quality assurance (in particular the test activities) phase by phase. Thus, it extends the waterfall model by phase-specific test levels.

Figure 3.2 shows the usual graphical representation of the V-model. It is certainly not difficult to see where the model got its name from. On the left side we see all the phases in which specifications are created, starting with the user requirements specification, which are detailed in further phases to technical specification(s) and design specifications as basis for implementation. The actual implementation is shown in the bottom tip of the V. On the right side we find the individual test phases, in which tests are performed against corresponding specifications of the respective left side. Thus, each design level is matched by a test level in which the contents of the design level are tested. The idea behind this is to identify deviations as early as possible, since correcting them at an early stage of the project is still comparatively inexpensive.

In Fig. 3.2 two other concepts are shown, that are closely related to the V-model:

- **Verification**

  Verification focuses on the question, "Did we develop the software correctly?" "Correctly" in this context means "according to specification." In other words,

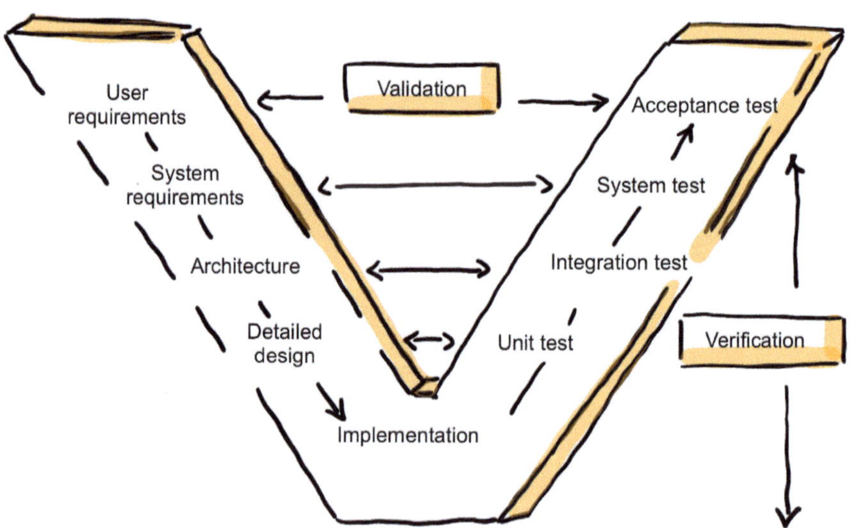

Fig. 3.2 The V-model

it is checked whether the implemented software fulfills the specified (product) properties.

- **Validation**

  During validation another question is in focus: "Did we develop the right software?" In other words, can the user goals be realized in the target context?

We will return to verification and validation in Chap. 8 "Quality Assurance."

Warning Especially in Germany, there is a risk of confusion. The V-model described in this book corresponds to the idea of having test levels assigned to specification levels, visually represented as "V." This idea inspired the German government and gave birth to an entire project management framework, the "V-Modell® des Bundes." Later, this framework became the V-Modell® 97 and since 2025 the V-Modell® XT 2.4 (Weit 2024). This framework is widespread in Germany and Austria, because it has long been the German de facto standard for public administrations.[1]

Project Management Frameworks in the European Union (EU)
The current project management framework for projects of the European Union is PM2, developed by the European Commission. In November 2016, the methodology was officially released under the name "Open PM2" in an open-access version, and it has since been made available to all interested parties, including EU Member States and the public (European Commission 2024).

Figure 3.3 shows the iconic "House of PM2," a structural framework highlighting the four foundational pillars that uphold effective project delivery. These pillars—governance, lifecycle, processes, and artefacts—form the structural supports of the methodology, while the PM2 mindsets act as archway, unifying and guiding the framework with shared values and attitude.

> **Hint** In Germany, a national variant of PM^2 exists: "PMFlex" (Bundesverwaltungsamt 2023). PMFlex is mandatory for projects involving German authorities and has largely replaced the V-Modell® XT in this domain.

PM^2 was initially a purely sequential project management framework, which is why we list it here. But even the EU is keeping up with the times. The PM^2-Agile Guide, version 3.0.1, published in 2021, represents the complete agile extension of PM^2 (European Commission 2021). Which brings us to the next topic.

---

[1] The Federal Ministry of the Interior provides the V-Modell® XT under a free license (Creative Commons BY 3.0 DE), which allows it to be used free of charge.

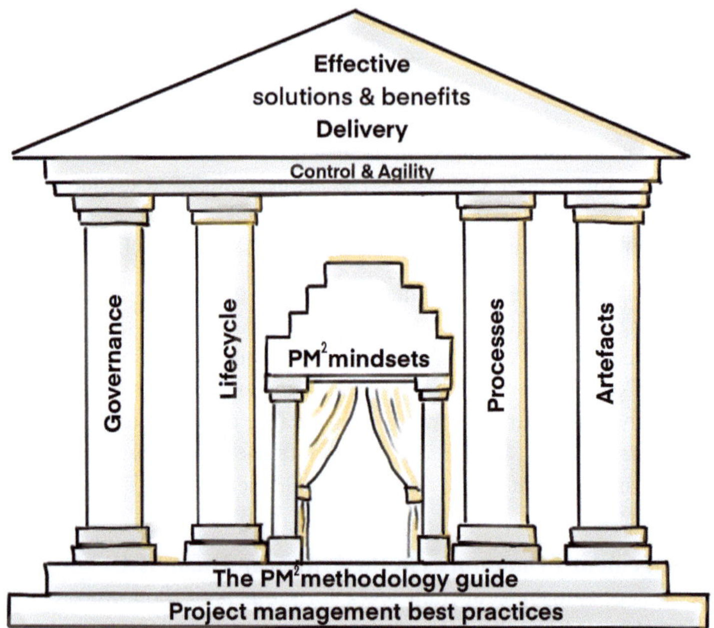

Fig. 3.3 The elements of the project management framework PM^2 of the EU

3.1.2 Agile Frameworks

Software development history has in its first decades not necessarily been a success story, as it was long associated with terms such as "software crisis." "application backlog" or "integration hell." The previously widespread—mostly sequential—project management frameworks are reaching their limits with increasingly complex systems and extensive relationships (interfaces) between individual software applications. The sequential frameworks (such as waterfall, V-model, but also sequential models to which an agile part was attached later on, like PRINCE2® or PM^2) increasingly appear less suitable for flexibly and quickly developing new applications and integrating them into existing architectures. Agile frameworks owe much of their current prevalence to this background.

Hint Don't be confused by the wording! Since agile project management frameworks do not primarily rely on structuring project processes in a suitable manner, but introduce other important dimensions, such as values, transparency, and user feedback, we do not call them agile process models but rather merely "agile frameworks" from now on.

"Agile frameworks" is the generic term for a flexible and lean development process. Agile software development focuses on delivering working software in small, iterative cycles, with close collaboration between teams and stakeholders, and a strong emphasis on flexibility and responding to change.

The "Agile Manifesto," which came into being in 2001, can be seen as the initial spark for agile software development (Agile Alliance 2001). As the name suggests, it is a manifesto in which the authors set out their fundamental convictions. The representatives of the Agile Manifesto appreciate (according to the wording).

- Individuals and interactions more than processes and tools
- Working software more than comprehensive documentation
- Collaboration with the customer more than contract negotiation
- Responding to change more than following a plan

However, "agile" does not mean that there should no longer be any documents and contracts at all. The representatives of the manifesto also make this explicitly clear. It is more a matter of weighting: although the representatives find the values on the right important, they explicitly rate the values on the left higher.

Agile frameworks assume in principle that significant parts of the requirements and the solution approaches are unclear at the beginning. Unlike sequential project management frameworks, however, agile frameworks do not claim to clarify these ambiguities before the start of implementation. Instead, they rely on the fact that this ambiguity can be eliminated by creating intermediate results. These intermediate results can be used to find the missing requirements and solution techniques more efficiently than by means of a long and abstract clarification phase.

The most commonly applied agile framework is Scrum, which we will focus on in the remainder of this chapter. But also Kanban and eXtreme Programming (XP) are used as agile frameworks today (Meyer 2014). Although Kanban as an approach is originally "lean" instead of "agile," this conceptual differentiation is irrelevant for the moment, as we focus on practice and "basic knowledge."

Kanban is originally a production process control method that can also be applied to software projects. Activities are controlled using six practices:

1. Visualize the workflow
2. Limit the amount of work-in-progress (WIP)
3. Measure and control the flow
4. Make policies for the process explicit
5. Promote feedback loops and leadership at all levels
6. Use models to identify opportunities for collaborative improvement and evolve experimentally

With Kanban there are no iterations. The core is the Kanban board, on which the work packages are physically pinned or stuck. The board visualizes the flow of activities or work packages (open, in progress, to test, done). Each employee pulls his or her own tasks. Attention is paid to ensure that there are not too many tasks running in parallel.

eXtreme Programming on the other hand, is an agile and iterative project management framework, which consists of values, principles, and practices. The values include communication, simplicity, feedback, courage, and respect. We will discuss the principles in more detail in Sect. 3.3.1 The practices include "pair programming," "test-driven development," "refactoring," "unit testing," "continuous integration" and—our favorite—"no overtime" (Beck 2000).

Both Kanban and XP have had an enormous influence on Scrum. We will later find both techniques (e.g., visualization on the board) and principles (e.g., spatial proximity) in Scrum.

The approach of Scrum is, in short, empirical, incremental, and iterative. Scrum consists of clearly defined rules. These rules define four events, three artifacts, and three roles that make up the core of Scrum. In Scrum, in addition to the product, the planning is also developed iteratively and incrementally. The long-term plan (the product backlog) is continuously refined and improved. The detailed plan (the sprint backlog) is only created for the next iteration. This focuses the project planning on the essentials.

3.1.3 Sequential or Agile?—The Agony of Choice

When should a sequential, when an agile project management framework be chosen? Of course, the respective context, e.g., factors such as industry or market and competitive situation of the company as well as the size and type of project play a role and must be considered. Therefore, the question cannot be answered categorically. The basic advantages and disadvantages as well as suitability ranges of the two are summarized in Table 3.1.

In practice, the distinction is often not that sharp. Many of the approaches and methods from the agile world are applied today as components in projects with a sequential approach (e.g., many of the practices of eXtreme programming). Especially in safety–critical domains and in projects that involve government authorities, the V-model (or its successors) with its initial requirements analysis and system architecture remains mandatory. The above table can therefore only serve as a first rough guide in decision-making.

This brings us to the next topic: the development, use, and adaptation of project management frameworks to the operational and project-specific needs.

Table 3.1 Advantages, disadvantages, and areas of suitability of the project management frameworks (ASQF CPPM 2025)

Advantages	Disadvantages	Suitability range
Sequential approach		
• Reduction of complexity by separating subtasks of the project into phases • Focus on external as well as hierarchical control options	• User feedback only after delivery of the system, leading to high costs of error correction • Separation of specification and implementation • High planning expenditure, but still low transparency on project progress/value add	• If requirements can be or must be clearly defined in advance
Agile approach		
• Early user involvement, relatively high fulfillment of user requirements • Relatively short development times to potentially shippable product • Approach that delivers executable software within few iterations • Approach in which changing requirements can be accommodated through iterative design	• Only successful if agile principles are understood and internalized by all management levels	• If the requirements cannot be clearly described in advance • If compatible with the organization's leadership principles

3.2   Company-Specific Software Development Processes

Example Do you remember our case study with the internal platform development mentioned at the beginning?[2] Initially, no project management framework was chosen. "After all, it's just an internal development" and "we know how to do it." After massive problems arose, Scrum was introduced in the project. In the end, it turned out that the way Scrum was used and "lived" in the project and in the organization was also suitable for larger tasks and projects.

This is a very typical progression that we observe in many companies. It shows us that the use of project management frameworks is helpful in structuring complex processes (and ultimately promotes project productivity) and that the general approach should be tailored to the organizational environment. The latter is commonly called "process tailoring."

---

[2] If not, you will find it at the end of the introduction of this book.

Definition Process tailoring

Process tailoring is the adaptation of the project management frameworks to specifics of the company, of the project and other factors to ensure the most suitable project process possible (ASQF CPPM 2025).

Possible factors to which the generic project management frameworks should be adapted are:

- Conditions of the industry sector
- Market conditions
- Competitive conditions
- Company mentality
- Willingness to take risks
- Development potential

The advantage of process tailoring is obvious: The "best practices" provided in the general reference processes of the various project management frameworks can be enriched with your own requirements so that they are meaningful and target-oriented for the specific project in the specific company environment.

Example Too abstract? Let us take our case study. When switching to Scrum, it turned out that one of the principles—spatial proximity—could not be fulfilled, as parts of the development were to be done off-shore. Without being in a room, however, it is difficult to visualize the work packages on the board. Software was therefore introduced to support agile development across continents.

Figure 3.4 shows the typical sequence of process tailoring, which always takes place on (at least) two levels:

- first at corporate level (this is where process and program management at company level, that is, for all projects is called upon), and
- then at project level (requiring project management).

Direct and unreflected adoption of the standard process with all its process parameters (left arrow) is generally not recommended. One of the most important strategic tasks of project management is to constantly review and adapt the project management framework and the associated project processes. Process tailoring takes place in close communication with other stakeholders and by no means only concerns "processes" in the narrow sense: methods, tools, and artifacts used in the project must also often be adapted to various factors, and must also be further developed at company level.

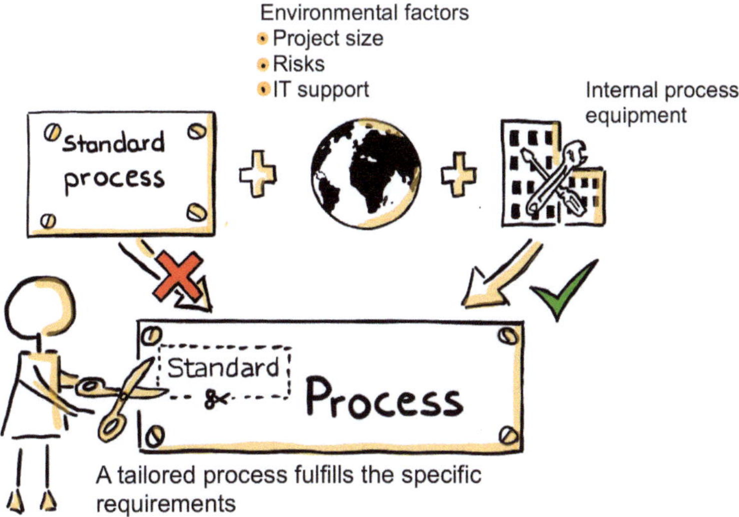

Fig. 3.4 Process tailoring procedure

3.3 Agile Frameworks Using the Example of "Scrum"

Agile project management is fundamentally characterized by the fact that communication and interaction of the people involved come to the fore. The basics and history of Scrum can only be briefly introduced here. Details are provided in other books and training courses, see e.g., Schwaber and Beedle (2002), as well as Beck (2000).

The term Scrum actually comes from the vocabulary of rugby and means something like "crowd." Scrum was first introduced at a scientific conference in 1995 by Ken Schwaber and developed together with Jeff Sutherland (Schwaber 1995).

3.3.1 Principles—What Characterizes Agile

All agile frameworks (including Scrum) share the guiding principles that were mainly and most clearly defined for eXtreme Programming (XP). These include:

- Rapid feedback
- Expect simplicity (from the team) and seek it yourself
- Incremental change
- Accept change
- Quality work
- Open communication

Rapid feedback means working with fast and honest feedback, both in relation to the evolving product (especially through early and repeated testing!), as well as within the project team and toward the customer.

Expect and seek simplicity, as a principle, means that you should always look for the simplest solution in both design and implementation, and you do not address things that are planned for later releases at the current time. In other words, you want to eliminate the work you do not *have to* do.

The two principles of incremental change and acceptance of change go hand in hand and dictate that adjustments to the product after each iteration are not only possible, but intended and welcome—even in late project phases! By improving in small steps (increments), it becomes possible to recognize more quickly whether the product development is on the right track.

Quality work is another guiding principle and also deserves an explanation here. It could be misleadingly assumed that speed takes precedence over quality in the agile world. The opposite is the case: quality (in the sense of conformity with customer expectations) is not up for discussion, which has to be ensured by close and repeated customer feedback, among other things.

Open communication in all directions—within the project team as well as with stakeholders, across hierarchical, social, functional, and local boundaries—is probably the most important principle without which successful agile software development cannot function. The classic "software nerd" who programs alone, omnisciently and turns in his code at the end is slowly dying out in the agile world (we will come back to this in the section "Scrum and agile human resource management").

In Scrum, nine elements can be identified, which are illustrated in Fig. 3.5.

The new concepts and roles in Fig. 3.5 show how the management and project culture as well as the basic understanding change on the way from sequential

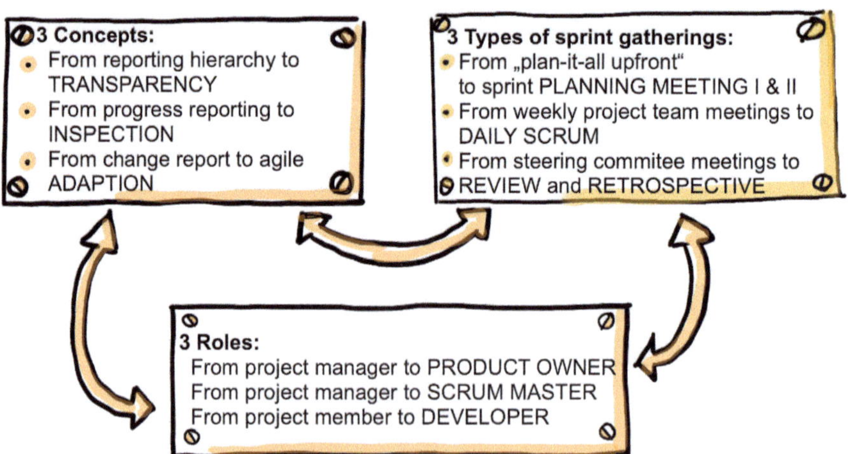

Fig. 3.5 Nine elements of Scrum, contrasted to sequential frameworks

to agile project business. Phase-oriented project management is characterized by reporting hierarchies, progress and change notifications, and a clear separation of responsibilities (management by one or more project managers at one level and execution by the developers at the other level). In contrast, in the agile world, transparency, (self-)review, and rapid adaptation to changes in requirements are the defining principles, which require integration of project management tasks into other project roles.

Also the way in which information is exchanged and important decisions are made is changing. In Scrum, regular sprint planning meetings with the team replace the upfront-planning formerly done by the "almighty" project manager. The typical weekly status meetings give way to a brief daily exchange within the team (Daily Scrum). At the end of the sprint, a sprint review is conducted to evaluate the sprint results, and a sprint retrospective to review the team efficiency and cooperation. These two gatherings are mandatory to ensure early feedback not only on product quality, but also on the development process itself.

Below, we elaborate on each of the nine elements in Fig. 3.5 in detail.

3.3.2 Concepts—The Agile Strategy

Scrum is based on three essential agile concepts: transparency, inspection, and adaptation. These are concepts that form the theoretical pillars of Scrum.[3] These three pillars come from the theory of empirical process control. It states that a complex system can be developed successfully if the status of the solution is always transparent, this can be checked in small, manageable steps, and adapted at short notice. This reminds us, for example, of the Deming Cycle (PDCA)[4] and other concepts of quality assurance and continuous improvement. The concepts are now briefly explained in the context of Scrum:

- **Transparency**

  Product development processes are transparent when the processes and, above all, their results are visible at any time to the person monitoring them. In Scrum, this means that the duration of many project processes is limited (socalled "time-boxing"), in order to be able to examine their intermediate results. In addition, it is clearly defined in advance when a process result is to be considered "completed." This definition, which is agreed upon by the team ("Definition of Done") usually includes not only programmed functionality but

---

[3] Scrum is partly inspired by the Toyota Production System (TPS) and the lean management approach, as well as its variant Kanban. (See Meyer 2014, pp. 133–137) for a brilliant comparison between Scrum, lean and Kanban.

[4] The Deming Cycle was developed by William Edwards Deming and includes the phases "Plan", "Do", Check" and "Act", which are widely used in quality management today (Deming 1982).

also at least successful testing of the code/unit tests based on previously agreed acceptance criteria from the user's perspective.

- **Inspection**

  Scrum differs from classic project management frameworks in that project progress is not simply queried and reported upwards, but is regularly inspected on a daily basis (with regard to progress) and bi-weekly (i.e., depending on the sprint length) for the product to be developed.

- **Adaptation**

  This concept refers to the culture of flexible adaptation (measured against previous or new requirements). It refers to results, processes, or methods that can no longer be tolerated. Scrum prescribes four events for inspection and adaptation: sprint planning, Daily Scrum, review, and retrospective.

3.3.3 Roles—Who is Responsible for What?

The goal of Scrum is to form project teams that organize themselves independently. According to Schwaber's and Sutherland's guide (Schwaber and Sutherland 2020), Scrum recognizes only three roles: the product owner, the developers, and the Scrum master. Taken together, these roles make up the entire so-called "Scrum Team."

Product Owner

The product owner has the task of defining the development goal and managing the project budget. He or she defines and prioritizes the so-called product backlog in which all task packages are recorded and for which he alone is responsible. Unlike in sequential project management frameworks, however, the product owner does not assign the task packages to individual team members. The team itself is responsible for this.

The main task of the product owner is to optimize the business value of the project result. In other words, he is responsible for the financial success of the product development, and should therefore see himself primarily as a "product visionary" and less as a project manager. A project manager in the classic sense (i.e., in the sense of a sequential project management framework) sees himself primarily as a controller of the scheduled execution of a project with a predefined goal. Since a completely predefined project goal does not exist in Scrum, the classic role of project management cannot be transferred entirely to the product owner but is distributed among several Scrum roles.

The product owner has a difficult and time-consuming task. He represents the customer and acts as the sole—in the best case constantly available—contact person for the project team. In this way, he can protect the project team from too much influence from the customer or management. He must create the product vision, identify, and prioritize stakeholder requirements, create a release plan, and approve or reject the releases at the end of each sprint. This is usually a "full-time job" for one person. Scrum explicitly prohibits this role from being delegated to a committee. Whether this is feasible in practice—we will get to that later.

Developers

The role "developer" includes all persons involved in the development. At the beginning of each sprint, the developer independently select work packages from the prioritized product backlog whereby packages are always drawn "from the top" (i.e., starting with the highest priority). The developer then break down the work packages into individual tasks and commit to completing them by the end of the sprint. Scrum does not provide for a hierarchy in the overall team (= product owner, scrum master and developer) and recommends a team size of three to max. nine people (ten in the latest version of the Scrum Guide 2024).

Apart from the product owner and the scrum master, all other team members are called "developers," even if the team should be interdisciplinary. The team is highly self-responsible and should organize itself. Since the team is supposed to see itself as a unit, it is explicitly intended that developers should work full-time on the project. What makes sense in theory often proves difficult to implement in practice, since long-standing experts often experience a "multi-project daily routine." In addition, the team should have a uniform and open workspace, both in physical and virtual space (= Internet). Only then can it really fulfill the team role according to Scrum.

Scrum Master

The Scrum master has the task of constantly monitoring compliance with the Scrum procedure. He should not be the product owner. Instead, he is a servant leader and the "protector" of the developers. In particular, he must prevent the product owner from making too many detailed planning specifications or exerting influence on the estimates and work of the team.

During a sprint, the Scrum master shields the team from new requirements or reprioritizations by the product owner so that they can work in peace. He is committed to the team and supports it in terms of the meaningful implementation of all Scrum processes and methods during the project. He controls the compliance with the principles, values, and rules of Scrum, and helps the team to organize itself. In short, he acts as "master of ceremonies" for the Scrum process.

The Scrum master has no authority to issue directives, but rather a comprehensive coaching role. He is supposed to remove all obstacles that can arise during the implementation of Scrum processes and that stand in the way of the project's success from the team's perspective.

Regarding the roles in Scrum, it can be rightfully stated that they are partially turned upside down and redesigned compared to classic approaches. In particular, managers in an agile environment are no longer distributors of orders, but rather explicit service providers and enablers for the project members. In the agile approach, responsibility, autonomy, and competence are shifted "downwards."

The importance and consequences of this role design will still shine through in many places in this book, for example in project planning and control as well as in human resource management.

3.3.4 (Sprint) Elements—The Sprint Flow

The overall system to be developed is created in successive iterations, which are called " sprints " in Scrum. The aim is to hand over to the customer a new software version at the end of each sprint. In Scrum language, these versions are called "increments."

> **Short Definition** Sprint
>
> According to Scrum, products are developed in iterations, so-called Sprints (ASQF CPPM 2025).

Sprints in Scrum have a consistent duration of usually 2–4 weeks.[5] "Consistent" is important in this context. Although the sprint length can be adjusted during the project, it should be kept as constant as possible.

Basically, according to the "time-boxing" principle, all mandatory meetings in Scrum should also have a maximum duration (i.e., planning meetings, daily Scrums, review, and retrospective). Each sprint runs in three phases, which are shown in Fig. 3.6. It starts with the sprint planning, followed by the sprint work phase, and ends with the sprint review and retrospective. During the work phase, a Scrum team should not be disturbed from the outside. We can now refine our initial, brief definition of a sprint.

> **Long Definition** Sprint
>
> A sprint is a time-boxed iteration (of fixed duration, typically 2–4 weeks) that serves as the container for all Scrum events, during which the Scrum team works to deliver a usable, ("Done") increment that advances the project goal, and which enables regular inspection and adaptation (Schwaber and Sutherland 2020, p. 7).

In the iterations, the work packages are distributed according to the pull principle.

The developers decide for themselves how much work and product parts they want to deliver within a sprint. Thus, each developer has control over what he or she gets as tasks. Before the first sprint can begin, of course, it must be

---

[5] Again, we find the concept of "time-boxing."

Fig. 3.6 Sprint flow: process of a sprint and the most important artifacts

at least roughly clarified what the development is intended to achieve. The so-called product backlog serves this purpose, often together with a product vision document.

At the beginning of a Scrum project, the product owner must describe the vision with a short description of the product, the basic architecture, and the design ("high level design"). In addition, a rough effort estimation takes place and a schedule for possible releases is set up. Then it should be decided whether the project should go into the first sprint.

As soon as this business decision has been made, the product backlog is created by the product owner (if necessary, with other stakeholders, especially the customer). For this purpose, so-called user stories are usually collected and prioritized. As we will see in a moment, user stories are requirements formulated in a certain way. However, Scrum does not prescribe the use of user stories. The Scrum Guide only mentions "product backlog items" in general.

If the product backlog contains some sufficiently clarified items, the first sprint can begin. Each sprint consists of three key activities: sprint planning, daily Scrums, and review/retrospective (see Fig. 3.6).

- **Sprint Planning**

  Sprint planning entails at least one, but usually two planning meetings (sprint planning meeting I and II). In the sprint planning meeting, the team decides which user stories from the product backlog are to be processed in this sprint (definition of the sprint backlog).

- **Sprint Working Period**

  During the working period, in which the development goals are implemented, the team meets daily for the so-called "Daily Scrum." In this short meeting, each team member gives a short summary of the previous day, informs the team about the planned activities of the current day and addresses any disruptive factors. The aim of the meeting is to inspect progress toward the sprint goal, trigger necessary adjustments of the product backlog and the planning, and to address impediments.

The Daily Scrum is time-boxed and should not exceed 15 minutes. To keep it from getting too comfortable, it is conducted standing up (especially for local team members), which is why it is also known as the "Daily Stand-Up." The Scrum master facilitates the Daily Scrum if necessary and takes care of the disruptive factors. Theoretically, the product owner has no authority to make decisions related to the sprint scope during the ongoing sprint working period. Exceptions should be limited to extreme cases, e.g., if the product owner prevents developers from working on outdated user stories.

- **Sprint Review and Retrospective**

  The result of the sprint is always a shippable increment or a release that comprises the sum of all increments completed to date. At the end of the sprint, the newly developed functionalities are presented to the customer or—if not available—to the product owner (and to other key stakeholders, if possible) in a sprint review and approved by them.

The purpose of the sprint review is to inspect th**Planning**e achieved outcome of the sprint and determine future adaptations. Of course, it can also happen that the product owner does not accept the results. In this case, rework must be done in the next sprint.

After the sprint review, a sprint retrospective is held to analyze what can be improved in the project during the next sprint. The focus of this meeting lies on team dynamics and continuous improvement, not on product quality. Here, the team can express improvement requests that may affect both the organization and the processes. For example, the team can request that the colleague from the opposite corridor finds a place in the team room. It is part of the Scrum master's job to implement these requests.

3.3.5 Scrum Meetings

Sprint Meetings

The sprint begins with sprint planning activities. According to Sutherland (2014, pp. 60–64), this consists of either one meeting with two sessions, or two separate meetings, sprint planning meeting I and II (Table 3.2).

While the first sprint planning session focuses on "what" to work on in the current sprint (i.e., which user stories from the product backlog and how much effort is likely to be required per user story), the second sprint planning session focuses on "how" to proceed in the sprint, i.e., which tasks result from the individual user stories and how much time these tasks require.

For effort estimation, the Scrum team uses a special, playful estimation method: the so-called planning game (better known as "planning poker"), which we will discuss in more detail in Chap. 5 (Table 3.3).

The result of the sprint planning session II is thus an updated sprint backlog and a corrected forecast of the sprint goals, and associated with this a promise ("commitment") of the team to the product owner.

Table 3.2 Overview of the sprint planning meeting I

Key data—sprint planning I	
Target	Iteration planning
Duration	5% of the sprint length
Subject	"What shall be developed?"
Participants	Product owner, Scrum master, team, (possibly later users)
Content	• Define sprint goals • The product owner shows prioritized stories • Team appreciates stories • Team selects stories for the sprint
Output	Sprintbacklog

Table 3.3 Overview of the sprint planning meeting II

Key data—sprint planning II	
Target	Iteration planning
Duration	5% of the sprint length
Subject	"How shall the product be developed?"
Participants	Scrum master, team
Content	• Define tasks • Estimate tasks
Output	Updated sprintbacklog

Standup Meeting/Daily Scrum

In the actual sprint work phase only daily "stand-up" meetings ("Daily Scrums") are mandatory (Table 3.4).

Sprint Review

At the end of the sprint, the Scrum master schedules a sprint review meeting. During this sprint review, the team presents the sprint results to the product owner and, if applicable, to other stakeholders, as they were defined in the "sprint backlog" at the beginning of the sprint. Important: Unstable or untested functionalities are not presented and are considered as "not delivered," because they do not meet the "Definition of Done"! (Table 3.5).[6]

In practice and in larger Scrum projects with extensive development environments and architectures, the requirement for the "shippable increment" for the first sprints can hardly be met, as it often takes up to two weeks for the project-internal development platform to be installed and configured. However, this does not diminish the usefulness of the "shippable increment" requirement for the first sprints as well, since the efforts are now transparent. It prevents the all too human temptation for developers to spend weeks setting up complex technical development environments instead of starting to implement functionalities.

Table 3.4 Overview of the daily scrummeeting

Key data—daily scrum	
Target	Team communication
Duration	Max. 15 min
Subject	"What did I achieve yesterday? What do I have planned for today? What do I need for it?"
Participants	Scrum master, team
Content	• Activities performed and planned • Impeding environmental factors
Output	None (pure exchange of information)

---

[6] See Sect. 3.3.2 on page 43 for details on the "Definition of Done."

Table 3.5 Overview of the sprint review meeting

Key data—sprint review	
Target	Increment feedback
Duration	2.5% of the sprint length
Subject	"What did we accomplish?"
Participants	Team, Scrum master, product owner (possibly also other stakeholders such as customer or later users)
Content	• System demo • Revision according to the sprint targets • Review of release burndown • Obtain customer feedback • Definition of changes for next sprint
Output	Sprintbacklog review list

Sprint Retrospective

The sprint review meeting should not be confused with the "sprint retrospective." The sprint retrospective is conducted to analyze improvement potentials in the Scrum project as a whole and especially in team collaboration. This is where the concept of adaptation introduced above comes into play, not only in relation to the product ("review"), but first and foremost regarding the team process (Table 3.6).

In the retrospective, the team can determine its "velocity" as a perceived rhythm of joint development, in effect observable as the number of user stories, work packages, or more generally, "story points" that it achieves per sprint. (We will elaborate on "story points" later in this chapter.)

The sprint retrospective is of enormous significance for the learning processes and autonomy of the Scrum team. Teams that consciously use the retrospective

Table 3.6 Sprint retrospective overview

Key data—Sprint retrospective	
Target	Improvement of teamwork
Duration	5% of the sprint length
Subject	"What can we do better/easier?"
Participants	Scum Master, team, optionally the product owner
Content	• Explain rules and procedures • Data collection (subjective/objective) • Analysis (root causes) • Action items • Agreements for the next sprint • Personal views • Relationships within the team/externally • Processes, meetings, tools
Output	Improvement list ("impediment backlog")

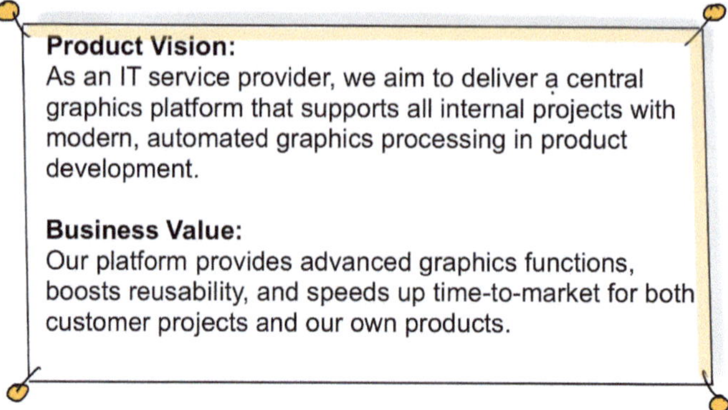

Fig. 3.7 Example of a product vision in our case study

to systematically increase their "velocity" from sprint to sprint can achieve significantly higher productivity and quality than other project teams. To transfer the insights from the previous sprint to the next sprint, the "Impediment Backlog" is a useful artifact, provided that it is actually taken into account at the start of the following sprint.

3.3.6   Scrum Artifacts

In this section, we want to deal with the most important Scrum artifacts[7] from the product vision to the Scrum task board. We do this in concrete terms and with examples, because even agile software development is not possible without documents and materials!

Product Vision
The product vision document can be seen as the motivation and at the same time the business case for the software product to be developed. It is created by the product owner, but extensive customer input is usually necessary. Although the product vision is not one of the artifacts required in the Scrum standard, it is a very important document, because the Scrum team and all stakeholders should have understood and acknowledged the vision as the project goal (Fig. 3.7).

---

[7] "All documents and materials created during the development process of a software product are called "Artifacts" (for a more detailed account, see Jacobson (1999).

User Stories

> **Definition** User story
>
> User stories are used in agile project management frameworks for the specification of requirements by the later users of the system (ASQF CPPM 2025).

User stories are requirements for the software product described by customers or stakeholders of the project with an added value from the user's perspective, which are documented as specifically as possible. They are deliberately formulated in everyday language. They should be formulated in the form of statements with a specified structure:

As a (who wants to accomplish something)

I want to (what they want to accomplish)

So that (why they want to accomplish that thing)

Part of the concept of user stories is that acceptance criteria and suitable test cases are also defined for each user story to be able to assess the implementation of the user stories as accurately as possible later. The underlying agile methods are the "Definition of Done" and "test-driven development."

> **Example** In our case study, a possible user story would be: "As a product manager, I want to use the Gouraud Shading feature so that I get smooth graphics."

Product Backlog

The product backlog is created by the product owner and continuously developed, i.e., new content is usually constantly added and the existing content is reprioritized.

> **Definition** Product Backlog
>
> A list of backlog items representing the requirements of the software or solution to be developed within the project (Schwaber and Sutherland 2020).

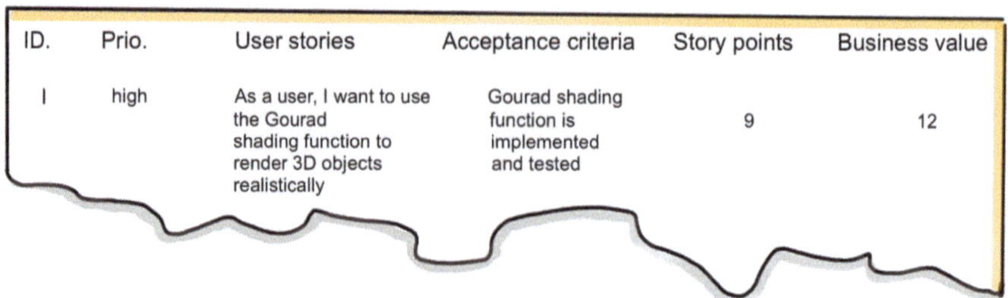

Fig. 3.8 Example of a product backlog (simplified)

To be more precise, the product backlog is a collection of all (currently) known requirements for the system to be developed within the project. Generally speaking, it contains backlog items, usually in the form of user stories. The notion of "user stories" originally comes from eXtreme Programming. Scrum is quite flexible in this respect and does not prescribe what the product backlog should look like. Accordingly, the Scrum Guide refers rather neutrally to "backlog items" (Schwaber and Sutherland 2020). The requirements could therefore also be entered in the product backlog in a different structure and according to other rules. Besides user stories it can also contain so-called "Epics."

Epics are requirements descriptions that combine multiple user stories because they are too large to be exhaustively described in a single user story. An epic often has such a large functionality that it requires too much effort for a single sprint. Therefore, it is usually split into multiple user stories later.

Figure 3.8 shows an entry in the product backlog from our sample project. In addition to its brief description and the acceptance criteria already discussed above, a product backlog entry includes an estimate of the associated effort (in so-called "story points," which we will explain later) and the business value.

How can you determine which user stories are important and should be implemented first and which should be postponed to later sprints? Answer: The product owner prioritizes them according to their business value and consequently defines a processing sequence for the upcoming sprints.

Sprint Backlog

As soon as the development team selects the user stories of the product backlog according to their prioritization for processing in the upcoming sprint, the sprint backlog is created. The team derives the "tasks" for the upcoming sprint from the sprint backlog elements. A task is always pulled for implementation by a team member according to the pull principle and runs through a regulated workflow from "Open/ToDo" to "Finished/Done."[8]

Only the project team decides which backlog elements it wants to work on in the upcoming sprint. After all, the team knows best which tasks are required

---

[8] Of course, the exact terms may vary depending on the project.

User story ID	Task ID	Task	Estimation	Assignee
01	03	Read specification and compare it to the story	5	Miller
01	04	Refining design	8	Brown

Fig. 3.9 Example of a sprint backlog

for their implementation and how long they will take. Therefore, it must not be overruled (Fig. 3.9).

Sprint Burndown

A sprint burndown chart illustrates the remaining workload in the sprint. It shows the ideal trend and the actual workload distribution of all tasks during the sprint so far. The sprint burndown should be updated once a day so that the progress can be visualized permanently. It implements two agile concepts at once: transparency and inspection (Fig. 3.10).

Fig. 3.10 Example of a sprint burndown chart

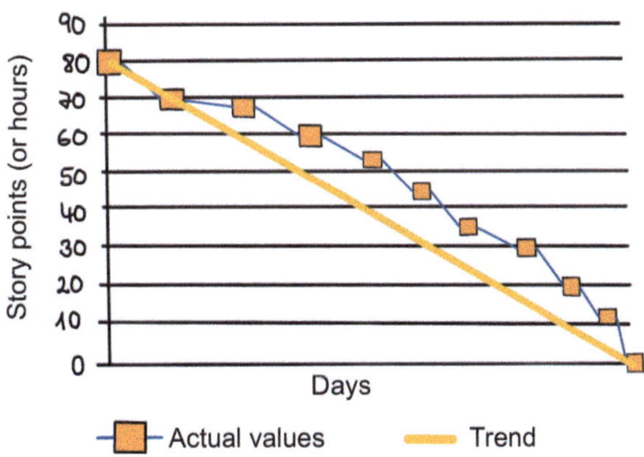

Both burndown charts (also the release burndown chart below) can use the unit "hours." In many Scrum projects, efforts are estimated by using the concept of "story points." These are more or less arbitrarily defined units that are used by the developers to estimate the size of a user story.

Definition Story Points

A relative unit of measure used by the development team to estimate the effort needed to complete a product backlog item, typically a user story (Cohn 2005, p. 36).

The remaining effort is usually expressed in story points, which have the advantage over hours that they quantify the size of the task, or complexity, of a user story, regardless of time. After all, an experienced team of developers may implement a user story in half the time compared to another, relatively inexperienced team.

Anecdote Since story points can be converted into working hours using velocity, teams sometimes find it difficult to view them as an abstract quantity. One of the teams we worked with in the past therefore decided to estimate in "gummy bears" rather than story points.

The burndown diagram in Fig. 3.10 illustrates the ideal, linear processing trend. The line starts at the top left at 80 story points estimated in the second sprint planning meeting. This is the value of the story points still to be processed on the first day of the sprint. Ideally, all story points are completed on the last day of the sprint. The line therefore ends at zero at the bottom right.

The actual values show that more story points were processed in the first two days than in the linear extrapolated plan, but that the team fell slightly behind the linear plan from the third day onwards.

The release burndown chart shows how quickly the team is working through the product backlog. It also shows how many sprints are expected to be necessary until the end of the project (Fig. 3.11).

Scrum Task Board

The product backlog and the sprint backlog are "living" documents. They should be updated daily. Although not explicitly prescribed by Scrum, the task board—a form of visualization for the daily management of the sprint backlog—has proven its worth.

Figure 3.12 shows a task board variant with the usual four columns. The first column shows (at least) the user stories of the current sprint from the product backlog (for small projects sometimes also the entire product backlog). The second column shows the tasks not yet completed and not yet in progress in this sprint, the third column shows the tasks in progress, and the fourth column shows

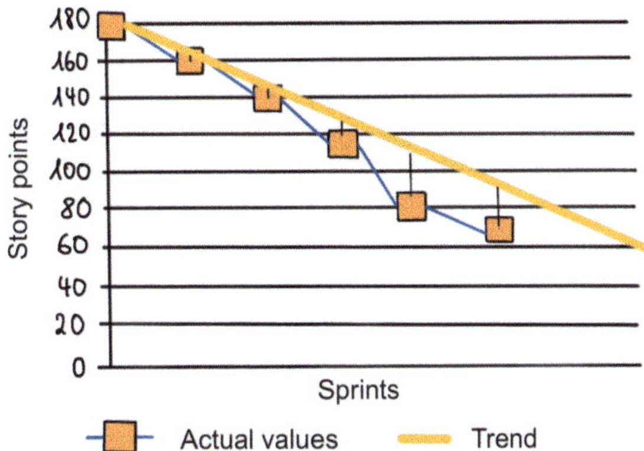

Fig. 3.11 Example of a release burndown chart

the completed tasks. In practice, haptic task boards such as pin boards are suitable for project teams at one location, while there are already a large number of software tools for locally distributed teams that realize work with digital task boards ("drag & drop" of cards, etc.).

The Scrum task board can be used for visualization during the daily Scrums and serves to raise transparency for everyone.

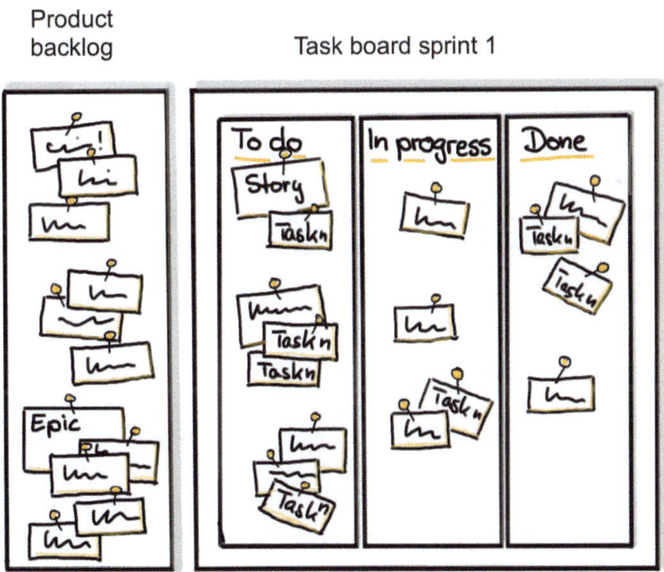

Fig. 3.12 Example of a Scrum task board

Table 3.7 Success factors for Scrum in human resource management

Values	Intrapersonal skills	Interpersonal skills
Openness	Personal responsibility	Ability and willingness to communicate
Courage	Self-reflection	Be able to give and accept criticism
Respect	Decisiveness	Helpfulness
Commitment	Willingness to learn	Delegation skills
Focus	Quality awareness	Trust
	Discipline	Be able to put common interests above self-interests

3.3.7 Scrum and Agile Human Resource Management

We have already determined that agile frameworks fundamentally reorganize the distribution of project management work. One could even say that they reverse it.

Agility calls for a fundamentally different approach involving the human resources function, the Scrum Master, and the entire team—from recruitment to separation—and a leadership style grounded in trust, see e.g. Shastri et al. (2021). Each individual in the Scrum team takes responsibility for project management tasks. On the other hand, Scrum teams require employees who are willing to take responsibility for many of the topic blocks and project activities described in this book and are capable of organizing themselves.

Communication, interaction, and social skills are generally very important in projects, but they are vital for survival in agile projects. We will discuss this in more detail in Chap. 10 "Human resource management." In this chapter, we will therefore limit ourselves to two remarks:

All team members should strongly identify with agile values, principles, and practices.

They should also have a high level of communication and interpersonal skills. Table 3.7, shows which competence areas this relates to. More details can be found in Maximini (2018).

3.3.8 Scaling Scrum

The "agile sweet spot" was identified as situations where agile methodologies excel: when a small, co-located team is developing business applications within rather short-term projects (Kruchten 2004). Thus, it may not be suitable for large-scale environments. Since hardly anyone wants to return to sequential project management frameworks, we need a way to scale Scrum.

The two best-known frameworks for agile synchronization across multiple teams are SAFe and LeSS. SAFe stands for "Scaled Agile Framework." It guides larger organizations to apply agile principles and practices on a larger scale. "Large-Scale Scrum" (LeSS) pursues the same idea, scaling up Scrum from one team to a larger group of teams.

LeSS, developed by Larman and Vodde (2017), emphasizes minimalistic scaling by maintaining a single product backlog, one Definition of Done, and a shared sprint cadence across multiple teams. It operates on two levels:

- Basic LeSS (2–8 teams) and
- LeSS Huge (8+ teams) each with slight structural adaptations.

LeSS encourages feature teams (cross-functional teams focused on end-to-end customer features) over component teams and promotes empirical process control through transparency, inspection, and adaptation.

Unlike other scaling frameworks, LeSS avoids adding layers of management or complex roles, instead focusing on whole-product thinking and continuous improvement. This sounds great! Let us summarize the most basic LeSS-rules so that LeSS can be understood with just a few words:

- One Product Owner for all teams
  There is only one Product Owner (PO) who manages the single Product Backlog for all teams. The PO prioritizes and clarifies requirements for all teams.
- Feature Teams instead of Component Teams
  Teams work across features (e.g., "login functionality"), not across technical components (e.g., "backend development").
- One Shared Sprint for All Teams
  All teams start and finish the Sprint simultaneously (e.g., every two weeks). There is a shared Sprint Planning, Review, and Retrospective for all teams.
- No new roles (except in LeSS Huge)
  In Basic LeSS, there are no additional roles such as "Release Train Engineer" (as in SAFe). In LeSS Huge (8+ teams), there are Area Product Owners (for sub-areas) and an Overall Product Owner (Fig. 3.13).

SAFe was designed by Knaster and Leffinwell (2020) to bring agile methods to large enterprises. It is continuously updated and has now reached version 6.0 (Scaled Agile 2025).

SAFe is built on lean and agile principles and includes a collection of best practices for large enterprises. It supports companies of varying sizes, and has extensions to enable flexibility for large companies. SAFe's organizational structure is large and has multiple hierarchical layers with many predefined roles and responsibilities. Some practitioners consider SAFe too cumbersome and complex. Some even say that SAFe is becoming "the new waterfall" (Uludağ 2022, p. 28) (Fig. 3.14).

Four pre-built SAFe configurations allow companies to tailor SAFe to their business needs:

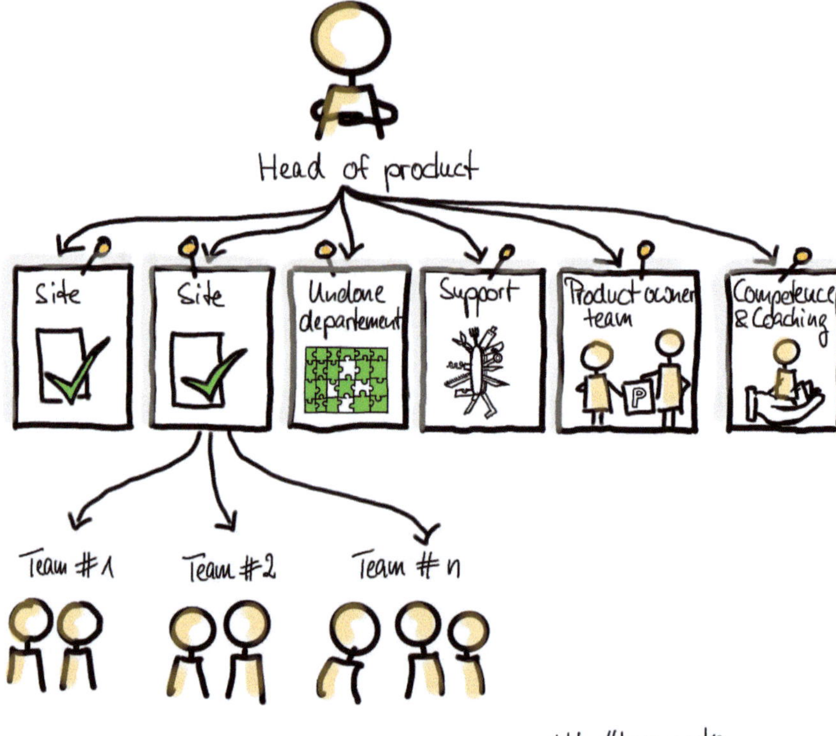

Fig. 3.13 Basic organizational structure of LeSS

- **Essential SAFe** is the most basic form of SAFe. It contains a minimal set of roles, events, and artifacts applicable at a team and program level
- **Large Solution SAFe** describes additional roles, practices, and guidance to build complex solutions. It includes Essential SAFe and extends it.
- **Portfolio SAFe** entails a set of competencies and practices that can fully enable business agility.
- **Full SAFe** represents the most comprehensive configuration to maintain portfolios of large solutions that typically require hundreds of people.

Depending on the selected configuration, four organizational levels integrate agile and lean practices, and are aligned with each other:

- The **Team Level** is the lowest level and describes how agile teams work. It suggests agile teams to use Scrum, Kanban, and XP techniques and two-week iterations.

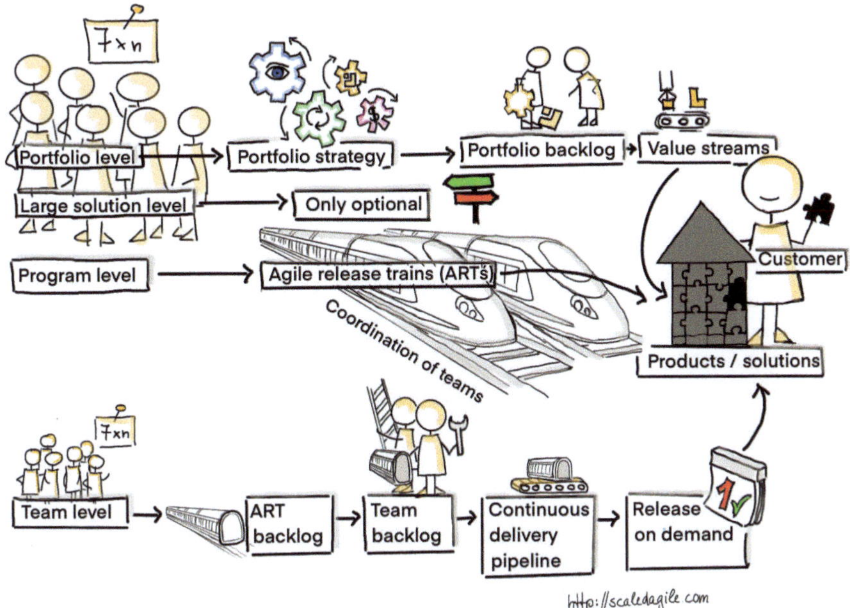

Fig. 3.14 Basic concepts of SAFe 6.0

- At the **Program Level**, teams are part of an Agile Release Train (ART), a group of 5–12 agile teams that delivers solutions in a 8–12 week Program Increment (PI).
- SAFe further entails a **Large Solution Level**. At this level, several ARTs are incorporated into a Solution Train.
- At the **Portfolio Level**, the enterprise oversees multiple programs.

Furthermore, SAFe comprises four core components (Knaster and Leffinwell 2020): principles, roles, events, and artifacts. As the reader will notice already, SAFe is much further removed from Scrum and is more complicated than LeSS.

More details of both frameworks—as well as some other successful large scale frameworks such as Scrum-of-Scrums (SoS), Disciplined Agile Delivery (DAD) developed by Amber (2012), or Scrum@Scale (Sutherland 2022) are beyond the scope of this book.

3.3.9 Scrum: A Success Story

Scrum can be considered a "success story" among the project management frameworks for software development projects, because it has established itself as the "agile standard" in practice.

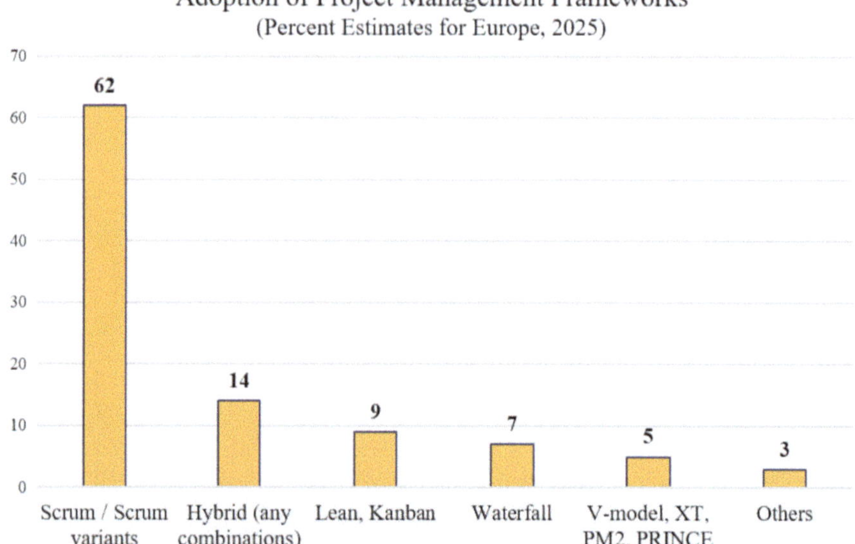

Fig. 3.15 Adoption of project management frameworks

Figure 3.15 summarizes the results of a meta-analysis from several sources and studies from the period 2019–2025, namely from Digital.ai (2022), Digital.ai (2024), Klünder et al. (2019), KPMG (2022), Parabol (2024), PMI (2025), and TechReport (2022). The results of those studies confirm a distribution of more than 60% for Scrum including Scrum variants (that is SAFe, LeSS, DAD, SoS, and others). In contrast, the most widespread pure sequential project management framework is still the general waterfall model.

Why is Scrum so successful? First, Scrum appeals as an agile framework because it not only addresses computer scientists and developers, but also the other stakeholders of today's product developments. Second, Scrum has adopted many successful elements from other frameworks and bundles their advantages. That is why it became the "de facto standard" for agile software development. Third, it greatly enhances the importance of the team as a value-creating unit.

Nevertheless, it is also a fact that the "sequential" project management frameworks have not "stood still" either. Many of the approaches and methods from the agile world are also used today in projects with sequential procedures, for example many practices of eXtreme Programming (XP), or PRINCE2® Agile. In addition, combining two or even elements of three project management frameworks has become an attractive option. We call this category "hybrid" approaches and will address it in more detail below.

The selection of a suitable project management framework for a project should not be based on general rules or a "black and white" exclusion procedure. Therefore, we want to end this section with a short list of the most well-known advantages and disadvantages of Scrum.

Advantages of Scrum

- The team bears full responsibility for the final product—this usually promotes the motivation of each individual.
- Daily Scrums increase the focus on Scrum goals, thereby increasing the efficiency of the team and reducing the so-called "idle power."
- The shippable product at the end of each sprint enables rapid and measurable customer feedback and thus accelerates product development.
- Clear rules and prescribed elements make the procedure relatively easy to learn and well structured.
- Scrum offers high planning reliability despite flexibility: transparency, inspection and adaptation in short cycles minimize risks for the customer—again compared to other project management frameworks.

Disadvantages of Scrum

- With large teams or many sub-projects, Scrum poses the risk of too much decentralization, i.e., the sub-projects becoming independent without an overall view. Approaches such as "SAFe," "LeSS," or "Scrum-of-Scrums" can remedy this, but must first be learned.
- The product owner must be available throughout the entire project and may become a bottleneck.
- Scrum projects develop a high dependency on the commitment and competencies of key roles, such as the product owner or the Scrum master.

Conclusion

To summarize the evaluation of Scrum—both in comparison to other agile and sequential project management frameworks—it can be stated that Scrum makes it possible to:

- Identify risks at an earlier stage.
- Implement and incorporate user requirements more effectively.
- Hand over responsibility and authority to each team member.

Agile frameworks are generally suitable when teams can and should work without hierarchical or central supervision, and when the requirements for the systems and products to be developed are still quite unclear.

Thanks to scaling methods such as "Scrum-of-Scrums," Scrum is nowadays suitable for all team sizes and project sizes where requirements are still evolving. The statement, which was still widespread in many textbooks after the turn of the millennium, that Scrum, along with other factors, is only suitable for small projects, is now simply outdated.

Nevertheless, there remain industries and areas in which elements of the V-model are in part firmly prescribed due to the high safety levels of the systems and corresponding high legal regulation of product development.

3.4   The Practice of Hybrid Project Management Frameworks

As we saw in the previous section, Scrum is widely used. However, a closer look at the study data reveals that hardly any company that has established Scrum or another agile project management framework has established it completely and in its pure form. Many companies today obviously do not want to miss out on the fruits of agile product development, and have therefore introduced parts of agile ideas, however without completely "throwing overboard" the proven advantages of sequential project management frameworks. In other words, we will rarely find a pure agile environment.

In addition, agile frameworks are not a panacea, and—as we have discussed above—demand some competencies and commitment from the acting people. To put it in the words of Ken Schwaber (Google 2006):

> However, Scrum works with idiots. You can take a group of idiots, that maybe didn't even go to school, don't understand computer science, don't understand software engineering techniques, hate each other, don't understand the business domains, have lousy engineering tools and uniformly, they will produce "crap" every increment. This is good! You want to know where you are at the end of every iteration.

In other words, even in case the people assigned were not optimally qualified and would hate each other, Scrum would still work in one respect: The management knows early on that there is no project progress.

However, the true potential of agile project management frameworks only comes to the fore if the management culture and the maturity level of the organization are in line with agile approaches (see also Chap. 11 "Maturity models").

Many companies and organizations are still in a process of change, and are therefore looking for mixed forms for the delivery of their projects.

These hybrid forms are mostly variants of the so-called "scaredy-cat model," which is also known as the "water-Scrum case" in the Anglo-American world (see Fig. 3.16): The V-model concept is combined with Scrum, in that the upper phases are processed sequentially, and only the lower phases are agile. The transition to Agile happens somewhere between the system architecture and the detailed design, depending on the specific characteristics of the hybrid model. Unit tests are clearly part of the agile iterations, while acceptance tests follow again the sequential approach.

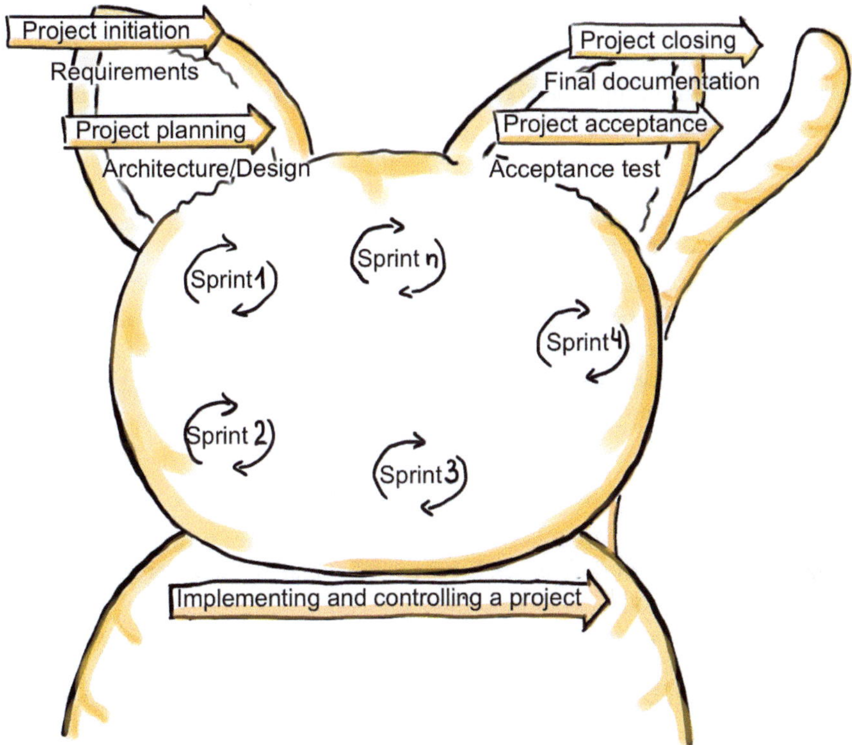

Fig. 3.16 Agile approach embedded in classic project phases

However, one thing must be clear: This is no longer an agile or Scrum project, and the very advantages that Scrum offers through its concepts of transparency, inspection, and adaptation are sacrificed here due to fears or concerns in favor of upfront planning and upfront architecture design, as well as downstream and sequential integration, system and acceptance test phases.

3.5   Summary

This chapter was about project management frameworks and how they provide heuristics, methods, and tools for the efficient execution of software development projects. We made a fundamental distinction between sequential and agile frameworks.

Sequential project management frameworks reduce the complexity of the project by separating subtasks of the project into phases, and basically provide for external as well as hierarchical control options.

Agile frameworks, on the other hand, offer a minimization of risks and an increase in product acceptance through the incremental approach.

A particularly popular agile framework is Scrum. It follows the agile principles. Important elements are the iterative approach (sprints instead of phases), the user stories (instead of detailed requirements) and the lean approach, which is also reflected in the methods used, e.g., for estimating effort (think of "Planning-Poker").

In any case, project management frameworks should be adapted to the specific company and project requirements as part of process tailoring.

In addition to the selection and adaptation of the general and specific project management frameworks, which together describe, in simplified terms, the HOW of the overall software development process, special requirements, standards, and norms must always be taken into account, which specify the WHAT—i.e., in particular which methods and documents must be used and created. Scrum, for example, does not describe any documents, which must nevertheless be created if a process or a standard requires it.

3.6 Exercises

1. What are the main differences between sequential and agile project management frameworks?
2. What weaknesses do sequential project management frameworks have? How are these circumvented in agile frameworks?
3. Name and explain two advantages and disadvantages each of sequential and agile frameworks.
4. What requirements should be met for the use of an incremental approach?
5. Assign the following models to sequential or agile project management frameworks: Scrum, waterfall model, V-model, Kanban, eXtreme Programming.
6. What are criteria that should guide process tailoring of a project management framework for a given company and project?
7. Explain why "process tailoring" should be done in every project.
8. Name and explain three guiding principles of agile system development.
9. In addition to agile guiding principles, agile frameworks also provide typical elements. Name these.
10. Briefly explain the basic ideas of agile system development according to Scrum!
11. Which three essential roles does Scrum define? Describe the tasks and rights of a role of your choice!
12. Outline the Scrum process and name four core events of Scrum.
13. Name and explain the tasks and outcomes of "Sprint Planning I und II."
14. What are the benefits of running a "Daily Scrum"?
15. Name and explain the tasks and outcomes of the "Sprint Review".

References

(Agile Alliance 2001): Manifesto for Agile Software Development. Available at: https://agilemanifesto.org/ (Accessed: 10 September 2025).

(Amber 2012): Ambler, S. W., Disciplined Agile Delivery: A Practitioner's Guide to Agile Software Delivery. IBM Press. ISBN: 978-0132819405.

(ASQF CPPM 2025): Project Management Foundations, Syllabus (EN), ASQF® Certified Professional for Project Management (2025) - Foundation Level, Version 3.0, 2025.

(Beck 2000): Kent Beck: Extreme Programming Explained – Embrace Change – 1. edition, Amsterdam, Addison-Wesley Longman, ISBN 978-0201616415.

(Boehm 1979): Boehm, B. W. (1979), Guidelines for Verifying and Validating Software Requirements and Design Specifications, in P. A. Samet, ed., 'Euro IFIP 79', North Holland, pp. 711–719

(Bundesverwaltungsamt 2023): PMflex-Projektmanagement-Leitfaden. Bundesverwaltungsamt. Available at: https://www.bva.bund.de/SharedDocs/Downloads/DE/Behoerden/Beratung/GrossPM/PMflex/PMflex-Projektmanagement-Leitfaden.pdf

(Cohn 2005): Mike Cohn: Agile Estimating and Planning, Prentice Hall, 360 pages, 2005, ISBN 978-0131479418.

(Deming 1982): Deming, W. E., Out of the Crisis. MIT Press.

(Digital.ai 2022): 15th State of Agile Report. Digital.ai, Lexington, MA. Available at: https://digital.ai/resource-center/analyst-reports/state-of-agile-report

(Digital.ai 2024): 17th State of Agile Report. Digital.ai, Lexington, MA. Available at: https://digital.ai/resource-center/analyst-reports/state-of-agile-report

(European Commission 2021): PM^2-Agile Guide v 3.0.1. Luxembourg: Publications Office of the European Union. Available at: https://op.europa.eu/en/publication-detail/-/publication/ed85debf-decc-11eb-895a-01aa75ed71a1

(European Commission 2024): PM^2 Project Management Guide 3.1. Publications Office of the European Union. Available at: https://op.europa.eu/en/publication-detail/-/publication/ed85debf-decc-11eb-895a-01aa75ed71a1

(Google 2006): Schwaber, K., Talk on Scrum, in: Google TechTalk, Sept. 5, 2006, https://www.youtube.com/watch?v=_47VWIvOKH8, accessed 03.10.2025.

(Jacobson 1999): Jacobson I, Booch G, Rumbaugh J.: The Unified Software Development Process. Reading, MA: Addison-Wesley.

(Klünder et al. 2019) Klünder, J., Hebig, R., Tell, P., Kuhrmann, M. et al.: Catching up with method and process practice: An industry-informed baseline for researchers, in Proceedings of the ICSE-SEIP2019. Montréal, Canada, IEEE Computer Society Press, pp.255–264. https://doi.org/10.1109/ICSE-SEIP.2019.00036

(Knaster & Leffinwell 2020): Richard Knaster and Dean Leffingwell. SAFe 5.0 Distilled: Achieving Business Agility with the Scaled Agile Framework. Addison-Wesley, Boston, MA, USA,2020.

(KPMG 2022): Agile Transformation Survey 2022. KPMG International. Available at: https://home.kpmg/xx/en/home/insights/2022/11/global-agile-survey.html

(Kruchten 2004): Kruchten, P. (2004). Scaling Down Large Projects to Meet the Agile "Sweet Spot". The Rational Edge, IBM developerWorks.

(Larman & Vodde 2017): Larman, C. & Vodde, B. Large-Scale Scrum: More with LeSS. 3. ed. Boston: Addison-Wesley Professional. ISBN 978-0-321-98571-0.

(Maximini 2018): Maximini, D. The Scrum Culture: Introducing Agile Methods in Organizations. 2nd edn. Springer International Publishing, Cham. ISBN 978-3-319-73841-3. https://doi.org/10.1007/978-3-319-73842-0.

(Meyer 2014): Meyer, B., Agile!: The Good, the Hype and the Ugly. Berlin, Heidelberg: Springer, https://doi.org/10.1007/978-3-319-05155-0

(Parabol 2024). Agile and Scrum Statistics 2024. Parabol Inc. Available at: https://www.parabol.co/resources/agile-statistics

(PMI 2025): Project Management Institute Pulse of the Profession 2025: Amplifying Impact in the Age of AI. PMI, Newtown Square, PA. Available at: https://www.pmi.org/learning/thought-lea dership/pulse

(Royce 1970): Winston D. Royce: Managing the Development of Large Software Systems, in Proc. IEEE, WESCON, 1970, www.cs.umd.edu/

(Scaled Agile 2025): SAFe® Explained: Succeeding with Lean and Agile at Scale. Scaled Agile, Inc., https://scaledagile.com/

(Schwaber 1995) Schwaber, K., The Scrum Development Process. In: Proceedings of the 1995 OOPSLA Conference.

(Schwaber & Beedle 2002) Schwaber, K., Beedle, M., Agile software development with Scrum, Upper Saddle River, NJ, Prentice Hall, 2002.

(Schwaber & Sutherland 2020): K. Schwaber, J. Sutherland: The Scrum Guide: The definitive guide to Scrum: The rules of the game, (U.S. English ed.). https://scrumguides.org/scrum-guide.html

(Shastri et al. 2021): Y. Shastri, R. Hoda, R. Amor, Spearheading agile: the role of the scrum master in agile projects, in: Empirical Software Engineering (2021) 26: 3, p. 2–31, https://doi.org/10. 1007/s10664-020-09899-4

(Sutherland 2014): Jeff Sutherland: Scrum: The Art of Doing Twice the Work in Half the Time, 256 pages, ISBN-13 978-1847941107

(Sutherland 2022): Sutherland, J. The Scrum@Scale Guide: The Definitive Guide to the Scrum@Scale Framework, Version 2.1, Scrum Inc. Available at: https://www.scrumatsc ale.com/scrum-at-scale-guide-online/

(TechReport 2022): Scrum Usage Statistics 2022. TechReport, Business Workplace Research. Available at: https://techreport.com/statistics/business-workplace/scrum-usage-statistics

(Uludağ 2022): Uludağ, Ö., Empirical Analysis of the Adoption of Large-Scale Agile Development Methods. PhD Dissertation, Technical University of Munich (TUM).

(Weit 2024): Weit e. V., V-Modell XT: System development standard for IT projects, Release 2.4. Bonn: Weit e. V. (released May 2024)

Project Initiation

4

4.1   And Now?—Project Initiating Activities

When does a project start? This question is not so easy to answer. At the beginning there is always some trigger—a customer inquiry, a new product or business idea, a change request regarding an existing scenario or an internal inquiry whether it would not be possible to develop something. Often, this is still a vision with no or few concrete goals.

As the discussions continue, we eventually concluded that something should be done and that it will involve costs. We said that a project begins when the implementing organization has completed the processes required to commission the new project, but none of the ISO standards provides information about the exact nature of these processes, as these depend heavily on the project organization and the intended project management framework. It might be a decision taken during a meeting as well as an official commissioning.

From this moment on, the first phase of the project begins, which we call "project initiation" in accordance with the said standard. In literature you also find the term "project start," but this term is misleading. "Project start" makes us think of a starting shot, e.g., in the context of a kickoff meeting. However, the official announcement of the start of the project is only one out of many activities of project initiation. In fact, project initiation essentially serves:

1. to gather sufficient information to identify and soundly assess the opportunities and risks of the project;
2. to obtain sufficient clarity about the requirements to be able to start the project work (i.e. do the planning and, later, start with the implementation);
3. to clarify contractual aspects;
4. to identify the project management framework to use;
5. to procure the necessary resources.

A. Johannsen et al., *Foundations for Software Project Management in Classic and Agile Environments*, https://doi.org/10.1007/978-3-032-16797-2_4

ISO 21502:2020 specifies purpose and activities of this phase as follows: "The purpose of initiating a project is to plan the project, define the project organization, mobilize the project team, define project governance and management, identify stakeholders, and verify the project is justified."

4.1.1 Identify and Weight Opportunities and Risks

Strictly speaking, it is not even certain that the initial idea will actually be implemented at the end of the initiation phase. It may well turn out that there are technical difficulties that cannot be overcome at reasonable financial costs. If there are doubts about the feasibility of the requirements, the development of a prototype is an option.

In addition to the feasibility study, prototypes are also used to clarify requirements, e.g., regarding the graphical user interface, in short: GUI. This does not even have to be a piece of programmed software. Presentations, HTML pages or "mockups" that can easily be created using collaborative design tools such as "Figma," "Miro," or "InVision" (see Feng et al. 2023) can also be used to "experience" the visual impression quite well (including the "click experience" thanks to hyperlinks). If you are considering a GUI prototype, you should do some research on the Internet. There are several commercial and freely available tools for web applications, mobile apps, and "classic" desktop applications. Since the market is changing rapidly, there is little point in going into more detail about individual tools here.

In addition to technical feasibility, there are several other criteria that can speak for or against a project. First, there is always the financial question: What will the development and production cost us? How much profit can we expect, or how high might the savings be? But there are also other, more strategic considerations: Does this product open a new market for us or give us a competitive edge? This can be the deciding factor to proceed with a project even if the financial invest clearly exceeds the profit to be expected in the short term. In that case, the project is an investment in the future, and opportunities and risks should be weighed up carefully. Finally, we may not really have a choice, for example, if the legal situation has changed and we must adapt our product to the new requirements.

Project initiation also marks the beginning of risk management, which we will discuss in more detail in Chap. 9. Risks are identified and evaluated as early as the initiation phase, and countermeasures are considered. At this early stage in the project, however, the procedure is not yet as systematic as we will see later in Chap. 9. One of the reasons for this is that not all the information required for a detailed risk analysis is yet available (e.g., the requirements specification).

4.1.2   Obtain Information for Project Implementation

During project initiation, the moment comes when the decision for or against further implementation is made. By now at the latest, sufficient information should be available for a core team to start working. However, the transition between the initiation phase and the planning phase is often fluid. One of the first tasks of the core team during the planning phase may be precisely to identify the requirements.

While the detailed requirements may not be fully captured until the planning phase, the project objectives should already be clearly worked out in the initiation phase. Although it is generally known that many projects fail because of unclear objectives, the definition of objectives is often treated stepmotherly, according to the motto: "We all know what we want, don't we." Unfortunately, this is usually not true. Goals that are not written down are neither tangible nor demonstrably aligned. Since the human brain has the property of filling in missing information with what is already known, this leads to implicit assumptions that may later turn out to be wrong. It is particularly unfortunate when different stakeholders have made different or even contradictory assumptions and this is only discovered during the acceptance test.

Thus, the first step is to clarify the goals together in close consultation with the customer. This "customer" does not necessarily have to be an external customer. The product manager from the internal marketing department or another business unit within the company also counts as a customer in this context. In the first case, the product manager represents many end customers, not all of whom could be reached; in the second case, the project is probably triggered by an internal need. It is important to clearly identify the project goals. Therefore, the product manager must know exactly what the goals of the end customers are.

Figure 4.1 shows the gradation between the strategic considerations and the global vision that triggers the project, the concrete(er) goals that are laid down during project initiation, and the detailed requirements that are derived either also during project initiation or later in the planning phase.

The way in which these requirements are elaborated and documented depends on the chosen project management framework. From sequential project management frameworks, we know the classic requirements specification. There is the claim that (almost) all requirements should be collected, analyzed, documented, and agreed upon in advance. However, since it can always be assumed that requirements will change during the project, a change process should be set up at the beginning of the project. Late, new or changed requirements represent a considerable project risk whose probability of occurrence can easily be set at 100%. It is therefore important to establish mechanisms for dealing with such late requirement changes.

Agile frameworks are better positioned in this respect. Requirements are captured in the form of user stories and it is sufficient to initially focus on the first release.

The change process must be documented and agreed at the latest in the project planning phase, and in the case of projects with external customers even at the

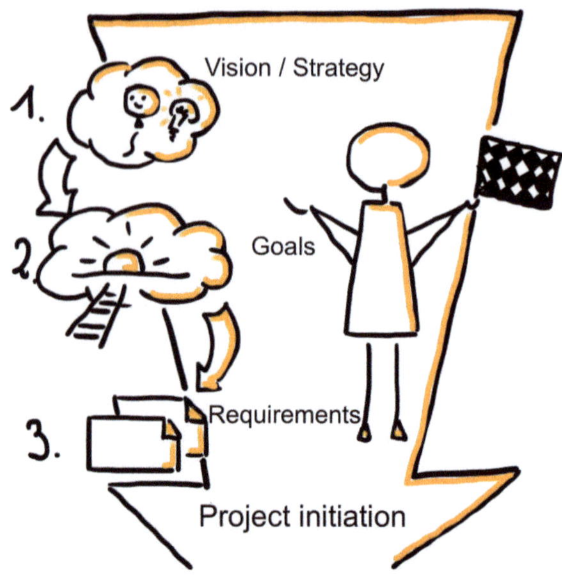

Fig. 4.1 Clarification of goals during project initiation

end of project initiation, as the handling of change requests should be part of the contractual agreements.

4.1.3 Clarify Contractual Aspects

For projects that are officially commissioned by a customer, obviously a contract must be drawn up. But even for internal projects, there may be contractual issues to clarify with partners, suppliers and/or service providers. Overall, the following points should be clarified unambiguously.

Scope of Delivery
The scope of delivery includes all hardware, software, and documents supplied by the contractor to the customer, as well as any services. Since experience shows that there are always different interpretations of the scope of delivery, it is important to clearly delineate the project and its limits. The contract should therefore state not only what will be done but also what is not part of the agreement.

In addition, it should be indicated how early feedback shall be collected/ provided. This is typically part of a document that should be signed-off by stakeholders. The precise name of the document differs from organization to organization. Some call it "project charter," we call it "project definition document" (see below).

> **Definition** Project definition
> Single overarching document, that describes the objectives and the management approach of a project, and thus serves as orientation for all stakeholders involved (ASQF CPPM 2025).

Milestones

Hardly any project is so small or so short-term that it can do without intermediate deliveries. In sequential project management frameworks, one of the first milestones is typically the release of the requirements specification. In agile frameworks, each sprint end represents a milestone. It should be clear which deliverable is expected at which milestone and how the acceptance of the (intermediate) delivery is done (e.g., by reviewing the specification documents or performing acceptance tests).

In agile projects, the acceptance of sprint results in the sprint review, which can have contractually binding significance. However, the prerequisite is that the client is actually closely involved in the agile approach. In this case, the selected project management framework and the resulting obligation of the client should be clear and contractually agreed. In practice, many projects are handled internally in an agile manner, but without delivery to the customer after each sprint. In this case, the customer is represented by an internal product owner (e.g., the product manager). Additional acceptance criteria should then be defined for the external deliveries, analogous to sequentially processed projects.

Costs

This point summarizes all financial aspects. It is closely linked to the two previous points.[1] It is important to clarify when and how much is paid for which service and what the payment conditions are. In general, there are two operating models: the fixed-price offer or processing according to time and effort. In sequential project management frameworks, the fixed price is usually based on the functional scope, while the "agile fixed price" is based on the number of delivery objects and/or the time.

Typically, payments are linked to milestones. The acceptance criteria of the deliveries defined for the milestones also serve as a measurement of whether the service has been performed correctly and to the desired extent (and should therefore be paid for).

Communication

In addition to the organizational and technical contacts of both contractual partners, the communication channels should also be clearly regulated. Is an e-mail sufficient as a written document or must at least an electronically signed document

---

[1] Together, the three topics form the classic triangle of scope/content, deadline/schedule, and cost/budget.

be sent if, for example, expected additional work or postponements are to be communicated? How is information exchanged on a regular basis? In most projects, a weekly status meeting is established via online channels. However, these should be supplemented by regular on-site meetings, as closer contact considerably simplifies communication and creates a basis of trust.

Reporting

Deadline delays and additional expenses become worse the later they are communicated, as the affected customer is given less opportunity to cope with the change. Therefore, it should be contractually clarified which indicators should be monitored and communicated at what intervals. Typically, the contractual partners define a set of metrics for this purpose. In addition to costs and deadlines, metrics for measuring the functional scope and its quality should also be recorded. Metrics on implemented requirements/user stories and on new/processed defect reports are also useful.

Dealing with Changes

There is no point in closing one's eyes to the fact that change requests will occur. However, changes are a considerable project risk, especially in sequential project management frameworks and in fixed-price bids. The CrowdStrike disaster mentioned in the introduction is only one out many examples where a small change had huge impact.

Every project should therefore have rules for dealing with changes from the start. Who decides what is still processed and what is not? What criteria are used to make the decision? How are change requests documented? It is important to find a viable compromise between total refusal ("wasn't part of the contract, we won't do it") and uncritical "obedience" to the customer. Ideally, the contract should specify the criteria according to which the contractual partners jointly decide whether or not a change is to be made, and if so, under what conditions.

Definition of and Handling of Serious Deviations

By "deviations" we mean all points in which reality "deviates" from the contractually agreed condition. These can be delays, additional costs, or faulty/absent functionality. In contrast to change requests, the negotiating position of the contractor is rather poor in the case of deviations. However, in this case, it does not help the client much to take the position that there should be no deviations. Instead, it should be contractually regulated how both (i.e., client and contractor) can find a constructive solution together.

Not every small software error is immediately a danger to the overall project. Even minor schedule delays can possibly be dealt with later. For this reason, the contractual partners should first determine at what point a deviation is so serious that there is a need for joint action. The metrics mentioned earlier can serve as a rule, for example by defining a traffic light system. As soon as a defined threshold value is reached, the traffic light goes to "yellow," then to "red" when the second threshold is exceeded. Yellow signifies, for example, that there is a risk of a serious deviation, while red can indicate that the serious deviation has occurred or is certain to occur.

Defining clear criteria prevents unnecessary recriminations and possibly financial claims later (according to the principle "You did not let us know soon enough"). After all, the goal is to establish a relationship based on partnership and to complete the project successfully for everyone involved. In practice, this clarification of the term "serious" is unfortunately often neglected. As a result, the traffic light color is assessed rather subjectively and misunderstandings can arise.

4.1.4 Determine the Project Management Framework

The choice of the project management framework influences all further project phases and must therefore take place during project initiation. As already mentioned, it may even make sense to anchor the project management framework in a contract.

In Chap. 3, we have already discussed the advantages and disadvantages of sequential and agile frameworks. The project manager must now ponder and decide on a concrete framework. In this context, we would like to warn against changing the project management framework prematurely. Agile frameworks require trained and motivated employees, a (really) available product owner (in the case of Scrum) and, in general, a change in thinking at management level as well. It is therefore not a good idea to switch to agile in the middle of a project if those involved are not already familiar with the new approach. Likewise, it is counterproductive to go back to the sequential approach after a few sprints, for example, because "agile has not proven itself." A project needs continuity. Any change, even within the same approach (sequential or agile) is a disruption that can be avoided by making a considered choice in advance.

Therefore, it is important to analyze and weigh all aspects during project initiation and then to clearly define the project management framework with all its project-specific adaptations.

4.1.5 Procure Resources

At the end of project initiation the project should be ready to takeoff. This also includes ensuring that at least the core team has been named and made available for the project, sufficient laptops are available, and the necessary infrastructure has been ordered (e.g., servers or hardware test systems). Additional employees may also need to be hired or suppliers or service providers commissioned.

The various aspects of personnel selection will be discussed in more detail in Chap. 10. So much in advance: it is up to the project manager to determine the need and, in close cooperation with the human resources department of his organization, to ensure that he or she obtains suitable (i.e., qualified and available) employees.

The way in which services are procured depends heavily on the organization in question. Many, usually larger, companies have established processes for how suppliers are selected, commissioned, and evaluated. In this case, the project manager must deal with the purchasing department of his or her organization, clearly define the needs, and ensure that the right service or object is ordered. In smaller companies, the project manager may be able to select and commission the suppliers or service providers himself. In that case, "Clarify contractual aspects" (Sect. 4.1.3) becomes important.

4.2   Project Definition and Project Order

As a result of the project initiating activities a project order is issued. It consists of one or more formal documents with the purpose to officially approve the project start (or a new phase of the project), to define the project manager with his/her responsibilities and authority, and to document the goal, budget, expected deliverables, and other business requirements (e.g., target date).

The third item corresponds to the project definition and documents the results of the project initiating activities (see Sect. 4.1). Its aim is to create a common understanding of the project among all stakeholders. In terms of content, the project definition contains the following points, among others:

- **Project Motivation**

  This section identifies the business reasons why the project is undertaken (e.g., profitability). In Fig. 4.1, the project motivation was presented as "vision/ strategy." It contains the business case behind the project. For the stakeholders it is important to know the motivation to be able to make the right decisions later (i.e., in the interests of the company) in case of doubt.

- **Quantifiable Project Goals**

  This point sets the bar against which the success of the project will later be measured. Again, we find the three aspects of costs/budget, schedule, and scope, which are often represented in the form of a triangle. For budget and schedule, it is relatively easy to set quantifiable goals. Functional scope is more difficult to measure, but it strongly relates to the number of requirements or user stories planned for a release.

- **Stakeholder List**

  If stakeholders are forgotten, sooner or later this will show up in the project. The list of stakeholders should therefore be thoroughly maintained, especially since it is an important input for the requirements analysis. However, not all individual persons must be listed by name, but all roles must be represented. Table 4.1 shows the stakeholder list of our sample project.

Table 4.1   Stakeholder list (example)

Name	Position	E-mail	Phone	Domain/expertise	Availability	Interview	Done
Bridget Boss	Head of department	bboss@mycompany.com	4565	Platform project line	Ask secretary	Pending	
Jane Doe	Project manager	jdoe@mycompany.com	2677	Customer project 1	?	tbd	
Ramakrishna Maier	Product manager	rmaier2@mycompany.com	7249	Marketing/sales	Only Monday and Thursday after 3 pm	2022/03/23 3:30–5:30 pm	x
Dr. James Want-Have	Project manager	james.want-have@customer.com	01234–999620	Client of previous project	Onsite in CW34	2022/03/25 10am– 12 pm	
Clark Strong	Assessor	clark.strong@customer.com	01234–999852	QA customer	On leave till CW36	tbd	
Natasha Yarovna	Quality manager	nyarovna@mycompany.om	7332	QA MyCompany	Monday to Thursday 8 am to 3 pm	2022/03/10 9-11am	x
Arthur Reckless	Functional safety manager	areckless@mycompany.com	5104	BU safety management	From CW 36 Tuesday to Thursday in the morning	2022/03/23 9-11 am	
…	…	…	…	…	…	…	…

- **Development Plan**

  The development plan contains the description of the planned approach and can be roughly divided into three aspects:

  (a) Processes (project management framework, roles and tasks, handling of changes, communication, reporting, etc.)
  (b) Planning (major milestones, rough scheduling, rough budgeting)
  (c) Deliverables (all deliverables such as code, user manual, installation instructions, but also specifications and development documentation)

- **Requirements Specification**

  The documentation of the requirements for the product to be developed, as far as they are already known. This point has already been discussed in Sect. 4.1.2.

- **Preconditions and Assumptions**

  All preconditions, boundary conditions, and all assumptions made, e.g., regarding the availability of people or the technical design of interfaces, should be recorded so that it is clear to everyone involved what the scope of the project is. This also includes documenting the identified opportunities and risks.

- **Project Organization and Project Team**

  What form of project organization has been decided? Who will be part of the project team?

Of course, many of those points will change later. For example, the project team may initially be only a core team. The planning will also change several times upon closer inspection. However, it is crucial that all stakeholders agree to the content of the project definition and that the general direction of the goal is understood and accepted by all. To achieve this, the stakeholders must be involved. This is where the implementation of a project start workshop has proven its worth.

It is no coincidence that many of the points mentioned have already been addressed in the section "Clarifying contractual aspects." In fact, the project definition can be part of a contract. At least, it takes on the character of a contract within the organization when the project order is issued. As such, it undoubtedly adds value regardless of the selected project management framework.

4.3   Contract Design—More Than Just a Nuisance!

To enable the various parties involved in a project to work together successfully, the exact manner of cooperation must be binding and, if necessary, also contractually regulated. In Sect. 4.1.3 we have already discussed which points belong in such a contract. In this section, we turn to the question of which form of contract is suitable in which context. The area of contract design in IT projects is vast—for more information see (Ulusoy and Hazir 2021, pp. 281–310), and (Cai et al. 2023).

We consider contracts in which the project manager acts as the client, i.e., buys in external support for his project. In general, we distinguish between four forms:

- **Commissioning of a General Contractor**

The idea of the general contractor originally comes from the construction industry. The client commissions the general contractor who takes over the task assigned to him completely under his own direction and delivers a finished product (in the construction industry, the turnkey building). The client may keep some possibilities of influence, but the basic idea is that the general contractor takes over the organization and thus also the responsibility for the development. If you want to prevent the general contractor from hiring poorly qualified but cheap subcontractors, you should settle the selection criteria and procedures contractually. The main advantage of awarding the contract to a general contractor is that there is exactly one contact person. In addition, the general contractor contractually guarantees deadlines and costs and assumes the warranty. The disadvantage is that the client has relatively little insight into progress. Finally, even agreed contractual penalties do not necessarily prevent delays. The award of a contract to a general contractor makes sense if the required know-how is only weakly developed or not available at all in the own company.

- **Involvement of Subcontractors**

If the client only wants to outsource parts of the project, the involvement of subcontractors is more appropriate. There are two forms: the contract for work and the service contract. In the contract for work, the delivery of a "work" is agreed. This can be, for example, a hardware or software component. Unless otherwise agreed in the contract, it is up to the subcontractor how the work is created. In contrast, in a service contract, a service is agreed without there necessarily being a guarantee of success. Service contracts are paid on a time and material basis, while contracts for work are generally paid based on an agreed fixed price.

- **External Personnel**

External personnel help to increase the project team as needed or to bring special competencies into the project. Many companies therefore work with freelancers or "buy in" employees on a temporary basis or via a service contract. External employees require a workstation, access card, etc., are on site or part of a virtual team, and are practically indistinguishable from other, internal team members.

- **Cooperation Within a Consortium**

Cooperation within a consortium is suitable when the project scope or the business risk cannot be handled by one company alone. In a consortium, partners with equal rights join forces. Together, they appoint a consortium leader who, as primus inter pares, constitutes the interface to the client. Depending on the distribution of tasks and risks, the individual partners assume more or less liability, which must be clearly defined in the contract. Externally, the consortium leader acts like a general contractor, whereby the client may (but need not) be aware of the existence of the consortium.

The detailed contract design, the types of documents exchanged, and the focal points set therein vary individually from project to project. The selected project management framework has a strong influence.

A classic basis for a contract are requirement specifications and functional specifications. The requirements specification contains the customer's wishes, while the functional specification corresponds to the contractor's binding commitment. Ideally, the requirements specification does not yet contain any technical solutions, but rather high-level customer requirements—in other words, what is to be done and why. The functional specification then translates the stakeholder requirements into functional requirements, which set out how the desired goal is to be achieved. In practice, however, many projects wrestle with either detailed requirements specifications or overly general functional specifications. In the first case, the contractor is deprived of the opportunity to choose a different, possibly more favorable solution. In the second case, the detailing is often omitted altogether, which can lead to problems in the further course of the project. Another disadvantage of this form of contract is that changes are usually not provided for.

Agile frameworks and service-oriented business relations focus on the contractual definition of the following points in addition to the rough definition of goals:

- coordinated (!) approach, especially regarding the prioritization of business opportunities, epics, story maps, user journeys and user stories
- communication channels and forms
- how to deal with changes and deviations.

To achieve a certain degree of dependability, boundary conditions must also be defined in agile projects. These include the system architecture or at least the basic principles of the same as well as usually a minimum guarantee that selected user stories will be implemented.

Regardless of the project management framework rights, duties, decision-making processes, and escalation paths must be clearly defined. In particular, it is important to clarify and agree on the client's duty to cooperate. Even the general contractor will need information and, above all, timely feedback. If, contrary to the original agreement, the project manager has to wait weeks for the customer to review a specification, something is definitely going wrong.

4.4 Requirements Analysis—No Chance Without It!

Unclear and missing requirements cause considerable risks in later project phases or iterations—even in agile settings. Unfortunately, this fact is still not generally accepted. Even companies that should know better from their own experience fall into the same trap again and again and start the implementation without clearly formulated and sufficiently detailed requirements. In most cases there is a requirements specification. However, this is too general to serve as a guideline or benchmark for implementation and quality assurance. At some point, the question arises as to how far the implementation has progressed. Without formulated requirements, however, progress is difficult to measure. Also, the question of whether the developed product does what it is supposed to do cannot be answered without precise specifications. In other words, without requirements, the project finds itself flying completely blind until one day it crashes more or less violently.

The requirements analysis for the system to be created must already be tackled during project initiation. This also applies to agile frameworks. After all, Scrum also requires a robust product backlog from the first iteration onwards. This does not mean that all requirements must be known at the end of project initiation, but that it is clear where the journey goes and which stakeholders are involved in the project. The exact elaboration can also take place during the project planning. In sequential project management frameworks, the project manager usually appoints a dedicated requirements engineer. In agile frameworks, the product owner takes on this task.

However, it should be clear to both that requirements analysis is more than just putting a few functional requirements down on paper. Requirements analysis is a structured process in which all stakeholders must be involved. In addition to the (obvious) functional requirements, there are also non-functional requirements. These include quality requirements for performance, security, testability, maintainability, etc., as well as technical and organizational constraints. The technical constraints include, for example, the specification of a programming language. Organizational constraints can be the required conformity to a law or a standard as well as a fixed budget or a deadline for availability. Non-functional requirements can be extremely important for the system architecture. If you neglect them, you are building on sand. The international standard ISO/IEC 25000 [(ISO 25000:2014), formerly ISO 9126] provides assistance on this topic.

The best-known requirements elicitation technique is certainly the stakeholder interview, in which stakeholders are asked about their needs. It is important to ask open questions and to separate wishes from requirements. Many interview partners tend to present technical solutions as requirements. Therefore, the requirements engineer should investigate less how something is desired, but rather why it is required, that is, the goal causing the wish.

Survey techniques such as interviews or questionnaires reach their limits when it comes to capturing subconscious or unconscious requirements. Subconscious requirements are requirements which the stakeholder take so much for granted that it no longer occurs to them to mention them explicitly. Observation techniques, in which the requirement engineer watches or even familiarizes himself with the field of action, are helpful to identify subconscious requirements.

Unconscious requirements are requirements that the stakeholder did not even know he could have. In requirements management, we speak of "attractive quality." There are a several creativity techniques for identifying such requirements.

Finally, there is the possibility of looking into the past or at the competition. Document-based elicitation techniques focus their attention on requirements specifications of the previous product, user manuals of the competitor's product, and other documents from which requirements for the new product can be gleaned.

Anyone who determines, documents, and manages requirements should be familiar with the topic right from the start. There are several training courses (e.g., the IREB® Certified Professional for Requirements Engineering—Foundation Level, (CPRE 2024)) and textbooks (Meyer 2022), the content of which we have only briefly touched upon in this section.

The exact process of requirements analysis varies as it depends on the company and the project. We have already discussed the influence of the project management framework. However, a few success factors can be denominated that apply to all projects and which the project manager should keep permanently in mind:

- Requirements must be sufficiently clear, documented and agreed. If they are not, there will almost inevitably be discussions and unpleasant surprises later in the project. Even in agile frameworks, the product owner must create a common understanding for all stakeholders. The ISO/IEC/IEEE 29148 standard helps with documentation (ISO 29148).
- Requirements must be clearly prioritized. This is done in agile projects as part of backlog refinement.[2] In the product backlog, the prioritization is determined by the order of the backlog items. In sequential project management frameworks, the priority is usually managed as an attribute.
- Stakeholders must be sufficiently involved (as input providers and reviewers). This sounds obvious, but it is often the reason why projects get out of hand. Therefore, it is important to have a complete list of stakeholders at the end of project initiation.
- The entire product lifecycle must be considered (including maintenance, deinstallation, etc.). It helps to consider all use cases. The German Wikipedia article

---

[2] "Backlog refinement" refers to the activity of the team together with the product owner to sift through, clean up, and prioritize the product backlog.

on change requests[3] beautifully illustrates what happens when use cases are neglected: "When testing a toll system, it is discovered that the distance recorder counts backwards when the vehicle is driving in the opposite lane due to road works."

- **Interfaces and delimitations must be clarified.**

  As mentioned earlier, the project manager can delegate the stakeholder and requirements analysis to a dedicated requirements engineer, but must continuously keep an eye on progress and mediate if necessary.

> **Example** As mentioned in the introduction, undocumented requirements were a major problem in our case study example. Apart from the project manager, nobody knew in which context the functions of the graphics library were to be used. Only when a team member decided to create a flowchart was it possible to clarify this point, at least. In general, graphical models are a good way to present requirements clearly and more unambiguously.

In the future, AI-based tools will be of great help, streamlining the elicitation process and creating documented requirements or user stories with acceptance criteria for us (Habib et al. 2025).

4.5   The Soft Factors—Required Soft Skills

Of course, part of the technical toolbox of a project manager is to know the various forms of contracting and methods of requirements analysis. However, the so-called "soft skills" are at least as important, if not even more. A project manager must be able to negotiate well, appear confident, and communicate skillfully. Particularly during project initiation, the opinions of the individual stakeholders on the exact implementation of the project often diverge widely. In this case it is necessary to mediate. In the following section, we therefore take a closer look at these "soft factors," as soft skills are also called.

4.5.1   Negotiation Skills

For the project manager, project initiation is characterized by negotiations at all levels: with customers, partners, service providers, and suppliers, but also within his own company. On the one hand, he must "loosen up" employees from other

---

[3] Retrieved on October 30, 2024.

departments, and on the other hand, he may need supplies or support, whether from purchasing, the HR department or hardware development. Negotiation skills are therefore among the most important soft skills that the project manager should possess in this project phase. Table 4.2 shows some principles of diplomatic conversation that are useful to know in negotiations and that can be learned.

4.5.2 Self-Confidence and Decisiveness

Particularly in negotiations, project managers are often faced with the difficulty that they do not quite know how far their decision-making authority goes. In addition, not everyone really likes to make decisions. There are three possible scenarios that can prevent a decision from being made:

1. The project manager does not have the necessary authority.
2. The project manager has the necessary authority, but does not dare.
3. The project manager does not dare because he is not sure if he has the necessary authority.

Depending on the scenario, different measures are required. In the first case, the decision must either be made by the supervisor or, better yet, the project manager must be authorized to do so. The second case is more difficult. Training measures and, above all, strong support from the supervisor can help. The third case is absolutely avoidable, but unfortunately occurs quite often in practice. In this case, the project manager must clarify the situation himself and, if in doubt, demand documentation of his decision-making authority in the project order.

4.5.3 Communication Skills

In addition to negotiating skills and self-confidence, the project manager requires facilitation and communication skills during project initiation. If necessary, workshops must be facilitated and documented. Its results must be communicated in all directions and feedback gathered. Figure 4.2 represents the communication directions in the project:

- Internally, e.g., during a kickoff event with the project team;
- Upwards in the context of management presentations;
- Externally, e.g., with the customer, but also with partners, service providers or suppliers.

Communication is more than sending your message well, but also about being able to receive. The project manager should be aware that his project team needs the background information, too. What is the purpose of our work? Is the client satisfied with what they have received? What plans are there to compensate for

Table 4.2 Principles of diplomatic negotiation

Principle	Explanation
Cultivate small talk	If you go like a bull at a gate, you are going to get in trouble. Instinctively, we therefore often start conversations with harmless topics. But as superficial as this small talk may be—it's always good to build up some personal relationship between the conversation partners. It may sound strange, but shared experiences such as children of the same age actually "bind"
Know your own goals	Be clear beforehand what you want to achieve and where your pain threshold lies. During the discussion, you may not be quick enough in your mind to decide whether a proposal is still acceptable or not. Therefore, prepare yourself well and, in addition to the optimal solution (for you), also consider possible alternative scenarios that you can also live with
Let the other person talk	Anyone who talks inevitably reveals information. Therefore, let the other person talk. If you speak yourself, only answer the specific question. Let the other person figure out for himself that you may not have found another supplier Ask questions that steer the conversation in the direction you want. Most importantly, never interrupt your conversation partner. If you do, you are unnecessarily giving up an advantage The more clearly you convey to your conversation partner that you are interested in what is being said, the longer he or she will talk. Head nodding, murmured acknowledgements, eye contact, and brief follow-up questions are among the techniques of what is known as "active listening"
Listen carefully	Listen carefully to what your counterpart is saying. Also pay attention to the body language and everything that is said between the lines or not said. Be very aware of what is being said and what you might have interpreted from your own experience. The latter can be completely wrong. If in doubt, ask. This also has the advantage that the other person is talking again
Let things evolve	Do not try to overcome several stages at once. Negotiations take time. If you bring all the arguments at the beginning, you will quickly run out of ammunition. Think of it as climbing a mountain peak: step by step, without haste
Appear confident and congruent	The less you pretend and the more you radiate self-assurance, the more authentic and convincing you will come across. Look your interviewer firmly in the eye. Do not try to play the tough businessperson if that is not your nature, but do not be intimidated either. There would be no negotiation if you did not have something to offer that your counterpart would like

(continued)

Table 4.2 (continued)

Principle	Explanation
Remain objective	He who roars has lost. So do not let yourself be lured out of your reserve. If your counterpart does not heed this advice, remain objective. But do not be resentful either. That is also part of "being objective" I-messages help minimize emotional reactions. "You just said that…" simply sounds different than "I heard that…" —especially if the second half-sentence is emotionally charged
Search win–win solution	Look for a solution that benefits both sides. To do this, you need to understand the other person's needs, which in turn requires you to let the other person talk and listen carefully yourself. Again, thorough preparation helps. It is advantageous for further cooperation if both negotiating partners are satisfied with the solution

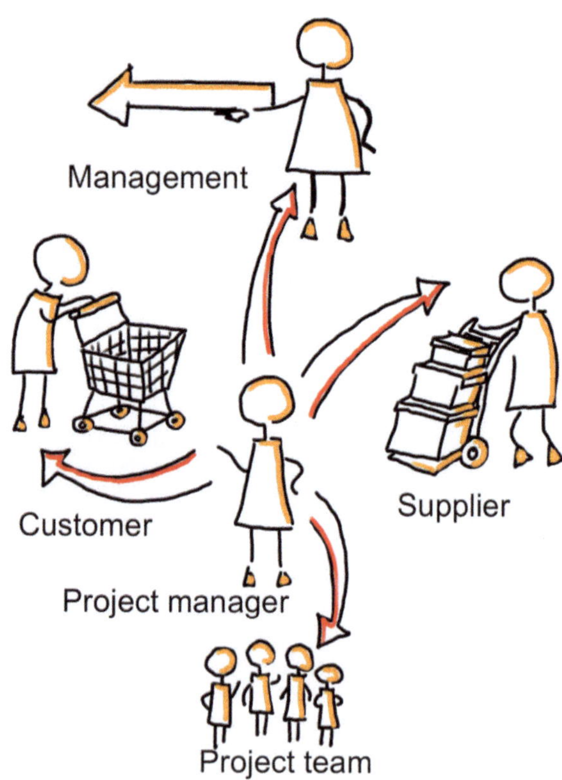

Fig. 4.2 Communication in all directions

the obvious work overload? These are questions that are discussed in the team and can divert attention from the actual goal. We will discuss this in more detail in Chap. 10.

It is important to create an open, fault-tolerant project culture right from the start. Projects in which errors are covered up and deviations are reported as late as possible are difficult to control. If an employee reports "I'm practically done" several times in a row, then this statement clearly does not have much validity. Late communicated schedule delays or additional costs are also a problem for the customer. It does not help to bury your head in the sand in the face of problems.

4.5.4 Facilitation and Visualization Techniques

While communication is a basic theme that runs through the entire course of the project, facilitation skills are required in workshops, especially at the beginning of the project and in times of crisis, e.g., to determine the project definition, for risk analysis, or to find solutions to conflicts or problems. The project manager should therefore have basic knowledge of facilitation methods and be able to visualize complex subjects.

Instead of presenting these methods one-by-one in this section, let us look at a concrete example. How could the project start workshop for our graphics platform project look like?

Our fictitious workshop is all about one crucial question: "What must the platform be able to do?" Preliminary discussions have already shown that views on this differ widely. Therefore, the workshop promises to be challenging. In addition, the project manager knows the participants and knows that some of them are rather quiet in meetings.

Thus, he decides to start by using pin-it cards as these help to involve all participants in a group. All participants write their ideas, objections, suggestions, or whatever is being discussed on colored cards. First, these are placed on the pinboard without any sorting so that everyone gets an overview. In a second step, the cards are then arranged thematically ("clustered") on the pinboard and given headings.

When it comes to the sequence of function calls, all participants are in danger of losing the overview. Everyone has a sequence in mind, but it is difficult to communicate this to the group. This is where flowcharts come in handy to illustrate the processes.

Flowchart are generally known. However, most project managers are less aware that they can also be worked out with small cards on the pinboard. The result may look rather unprofessional at first glance; however, the discussion with haptic cards is much livelier and more creative than it would be the case with some professional-looking software. Flowcharts as a visualization technique are also suitable when seeking for optimization potential in existing processes.

One of the requirements identified so far is: "the user interface should look modern." This is too vague for the project manager. What does "modern" mean for the participants? Perhaps there is even an opportunity to develop new, creative ideas.

Brainstorming is probably the best-known creativity technique. All workshop participants throw ideas at each other about what the platform could look like. "Kidding around"—i.e., coming up with obvious, but funny nonsense—is explicitly allowed, negative criticism, on the other hand, is explicitly forbidden. All suggestions are noted without evaluation. Later, the wheat is separated from the chaff. The basic idea is that participants stimulate each other to come up with creative suggestions.

Above all, our project manager wants to avoid developing the platform without taking the user's needs into account. Therefore, he asks an absurd-sounding question: "How do we fail best? What must we do so that no one can use our platform?" and has the group "brainstorm" on this. This method is known as "reverse brainstorming" or "brainstorming paradox." It is well suited for identifying risks. The rules are the same as for brainstorming.

To structure the brainstorming results, our project manager uses mind maps. Today, mind maps are part of the standard repertoire of every manager. Well prepared, they can also serve as a checklist or agenda for a workshop and be filled with life during the discussion. Ideally, the tool allows to convert the mind map into a text file, which considerably simplifies the preparation of a formal, final report (e.g., for the customer).

Toward the end of the workshop, the requirements are to be prioritized. Although the last break was not long ago, the participants seem tired. The ten most important requirements are quite easy to identify, but the fine-tuning is proving tough. Our project manager therefore resorts to dot-voting, which allows him to get a picture of the group's mood within a very short time and with little effort. All he needs are enough dot stickers and a flipchart.

Since there are ten requirements, each participant receives 6 dot stickers.[4] The participants can now decide whether to distribute their points or to put all their points on the scale for one topic.

As in any meeting, it is important in workshops to come to a conclusion and clearly identify next steps. Our project manager therefore creates a classic to-do list on the flipchart. Thus, he keeps a visible record for everyone of who must do what and by when.

---

[4] The general formula for the number of dot stickers per participant is: Number of topics/2 $+$ 1 $=$ Number of dots per participant.

4.6 Summary

This chapter covers the first phase of a project, project initiation. The aim of this phase is to identify and evaluate the opportunities and risks of the project, to decide for or against implementation, to obtain the necessary information for further implementation if necessary, and to sort contractual matters out.

The project definition is part of the written project order. It contains information about the project motivation and goals, the stakeholders, the development plan, the requirements to be implemented (if known), preconditions and assumptions, and the project organization.

There are several different contract forms, all of which should be regulated in writing. In addition to content-related aspects, a contract specifies the procedure, particularly regarding the prioritization of work packages, the communication channels and forms, and the handling of changes and deviations.

Various elicitation techniques exist for requirements analysis, but they are beyond the scope of this book.

The "soft factors," i.e., soft skills, play an important role in project initiation.

4.7 Exercises

1. Explain the importance of project initiation.
2. Name and explain three key project initiating activities.
3. Explain why negotiation, facilitation, and communication skills are required during project initiation.
4. Name and explain three aspects that should be covered as part of the project definition.
5. Explain why it should be contractually regulated how to deal with subcontractors or freelancer.
6. Which aspects should be contractually fixed in any case? How could you contractually anchor these aspects in agile frameworks?
7. Explain possible consequences resulting from an unsystematic requirements analysis.

References

(ASQF CPPM 2025): Project Management Foundations, Syllabus (EN), ASQF® Certified Professional for Project Management (2025) - Foundation Level, Version 3.0, 2025.

(Cai et al. 2023): Cai, X., Hall, N.G., Wang, S. & Zhang, F. (2023). Cooperation and contract design in project management with outsourcing. Journal of Systems Science and Systems Engineering, 32(1), 34–70. https://doi.org/10.1007/s11518-023-5548-x

(CPRE 2024): International Requirements Engineering Board, IREB® Certified Professional for Requirements Engineering – Foundation Level, V 3.2.0, February 2024, https://www.ireb.org/en/cpre/foundation/

(Feng et al. 2023): Feng, K.J.K., Liao, Q.V., Borenstein, J., Li, J. & Liu, Y. (2023) Understanding Collaborative Practices and Tools of UX Professionals. In: Proceedings of the 2023 CHI Conference on Human Factors in Computing Systems (CHI '23). New York: ACM, pp. 1–16. https://doi.org/10.1145/3544548.3581273 (dl.acm.org).

(Habib, Graziotin & Wagner 2025): Habib, M.K., Graziotin, D. & Wagner, S. (2025) ReqBrain: Task-Specific Instruction Tuning of LLMs for AI-Assisted Requirements Generation. arXiv preprint arXiv:2505.17632. Available at: https://arxiv.org/abs/2505.17632

(ISO 25000:2014): ISO/IEC 25000:2014 – Systems and software engineering - Systems and software Quality Requirements and Evaluation (SQuaRE) - Guide to SQuaRE. Available at: https://www.iso.org/standard/64764.html

(ISO 29148:2018): ISO/IEC/IEEE 29148:2018 – Systems and software engineering — Life cycle processes — Requirements engineering. Available at: https://www.iso.org/standard/72089.html

(ISO 21502:2020): International Organization for Standardization (ISO), ISO 21502:2020(E) – Project, programme and portfolio management — Guidance on project management. Geneva: ISO.

(Meyer 2022): Meyer, B.: Handbook of Requirements and Business Analysis. Cham: Springer. https://doi.org/10.1007/978-3-031-06739-6. eText ISBN 978-3-031-06739-6.

(Ulusoy & Hazir 2021): Ulusoy, G. & Hazır, Ö. (2021). An Introduction to Project Modeling and Planning. Springer Nature. https://doi.org/10.1007/978-3-030-61423-2

Project Planning 5

5.1   On the Importance of Planning

If one does not know to which port one is sailing, no wind is favorable. (Lucius Annaeus Seneca, 4 B.C. to 65 A.D.)

Seneca's saying is not new wisdom and yet it is still valid today. Only those who know their goal can take the right path. But the reverse is also true: Only those who plan their route will reach their goal quickly and with certainty.

In addition to the problems that automatically arise from poor or missing requirements, a lack of sound planning will inevitably end in a situation that is universally feared, but unfortunately regularly encountered: chaos.

If all this has been known for so long, and if chaos is so feared, why do so many projects end up in this state? There could be two reasons:

- The people in charge are inexperienced and do not know what steps they need to take to get their project on track
- Or worse, it's the so-called "heroes at work" syndrome.

The latter are those species that settle down in disorderly and thus non-measurable conditions—because they can then draw attention to themselves through ad hoc measures, or because they simply refuse to accept measurable conditions.

In such an environment, sound project management will not be possible. In any case, reliable project results cannot be predicted.

To engage in project management means to embrace a methodology that allows for making statements about the state of the project and its anticipated future course at any given time. Those who settle into chaotic conditions live in day-to-day business. A planned approach does not take place.

A typical statement is: "Somehow we still made it." This is the attitude of the person who jumps from the 20th floor and then, when he passes the tenth floor,

© The Author(s), under exclusive license to Springer Nature Switzerland AG 2026   91
A. Johannsen et al., *Foundations for Software Project Management in Classic and Agile Environments*, https://doi.org/10.1007/978-3-032-16797-2_5

is satisfied to find that everything has gone well so far. Everyone will realize that thinking during the fall about what strategy to use to survive the impact does not sound like a planned course of action. One might even call it foolish. And nothing becomes more right by doing it wrong for years.

So what will happen in reality when you try to run projects on a "day to day" basis? Probably something will be delivered, however.

- The project scope might be reduced,
- Team size must be increased in late phases,
- The budget will be exceeded,
- The quality—at least that of certain parts—will not meet expectations, and
- The project team members burn out.

The heroes are not those who try to control chaos, but those who prevent it!

To be clear: this applies to both sequential and agile approaches.

Sound project planning plays a central role in project management. It is all about being equipped for thorough project controlling. Its importance cannot be emphasized enough! Without project planning there can be no project controlling.

We should be clear about one thing: project planning costs time and therefore money. Omitting it or not carrying it out with due diligence, however, will certainly be many times more expensive! What is missed in the early phases of a project can hardly be made up for later (or if it is, only incompletely and with much effort)—not to mention the resulting problems. Taking the steps at the right time, on the other hand, is a relatively inexpensive matter.

No sailor would set sail without first planning the route! How else should they be able to determine on the way that they have deviated from the course to then initiate a course correction? Who now claims that this comparison is lame because experienced captains do not have to plan known routes, forgets that by definition no project is like another. So, there is no known route for our navigator to use.

In the following, the individual steps of a sound project planning as well as their importance will be described. Not every step has to be carried out in the same way for every project, but each has its own important significance, and none should be omitted completely.

5.2   Defining the Project Scope

Project planning is a continuous activity that starts at project initiation when the project definition is created. During the project, this project definition or parts of it are revised and further detailed as the understanding of the project scope increases. The activities and artifacts described in this chapter are closely related to the management practices "Planning," "Costs," and "Schedule" of ISO 21502:2020 and form the basis for subsequent controlling.

Let us be more concrete. When we start planning for our project, the first step should be to check whether the project definition is still up to date or whether it needs updating. This becomes even more important the more time has elapsed between the creation of the project definition and the start of planning. Only in this way can we subsequently rule out, to the best of our knowledge and belief, that there are no remaining gaps in the understanding of our project; i.e., that the scope of the project is clear to us.

All project documents—including documents created in the planning phase—must be consistent with each other. If there are deviations, it is not foreseeable on what basis the substantive decisions will be made.

Next, a rough roadmap for our project must be established from the information contained in the project definition. (We will explain the reasons for that later.)

5.3   Milestone Planning—What for?

Many projects require overarching scheduling, often in the form of a milestone plan. We have to make sure that the time frame we determine matches the one our clients—whether internal or external—have in mind. If this does not happen, major problems are pre-programmed from the beginning. It is, therefore, a good idea to define markers that we can use to validate our common understanding of the timing with our stakeholders.

The markers we use in project management are called milestones. They mark important events during the project and divide the project into meaningful sections.

> **Definition** Milestone
> A milestone is an event of special significance in project management (ASQF CPPM 2025).

Milestones describe not only deliveries, but also transitions between project phases as well as internal quality reviews. Typical main milestones are project start, start of implementation, first delivery, etc. In addition, there are also milestones that serve more for internal coordination such as the availability of certain components.

Milestones have an important function. On the one hand, they help to minimize the risk of undesirable developments by forcing the monitoring of project progress. On the other hand—and this should not be underestimated—they enable the team members to experience success.

Milestones give a project a time structure and facilitate coordination and communication with stakeholders. However, they can do even more, as we will see when dealing with progress monitoring.

Once the milestones have been identified, the question of documentation arises. This is, where the milestone plan comes in. It is established from the project goals and compared with predefined milestones, if existing.

The simplest form of a milestone plan is a list as shown in Fig. 5.1.

	A	B	C
1		**Milestones**	
2		Requirement specification	January 8, 2024
3		Order placed by customer	January 19, 2024
4		Project start workshop	January 26, 2024
5		Q1 Gate	February 14, 2024
6		End of system requirement analysis	February 23, 2024
7		End of software requirement analysis	March 18, 2024
8		End of hardware requirement analysis	March 18, 2024
9		Design freeze A-Sample	July 12, 2024
10		Q2 Gate	July 17, 2024
11		Pre-Release A-Sample	July 22, 2024
12		Release A-Sample	July 31, 2024
13		Q3 Gate	October 5, 2024
14		Design freeze B-Sample	November 21, 2024
15		Pre-Release B-Sample	December 16, 2024
16		Release B-Sample	December 20, 2024

Fig. 5.1 Documentation of milestones in a list

This presentation form ensures that the information is documented in a reliable manner, can be discussed and agreed with the stakeholders and is available at any time.

The milestone plan includes the main milestones (e.g., start of project initiation, agreed requirements, agreed system architecture, coordinated deliverables and others), as well as supporting, internal milestones depending on the circumstances.

Definition Deliverable

ISO 21500:2012: A deliverable is a unique and verifiable element that is required to be produced by a project.

This includes deliverables of work packages or deliverables at milestones. Deliverables define the required outputs and outcomes of a project, and correlate to either tangible or intangible objects that have to be delivered by the project.

However, it is problematic that the milestones are written down separately and there is no link to the other planning data. There is a risk that the list diverges from other planning documents. If necessary, checks and reconciliations must always be carried out manually with other information (e.g., the availability of employees), which is time-consuming and involves the risk of errors.

	Milestones	March 2024	April 1, 2024	May 2024
1	**Milestones**	**March 2024**	**April 1, 2024**	**May 2024**
2	Requirement specification	January 8, 2024	January 8, 2024	January 8, 2024
3	Order placed by customer	January 19, 2024	January 19, 2024	January 19, 2024
4	Project start workshop	January 26, 2024	January 26, 2024	January 26, 2024
5	Q1 Gate	February 14, 2024	February 14, 2024	February 14, 2024
6	End of system requirement analysis	February 23, 2024	February 23, 2024	February 23, 2024
7	End of software requirement analysis	March 18, 2024	March 18, 2024	March 18, 2024
8	End of hardware requirement analysis	March 18, 2024	March 18, 2024	March 18, 2024
9	Design freeze A-Sample	July 12, 2024	July 12, 2024	July 12, 2024
10	Q2 Gate	July 17, 2024	July 17, 2024	July 17, 2024
11	Pre-Release A-Sample	July 22, 2024	July 22, 2024	July 22, 2024
12	Release A-Sample	July 31, 2024	July 31, 2024	July 31, 2024
13	Q3 Gate	October 5, 2024	October 5, 2024	October 5, 2024
14	Design freeze B-Sample	November 21, 2024	November 21, 2024	November 21, 2024
15	Pre-Release B-Sample	December 16, 2024	December 16, 2024	December 16, 2024
16	Release B-Sample	December 20, 2024	December 20, 2024	February 3, 2025

Fig. 5.2 Milestones as a trend

An extension of the list-based milestone planning allows to record a trend over milestones (see Fig. 5.2). Here, the focus of the statement is rather on the development of the dates over time.

So, there is more information in the list. However, the problem of the missing link to the further planning data remains.

In Fig. 5.2, we see how at regular intervals the milestone date was re-evaluated. The recording of a milestone-trend serves as input for progress monitoring at the project level. More about this later.

So, what is the easiest way to link the milestones to the other essential planning data? By saving both in the same document, for example, and linking them there! For this, the activity time planning is suitable, which—as we will see later—is indispensable in project management and which is closely linked to the so-called work breakdown structure.

Definition Work Breakdown Structure (WBS)
Decomposition of the defined scope of a project (...) into progressively lower levels consisting of elements of work (ISO 21502:2020).

The work breakdown structure (WBS) is used to create a picture of a project based on its deliverables. The purpose of the work breakdown structure is to identify all deliverables and prevent components and work packages from being overlooked.

In the definition above, we just used the term "work package." This term is not difficult to picture and imagine. You certainly think of a "bunch of work" to be done. However, it is important to know how much work professionals connotate with this term, so we better specify this term more precisely:

> **Definition** Work package
> ISO 21500:2012: A group of activities that have a defined scope, deliverable, timescale, and cost.

Now it becomes clear, that a work package always entails some activities, and is the lowest level to be shown in a WBS, which implies that it belongs to a level above the activity level:

> **Definition** Activity
> At the lowest level, the WBS defines the work packages from which the activities are derived, which must be estimated and planned out in detail. As the smallest unit, the planned activities later form the basis for project control (ASQF CPPM 2025).

Activities have a length and are arranged over time depending on various influencing factors. In the sequential world, this typically happens in a planning phase preceding implementation (we call this upfront planning), whereas in the agile world, identification and planning of activities only happens for a very short period of time (an iteration). Also, the possibilities to plan milestones and activities together differ fundamentally.

5.3.1 Milestone Plans in the Sequential World

In the early years of software projects, a method was sought for documenting activities and associated milestones graphically. Due to a lower complexity and a significantly smaller scope compared to today's software solutions, it was possible at that time to fall back on a technique that was known from general project management: The network plans.

In network plans, each activity (also called node) is represented by a box containing parameters related to the activity. These are the earliest and the latest possible starting point, the earliest and the latest possible ending time, the buffer, and the duration of the activity. Network plans are used to arrange activities depending on external frame conditions and internal dependencies and allow the representation of processing paths by bringing the activities into a relationship.

To use network diagrams, the scope of activities should remain manageable and the duration of activities should be sufficiently long. Otherwise, the plans become so confusing that the overview is lost. To this day, network plans are often used in the construction sector, for example, when the activities of building a floor have to be planned in the necessary sequence.

In software projects, the network planning technique has reached its limits. The challenges are too complex, the number of activities and the interdependencies are too high. Also, the estimated duration of the activities is usually too short to use network diagrams in a meaningful way. A clear representation is simply no longer possible here, especially since all nodes have the same size and the duration must be read off. This makes a simple and quick interpretation of the overall situation enormously difficult.

Another technique from the early twentieth century turned out to suit better. The bar chart developed by Henry L. Gantt (from 1910 on) and named after him proved to be very well suited for displaying small-scale planning. Today, a wide variety of software tools can be found that support Gantt charts.

We will have a closer look at Gantt charts in the context of activity time planning in the sequential environment. In this section, we will concentrate on the question how they elegantly solve the question of joint documentation and planning of milestones with the other planning data.

Gantt charts allow documentation of milestones by simply using a different definition: Milestones are activities of length zero. So, it is possible to insert an activity in the Gantt chart, give it a length of zero and from that moment on, it will be usually displayed by tools as a milestone in the form of a diamond (see Fig. 5.3). In this way, it is possible to insert the milestones into the common Gantt chart and to bring them into a relationship with other planning data such as activities. This also means that the activities can be assigned to their respective milestones. It is therefore no longer necessary to manually reconcile the information.

5.3.2 Milestone Plans in the Agile Environment

There is no upfront planning at activity level in the agile environment. But what about the milestones?

The central document to be able to look into the future in agile methodologies—especially in Scrum—is the product backlog. The user stories (short: "stories", as we will call them from now on) that are already known are prioritized and thus arranged in a chronological order.[1] The form in which a product backlog is maintained is not prescribed by the Scrum Guide. Some project teams prefer to use a haptic board with notes on a wall, others (especially when a project exceeds a certain size) rely on the use of a software tool.

It is important to consider that milestone planning typically plays a key role in the project and is sometimes taken on by employees who may not necessarily be in an agile context. Let's take an overall project manager, for example. This person has to coordinate joint planning with internal or external stakeholders, who often work in a plan-driven, sequential manner. Here, the problem of linking the milestones with other planning information arises again—in this case with the

---

[1] Remember that user stories are units of software functionality which are valuable to the customer, testable and understandable to both customers/users and developers.

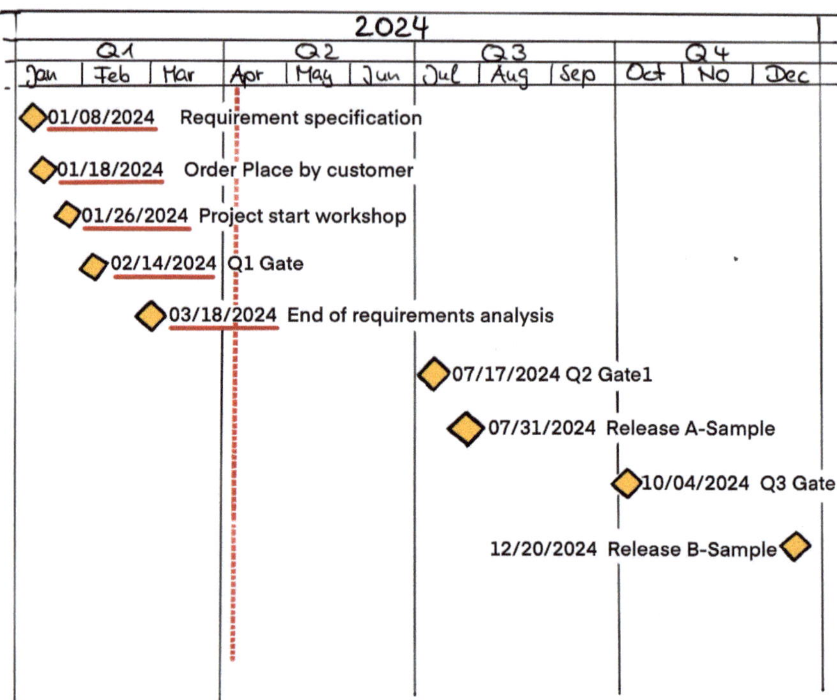

Fig. 5.3 Milestones in the Gantt chart

stories. Without a suitable link, there is a great risk of coordination problems and incorrect planning.

It is strongly recommended that the higher-level roles use the same tool for milestone planning that is used by the product owner to maintain the product backlog. Most software tools allow the product backlog to be structured in order to implement release planning. If you define that the milestones are managed as releases, you have a wonderfully lean solution that causes no disruption in the tool chain and is consistent a priori.

But what about haptic product backlogs with stories as paper cards on a physical wall? It is of course possible to perform, e.g., a release planning using cards on haptic boards. The related method is called "Story Mapping". Prioritizing the stories, taking into account different releases, is part of the daily work for experienced product owners.

Preferably, it should be possible to link all user stories or other items of planning to the higher-level overall planning structure, usually the milestone sections, i.e., every user story should be linked to a release and/or milestone.

5.4   Big Picture—What is the Structure of the Project?

Every project—no matter how complex, how large or how complicated—must be able to be represented in the form of a clear presentation. This is just as true for the development of a small web application as it was for the "Apollo program" to realize the moon landing. Admittedly, the pictures representing the project will be of different complexity and probably not the same size, but both projects can be presented in a structured way. If people involved feel unable to establish this structure completely, this is an alarm signal.

5.4.1   The Work Breakdown Structure

So we need something that we call in technical jargon the work breakdown structure (WBS). It is created from all the information gathered in previous steps. Combining this information, we have all the insights: what our project is about, what the challenges are, what its scope is, and what ultimately needs to be delivered. Requirements, project goals and the results of milestone planning, as well as any assumptions, lead to a big picture of our project, an overview of what needs to be accomplished in the course of the project. If individual pieces of information are missing, the work breakdown structure cannot be fully described, and the big picture is incomplete.

Creating a work breakdown structure is not very time-consuming. The cost–benefit ratio is very good. A workshop of a few hours with experienced personnel usually already delivers very good results for smaller projects, which can be updated or refined in later phases. The workshop participants usually follow a top-down approach in which the project is broken down from the higher-level structures to the lower levels.

A work breakdown structure is composed of what we call the list of deliverables of the project. Work packages are a set of activities that generate effort and require planning. Therefore, the name is misleading. Not all of them have a purely functional character. Some of them are only indirectly part of a delivery. "Quality" is a good example. We will probably not find "quality" listed as deliverable. However, if quality is missing in the delivered features, the delivery will certainly be refused just as if the features were missing.

Similarly, we plan work packages for project management, configuration management and so on. As soon as we have to schedule employees for the work packages, the work packages are part of the work breakdown structure. What is not in the WBS, is by definition not part of the project.

The purpose of this step is to make sure that nothing is forgotten in the project. If we follow the rule described above and if competent people participate in the definition of the WBS, the resulting document will show what must be achieved during the project. Therefore, the WBS is an important document which should also be subject to review.

5.4.2   Presentation of the WBS

There are several ways to build a work breakdown structure. The international standard for WBS creation (ISO 21511:2018) helps organizations to increase project transparency, alignment, and efficiency by ensuring that all work packages are clearly defined, organized, and traceable throughout the project lifecycle. While the standard is neither compulsory nor always applied in its entirety, some basic rules apply to all possible forms of a WBS:

- The representation should be graphical.
- As the name suggests, it is a structured, hierarchical representation.
- The structure should always be broken down until the elements at the lowest level become manageable. Those elements are then called features or (depending upon context) components.
- The work breakdown structure shows a very rough and preliminary architecture.

Usually, the WBS is documented in a tree structure, but mind maps are equally helpful.

Example To leave the theory behind, let's create a work breakdown structure for our project example, which uses a normal tree structure. The result is shown in Fig. 5.4. The starting node is our project itself. Below this are the individual domains with their components as columns (of course, this example does not claim to be complete).

In Fig. 5.4, the tree structure focuses on delivery items. Alternatively, the tree could also reflect the question, who is in charge. The WBS presentation with a function-oriented structure, in which the organization or the executive bodies are put forward, is rather rare, but may make sense in individual cases.

Figure 5.4 also shows how the WBS reflects a simple preview of a later system architecture.

The lowest level nodes (i.e., the leaves of the tree) represent the work packages that require resources and need planning. This is where the effort will occur. Do not go too much into detail at this level. It will be expensive and you will lose the overview. Keep the concept of components in mind!

In general, it should be possible to estimate at the work package level. Effort estimates at the work package level are very often necessary when the work breakdown structure is used to prepare a quotation. Bidding usually takes place at a very early stage of planning and may need to be done quickly. There is usually not enough time for an estimate at activity level.

However, due to the fact that work packages are not so detailed, this will result in relatively rough and inaccurate estimates that will need to be refined later, based on the activities. (Remember: We are still on a high-level planning. Work packages are sets of activities, and the latter will be the basis for detailed project planning.).

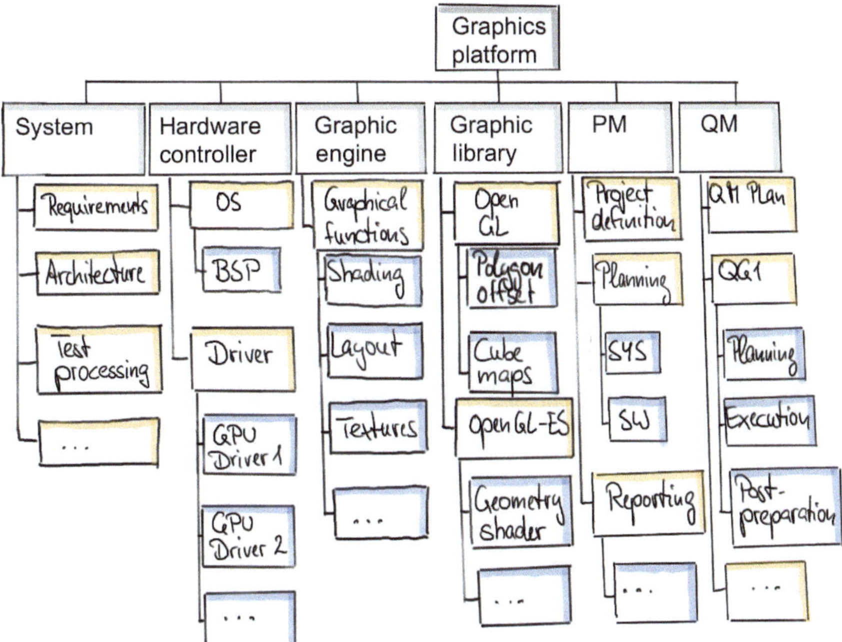

Fig. 5.4 Example of a work breakdown structure in tree structure

The packages are simply still too large to achieve comparable accuracy with activity-level estimates. Ultimately, this also means that we must be aware that we will find deviations when we estimate in more detail later. For this reason, assumptions and exclusions that led to the creation of the work breakdown structure must be documented and included in the offer.

Has a work breakdown structure always to be documented in the form of a graphic? Our first rule emphasizes this. After all, it is the aim to ensure the overview. However, in case the overview does not suffer, it is also possible to enter the work breakdown structure directly as a hierarchy in the form of headings in the Gantt charts. In smaller software projects, this is definitely a viable approach.

It is important that each component of the WBS has a unique identifier to which all other documents (e.g., activity scheduling) refer.

5.4.3 The WBS in Agile

Agile projects use different terms, but follow the same idea of breaking down larger work packages into smaller items. Typically, a product backlog with items is created, which will be continually updated and detailed. Epics are detailed in user stories and may be represented as story maps.

A story map is a visual representation of a product backlog that organizes user stories along the horizontal axis by the user's workflow and along the vertical axis by priority, importance or chronological order. It helps teams understand the big picture of product functionality, plan releases, and identify gaps in the user journey (Patton 2014).

Figure 5.5 shows these axes:

- The horizontal axis represents the user journey. The activity corresponding to the epic is broken down into its individual steps. The sequence of steps forms the "narrative line" (see Fig. 5.5) or "backbone," as it is often called. The distribution of user stories on the horizontal axis is determined by the position of the corresponding step.
- The vertical axis represents the release planning. What goes into which release is determined by the priorities of the user stories. Most essential stories should be part of the first release which corresponds to the minimum viable product.

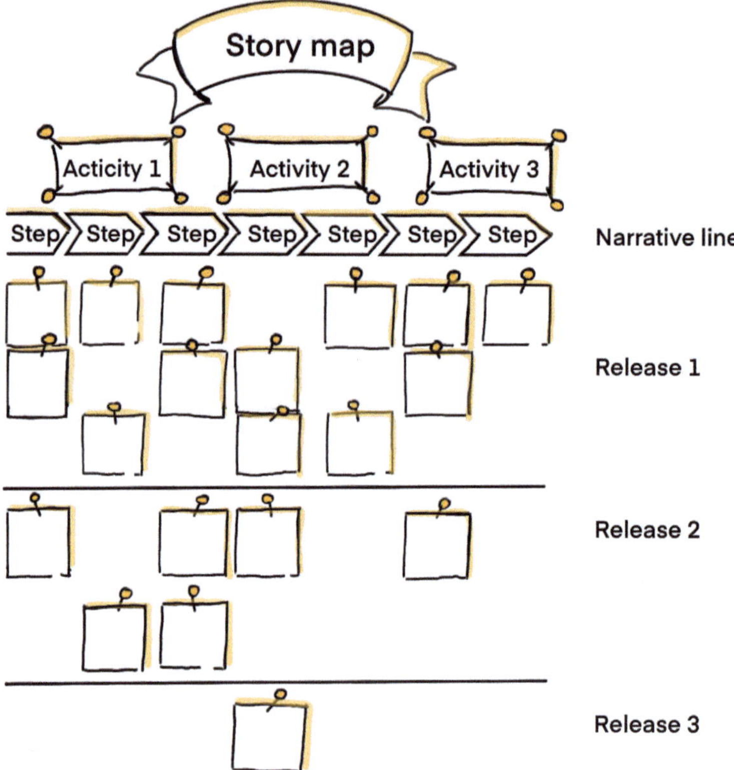

Fig. 5.5 Release planning using a story map

Stories with lower priority can be developed in later iterations, even if they belong to the same step as the one included in the first release.

However, story maps do not represent the entire scope of a project. This is precisely why a WBS can also be valuable in agile projects.

Even in agile frameworks we obtain a considerable benefit from having a WBS, because it is a perfect starting point for the product backlog creation and helps to create an initial estimate of the expected effort for the project.

> **Example** Remember our WBS in Chap. 5. Among the graphics functions, there were "Shading" and "Textures." "Shading" could directly become a story in the product backlog, whereas the "Textures" work package is more like an epic, since it is likely that the individual textures can still be broken down into individual stories.
>
> In sequential project management frameworks, we find a similar situation. "Shading" could serve as a work package in an activity schedule as an umbrella term or cluster of associated activities, "Textures" would need to be further subdivided.

5.5 The Path to Realistic Effort

In software projects, the costs are generated by one main factor: The development effort. Software development is the only discipline in which the product is already created during development—solely by writing or generating code of the required quality and then testing it. In hardware development this is different. Here, the architecture and design are developed first, which then serve as input variables for the actual hardware production.

Thus, no manufacturing employees, production lines or machines are necessary to produce software. As long as AI agents cannot fully create software without human involvement (refer to Chap. 8 concerning AI agents), we can draw a very simple formula to determine what costs our software product will incur in production:

> The majority of the costs for a software product originate from the labor expenses in the development and test phase.

The conversion of labor expenses into costs is usually very simple, since fixed hourly rates exist. It is therefore clear what a work hour costs for a particular role or person, so the only question that remains is how much labor to expect!

To say it in advance: This is where you can see who has mastered their craft. Deviations of 20% in the calculation of expenses may be painful for a software project with a total volume of 10,000 Euros, but for a total volume of one million they can lead to disaster. Obviously, it makes sense to deal with the subject, to take it seriously and to carry out the estimates with due care.

There are different methods to determine the effort of work packages or activities. Some require experts, others statistically relevant historical data. However, they all have one thing in common, and one should be clear about this: They are estimates and **estimates are only estimates**. Those who expect mathematical accuracy will be disappointed. Fortunately, there are effective ways to address this issue. We will return to this topic later.

Since different tasks mean different challenges, which in turn can be solved in different ways, it is unfortunately not possible to simply talk about "labor expenses." Let us consider an example.

Example We expect that the development of a web page with 1000 lines of HTML5-code is easier and faster to master than 1000 lines of C-code for an I^2S driver,[2] which is written to run on an embedded operating system. On the one hand, the more demanding task will take longer and thus generate higher effort; on the other hand, there is also the question of available skills. An experienced driver developer will not necessarily have the best prerequisites for developing a web page and vice versa. Knowing how long it typically takes to develop a work package is therefore one side of the coin, whether experienced staff can be called upon is the other. This must be considered in the effort estimate.

Our work breakdown structure gives us a very good idea of the skills we need to assemble in our teams and how much personnel will be required. In our example, we might know from experience that a single employee can do the implementation of the Ethernet drivers, but for the textures, we will certainly need two employees.

5.5.1   How Do We Estimate?

The world of estimation methods is divided into methods based on expert knowledge and those requiring very well-maintained historical databases. In addition, there are so-called advanced methods which have been developed for special purposes. Each method has its justification. Which one is ultimately used depends on the project-specific environment and other input requirements.

Before we start, however, the question arises: What do we estimate? The results of estimates are always efforts. In software project management, we never estimate costs, time spans, or the duration of a work package. These parameters emerge in later phases of planning.

---

[2] I^2S stands for "Inter-IC Sound" and refers to the audio data interface between two integrated circuits (IC).

5.5.2 Size Estimates

For size estimates, maintained data are consulted instead of estimating individual work packages to achieve quite good results, even for large packages. The procedure is similar to that in used the construction sector, where nobody counts individual bricks, steel mats and shovels needed. Instead, it is possible to quantify what a cubic meter of enclosed space will cost based on documented empirical values. Of course, this requires differentiation according to a wide variety of parameters. Depending on materials and location, different values will result. It is easy to see that a cubic meter of bicycle shed has a different price than a cubic meter of noble converted attic.

In software projects, size estimates are used primarily when figures must be available for a high number of work packages in a short time, for example, in order to prepare a quotation. Similar to the construction example, we have to determine a size that is used for evaluation. Theoretically, there are several possibilities for the software, such as the number of expected lines of code, input fields or masks and other interfaces, or reusable modules. This number is multiplied by an empirical value to determine the estimated effort.

Often enough, however, this is exactly where the errors in estimation happen. How many lines of code will it actually be? However, if we are able to say that:

- One Ethernet driver typically corresponds to 2800 uncommented lines of code,
- We know what a line of code means in terms of effort,
- The high-level interface is available,
- To our knowledge, an experienced driver developer is available,
- The specification of the Ethernet driver is available, the technology is not new to us, and
- All other relevant conditions are recorded,

then we may venture a statement. However, the question of risks remains. What is the probability that the above assumptions will come true? If they turn out to be wrong, what deviations will result?

Agile projects perform effort estimations at user story level, but refine them during sprint planning. Then, the team determines the necessary tasks, which may lead to an updated estimate.

In Scrum, the effort is not seen as a constant that only depends on the duration of the sprint and the team size. Rather, the productivity is considered to be a variable that relates to the velocity of work within the team. Mike Cohn introduced the term "velocity" in 2005 as "the amount of work a team can tackle during a single sprint." Many see this as the key metric in Scrum (Cohn 2005).

When the efforts for entire stories in the product backlog are estimated, this is, strictly speaking, an estimate of the size, since these estimates precisely meet the criteria for size estimation. On the one hand, the stories are usually too large for exact estimates. On the other hand, the teams use comparative figures for the evaluation. Ultimately, everyone involved is also aware of the relative inaccuracy.

In any case, size estimates must be based on qualitatively and quantitatively reliable and maintained historical data. As stated above, in Scrum, the team regularly determines its own "velocity".

In sequential project management frameworks, empirical values must be collected and made available for follow-up projects. This is precisely the reason why size estimates should be handled with care, especially since they are always used in software projects when there is time pressure anyway.

Again, estimates of large packages will generally tend to give less accurate values than those of smaller ones.

5.5.3   Expert Estimates

But what good is the knowledge that smaller work packages normally provide better estimates if we only have large work packages? Strictly speaking, it is not so much a question between large and small as between coarse and detailed. It is obvious that detailed packages have more information available that can be used in the estimation.

This is precisely the information that is important for expert estimates. Expert estimates are based on assigning the estimate to people who can quantify the efforts based on experience. Basically, it is all about the experts' "gut feeling." Thus, if one wants to ensure that the estimates provide the most accurate results possible, detailing must take place.

In sequential project management frameworks, the delivery objects (i.e., the lowest level of the WBS) could be included in our planning as features and used there as a container or as a heading before they are subsequently split into activities. Figure 5.6 shows this process schematically.

In Fig. 5.7, the delivery objects were transferred from the work breakdown structure to a project management tool and can be found there, typically in a Gantt chart. Again, they are broken down into activities and documented directly in the Gantt chart. Apart from the fact that we keep information together in this

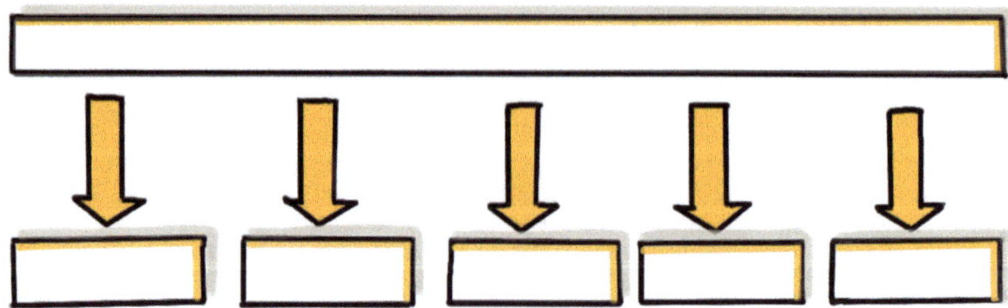

Fig. 5.6 Splitting features into activities

way, this representation has another advantage: The activities are used later in the context of activity scheduling to arrange them over time.

Activities are the smallest unit in project management on which progress monitoring takes place. At the same time, activities have the perfect size for an expert estimate, as they can usually be assessed very well by the experts.

To a certain extent, the following is true: the smaller the activities are, the more accurate the estimates become; however, only to a certain extent. Many small estimates can grow rounding errors, and sooner or later, they become impractical. Apart from this, the effort required to perform the estimates increases enormously, especially if we have many activities. For this reason, we have to weigh things up. Values between a few days and a maximum of two weeks provide good results in terms of estimated values and subsequent monitoring. In addition, the effort for the estimates is kept within limits. The more innovative the topic is, or the less experience we have with it, the more detailed the activities for this feature should be broken down.

Expert estimates follow these general rules:

- Estimates are only estimates! If many small activities exist, the errors average out.
- Estimates require experience! Employees should be given time to learn this.
- Estimates should NEVER be made by only one person! Several experts should agree on a value for an activity.
- Estimates should always be made by the person subsequently appointed to the task, if possible.
- Expert estimates are bottom-up estimates.

In general, expert estimates are based on the fact that experienced personnel can draw on experience when a known technology needs to be evaluated. If it is a completely new matter for the staff or the organization, even an expert estimate will possibly yield very unreliable results. However, whenever we have to determine expected effort, it is still preferable to the other methods described in this book. The inaccuracy of the results is then due to uncertainty. We must be aware of this.

The Delphi Method

An established procedure for expert estimation is the Delphi method (see Fig. 5.8). This is a defined procedure in which, for example, the facilitator role is described. The facilitator prepares the activities, distributes them to the experts, who estimate separately and anonymously. The facilitator then combines the results and presents them to the experts. If there are discrepancies, the facilitator must reach an agreement and, if necessary, convene a second round of estimation.

This method is quite formal and laborious, but it forces a certain discipline and provides agreed estimates in any case.

GPU Driver 1	04/08/2024	07/10/2024	41
	04/08/2024	06/10/2024	34
Analysis of Specification	04/08/2024	04/12/2024	2
Development environment	04/08/2024	04/15/2024	3
Software requirements	04/15/2024	04/19/2024	5
Design	04/22/2024	04/26/2024	4
Implementation High Part	04/29/2024	05/22/2024	11
Implementation Low Part	05/01/2024	05/27/2024	13
Preparation Unit Tests	05/28/2024	06/03/2024	5
Performing Unit Tests	06/04/2024	06/06/2024	3
Code Review	06/07/2024	06/10/2024	2

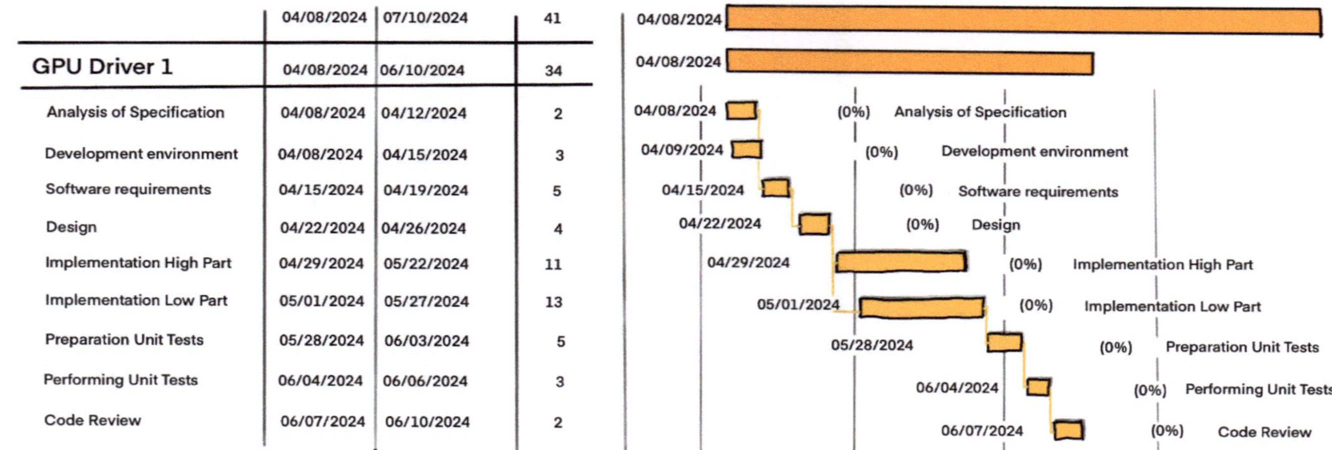

Fig. 5.7 Detailed features in Gantt chart

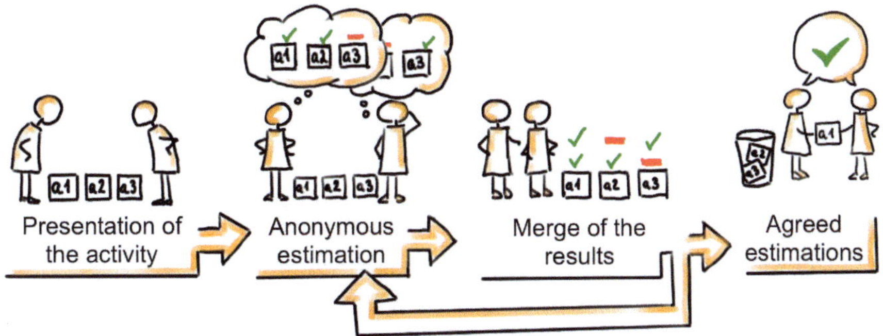

Fig. 5.8 Procedure of a Delphi estimation

The Informal Expert Estimation

If you do not want it to be quite so formal—or if the situation does not allow it—you can also resort to a very widely used method based on the Delphi method principles. We call it the informal expert estimation. There are no rules for a formal description of the activities to be estimated and, except for the experts, no specified roles are mentioned. Still, the general rules described above must be followed to obtain reliable results. Informal expert estimation not only requires less effort, it is also leaner and faster than the Delphi method.

Planning Poker

The expert estimates introduced here were traditionally designed for sequential project management frameworks. However, examining the Delphi method procedure reveals similarities to planning poker as described in Scrum.

In planning poker, the team members (the experts) get playing cards with so-called story points on them. The basic idea of story points is to move away from estimating the effort of stories in the product backlog in hours or days, but rather to evaluate the complexity of a user story. The basis for this should be a reference story, the complexity of which is known to all team members and for which the number of story points is set. During a planning poker session, each team member compares the story to be estimated with the reference story. The conversion of story points into person-hours can be done later by the Scrum master using the team velocity. In practice, however, it has turned out that most teams do think in terms of time. Experience shows that it is quite possible to have the teams estimate in hours or days.

The same cards are also used to estimate the effort of the tasks derived from the stories. Since these are small enough, the points printed on the cards should be interpreted as hours here.

The "Poker" cards have another special feature. The series of numerical values printed on them is not linear but based on a Fibonacci sequence[3] (e.g., 0, 1/2, 1, 2, 3, 5, 8, 13, 20, 40, 100). This accounts for the fact that larger packets cannot be estimated as accurately. So there is little point in arguing at length about whether it will be 40 or 60 h. Thanks to the limited card values, only "rather 40" or "rather 100" can be given as estimates. "Rather 100" signals: "rather inaccurate."

First, the product owner presents the story to be estimated and clarifies any questions. The experts then place their estimates face down on the table. Everyone reveals their cards at the same time. The experts with the lowest and highest estimates explain their reasons. If no agreement can be reached, the team estimates again until the deviations are small enough. Finally, the team agrees on the best value.

Although the experts do not estimate anonymously, the separate, hidden estimation achieves the same advantage as the Delphi method: there is no mutual influence. Both methods provide only one value for each activity, which is ultimately confirmed by all experts.

The Three-Point Estimate

If, when analyzing the activity, the experts determine that the description is not of sufficient quality or that the activity itself is too risky, another method offers a way out.

The three-point estimation is not an estimation method in its own right. It extends the possibilities of Delphi and informal expert estimation by requiring three estimated values for each activity: one pessimistic, one realistic and one optimistic. Again, the experts agree on the respective values and determine what they mean. To obtain an agreed estimate afterward, the equation shown in Fig. 5.9 is recommended.

Since the realistic value enters the equation with a factor of four, it is given a special weighting. If the optimistic or the pessimistic value do not show any particularly strong swings, the calculated value will probably be close to the realistic value.

However, the effort for the estimation triples here, which is why this should only be done for selected activities.

5.5.4   Save Time with Analogy Methods

It is easy to imagine that the effort involved can be very high if all activities are evaluated based on expert estimates. For larger projects, this can quickly add up

---

[3] In the Fibonacci sequence, each number results from the sum of the two preceding numbers. For Scrum, however, this is usually modified for numbers greater than 13 to make the distance even greater. The value 1/2 also does not correspond to the Fibonacci sequence.

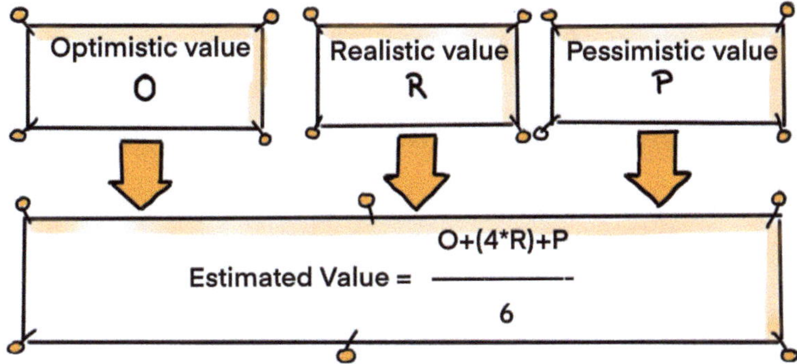

Fig. 5.9 Calculation formula of the three-point estimate

to an effort of many calendar days. Multiplied by the number of experts involved, this results in a considerable effort.

Therefore, we would like to present two more methods that can help to save time. These are the so-called estimations by analogy which are based on data from the past. Knowing those historical data, analogies can be drawn and expected efforts determined.

Established methods for this are the multiplier method and the percentage method. In both cases, only partial steps are estimated, and the missing data is calculated according to the method.

The Multiplication Method

The idea of this method is to find a quantity that can be estimated relatively easily based on up-to-date empirical values, and then convert it directly into an effort estimate.

The attentive reader will notice the similarity in essence to the size estimation. In software projects, the multiplier method uses the same data as the size estimation. Since there is a certain relationship between the number of lines of code of a software module and its effort, this is usually the size of choice. Of course, another size can also be chosen.

In contrast to the size estimation, however, the multiplier method places higher demands on the quality of the conversion to the associated effort by requiring a separate multiplier for conversion for a wide variety of tasks.

Example Table 5.1 shows an example table for the multiplier method. Obviously, the bootloader component has the highest number of weighted lines of code, although it has the lowest number of estimated lines. The high weighting factor of 2.6 indicates that a high effort is expected, that is, 2.6 times higher than expected for the development of an HTML page.

Table 5.1 Example table for the multiplier method

Component	Category	Estimated amount of coding lines (LOC)	Factor	Weighted LOC
GPU Driver 1	Hardware-related	1700	1,8	3060
GPU Driver 2	Hardware-related	1700	1,8	3060
Bootloader (BSP)	Assembler	1200	2,6	3120
Shading	C code with registry access	1800	1,6	2880
Polygon offset	Library/API level	2200	1,4	3080
Test page	HTML	1800	1,0	1800

Two parameters used in this method must come from very well-maintained and reliable historical data: first, the weight factor, and second, the value that indicates the effort actually caused by a weighted line of code. Finally, the sum of calculated weighted lines is multiplied by this value. If we assume that an average developer needs two minutes for a weighted line of code, we get an effort of approximately 70 person-days just for this subset of our project.

The challenge is to calculate a total cost from three parameters, all of which are either estimated or based on historical data. If you already feel unsure about one of those parameters, trouble is in sight.

In agile project management frameworks, T-shirt size estimation is a popular technique that resembles the analogy-based multiplier method. Rather than estimating each work item in isolation, the team agrees on the relative size of the epics, user stories, or features. The multiplier for the T-shirt sizes XS, S, M, L, and XL is then derived from the historical empirical values.

Strictly speaking, even planning poker relies on an empirical multiplier. The expert estimate yields the number of story points that are presumably required to implement a work item. To convert this effort estimate into working hours, it must be multiplied by the average number of hours required per story point, which depends on the velocity of the team.

The Percentage Method

In the case that good and reliable experience about the typical distribution of the efforts of the activities within a work package is available (as shown in Fig. 5.10), you can resort to the percentage method, which helps enormously to save time and thus estimation effort. The percentage method is also a estimation method by analogy. It is actually not an independent estimation method but extends (and accelerates) expert estimates.

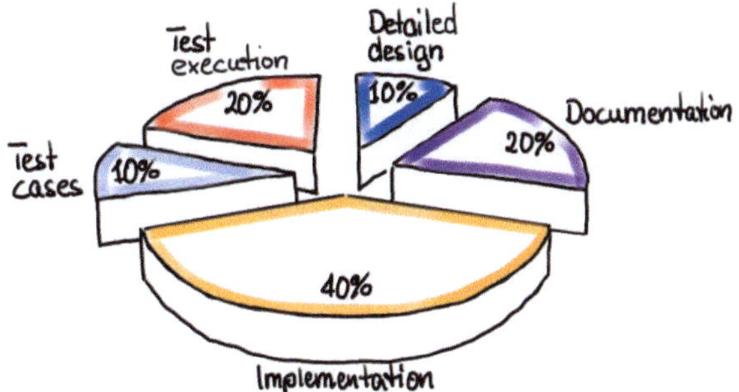

Fig. 5.10 Activities of a work package with percentage efforts

> **Example** Let us stay with our case study. Assuming that we have gathered the experience that for a typical OpenGL[4] graphics library function, the effort for all unit test activities is 10% and the effort for the actual implementation of the code is 40% of the total effort of the work package, one of the two can be calculated if the other is estimated.
>
> If, in addition, we have good historical data for the other activities, the remainder of the work package can be calculated by estimating one type of activities alone.

It is not uncommon to accelerate effort estimates in this way. Again, the challenge is to obtain reliable historical data. If the percentage breakdown is not correct, there may be noticeable deviations from the actual effort required.

However, the percentages may be adjusted rapidly, if work is done iteratively and early feedback is provided.

In any case, the error rate can be minimized by always estimating the largest proportion. The parts to be calculated will then cause a relatively small damage in case of an error due to their smaller size. In our example, we would estimate the implementation and almost half of the total package would have an estimated value with the precision of an expert estimate.

5.5.5   Advanced Methods

A comprehensive work on all aspects of software effort estimation, which can be recommended as further reading and which provides a good overview of methods ranging from planning poker to COCOMO II (see below), is (Trendowicz and Jeffery 2014).

---

[4] OpenGL stands for Open Graphics Library and refers to the specification of a "cross-language, cross-platform application programming interface (API) for rendering 2D and 3D vector graphics." (Wikipedia).

Table 5.2 Advantages and drawbacks of COCOMO II

Advantages	Drawbacks
Well-documented, widely validated in industry practice	Requires extensive and reliable historical data
Supports systematic and repeatable effort estimation	Less suitable for very small or agile projects with high uncertainty
Different modes (organic, semi-detached, embedded) allow flexibility	Can be perceived as complex and resource-intensive to apply
Applicable to integration with Function Point Analysis and other methods	Estimation accuracy depends strongly on calibration of cost drivers

Among the estimation methods are models that have either been developed for specific purposes or are used in targeted industries or use cases. To explain these advanced methods in detail here is beyond the scope of this book. Nevertheless, every project manager should have heard of them at least once.

The COCOMO model (Constructive Cost Model) is an algorithmic cost and effort model in which mathematical functions are used to establish a relationship between certain software metrics and the effort to be determined. Company-specific parameters must also be included in the calculation and, again, these must be based on very solid and well-maintained data.

COCOMO is used primarily in large software projects when the scale no longer permits other estimation methods and the effort for algorithmic modeling can be justified. An updated and widely applied version also suited for medium-sized projects is COCOMO II, introduced by Barry W. Boehm and colleagues in 2000 (Boehm et al. 2000). This version refines the original approach and adapts it to modern software engineering practices, including iterative development and component-based systems. Table 5.2 summarizes the advantages and disadvantages of COCOMO II.

The Function Point Analysis is another advanced method one should have heard of. It attempts to draw conclusions from the purely functional perspective of a user to determine which functions available to the user cause the underlying effort. These functions are called function points. These are not—as one could assume—function calls in the sense of the software architecture, but functionalities, for example, the views or dialogs of an interface. If the requirements for these dialogs are broken down into elementary processes that are meaningful for the user, they each receive a defined point value. If these are added up, the result is the so-called functional size.

The function point analysis was originally introduced by Allan J. Albrecht as a means of determining the productivity of projects. Its use in the context of effort estimation came later, when people realized that the functional size was well suited as an input value for the actual estimation procedure. This shows that the function point procedure is not an estimation procedure in its own right but is only used as a preliminary step for determining the input parameters in order to then convert the functional size into effort, for example, using COCOMO II.

As of today, function point analysis and COCOMO II are mainly used in large and very large projects, mostly with a commercial background. Today's software project managers rarely come into contact with it.

However, in the context of digital transformation and increasing complexity of large-scale IT systems, both COCOMO and function point analysis are regaining importance. They serve as systematic, data-driven estimation approaches at a time when organizations seek more reliable cost and effort predictions in complex environments. Using AI, the potential to efficiently estimate efforts will rise significantly in the near future (Rankovic et al. 2024).

> **Example** COCOMO II estimation software
> With a free demo version of the software SystemStar 3.0, COCOMO II application examples and estimates can be generated with a limited code size, see https://www.softstarsystems.com/demo.htm

5.5.6 Dealing with Risks in Estimation

Regardless of the method used to estimate the effort—uncertainties remain, as the values determined are either based on expert knowledge or are based on calculations whose basis is also subject to imponderables. In this context, we speak of risks, which means that we have to counter these risks with measures.

The trick is first to assess the risks. How big is the probability that the calculated effort will have an error? How important will this error be?

Causes of inexact estimates are insufficiently specified requirements, new technologies and insufficiently experienced personnel available for implementation. If one is able to estimate the resulting deviation and its probability, one can define a measure to counter the risk.

The most widespread measure is certainly to add a buffer to the estimated values. Of course, the question arises as to how big the buffer should be. Again, be pragmatic! As with the estimated values themselves, it is safe to assume that the errors in the buffer estimates compensate for each other, as swings in both directions are to be expected.

Unless you make generic mistakes by setting all the buffers too high or too low. This is where experience comes into play again. However, there is also a strategic aspect that needs to be considered. If the buffers are generally too high, the bid price may not be competitive or the calculated end date may not be acceptable to the customer. If they are too low, planning and cost risks remain.

Ultimately, the quality of the effort estimate stands and falls with the knowledge of all conditions and remains a matter of experience. Agile projects have a clear advantage. Here, experience is built up systematically and quickly, since the short iterations provide rapid feedback on the quality of the estimated values. This experience can then be incorporated into the detailed estimates for the next iteration.

5.6   Where Do Costs Arise in a Software Project?

In the previous step, we have determined the effort of the activities using a selected method. We are thus able to plan the activities over time according to the known project conditions.

However, in the course of project planning, we also need to clarify what the financial implications will be for our project, or, in short, what costs it will cause. Under certain circumstances, the cost estimate is already necessary because a bid must be submitted. In any case, we need it to determine the required budget.

When we talk about software projects, we can take advantage of the fortunate circumstance that there is the one main factor that causes the costs in the project. As already mentioned above, there is a direct correlation between the determined effort and the resulting costs: the labor costs. Even if we have to use different hourly rates for different roles or salary classifications, we have all the information we need to calculate the costs directly from the effort. It could hardly be simpler. All we have to do is multiply the estimated effort by the assigned hourly rates. Any evaluation in terms of experience, knowledge and risks is already taken into account in the effort.

Other cost factors such as training, licenses, test equipment or development tools usually play a subordinate role and can be added to the personnel expenses. In addition, these can usually also be determined relatively easily and accurately.

There is one point you should keep in mind: the costs calculated from the efforts indicate the budget required to implement the project. In customer projects, this is usually not the same as an offer price, for which further strategic and commercial considerations may play a role.

5.6.1   Cost Estimation and Project Management Frameworks

Strictly speaking, all of this only applies to projects managed in sequential models, because only here are all estimated efforts known before the implementation starts.

Is this a dilemma for agile projects? Only if you try to apply the standards of sequential planning to the agile world. If there is a requirement to have an "exact" value regarding the total costs before starting the development activities, we are a priori in a sequential or even plan-driven environment. In such cases, the application of an agile model is not advisable, or should at least only be ventured with appropriate experience.

The adjective "exact" was deliberately qualified above. It would be more than naive to rely on the fact that effort estimates and the resulting costs are exact values that remain valid over the entire project duration. Even in sequentially executed projects, it will only become clear during the project duration how accurate the estimates actually were. Experienced project managers are ready to acknowledge and counteract the deviation. Agile frameworks are not more inaccurate or sloppy than sequential frameworks, they are simply more honest in that they put predictions about far-future commitments into perspective.

So, what is the budget of an agile project? That budget, which was originally agreed at the beginning of the project (based on the facts known at that time). Further provision of budget or adjustments to the feature scope are then made by mutual agreement with all stakeholders. This is a core element of the agile approach. If this is not possible, you are in a sequential environment.

5.7 Activity Schedule or Task Board—Creating the Basis for Controlling

The following section describes what is probably the most important step in the chain of planning activities, although the previous ones were necessary to make it possible. Now, we determine our course along which the project is to be steered. Sequential and agile methods differ fundamentally here, which is why we will focus more on the different aspects.

In sequential project management frameworks, activity scheduling is characterized by the fact that the planning of activities for the entire following period precedes the actual implementation. This so-called upfront planning has the disadvantage that the uncertainty is very high for longer periods. This disadvantage can be mitigated by dividing the implementation into several sections and only carrying out shorter detailed planning for the subsections.

In practice, however, this procedure cannot always be implemented because it potentially collides with the interests of plan-driven stakeholders. Anyway, the advantages of an incremental, iterative way of working are not fully realized because the cycles are still much longer than in agile frameworks.

5.7.1 Influence of Activity Scheduling on Project Controlling

Let us first consider the case of sequential processing. In the course of the effort estimation, the work packages have already been transferred from the work breakdown structure to our planning tool and activities have been derived from them. It is precisely these activities that give activity scheduling the name. Entities that allow us to monitor the progress of the project very precisely on a detailed basis.

At this point, we are getting a little ahead of ourselves. We already know that activities need to be small enough to allow for the most accurate effort estimates possible. Once we look at project controlling, we discover another important aspect: we need transparency regarding the progress of individual activities. All attempts to measure the progress of an activity during its execution inevitably end up in an attempt to track the percentage of completion. In most project management tools, you can enter a percentage of completion for each activity in the Gantt chart. This shows that this procedure is not unusual.

However, a closer look reveals that tracking the percentage of completion not only provides a deceptive sense of security, but also generates expenses that are not justified by a corresponding benefit.

> **Example** Too theoretical? Here is an example. Let us say we want to monitor the progress of an activity that has a length of two months. We will therefore have no choice but to measure how far our activity has progressed at regular interval. If no better method exists—and this will be the rule—we will ask the person in charge to communicate the progress.

Problem #1: Where Does the Value Come From?

Unfortunately, the developer also has little methodological means to make a sound statement. On what metric should he base his statement? Number of lines written compared to lines yet to be written? Number of implemented functions compared to functions yet to be implemented?

Let us be honest: His answer will not be based on reliable numbers, but purely on his gut feeling. First, the comparative value (e.g., the number of functions to be implemented) is usually missing. Second, we cannot call for an estimation session for every intermediate state. Third, the developer is forced to make a statement that actually does not belong to his current area of responsibility.

Problem #2: What Does the Value Mean?

After being backed into a corner, the developer gives the project manager a figure: 50%. Only, what does 50% percentage of completion mean? 50% of the time? 50% of the lines of code?

Apart from that, we still have no idea of the time duration. After all, it is not said that the remaining 50% will take as long as the first 50%. Let's face it: You cannot build a solid progress monitoring on this procedure. Nevertheless, it is all too often common practice, and that, although this procedure has a problematic effect, which even has its own name.

Problem #3: The Asymptotic Approach

The past teaches us that the first statements of the person in charge are usually much more optimistic than those closer to the end of the activity. After all, as time goes by, the developer gains more and more insight into the functionality to be developed and the difficulties that may be involved. Toward the end, they say: "I'm almost finished!" Unfortunately, after a week it is: "Only a very small part is still missing" and so on. This leads to an asymptotic approach of the percentage of completion to the 100% mark. The effect is called the 90% syndrome.

The Possible Way Out

In sequential project management frameworks, a solution can serve as a way out, which is an established standard in agile frameworks—especially in Scrum.

There is only one reliable reference point for measuring the degree of completion of an activity: its end. When the person in charge reports that the activity is complete, we know its concrete status: 100%. Up to this point we were flying blind with regard to its degree of completion.

Therefore, the activities should be as short as possible. If the activity is two months long, we are flying blind for months, but if it is only a few days long, this period of uncertainty is drastically shortened. In addition, there is probably still enough time to counteract if the activity overshoots its planned end.[5]

This procedure is manifested in Scrum, where the duration of activities (called tasks) range from a few hours to a few days. The damage in case of a planning mistakes remains very low.

Conclusion

To summarize, the duration of an activity is critical and makes our lives easier when it comes to measuring project progress at the activity level.

This digression into the subsequent Chap. 6 was necessary because otherwise we create problems in the activity planning that then have to be dealt with later in project controlling.

5.7.2   Arranging Activities Over Time

We remember: At the beginning of the chapter, we talked about the need to document and link the milestones together with "further planning data." We speak about the activities, which we now have to put into a chronological order. We also have to define the dependencies between the activities (this is called the "relationship") and link them to the milestones. This is called activity scheduling.

The chronological order of the activities follows a number of criteria. First of all, a mandatory sequence is derived from the work breakdown structure, that is based upon the priority of the work packages. The milestones determine which features or components belong to the content of each milestone. This is always the case in sequentially executed projects. Even in agile project management frameworks, release planning is the most important specification we have for the arrangement of the stories in the product backlog.

Furthermore, there are mandatory dependencies between the work packages as well as within a package among the activities. It is easy to see that the first floor of a house cannot be built before the ground floor has been completed. Finally,

---

[5] However, the activity must not be on a critical path, because then the end date of the project is inevitably postponed. We will return to this topic later.

external boundary conditions influence the arrangement of a work package and its activities, for example, if we have to wait for supplies provided by the customer (so-called provisions) or if required employees are only available at a specified time.

Activity Scheduling in Sequential Projects

Sequential and agile frameworks differ in one essential point: While in agile frameworks no information has to be given about the type of relationships, in Gantt charts different possibilities are documented.

The most important and most frequently used relationship is the so-called normal sequence, or Finish-to-Start relationship. Here, the following activity can only be started when the preceding activity in the dependency has been completed. In a bar chart, the arrow will then point from the end of the preceding activity to the beginning of the following one.

Other relationships can be the end sequence, where multiple activities must end at the same time, and the start sequence, which marks that multiple activities must start at the same time.

> **Example** Figure 5.11 shows a section of the activity schedule of our case study. All activities identified for work package GPU1 are now in the correct sequence. Almost all activities follow the normal sequence, except for the two implementations that may start simultaneously, since obviously two persons may work in parallel. These two activities follow a start sequence that depends on the design. Figure 5.11 also illustrates that the development environment can be set up independently of all other activities, while requirements still need to be derived and the design created until the implementations start.

We could also have linked the start of both implementations with the completion of the development environment. However, the representation in the Gantt chart can also become very confusing due to the large number of arrows. Yet as soon as the development environment is delayed, the missing relationship should be added.

Figure 5.11 also shows how the start and end dates of the activities result from their dependencies. If the requirements analysis takes longer than expected, the start of the design is automatically postponed. This is where the great advantage of project management software becomes apparent. Those software packages or apps automatically calculate such delays. In general, activity scheduling should be easily adaptable.

As already mentioned, the availability of employees is an important parameter for scheduling of activities. An activity can only start once it is sure that the associated expert is available. Of course, other resources can also lead to dependencies or even bottlenecks. However, employees are by far the most important resources in software projects because they carry out the activities.

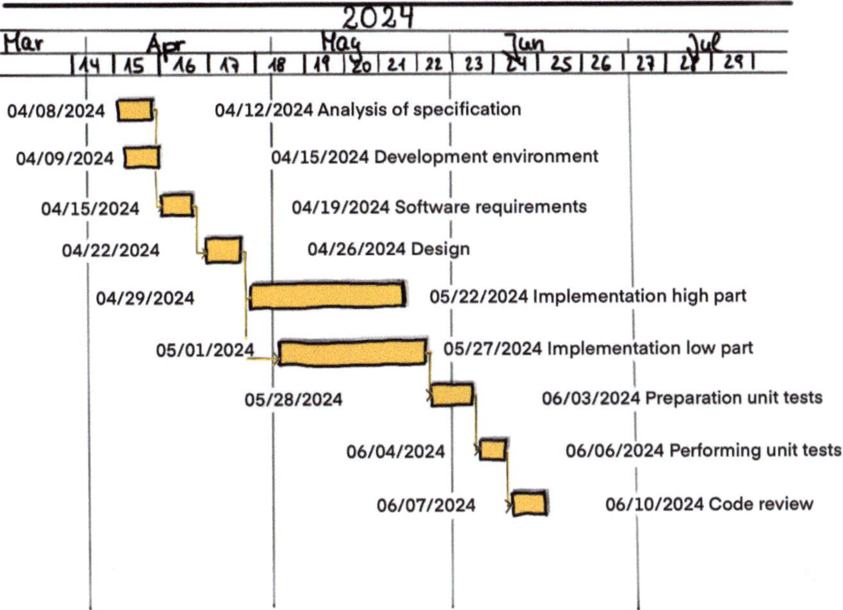

Fig. 5.11 Activity schedule as a Gantt chart

> **Example** In the case of the "High Part" and "Low Part" implementations in our example in Fig. 5.11, we can see that this arrangement was only possible because there are obviously two employees available. Likewise, it will be possible to build the development environment in parallel with the specification analysis and software requirements elicitation.

Note that the duration of an activity may differ from the determined effort if the activity is not scheduled full time, or planned wait times occur. However, it is the duration that determines the activity schedule.

Activity scheduling is not complete until the bar chart fully documents which dependencies have been identified and how they have been accounted for.

Activity Scheduling in Agile Projects

Figure 5.11 represents a typical activity schedule in sequential projects. In the agile world, there is no detailed upfront time planning. Rather, the closer we get to the delivery of an increment, the more detailed the planning becomes. This is known as the agile planning onion (Cohn 2005).

In agile projects, the order of the stories in the product backlog will primarily be determined by the product owner based on priority. The assignment to specific releases plays a decisive role. Technical dependencies between stories are resolved in collaboration with the team.

Even the effort estimation in agile projects differs from sequential projects. The stories are only roughly estimated by the team during release planning. Detailed planning always takes place at the beginning of the sprint in the sprint planning meeting. Here, the team determines which tasks to be implemented in the sprint. There is therefore no pre-prepared activity schedule. Instead, the project is controlled by prioritization. Since the team works through the product backlog in a prioritized manner, critical components can be processed at an early stage.

Agile projects use different tools than sequential projects. During sprint planning, the sprint backlog is determined and made transparent to the entire team using a task board.

> **Definition** Task
> Tasks are activities in agile frameworks that are derived by the team from the user stories at the beginning of an iteration (ASQF CPPM 2025).

Each task is represented by a card which is pinned to the column of its current status. By default, this is "ToDo." When the assigned team member moves the card into another column, the task is given a new status. This procedure is available both haptically on the wall and in software tools that simulate the procedure of cards on the board. In this way, agile frameworks avoid unnecessary effort for rescheduling. In a sequential framework with upfront planning, these expenses are inevitable.

Staff availability is usually not a topic in agile frameworks. In sequential project management frameworks, we need a sound strategy to ensure that the appropriate resources are available at the right time. Instead, Scrum assumes stable teams that are available throughout the entire project. This is an important aspect and, incidentally, has other advantages. Once practiced, stable teams can concentrate fully on the task at hand and develop considerable momentum.

Common Mistakes

A common mistake in activity scheduling is to automatically equate the effort of an activity with its duration. This can only work theoretically if the employee would work full time every day at a stretch on the activity assigned to him. However, since there are also employees with part-time agreements and employees cannot always work the entire working time on the activity, deviations will occur.

Please remember that employees sit in meetings, need rest breaks, and are sometimes also involved in administrative activities. In practice, it has proven successful to schedule a maximum of 80% of the available working time, even in the ideal case.

In sequential project management frameworks, another important aspect must be taken into account. Project management tools allow the specification of a percentage of an employee's participation in an activity. In this way, one can document that the employee is either working on several activities in the project at the same time, or is only available to the project to a certain percentage. The latter is often accepted as God-given, although there is usually a way out of it. The former can certainly be described as a serious error in craftsmanship.

When an employee has to perform several activities at the same time—whether in the same project or in different projects—context switches occur. It is well known that context switches are problematic for activities and no one doubts it. Nevertheless, employees are regularly assigned to several activities at the same time.

This creates a deceptive sense of security, as the plan gives the impression that several activities can be completed at the same time. However, when viewed soberly, the activities are completed later in total, due to the context switches, than if they were processed by the same employee one after the other.

> **Important** Often enough, the above-mentioned mistakes creep in because they allow to conceal fundamental problems.

There are activities that, in principle, have to be performed by several employees. Let us just take the example of a code review in which three people are involved (see Fig. 5.12).

When three employees share an activity, the project manager is missing important information. What was the reason that the activity "Code review GPU1" was not finished in time? How could one have taken countermeasures? If each employee has his own activity, it would have been possible to recognize that the facilitator was still held up by another activity and perhaps even replace him in time. Thus, a completely different picture of the project's progress emerges.

Please keep in mind that the work invested in activity scheduling is for later project controlling. But how do you want to evaluate the progress of activities that are only processed to a certain percentage? Who can guarantee that this percentage will be adhered to? Therefore, always observe the following golden rules:

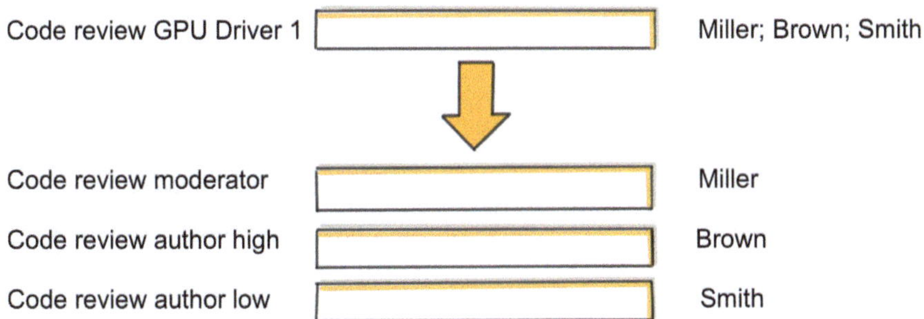

Fig. 5.12 One activity per employee

Important Golden rule
Only one activity per employee at a time!
and
Only one employee per activity!

Unfortunately, people very often deviate from this recommendation, which regularly results in problems or even blatant deviations. If you still feel tempted to break these golden rules, look for the root cause.

If an employee is only available to a project on a pro-rata basis, there is often a better option than assigning him or her to an activity with the same percentage. Here too, the root cause should not be evaded.

That someone works on a project proportionally does not necessarily mean that he is only available for three hours every day. It could also mean that he first completes his activity in our project, which only lasts a few days, and then works on another activity full time in the second project.

One problem remains, however, which is why this division between projects is also not really satisfactory and should be avoided whenever possible. How can the project manager be sure that the share promised to him will be kept? Practice shows that this is often not the case because the desert is burning in the other project or the employee still needs time for his work.

As said before, we are talking about sequential frameworks here. Agility prescribes stable teams. Who is surprised?

5.7.3   The Critical Path

Activity scheduling is an iterative process. In most cases, it turns out that after the activities have been arranged, final deadlines are calculated that are not compatible with the milestone planning. In this case, the planning must be optimized. Maybe one can start with the test specification while the implementation is still ongoing? Of course, one then needs another employee in the project. It may also be possible to break up activities and define intermediate deliveries, which in total extend the original activity, but attenuates the effect of dependencies.

If there is the possibility that activities can be strung together directly (since there are no other restrictions), you get a very dense and maximally compressed activity schedule. It cannot be more optimal, and unfortunately not riskier!

This is especially dangerous when the chain of activities directly determines a milestone. If delays occur in one of the activities, it must be expected that the milestone will be exceeded. Such constellations arise from time to time, but must then be re-evaluated. We are talking about risk here—and risks in project management must always be minimized or, even better, eliminated altogether.

In any case, a path that ends at a milestone without gaps between activities is an alarm sign. Here, things have been sewn on the edge, and hopefully not for avoidable reasons, because otherwise, at least in this section of the project, there is an imbalance. We should be able to rectify such paths and allows for sufficient buffer times between activities. Otherwise, we speak of a "critical path."

> **Definition** Critical path
> ISO 21500:2012: Sequence of activities that determine the earliest possible completion date for a project or phase.

If we have several parallel paths in the project, typically one of them is the critical path. It is the path with the smallest buffer, which determines the end date of the project. Activities on this path require special monitoring in order to detect problems at an early stage and to be able to take countermeasures.

Critical paths can be rectified if sufficient resources are available. If the number of employees cannot be increased, for example to parallelize activities, serious thought should be given to moving work packages to the next milestone. If this is not possible either, we have to live with the risk. However, this is not a good thing, because unexpected things often happen!

5.7.4 Conclusion

At this point, we conclude our section on activity scheduling and summarize the effects of the two approaches—sequential and agile:

In **sequential models**, activity scheduling is done in advance and often for the entire course of the project. This automatically leads to the problem that changes must be expected, which means that a certain part of the planning effort has to be repeated.

It is not possible to predict whether late-scheduled, critical activities have to be processed in a phase in which a high load of non-plannable events has occurred.

This is countered by **agile frameworks**: In the agile world, there is no detailed upfront time planning. Rather, the closer we get to the delivery of an increment, the more detailed the planning becomes. Work packages (often in the form of epics, features, or user stories) are only roughly estimated during release planning. Detailed estimation and planning takes place at the start of each iteration (e.g., a sprint in Scrum). This avoids unnecessary effort for rescheduling and critical components can be prioritized and processed during early iterations.

5.8 Workforce Planning

Parallel to the activity schedule, the workforce planning is created, which is defined rather informally or formally depending on the project. In the sequential environment, employees are usually assigned to activities in the Gantt chart (see Fig. 5.12). In agile projects, the team is fixed and team members write their name on the task card on the Scrum board at most. Whether and how workforce planning is documented also depends on the size and complexity of the project and the environment.

The personnel resource plan can be defined informally or formally, depending on the requirements of the project. Its level of detail depends on the complexity of the project and the management framework.

Especially in (sequential) upfront planning, activity scheduling, and workforce planning are closely interwoven and take place simultaneously. Project managers must know how many employees with which qualifications are available to them from when to when and to what extent in order to be able to put the activities in a meaningful chronological order. Conversely, they must know which activities should be carried out when in order to be able to ask the HR department for suitable employees in the first place.

In principle, employees should preferably have only one project at a time and be available to it as constantly as possible, since every context switch costs time. In sequential projects, however, this "low fluctuation course" is not an end in itself. The deployment of resources can also be oriented toward the planned feature packages if it is not possible the other way around.

Otherwise, it is important to avoid the common mistakes that we have already discussed in Sect. 5.7.2.

5.9   The Transparent Course of the Costs

Some stakeholders have a vital interest in knowing the expected development of the costs incurred as part of the project. Again, solid monitoring prevents surprises. Anyone who is startled when it is too late has not done a clean job. For this reason, the project manager should maintain a so-called cost plan.

In sequential project management frameworks, we receive a nice gift by doing the preliminary work for this step. Namely, all information is available to us. In the activity schedule, all activities are planned over time. For each of these activities we know the effort and via the duration we can read off which efforts will be performed in which time period. This automatically results in an increasing cost progression over time when the efforts are cumulated and multiplied by the hourly rates.

The curve created in this way shows whether the expected costs still match the budget planning. If deviations are detected, they can be counteracted. We call this "cost tracking."

In agile projects, the situation is different. Agile projects often start with a budget that is based on assumptions known at the start. But instead of establishing a detailed upfront cost plan, the partners involved agree that in case of doubt, either the budget must be re-evaluated or restrictions on the features planned at the beginning may be necessary.

Despite this fundamentally different approach, a basis for cost tracking exists in agile projects as well. The stories in the backlog are regularly evaluated by the team with regard to their quality and the expected effort. This results in a rough

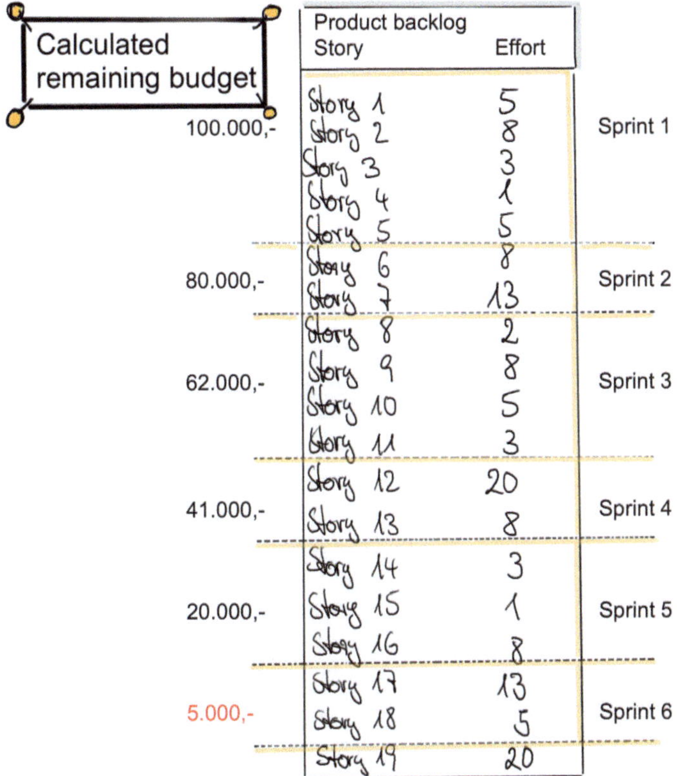

Fig. 5.13 Cost tracking in agile projects

estimate that can provide quite good values for experienced teams and known technology, although the stories usually contain few details.

If the team velocity is known, i.e., the sum of the efforts that a team typically achieves per sprint, it can be predicted in which sprint which stories will be completed and which efforts are associated with them. The costs are then derived from the efforts of the stories multiplied by the hourly rates. Figure 5.13 shows an example of cost tracking in agile projects. The figure also shows that approximately 20,000 Euro are required per sprint, but only 5000 euros are available for sprint 6.

5.10   The Project Plan is Created

The project planning steps described take place at a very early stage of the project. What has emerged here not only brings clarity about the further procedure and the framework conditions of the project, but also provides a whole series of important documents in which the results have been recorded.

From the milestone plan to the work breakdown structure, the evidence of effort and cost estimates to the activity schedule and cost plan, our strategies and their results were documented here. The project definition also finds its way here.

All these documents are not only important at the time of creation. They remain so throughout the life of the project, and even beyond, because they document decisions. Information is stored that helps us to pass on experience so that future work can build on the results of the current project.

All these documents must be collected and managed centrally to ensure availability. The form in which this is done is of secondary importance. However, it is important that a central reference to the collected documents exists. This can be a simple file or an article in the document management system.

We call this reference the project plan or, more commonly, the project manual. All decisions and insights are collected here—either directly or as a reference to the applicable documents. Now the documents can also be checked for consistency and conformity and updated if necessary. Ultimately, this collection forms the basis for all aspects of subsequent project tracking.

The project plan is not finished after the planning phase. With each step in the project, all new documents will be attached and decisions made will be documented that way. In particular, other planning documents will be added, such as the software quality assurance plan, the risk management plan and others.

The project plan should also regulate communication within the project as well as externally. Although this can also be done informally (for example, as a decision in a meeting), it should definitely be recorded in writing—ideally in the form of a communication plan, which in turn is included in the project plan.

Clearly, the project plan is an extremely important document. Therefore, it should be reviewed and formally approved. In addition, it must be known to all those affected and be available as required. Since it is permanently updated, it must be recorded in configuration management. After all, everyone should work with the currently valid version.

5.11   Summary

In this chapter, the individual planning steps were explained. Depending on the project management framework, they differ significantly in some cases. Figure 5.14 once again provides an overview of the similarities and differences between sequential and agile frameworks.

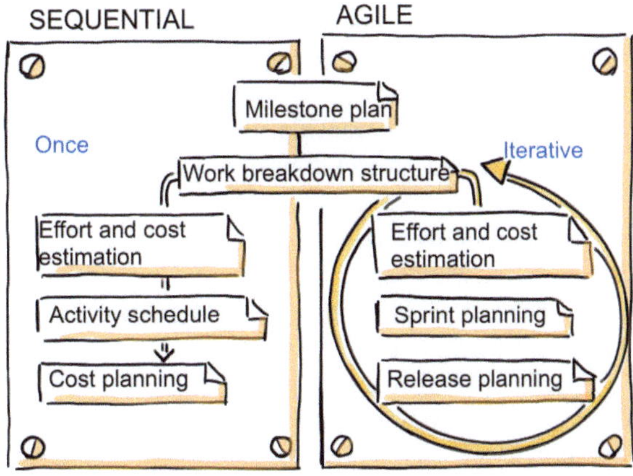

Fig. 5.14 Overview of the planning steps depending on the project management framework

Whereas in sequential projects there is upfront planning, in agile projects there is no complete activity schedule. Nevertheless, projects carried out in an agile manner tend to be more transparent and less risky, since changes and deviations can be reacted to quickly and without complications.

5.12 Exercises

1. Name and explain three key project planning activities.
2. Explain what aspects and relationships are represented within milestone schedules.
3. Outline a work breakdown structure for our case study.
4. Using a self-selected example, explain non-functional delivery objects.
5. Explain how the work breakdown structure could be referenced in subsequent planning activities.
6. Explain the difference between effort and cost estimates. What is the connection between the two?
7. Using a self-selected example, explain when the use of size estimation is appropriate.
8. Explain under what circumstances expert estimates are used.
9. Name the different methods of expert estimation and explain one.
10. A key principle for successful expert estimation is to obtain multiple opinions. Name other rules for successful expert estimation.
11. Explain the methodology of analogy estimation and under what circumstances it should be used.
12. Name the different types of analogy estimates.
13. One of the advanced estimation methods is called COCOMO II model. Name another advanced estimation method.
14. Explain what impact estimates have on project costing. What challenge arises in this context?

15. Name and explain benefits of using an activity schedule.
16. Explain the concept of the critical path.
17. Name different types of workforce planning.
18. Explain the relationship that exists between project planning, milestone planning and project control.
19. What are the basic rules for successful activity scheduling? Describe one of them in more detail.
20. Explain what specifics need to be considered in activity scheduling in sequential project management frameworks.
21. Explain what specifics need to be considered in activity scheduling in agile project management frameworks.
22. Explain how cost planning differs in different project management frameworks.
23. Name content that you define as part of a project plan.

References

(ASQF CPPM 2025): Project Management Foundations, Syllabus (EN), ASQF® Certified Professional for Project Management (2025) - Foundation Level, Version 3.0, 2025.

(Boem et al. 2000): Boehm, B.W., Abts, C., Brown, A. W., Chulani, S., Clark, B.K., Horowitz, E., Madachy, R., Reifer, D.J. & Steece, B. (2000) *Software Cost Estimation with COCOMO II* (with CD-ROM). Upper Saddle River, NJ: Prentice Hall. ISBN: 0-13-026692-2. https://doi.org/10.5555/557000

(Cohn 2025) Mike Cohn: Agile Estimating and Planning, Prentice Hall, 360 pages, 2005, ISBN 978-0131479418.

(ISO 21500:2012): International Organization for Standardization (ISO), ISO 21500:2012(E) – Guidance on project management. Geneva: ISO.

(ISO 21502:2020): International Organization for Standardization (ISO), ISO 21502:2020(E) – Project, programme and portfolio management — Guidance on project management. Geneva: ISO.

(ISO 21511:2018): ISO 21511:2018(E)—Work breakdown structures for project and programme management. International Organization for Standardization. Available at: https://www.iso.org/standard/71028.html

(Patton 2014): Patton, J. User Story Mapping: Discover the Whole Story, Build the Right Product. Sebastopol, CA: O'Reilly Media.

(Rankovic et al. 2024): Rankovic, N., Ranković, D., Ivanovic, M. & Lazić, L. (2024) Recent Advances in Artificial Intelligence in Cost Estimation in Project Management. Cham: Springer Nature. Artificial Intelligence-Enhanced Software and Systems Engineering, Vol. 6. https://doi.org/10.1007/978-3-031-76572-8

(Trendowicz and Jeffery 2014): Trendowicz, A. and Jeffery, R., Software Project Effort Estimation: Foundations and Best Practice, Guidelines for Success. Berlin: Springer. https://doi.org/10.1007/978-3-319-03629-8

Implementing and Controlling a Project   6

6.1   The Importance of Project Controlling

Once all activities of project initiation and project planning have been successfully carried out, we finally enter the phase of actual project execution. All the tasks that were identified and planned in earlier phases are put into action. In software projects, this is not only the implementation and testing of the software product, but also the preparation of all quality proofs, reports, and deliveries. All of this is recorded and controlled by project controlling.

The aim is to determine the project status efficiently and as smoothly as possible, to identify deviations from the planning and to initiate suitable measures to return to the path that was set in the planning. However, it may also be necessary to adjust the planning if the actual status proves to be unacceptable.

Project controlling can easily be described as the core task of the project manager, because no other task requires as much effort over such a long period of time as this one. Even if he or she is involved in all the steps of project initiation, planning, and later project closing, these will certainly only account for a fraction of the total time spent. Anything else would be a clear indicator of imbalance, because it would mean that planning takes longer than project execution.

The primary goal is to successfully complete the project in terms of schedule, scope, and budget. Widely established under the term "in time and budget," this goal is the most important and final milestone for our project. To achieve this is the essential task of the project manager.

Thanks to project planning, we have all the means and prerequisites in hand to be successful. It provides us with the necessary information that enables us to determine where we are with the project and what measures are necessary to actively steer in the right direction. In the previous chapter, we already forcefully emphasized how significant planning is for subsequent project controlling. Even a goal that is a small distance away can be missed if no one has planned the route in advance.

© The Author(s), under exclusive license to Springer Nature Switzerland AG 2026   131
A. Johannsen et al., *Foundations for Software Project Management in Classic and Agile Environments*, https://doi.org/10.1007/978-3-032-16797-2_6

Unfortunately, project implementation does not usually take place in a protected environment. Projects are subject to a wide variety of imponderables and challenges. What was planned at the beginning of a sequential project will almost never fully materialize. Being prepared for unforeseen changes in any area of our project is what makes a good project manager—being able to handle these situations without being thrown off track is what makes an experienced one.

It has been one of the driving forces behind the development of agile methods to deal with these very uncertainties. Therefore, just as in the previous chapter on project planning, we will emphasize the differences between sequential and agile project management frameworks. In fact, the different characteristics are again clearly evident in project controlling. However, we will also show how agile approaches can be applied in sequential methods and frameworks.

6.2   Execution in Various Environments

While the team is working on the execution of the project, the project manager has mainly one task: to keep the overview. Agile and sequential frameworks provide different answers as to how this can be achieved.

While sequential project management frameworks are characterized by the fact that planning activities take place before project execution, agile frameworks are known to rely on the iterative incremental approach.

Upfront planning before execution requires not only time and effort, but also knowledge of the qualifications and confidence in the promised availability of the identified employees over the entire planning period. None of the established sequential project management frameworks specify rules on how to achieve this. Agile does this very well.

The timing and nature of when each required employee is available to the project and how this is achieved is thus strikingly different in both worlds.

> **Definition** Push system
> In a push system, employees are assigned to activities during planning at the beginning of the project. Sequential frameworks are push systems (ASQF CPPM 2025).

They also remain push systems if this is done in coordination with the employees involved and agreed with them, because the assignment at the time of planning is what characterizes push systems.

In order to maintain an overview in sequential project management frameworks, it is the project manager's task to record and document the degree of completion at the activity level. As soon as deviations are detected that turn out to be serious, the planning must be updated.

Any necessary rescheduling—whether due to changes, additional efforts, or an unexpected, temporary, or permanent absence of an employee—may potentially double the already invested planning efforts for the affected activities. In less severe cases, this can nevertheless generate noticeable expenses, and in extreme cases can plunge a project into severe turbulence. Basically, we are in a plan-driven environment. Therefore, we have to be prepared for these kinds of "nasty surprises" and be able to deal with them.

In agile environments, this looks different. Here, we have rules for the structure of the teams and the deployment of the employees. Agile frameworks—above all Scrum—emphasize stable teams. While sequential project management frameworks allow employees to join and leave a project team as needed, this is not desired in agile frameworks.

Agile frameworks are pull systems in which the activities initially go into execution without assignment by the project manager. It is up to the team to decide which employee handles which activity.

> **Definition** Pull system
>
> Agile project management frameworks are generally "pull" systems. In a pull system, tasks are initially put into an iteration without being assigned to an employee. They are then "pulled" by individual team members as they pull tasks to execute them. Agile frameworks are generally pull systems (ASQF CPPM 2025).

In this context, specialization takes a back seat. The various tasks must be solved within the team. One speaks of "cross-functional teams," of interdisciplinarity or also of generalization. The idea is that the unchanging Scrum team must complete all tasks that arise within each sprint. In addition, since the team structure should remain stable, each team member should in principle be able to "pull" each task.

Obviously, this idea reaches its limits as soon as extreme specialization is required. In this case, one will still have to rely on one or the other specialist within the teams (in our case study, it was the driver developer). This may then only be the case for a limited number of iterations. Such an undogmatic approach does not necessarily stand in the way of the advantages of agility.

But where does this leave the project manager and their responsibility to maintain an overview, identify emerging issues early, and implement appropriate countermeasures? In agile frameworks, this role is deliberately dispensed within the execution. Team members work on their own responsibility and steer themselves. They take responsibility for the iteration goals.

Due to the short iterations, the product owner, who in practice still most closely fulfills the tasks of a project manager in this environment, receives quick feedback and can make changes to the product backlog as needed.

6.3   The Art of Tracking Project Progress

In Chap. 5, we already mentioned some pitfalls that—if not taken into account—can stand in the way of a reliable tracking of a project's progress. Just think of the assignment of several employees to one activity, which we strongly reject here once again.

The aspects that enable the project manager to record the project progress in a time-saving, smooth, and, above all, reliable manner are now to be dealt with in greater depth. The structure of the activity schedule we discussed earlier is important, but there are also different levels of project monitoring to consider.

In any case, it is essential to know how these levels are linked and how information should flow between them.

6.3.1   General Rules

The effort spent on tracking the current status and progress of a project should bring a benefit. Strictly speaking, the related efforts should be reduced to a minimum, but of course we do not accept any compromise in the quality and completeness of the recorded results.

The term "project controlling" describes what happens in the course of this phase. However, we understand this to mean less the "control" of employees and more the collection of data for controlling projects. Trying to collect data by means of a literal "control" carries risks, because a culture of control hampers transparency. The project manager will only ever find out exactly what he asks for. But this may not contain everything he should know. He will only be provided with reliable values if a culture of transparency is created.

The frequency of the survey is an important parameter. If the collection periods are too far apart, there is a risk of not being able to react in time. If the survey is too high frequency, the effort of all persons involved increases. In general, of course, the survey cannot be high-frequency enough if critical operations (i.e., activities on a critical path) are involved. However, the project manager must weigh very carefully whether the effort is worth it.

> **Example** In our case study, the project manager initially thought he had a—from his point of view—very legitimate interest in asking every hour whether a critical activity would really be finished on time. After a while, however, he realized that he was disrupting operations, to say the least. That was his good fortune. After all, if this happens in a stressful situation for everyone involved, there is a serious risk of tempers—and possibly a few objects "flying" (i.e., serious conflicts).

Of course, there may be situations in which it is necessary to have the information about progress of an activity available very promptly. Permanent inquiries, however, are of little help in such cases. It is better to rely on another means: Transparency.

Transparency enables reliable progress recording, but requires trust. For this reason, the project manager should establish a culture that can help him and the project out of trouble in difficult situations.

A culture of fault tolerance helps when the project manager must be able to rely on his team to proactively report to him the status of things. This starts with the indication that an activity has been completed and goes up to the message that further problems have occurred—and thus further delays are to be expected. This is essential not only under time pressure, but in general.

In general, collected data should correspond as closely as possible to reality. If employees fear unpleasant questions, they will always try to evade the situation by providing embellished information about the status of activities or features.

It is easy to understand that this is not sustainable. Nevertheless, this phenomenon will occur. The consequence is that measures are delayed or, in the worst case, even fail to materialize.

6.3.2 The Project Internal Progress Tracking

With project-internal tracking of the project progress, an information flow begins, which continues beyond the boundaries of the project to the last stakeholder.

Activities are the smallest units in our project by means of which the project is planned and controlled in detail. Progress monitoring also begins at the so-called activity level.[1]

In our preview in Chap. 5, we stated that activities should have a maximum size of a few days so that reliable progress monitoring is possible. The reason is that it is almost impossible to really accurately determine the progress of an activity until it is completed. Any attempt to arrive at a robust number will inevitably end in a percentage estimate.

So, the project manager asks, "How far along are you?" In response, he receives a value that is supposed to reflect the degree of processing: let's say 50% (see Fig. 6.1).

However, what sounds like a reliable assessment is deceptive, since this value probably corresponds more to a gut feeling than to a well-founded observation.

In Chap. 5, we have already outlined the problem and the way out. Instead of measuring progress at the level of <u>one</u> activity, we need to look at it at the level of <u>**all**</u> activities. The prerequisite for this is that we have divided our work packages into small, manageable activities. Then it is sufficient to consider only two states

---

[1] We distinguish the activity level from the project level. Progress monitoring at activity level looks internally at the smallest units of our planning, which were derived from the work packages of the WBS. Progress monitoring at project level is the view from the outside on the project and focuses on deadlines, costs and functionality. It is therefore about the project as a whole. At best, the work packages of the WBS are considered.

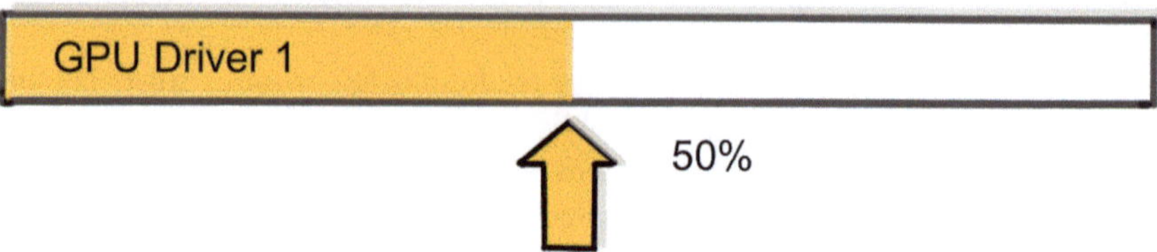

Fig. 6.1 Percentage measurement of an activity

per activity with regard to progress and compare them with the planning status: "not yet completed" and "completed." In the first case, the progress is 0%, in the second case 100%.

If this were done with long activities, feedback on the status of an activity would come very late. With a bit of bad luck, a milestone is looming just ahead and the dilemma is pre-programmed, as it may be too late to initiate any action.

In Sect. 5.7.1, we already mentioned the 90% syndrome (Hamid 1988). This term describes a condition that often occurs when percent progress is requested from someone. The effect is shown in Fig. 6.2. Initially, the worker does not know much more than at the time of the effort estimate. There were no serious problems yet, so he estimates that everything is still on track. However, as the activity progresses, the awareness increases that there is still a lot of work to do. The estimate becomes more and more pessimistic, but nobody dares to go below the value already mentioned last time (which would probably be the truth, though). The asymptotic effect shown in Fig. 6.2 arises.

If, for some reason, an activity cannot be detailed further so that it takes significantly more than a few days to complete—or if it is on a critical path—the project manager may not be able to wait for it to be completed. This is a special situation, which we would like to consider as an exception. Of course, exceptions do exist, but we should always clearly distinguish them from the rule.

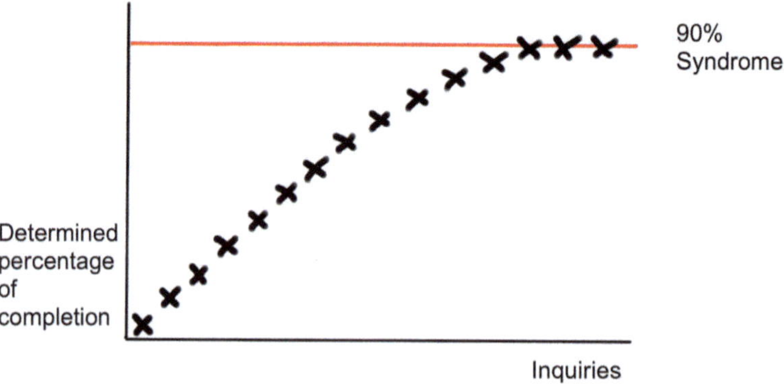

Fig. 6.2 90% syndrome

In this case, the project manager should rely on daily estimate of the remaining efforts (as opposed to the progress). Ideally, the developers estimate before the end of the work how much time they think they still have to invest in this activity. This estimate generates a new value every day, which is getting closer and closer to the final result.

Where is the difference to the 90% syndrome? The employee does not have to put the work already done in relation to the supposed remaining work. In other words, they do not have to perform an analysis of the work already done, but only an estimate of the remaining effort. It goes without saying that the employee should not be blamed for the fact that the values change on a daily basis, even if large leaps become visible. That would simply be the result of new knowledge.

As mentioned, this procedure should only be used for critical activities, because it creates a certain burden and uncertainties always remain. As before, only one thing is certain: The end of an activity.

Again, sequential project management frameworks can borrow methods from agile frameworks, where short tasks with seamless progress control are typical. Short inspection of progress should be achieved in the Daily Scrum, by status updates on the (haptic or tool-based) Scrum board and possibly by using a sprint burndown chart (Meyer 2014). Another regular opportunity to reflect on the causes of effort deviations and to initiate countermeasures is the retrospective.

> **Important** Daily standup meetings are not suitable for talking in detail about remaining effort estimates. That is simply lost time for everyone else. Use the sprint burndown chart to track the progress!

The "sprint burndown" (open versus done tasks within a sprint) is a daily metric used by Scrum teams to track the progress (Fig. 6.3). To achieve a smooth sprint burndown curve, each team member updates the status or estimates the remaining effort for their current task at the end of each day. Combined with the effort of tasks not yet started in the sprint, this provides an accurate and transparent picture of the remaining work and overall sprint progress. Again, transparency and inspection are essential in Scrum.

> **Definition** Burndown chart
> A burndown chart visualizes the amount of remaining work over time and helps identify trends or deviations in the team's velocity and delivery pace (ASQF CPPM 2025).

Note, that estimating the remaining effort for unfinished tasks is not mandatory in Scrum. Strictly speaking, the Scrum Guide does not stipulate a daily progress recording of the tasks, but it does require the team to inspects progress toward the sprint goal regularly. However, we recommend it for tasks that exceed a day.

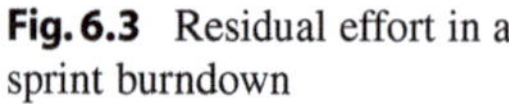

Fig. 6.3 Residual effort in a
sprint burndown

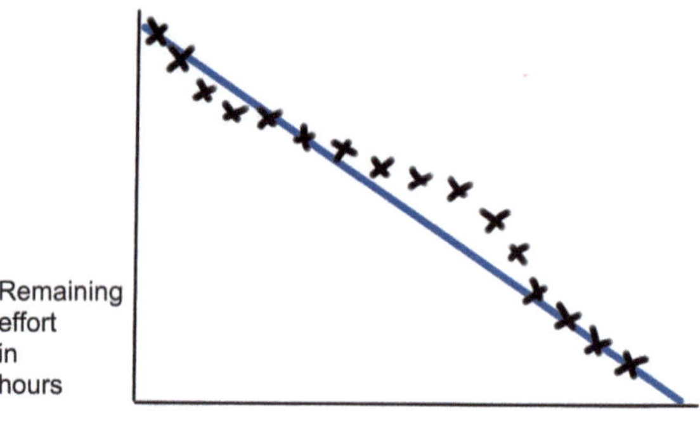

In any case, be it in sequential or agile environments, the recording of the
progress should be as seamless as possible. Scrum focuses on value-adding
activities and sequential projects should do the same.

Tool support for tracking the progress of activities is helpful. Ideally, a kind of
automatism develops: Shortly before the developers leave, they launch the project
tracking software, bring their coffee mug to the pantry, enter (depending on the
tool) the current status or the remaining effort, and then shut down the computer.
If the team is working with a haptic board, they can add their task to the "Done"
column on the way out or note the remaining effort with a pen.

Without such a tool (be it software-based, be it haptic), we are again at the
point where the project manager must ask for progress verbally and thus, to say
the least, is annoying or even hinders the work.

So far, we have only talked about the progress of individual activities. When we
add these up, we obtain information about the progress of the entire work package.
The project manager is now able to assess if it is necessary to take any actions
for the work package as a whole. This information must then be communicated
externally to the stakeholders, who are dependent on this information.

The question then naturally arises: In what form should this take place?

6.3.3 The View of the Project from the Outside

The internal tracking of progress is done in detail and is rightfully referred to as
the activity level. What stakeholders need, however, is an external view of the
project. We call this the project level.

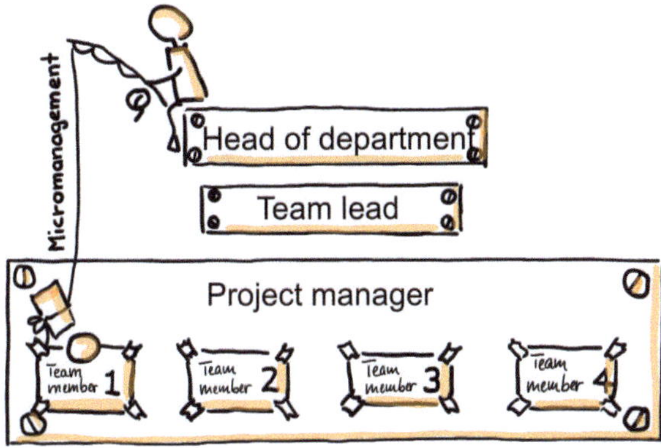

Fig. 6.4 Meddling in the project through micromanagement from the top

In contrast to the activity level, we do not use the smallest units to measure progress at the project level, but units from the language and the world of understanding of the stakeholders. Project managers who report progress at the activity level to stakeholders risk falling into several pitfalls. On the one hand, they risk overburdening the stakeholders by forcing them to familiarize themselves with this level. Second, they make their work more vulnerable to criticism. Once stakeholders are drawn into evaluating progress at the activity level, they may feel compelled to contribute at that level. However, this is not their task, since these are project internals that only the project team can reasonably assess.

If the two levels are mixed, a state arises from which it is difficult to escape. This is called micromanagement (see also Fig. 6.4). In this case, decisions are made at project level that have an impact on the activity level without any well-founded knowledge. The project manager is overridden and the team is poorly able to defend itself without entering into conflicts with higher levels of the hierarchy.

Organizations that have established micromanagement are not suitable for executing complex software projects.

The units that stakeholders use to assess their progress are those that govern their daily lives. These can be a wide variety of aspects or objects. The stakeholders who are interested in the technical progress of the project will rely on the deliverables (the features) from the work breakdown structure.

When project managers report the progress at project level, they should therefore rather refer to the progress of the work packages, which in turn is based on the progress of the assigned activities. Figure 6.5 illustrates this "condensation" using the example of our GPU driver.

> **Example** The project manager in our case study had to report the technical progress of his project to line management stakeholders on a weekly basis. He used the findings from his activity-level progress monitoring to report that the GPU 1 driver was in "green" status. "Green" in this context means that no deviations are visible so far.

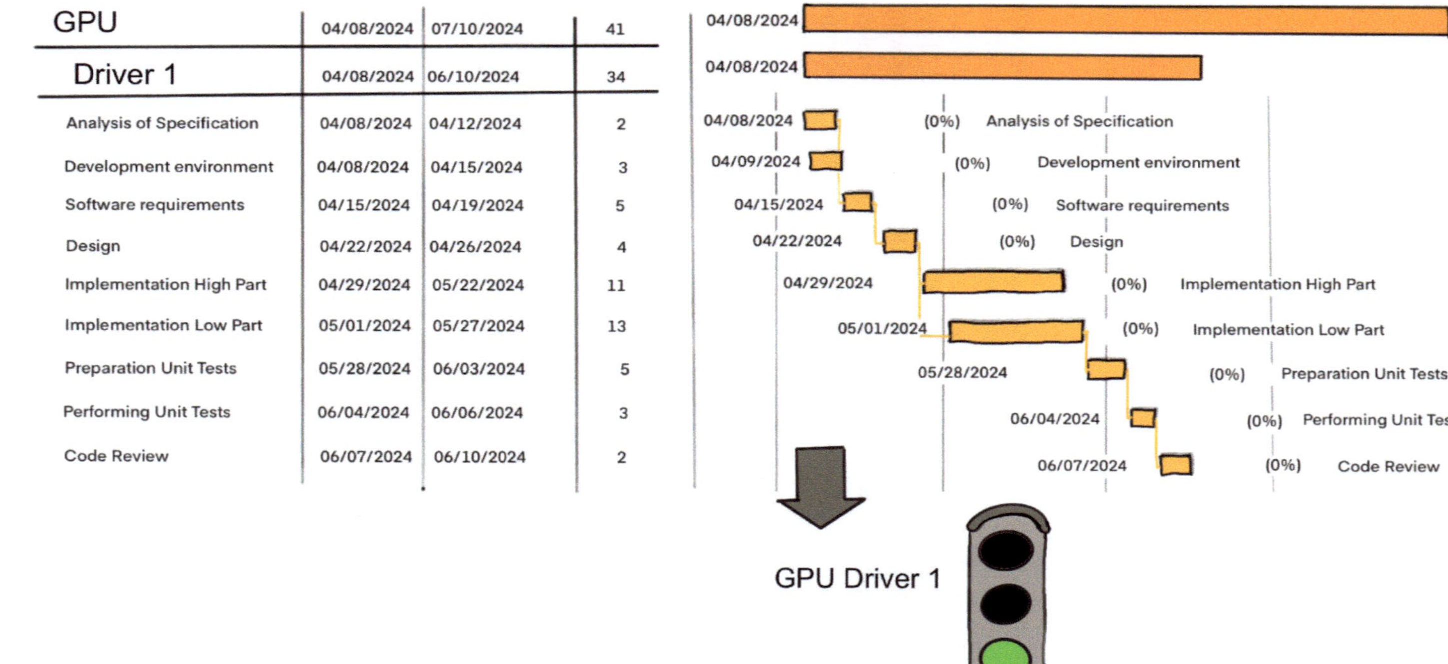

Fig. 6.5 Status of a feature derived from the activities

For most stakeholders outside the project, this information is sufficient. Many top managers are even allergic to more details. In discussions, this then manifests itself in impatience and the sudden question: "Are we on schedule or not?".

Only when the condensed information fails to materialize or proves unreliable, interest awakes. Since his need for information has not been met, the stakeholder demands further details.

This clearly illustrates how important it is for a project manager to condense complex technical details and translate them into language stakeholders can easily understand. This need is even more evident, if we consider that line managers usually have to supervise a large number of projects. If they are well informed, their focus remains at project level. If they are not, they dive into the activity level. This means:

- More discussions,
- More justification,
- More disturbances,
- More time needed.

In Scrum, the transition from the activity level to the project level is clearly regulated. The assessment of the project progress on project level is based solely on the state of the product backlog and the course of the sprint reviews, whereas the processes within a sprint based on the tasks are solely a team matter. Interference of stakeholders, even of the product owner, in a sprint is explicitly forbidden. The team, on the other hand, is obliged to answer questions about the status of the project based on the stories.

6.4   Progress Reporting and Information Exchange

Having understood how important it is to have the status of our project tracked in an efficient and smooth way, we need to address the issue of how this information can be transferred to the stakeholders with as little effort as possible. Here, we are not only talking about the progress reports mentioned in the title, but also about how to communicate progress in meetings.

The question immediately arises: Why should a book address how information can flow with minimal effort? Anyone who has spent time in a project management environment knows the answer. The efficiency of report generation is rarely questioned—even though it is clearly a matter of great importance. The result is that reports can be unnecessarily long, they do not contain the desired content, they are incomprehensible to the addressee and are therefore often not read. Which project manager wants to spend an unnecessary amount of time reporting on the status of the project if the effort involved is hardly worthwhile? If this is the case, reporting inevitably causes displeasure.

Warning It is tempting to have reports generated using generative AI. In fact, automated, AI-supported reporting works quite well. However, the reports generated are often quite long. This carries the risk that no one will read the text. Information can often be conveyed more effectively through dashboards and other graphical representations.

6.4.1   Efficient Status Reports

Definition Status report
Formal status reports address external stakeholders in order to provide optimally condensed information in their language and vocabulary (ASQF CPPM 2025).

Have the Addressee in Mind!
Status reports should always be oriented in scope and content to the needs of the addressee. The goal should be that the addressee is genuinely curious to open and read the report. If this is the case, all parties have done their job well. Progress reports carry information from the activity level into the project level, and as described earlier, these two levels should not be mixed. The ability of the project manager to manage an appropriate translation helps both to keep the addressee well informed and to do this with a reasonably low effort.

At the beginning of the project, i.e., during project initiation, take the time to discuss the form and scope of the report with the addressees. Agree with them what information—and only that information—is important and in what form it should be presented. For example, how much text should be included? Is text only necessary when more detailed explanations are appropriate? All this can be clarified quite quickly and subsequently saves time. If necessary, specify the report form contractually.

It should also be noted that the compression of the report increases the higher up in the hierarchy it is presented.

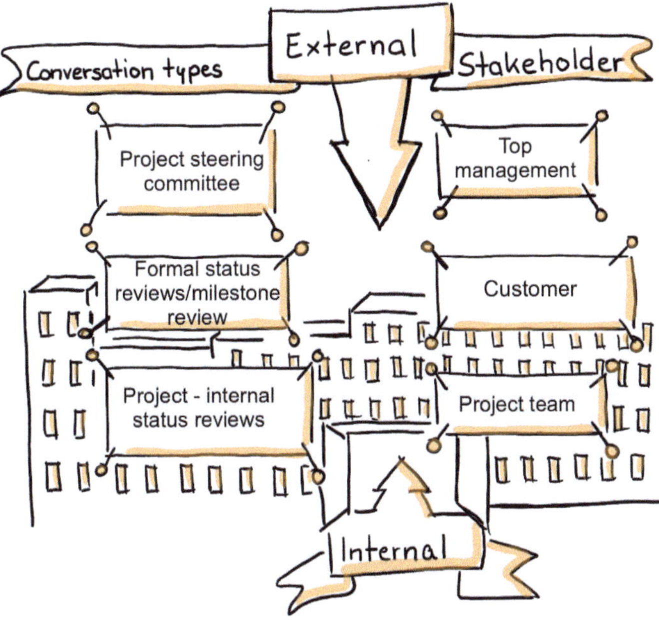

Fig. 6.6 Different levels of meetings and groups of participants

Figure 6.6 shows a nice example of this hierarchy. At project level, we talk with stakeholders or managers from the parent organization. They have no interest whatsoever in the progress of individual activities within the GPU 1 driver work package. The well-founded assessment of the project manager—based on a solid tracking at the activity level—is sufficient to communicate that the driver is in status "green."

It is likely that all parties involved interpret "green" more or less clearly the same way. However, if we want to use the remaining colors of a traffic light, it makes sense to define what they mean. Everyone should know what is meant by "yellow." Do yourself a favor and note these meanings as a legend directly in the report to prevent misunderstandings and unnecessary inquiries. The following definitions can help:

- **"Red"** = The project team and its project manager cannot solve the mentioned problem alone.
- **"Yellow"** = There is a need for action, but problem can be solved within the project.
- **"Green"** = Work packages advance according to plan.

Such a legend creates clarity and helps to initiate necessary actions, avoid unnecessary ones on the contrary.

Pure traffic light reports are very efficient, provided they are sufficient. They are also easy to interpret. As soon as the traffic light turns "red," you have to expect excitement to follow. Everyone immediately understands that something is about to go wrong here. Therefore, the color should be chosen carefully. There are no shades, so be careful! A "red" has as a desired effect that the stakeholders are involved. Use this only when it becomes necessary. This is a highly effective monitoring tool.

Keep an Eye on the Effort!

Let's consider the counterexample. If a project manager spends half a day a week creating one or more reports, something is probably wrong. Either the project is actually in trouble or the reporting is simply inefficient.

The contents of the report to be created later should be collected directly while the activity status data is being entered. This way, there is no need to act retrospectively—which carries the risk of information loss and errors—and the creation is actually efficient.

> **Example** In our project example, after the conversion to Scrum, the progress was recorded in a software tool. The project manager only had to build a report template that collected the necessary information for him. A spreadsheet did the rest. The graphs were copied into a presentation and sent to line management and the project owner of the project along with a list of the top 3 advances and top 3 risks.

Are Reports Always in Writing-Only?

The written form of a report is persistent and serves the purpose of careful documentation. However, the pure written form has its limitations. It is often important and valuable to discuss the project report with the addressees. In a conversation, participants may ask questions and exchange additional information beyond what a written report can cover.

A typical example of an oral reporting form is the steering committee. By this, we mean status meetings at project level that are held with management or customers. They serve to discuss topics that are of particular relevance to the specific group of participants (e.g., progress at feature level, main milestones, budget).

Stay within the terminology of the addressee! If the customer or the manager has the feeling that they have to dive deeper into the project to understand your explanations, you are not doing yourself any favors. There is a risk of micromanagement!

In agile frameworks, the sprint review is the fixed institution in which the results of the past sprint are formally presented to the stakeholders.

Oral reports also maintain the project's network by building and strengthening relationships. Last but not least, they offer the opportunity to place information that should not appear in written reports—and yes, such situations do occur.

> **Example** In our case study, an employee was removed from the Scrum team because he could not handle the high level of ownership. However, there was never a written report calling for the replacement of this employee.

Use oral reporting for upward marketing. Stakeholders, especially upper management, also need good news. Report successes, your project partners will love it! Do it often, even if it's just small things. It pays off. There is truth in the phrase "Do good and talk about it."

6.4.2 Meetings that Make Sense

In addition to daily communication within the team, there are meetings. Meetings are a more formal means of communication and should never be left to chance. Their balanced use determines whether they make sense or not. Some professionals sit in meetings all day long (Mroz 2018). This is not usually the case for project managers. If they spend most of their days in meeting rooms, something is wrong in the project environment.

We generally distinguish between two types of meetings:

- Meetings focused on sharing information,
- Meetings focused on developing solutions.

The first type includes pure information events, but also meetings for progress control or budget monitoring. The second type includes all workshops as well as problem discussions or project reviews to capture lessons learned.

The two types of meetings should not be mixed. Otherwise, it is likely that the group of participants has been poorly selected, resulting in some people's time being unnecessarily wasted.

Employees with a technical background are more allergic to inefficient meetings than those from a management background. If the meetings slide into long strategic discussions, they start studying the ceiling, for example, and wish for nothing more than to be back at their desks.

So, choose the group of participants to match the type of meeting you are planning. Figure 6.6 shows different meeting levels as they are common in larger projects. These meetings differ not only in their group of participants, but also in their frequency. Milestone reviews take place, as the name suggests, at selected milestones with the involvement of customers, product management, and higher management.

The project steering committee or steering committee is the highest decision-making body in the project organization. They usually involve top management.

If the presence of developers is required in their role as experts during an organizational meeting, it is advisable to limit the duration of their participation. This can be achieved through careful planning that allocates specific time slots, ensuring the appropriate participants are present for each topic. "Starting at 10 a.m., we will deal with topic B."

Nevertheless, mixing meeting levels should remain the exception, because even if the time slots can be planned quite well, they are not always adhered to. In fact, in our example, topic B does not come up until 10:30 a.m. If we are talking about a rule covering most cases, it is always better to deal with only one topic per meeting. If it is planned that several topics will be dealt with, several, consecutive meetings should be scheduled. This has another advantage: You avoid inappropriate scheduling.

If meetings take place without planning, they often tend to last forever, and in the best case, they are limited by the fact that the meeting room is needed by the next group. Sounds familiar, doesn't it?

Please consider the following: To the extent that meetings are organizational in nature, they represent non-productive time. So, for the sake of everyone, we should feel obliged to use this time efficiently. Especially employees who are measured by their productivity—usually this will be the developers or testers—suffer from ineffective or inefficient meetings. We do them no favors when we demand their participation and possibly plunge them into serious conflict. For this reason, the following basic rules should be followed to avoid dissatisfaction in the project:

- **Organize meetings to distribute information properly**.

  They should be very short and have rules for speaking time. Daily stand-up meetings in Scrum are the best practical example. If detailed discussions arise and exceed a tolerable duration of a few minutes, move the discussion to the follow-up. The other participants will thank you for it.

- **Distinguish informational meetings from workshops where results are developed**.

  This type of meeting is intended to be productive and requires a special group of participants, which is usually also smaller. No one should participate here who cannot contribute anything constructive.

- **Give all your meetings a time frame**.

  A defined start and especially a defined end force discipline and thus promote efficiency. In Scrum, we call this "time-boxing." It can be applied in all project management frameworks.
  Time-boxing means punctuality in every respect. For a meeting this means: It starts on time, even if not everyone has arrived, and it ends on time, even if the material has not been worked through. This greatly promotes discipline, as most people find it unsatisfying to leave topics they have started unfinished.
  The effectiveness and success of meetings are determined not only by how efficiently they are conducted. We distinguish three phases in the meeting

management process, all of which are equally critical to achieving successful outcomes (Mroz 2018):

- **Preparation**

Good preparation is half the battle for a successful meeting. Avoid going into meetings unprepared, especially if you are the organizer. If it is not defined what the meeting is about, what the agenda looks like, and what outcome will mark the meeting as successful, you can imagine how it will go.
The group of participants should also be selected with care and adequate invitations sent.

- **Execution**

Efficient execution increases the value of the meeting for all participants. Using time-boxing can also teach punctuality in sequential projects. You will be amazed at how quickly this works. Set rules for everyone's flow and attention. Meetings in which participants sit in front of their notebooks and work on mails, for example, are pointless in large parts! If decisions are made, write them down and assign people to be responsible for tasks.

- **Postprocessing**

A goal-oriented follow-up ensures the benefit of the meeting. Distribute the resulting minutes, or otherwise make them available to participants. Set up a mechanism to ensure follow-up on tasks.

6.5   Trend Systems

In Sect. 6.3, we discussed a reliable progress tracking of our project at the activity level. Apart from the project manager, however, other stakeholders such as the customer or higher-level managers are also entitled to information. They too want to feel that they are in "control" of the project entrusted to them. Good project managers concede this to the project level.

Progress reports convey the impression that the project manager has gained from monitoring the progress of activities at the project level. They represent a form of communication.

What the pure progress reports lack, however, are metrics and predictions based on calculations using the progress data. Line managers who oversee multiple projects in particular need a way to compare them. Since they cannot collect the necessary data themselves, they rely on the project manager to assist them. He or she should also do this, because transparency prevents micromanagement.

Methods that enable such predictions are called trend systems. These systems provide a high-level analysis of selected project parameters and create a sufficiently accurate picture of the project to enable a quick and meaningful overview.

There are several established methods in the context of software development, which differ in effort and benefit. We present the two most widely applied systems: The milestone trend analysis and the earned value analysis.

6.5.1   The Milestone Trend Analysis

Definition Milestone Trend Analysis (MTA)

The milestone trend analysis (MTA) is used to provide a graphical overview of project progress based on milestones in the project status report (ASQF CPPM 2025).

The milestone trend analysis—also called MTA for short—is an extremely low-effort method for graphically depicting the expected trend of the most important milestones (Wysocki 2019). It is particularly useful when stakeholders focus on monitoring deadlines.

In Chap. 5, we already demonstrated how the milestone plan—when maintained as a list—can be used to periodically re-evaluate the originally defined milestone dates. The most desirable outcome of a reassessment is that no adjustments to a milestone are necessary. Its date remains unchanged. However, if new information emerges, the milestone can be rescheduled—ideally as early as possible and well in advance of its planned date.

In the example of the Fig. 6.7 a reassessment of the milestone "Release B-Sample" took place at the beginning of May. It was postponed early from December 20 to February 3. Action is needed because under the currently known conditions, there will be a delay. However, since we recognized this early (nine months ahead of the original target date, after all), there is still time to intervene.

However, the new value in Fig. 6.7 is not really eye-catching. You have to go through all the values line by line. There is a real danger that changes will be overlooked. For this reason, there is a graphical representation that gets around this shortcoming. Figure 6.8 shows an example. In the diagram, the reporting periods are plotted on the X-axis and the current deadline forecasts on the Y-axis.

The diagram can be created by a tool, but can also be realized very easily with a standard spreadsheet program. The list from Fig. 6.7 directly serves as input for the diagram.

Figure 6.8 shows the diagram of a fictitious MTA. If we take a closer look at the series shown, we can see different possible cases of milestone progressions:

- The trend of the specific milestone represented by a diamond shows the optimal course. The predictions for its date never changed; the milestone was actually reached in week 17.

	Milestones	March 2024	April 1, 2024	May 2024	June
2	Requirement specification	January 8, 2024	January 8, 2024	January 8, 2024	
3	Order placed by customer	January 19, 2024	January 19, 2024	January 19, 2024	
4	Project start workshop	January 26, 2024	January 26, 2024	January 26, 2024	
5	Q1 Gate	February 14, 2024	February 14, 2024	February 14, 2024	
6	End of system requirement analysis	February 23, 2024	February 23, 2024	February 23, 2024	
7	End of software requirement analysis	March 18, 2024	March 18, 2024	March 18, 2024	
8	End of hardware requirement analysis	March 18, 2024	March 18, 2024	March 18, 2024	
9	Designfreeze A-Sample	July 12, 2024	July 12, 2024	July 12, 2024	
10	Q2 Gate	July 17, 2024	July 17, 2024	July 17, 2024	
11	PreRelease A-Sample	July 22, 2024	July 22, 2024	July 22, 2024	
12	Release A-Sample	July 31, 2024	July 31, 2024	July 31, 2024	
13	Q3 Gate	October 5, 2024	October 5, 2024	October 5, 2024	
14	DesignFreeze B-Sample	November 21, 2024	November 21, 2024	November 21, 2024	
15	PreRelease B-Sample	December 16, 2024	December 16, 2024	December 16, 2024	
16	Release B-Sample	December 20, 2024	December 20, 2024	February 3, 2025	

Fig. 6.7 Reassessment of a milestone

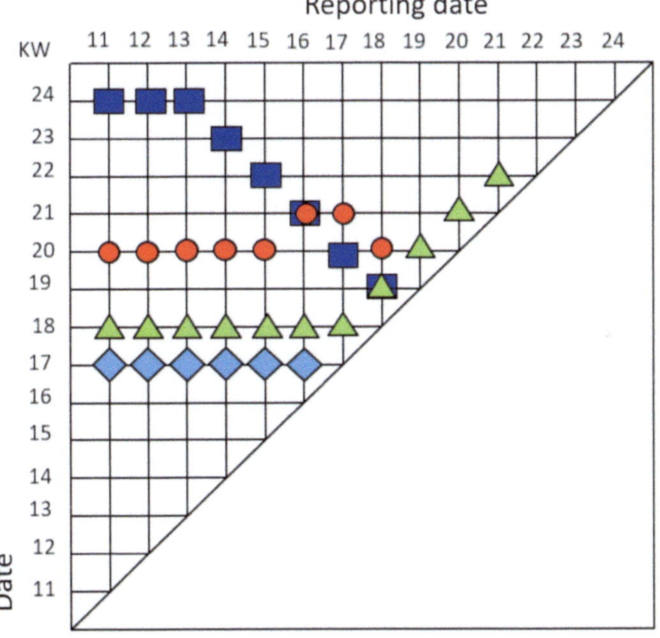

Fig. 6.8 Example of the diagram of an MTA

- The milestone symbolized by the circle had a deviation of one week for two weeks. Here, however, the situation could still be turned around. After suitable measures were initiated, it could be reset to its original date in week 20.
- The situation was different with the squares: the deadline was shortened by one week every week. Obviously, far too large buffers were included here. The milestone was reached much earlier than planned (in week 19).
- A special course is that of the milestone which is represented by the triangles. Here, the milestone is pushed forward week by week. This strongly resembles the "90% syndrome"—only applied at the milestone level.

6.5.2   The Earned Value Analysis

Hint The earned value analysis (EVA) is a project progress evaluation method based on the actual value of work performed and is mainly used in cost tracking in larger projects.

The earned value analysis (EVA) is a method of monitoring progress at the project level that relates the currently tracked status of a project (i.e., the actual value of performed) to its planned values (Vanhoucke 2014). The idea is to make predictions about further progress of the project. All this is done on a rather abstract level, without direct access to activity level insights.

The earned value analysis is widely used among controllers who have to present a comparative economic evaluation for larger projects in a segment, regardless of the sometimes very different nature of those projects. Of course, the project managers must provide the necessary parameters to the controller. Even if they do not perform the earned value analysis themselves, they are still the ones who provide the values.

In some circumstances, earned value analysis is part of existing software tools that controllers work with. However, the basic rules are so simple that they can easily be implemented in a spreadsheet. In fact, EVA requires only three parameters to perform subsequent calculations:

- The planned value (PV) indicates which expenses should have been incurred at the current point in time. This value can be taken from the cost planning.
- The actual costs (AC) quantify the value of the expenses currently incurred, i.e., what the project has actually cost to date. They result either from the current activity schedule or—even better—from the company's internal time recording.
- Finally, the earned value (EV) shows the value actually generated by the project at the reporting date.

And this is where it gets tricky!

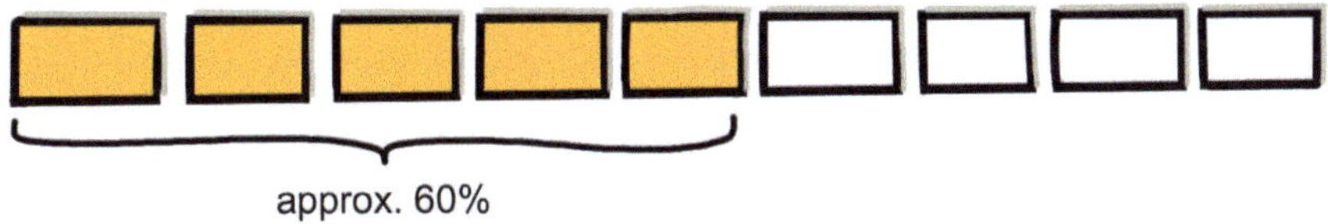

Fig. 6.9 Determination of progress from the sum of activities

Earned value analysis expects the project manager to know the actual value generated in terms of project progress. Obviously, this leads to the same problem encountered when estimating the percentage of completion for an activity. In earned value analysis, the project is treated like a single, huge "activity." In fact, EVA knows nothing about the work packages or activities in terms of activity scheduling. For this reason, the literature often refers to the "percent complete" of a project, see e.g. (Vanhoucke 2014, p. 50).

Experienced project managers know that they can never reliably ask for the percent complete. However, they can help themselves by taking the sum of all activities as a basis. As described in Chap. 5, these individual activities should be so small that their progress can be reduced to two possible values: not yet finished or finished (Fig. 6.9).

The best approximation of the progress of the entire project still comes from the project manager putting the completed activities in relation to the total. This gives a value that can only claim to be partially accurate, but is better than any estimate. Even if activities of different lengths exist, the errors will average out the more activities are included.

From the three parameters, simple mathematical formulas can now be used to calculate various indices that allow the project to be evaluated. However, we would like to concentrate here on two parameters that are intended to illustrate the principle.

- The **cost variance (CV)** is calculated from the difference between earned value and actual costs. It is therefore the difference between the earned value and the actual costs incurred. The formula is:

$$CV = EV - AC$$

- The **schedule variance (SV)** corresponds to the difference between the earned value (EV) and the planned value (PV). The formula is:

$$SV = EV - PV$$

A positive value for the Cost Variance CV means that the project promises to be more favorable than planned. Conversely, a negative value means that additional costs are to be expected.

The relationship between schedules and costs is less obvious. A positive schedule variance SV means that the project is ahead of schedule in terms of value added. If we extrapolate this, we can assume that the work will be completed earlier. A negative schedule variance, on the other hand, indicates that more time than planned must be spent to develop the desired functionality.

Controllers—if not the project manager himself—will draw conclusions about the progress and profitability of the project from these and other values. The project manager should therefore familiarize himself with this procedure so that he is aware of what the data he communicates is used for.

The earned value analysis becomes much more complex if we assume non-linear cost progressions. Let's take a simple example: we have already spent 75,000 euros in our project since the start, although only 50,000 euros were planned. This results in a negative cost variance and immediately the alarm bells go off: "The project will be 50% more expensive than planned."

However, this type of statement may only be made if it can be assumed that the cost trends are linear over the period under consideration. As long as the same amount of expenses is planned and incurred each month, the direct prediction into the future works. However, since this is rarely the case, the user of the method should use interpolation to subdivide non-linear progressions into those that can be approximated as linear. The procedure is shown in Fig. 6.10.

This does not make the procedure any easier. Above all, the result becomes less precise. It is good (only) for those who can carry out an evaluation in their organization on the basis of a tool that provides for non-linear processes.

Do not forget that the EVA is a trend system. A level calculated once may reflect an exceptional situation. Therefore, the calculated parameters should be observed over the entire period of the project.

Fig. 6.10 Linear interpolation of the cost

6.5.3   Release Burndown—The Agile Way to Track the Trend

EVA and MTA are trend systems that apply to any project, as they consider progress are on a rather high level. Agile projects have another way of keeping track of the progress: the release burndown chart already presented in Sect. 3.3.6 of this book (see also Fig. 3.11).

The release burndown chart shows progress toward a release goal. It visualizes the amount of remaining work over time and helps identify trends or deviations in the team's velocity and delivery pace. Similar to the MTA, you can literally "see" the project's progress when looking at the release burndown chart.

6.6   Change Management

The Greek philosopher Heraclitus must have been a project manager. At least one of his central statements, "There is nothing permanent except change," hits the mark. Moreover, Charles Darwin spoke of the "survival of the fittest" in his book "On the Origin of Species." What he meant, however, was not the strongest, but the most adaptable.

Since projects—as Heraclitus already recognized—are permanently subject to change, we should be prepared for this and be able to adapt. This is basically accomplished in very different ways in sequential and agile frameworks.

6.6.1   Sequential Project Management Frameworks

In sequential project management frameworks, changes are—basically undesirable—deviations from the initially analyzed and agreed requirements. All activities related to project definition (requirements and scope) and the corresponding project planning are aimed solely at ensuring that project execution achieves the project goal as precisely as possible—a true "precision landing"—while staying within the planned effort.

However, changes are unavoidable. Since they were not originally planned, additional efforts are incurred in the sequential scenario as a result of changes:

- Repeated analysis
- Rescheduling
- Possible rework, and (due to this)
- Additional errors.

The probability that changes will lead to new errors and thus to further rework is high. Since we do not want to discover these errors only after delivery of the product, we have to safeguard ourselves. For this reason, plan regression tests, i.e., repetitions of tests that have already been performed—and plan them at module, system and integration level!

But even if the product has been tested extensively, additional errors may occur when processes that were previously well coordinated in the project are neglected or even undermined. In other words, the software design was properly documented all along, but due to late changes, it was "sloppy" in the end and the documentation is partly wrong (because it is outdated).

Therefore, it is important not to underestimate the effort required to make changes!

For sequentially executed projects, it is essential to establish a well-defined change management process supported by appropriate software (as part of the project infrastructure). Such a change management process is a basic prerequisite for proper project execution. Maturity models explicitly prescribe a change management process.

Dealing with Major Changes that Affect the Project Scope

We distinguish two levels in change management. The first level, typically involving higher management levels, addresses changes that affect the overall scope of the project. These include changes in requirements, changes in milestone dates or changes in costs. The change process goes through the following steps:

1. The change is recorded and categorized.
2. The proposed change will be analyzed for its impact on existing agreements. If the scope of the project is changed, a formal change request is prepared. The change request is the central document to control changes to the project and deliverables and to formalize acceptance or rejection of these changes.
3. The change is adopted, deferred or rejected. The decision is made and documented by the Change Control Board (CCB).
4. For the adopted change, impacts on plans, work products, and activities are identified, documented, and communicated by project management.
5. The change is implemented by the project team.
6. The change will be tracked to completion.
7. The project definition and the time-related cost plan are updated accordingly.

> **Definition** Change request
> ISO 21500:2012: A documentation that defines a proposed alteration to a project.

The seven steps mentioned seem logical and therefore simple, but note that the "Implementation" step can involve massive testing activities. In addition, we introduced a new project committee through the back door: the "Change Control Board" (CCB).

For the project manager this means that, beyond the technical project level, there can also be significant additional effort to take into account at project control level, since in medium-sized or large projects, the CCB may need to decide on several hundred change requests within just a few months.

> **Definition** Change Control Board (CCB)
> Change control board that decides or rejects changes and documents the decisions made (ASQF CPPM 2025).

Figure 6.11 shows an example of how different changes pass through the seven steps.

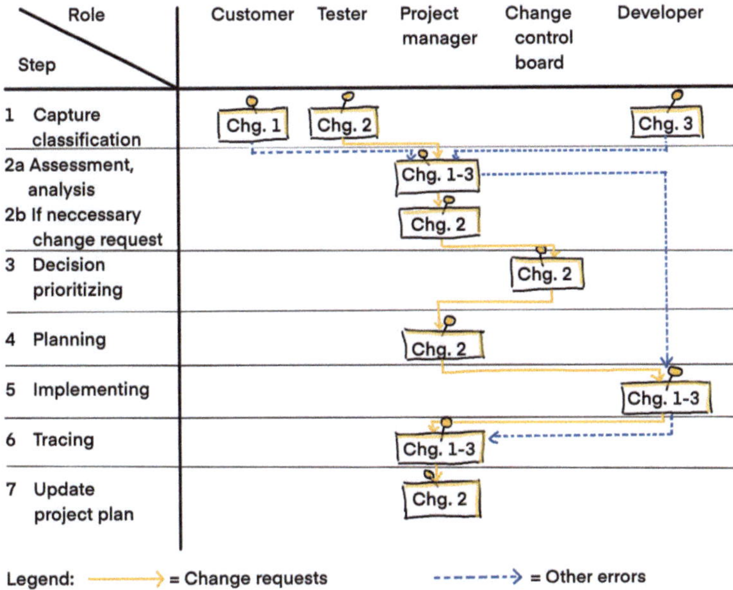

Fig. 6.11   Processing of changes in the change management process

Dealing with Minor Changes Without Impact on Project Scope
The second level handles changes that do not change the scope of the project. This level is typically lower in the organization, as the project team and the project manager can jointly decide how to handle the change.

In most cases, these are changes to components that have already been implemented, i.e., bug fixes. Software developers have different names for these errors: Bugs, problem report, defects, issues. They are discovered during the project's internal verification activities or, worse, by the customer (e.g., during validation). The latter can lead to considerable image loss and become extremely expensive.

Basically, the change procedure for bugs should follow the same steps as described above. Even small changes should be recorded, analyzed, implemented, controlled, and documented. However, this is usually part of the operational project work.

One difference between major and minor changes is the decision-making process. Depending on the environment, the decision to implement small changes—those that do not influence the project scope—does not need to be formally approved by a change control board, regardless of its size. In many projects or project phases, the developer themselves decide, in others it is the project manager, and in safety–critical projects there may also be a CCB for small changes.

The timing of the change also plays a role. The closer the end of the project is in sight, the more stakeholders should be informed about the planned change before it is implemented.

By definition, these "minor" changes do not cause a change or update to the project plans, as they do not affect the project scope.

The Change Request
Figure 6.12 shows an example of a change request that can be initiated by a customer or an internal entity. Today, a wide range of software tools manage the entire process through defined workflows, from the submission of a change request to the tracking of its implementation.

6.6.2 Agile Frameworks Have Fewer Problems

A key to the development of agile frameworks was the realization that modern software projects are subject to a large number of changes and a method is needed to deal with them well. This was solved by the core element of agility par excellence: Iterations.

The shorter the iterations, the more flexible the project. The length of the iterations therefore strongly depends on the environment. Projects in an environment with a high rate of change should schedule the sprints shorter than those in a stable environment so that feedback on the effects of a change can lead to action more quickly. If the project is in an environment with a lower change rate, the sprint length can be set longer.

CR ID 0001	Title: Recording as jpg format		
Product:	Graphical library	**Component:**	GraphicsExporter
Requested by:	John Doe	**Request date:**	Oct. 10th 2025
Affected items	Graphics library	**Release / Build:**	V1.12.6542
CR Type:	☐ Emergency ☒ Normal ☐ Standard	**Category:**	☐ Hardware ☒ Software ☐ Documentation ☐ Other __________
Description:	*<short description, possibly referring to attachments>*		
Priority:	☐ Critical ☐ High ☒ Medium ☐ Low	**Reason for change:**	*<explanation of business or user impact>*
CCB decision			
Decision:	☐ Approved ☐ Rejected ☐ Deferred	**Target release:**	
Date:		**Assigned to:**	
Closure			
Status:	☐ Planned ☐ In progress ☐ Implemented ☐ Validated ☐ Closed ☐ Aborted	**Comment:**	
Release date:		**Release version:**	
Approver:		**Date and signature:**	

Fig. 6.12   Structure of a change request

In principle, agile frameworks such as Scrum do not distinguish between user stories that find their way into the product backlog as a result of requirements and those that result from changes and overwrite existing stories or affect software parts that have already been implemented. Since there was no upfront planning, there is initially no additional effort for planning, since the changes can be processed in the course of the next sprints. The agile process is structured in such a way that all the above-mentioned steps for evaluating and processing the change can or even must be run through. However, even agile projects may have to follow additional formal change management processes that are not part of the general Scrum rules, due to company guidelines or regulatory requirements.

> **Example** In our case study, one of the projects requested the change on function that was already implemented. The development team did not see any problem and immediately agreed to do the change. Fortunately, the organizational processes required a formal change request. When the CCB analyzed the change, they discovered that the first version of the graphics library was already deployed. Changing the interface would have affected several other team. The change was therefore rejected.

Urgent changes are automatically processed in the next sprint, since they are at the top of the prioritized product backlog. However, this may already be too late. For example, if the sprint length is three weeks and the current sprint has only recently started, this means in the worst case that the change will be implemented in six weeks at the earliest. Although this is a clear statement, it can be too late in urgent cases if the change is a so-called "show stopper" that needs to be fixed immediately.

Experienced teams have found ways to deal with this, because being able to run agility effectively in a real-world environment is essential. One of these ways is to plan for buffers.

A team can usually estimate how tight the situation is in which a project finds itself. Thus, based on this assessment, a buffer can be kept for very urgent changes that have to be completed within the current sprint. This is done by not scheduling the entire availability of the team members. The team will be able to judge how much buffer is needed.

If no buffers have been included, or if they are exceeded, the team can agree on rescheduling with the product owner. The change will then be incorporated into the current sprint anyway. In return, the product owner accepts the risk that the story with the lowest priority will not be part of the sprint result and will therefore automatically move to the next sprint. This is also the case if only individual tasks of a story are unfinished. In this case, the entire user story moves to the next sprint and its priority is re-evaluated.

If a very urgent change becomes necessary, which leads the goal of the entire current sprint ad absurdum, there is the possibility that the product owner and team agree to cancel the current sprint. The next sprint would then be scheduled and the sprint cycles would start at a new rhythm.

Show stoppers do not necessarily have to wait for the end of the sprint, but can also be delivered before (possibly even have to). This must be taken into account when evaluating the change, as the additional delivery could have an impact on the achievement of the sprint target if additional effort has been incurred here.

6.7 Summary

In the course of the project control phase, the collected actual data ("As-Is" values) are compared with the results of the previous planning ("Planned" values). In this way, deviations from the planning can be reacted to.

A sophisticated and efficient reporting system creates transparency. Progress monitoring should always distinguish between the activity level and the project level. The structure and size of activities are generally decisive for reliable progress monitoring.

Two methods in particular, also known as trend systems, have become established in practice for monitoring and predicting progress at the project level. These are the "Milestone Trend Analysis" (MTA) and the "Earned Value Analysis" (EVA).

Changes to the previous planning in the project can occur at any time. On the one hand, these can be changes in the project scope at the project management level, and on the other hand, smaller changes at the operational level that occur, for example, as a result of bug fixes, but do not change the project scope. Changes must be systematically recorded, evaluated, decided, implemented, and tracked in both the sequential and agile approaches.

The difference between the two project management frameworks is that in the sequential project environment, changes are generally undesirable, represent a disruption to the process, and are subject to an elaborate, formalized process by means of change requests and committees (especially the Change Control Board). In the agile environment, changes are generally expected and can, with a few exceptions, be handled within the iteration planning.

6.8 Exercises

1. Explain the consequences of poor project controlling.
2. Name the essential components of project controlling and describe one of these components.
3. How can the tracking of project progress be put on a reliable basis?
4. Outline how you might collect progress data in each of sequential and agile projects.
5. One possible form of reporting is the so-called traffic light system. Name other forms.

6. Explain why the use of regular progress reports is useful.
7. Explain what benefits target group-oriented meetings have.
8. What points do you consider to make a meeting effective and efficient?
9. Explain why Milestone Trend Analysis is appropriate for time-oriented progress monitoring.
10. Explain how the release burndown chart visualizes project progress.
11. Describe the impact of changes in sequential and agile projects and how you will deal with them.
12. Name two levels of change management in sequential project management frameworks.
13. Name change management activities that typically occur in sequential frameworks.
14. Explain the specifics that arise for change management in agile frameworks.

References

(ASQF CPPM 2025): Project Management Foundations, Syllabus (EN), ASQF® Certified Profes286 sional for Project Management (2025) - Foundation Level, Version 3.0, 2025.

(Hamid 1988): Abdel-Hamid, T.K., Understanding the "90% syndrome" in software project management: A simulation-based case study', Journal of Systems and Software, 8(4), pp. 319–330. https://doi.org/10.1016/0164-1212(88)90015-5

(ISO 21500:2012): International Organization for Standardization (ISO), ISO 21500:2012(E) – Guidance on project management. Geneva: ISO.

(ISO 21502:2020): International Organization for Standardization (ISO), ISO 21502:2020(E) – 292 Project, programme and portfolio management — Guidance on project management. Geneva:293 ISO.

(Meyer 2014): Meyer, B., Agile! The Good, the Hype and the Ugly. Berlin, Heidelberg: Springer, https://doi.org/10.1007/978-3-319-05155-0

(Mroz 2018): Mroz, J. et al., Do We Really Need Another Meeting? The Science of Workplace Meetings. Current Directions in Psychological Science. 27. 096372141877630. https://doi.org/10.1177/0963721418776307. Available at: https://www.researchgate.net/publication/328399884_Do_We_Really_Need_Another_Meeting_The_Science_of_Workplace_Meetings

(Vanhoucke, 2014) Vanhoucke, M., Integrated Project Management and Control: First Comes the Theory, then the Practice. Berlin, Heidelberg: Springer. https://doi.org/10.1007/978-3-319-04331-9.

(Wysocki 2019): Robert K. Wysocki: Effective Project Management: Traditional, Agile, Extreme, Hybrid, 656 pages, ISBN-13 978-1119562801.

Project Acceptance and Closing 7

This chapter essentially deals with the question: "What tasks arise at the end of a project (or milestone or iteration, depending on the project management framework), what problems can occur and what can be done about them?" As banal as it sounds, a project cannot be successfully completed until the project customer (client) has declared to the contractor (service provider) that the project result has been achieved. In this context, we speak of "project acceptance."

7.1   Project Acceptance

Project acceptance serves to formally establish and document that the project results have been accepted directly by the project customers or third parties specifically commissioned for this purpose. As a rule, this presupposes that the requirements have been implemented correctly and completely in accordance with the specification, or that any deviating implementation complies with the mutually agreed arrangements. Accordingly, project acceptance determines whether the results produced are free of defects.

The determination of defects is of central importance for liability claims. Which legal claims are decisive depends on the form of the contract and the legislation (for example the German Civil Code). We will discuss this further below. Some contractual aspects have already been discussed in Chap. 4. From the contractual agreements, we can determine whether and how project acceptance must be carried out in technical and contractual terms.

Project acceptance is an essential prerequisite for project closing and therefore always precedes it. As a general rule:

© The Author(s), under exclusive license to Springer Nature Switzerland AG 2026   161
A. Johannsen et al., *Foundations for Software Project Management in Classic and Agile Environments*, https://doi.org/10.1007/978-3-032-16797-2_7

- Project acceptance must be planned well in advance (time, responsible persons, resources, location, procedure).
- Project acceptance can only be performed if clear acceptance criteria exist (contracts, requirement specifications).
- Project acceptance can be graduated (e.g. "Acceptance without defects," "Acceptance despite minor defects" up to "No acceptance due to major or significant defects"). Any additional measures required to remedy identified defects must at least be defined in a list of deviations and the activity plan must be supplemented accordingly.
- Effects of necessary changes with regard to costs incurred and times required must be determined and added to the project plan (project controlling).
- Contractually agreed measures are to be implemented.

Project acceptance can thus require extensive project controlling activities and is therefore closely interwoven with change management (see Chap. 6 "Implementing and Controlling a Project")!

7.1.1 Functional Acceptance

Software must undergo various tests (module/component test, integration test, system test, etc.) regardless of the project management framework selected. These tests all precede the actual project acceptance. This also applies to the acceptance tests specified in the V-model as part of verification and validation (see Chap. 3). The project acceptance merely involves the final acceptance check of the test results and test documentation of the preceding respective technical acceptance tests, which were usually run in previous project phases or—in the agile scenario—in the iterations that have taken place so far.

The list of deviations already mentioned above should include, among others, the following information:

- Project name
- Unique ID
- Priority (from the customer's perspective, must the deviation be corrected rapidly?)
- Date (when was the defect recorded?)
- Examiner (by whom?)
- Description (which requirement was not fulfilled due to which errors?)
- Classification of the deviation (significant/negligible—taking the effort into account)
- Assignee (who is responsible for eliminating the deviation?)
- Date of correction (till when?)

There are considerable differences between sequential and agile project management frameworks. In projects following the agile approach, project acceptance

Table 7.1   A list of deviations for our case study as an example

Deviation list					Project: graphical platform		
ID	Prio	Submitted	Examiner	Description	Category	Assignee	Until when
1	1	2025-01-24	FMB	Various errors when merging databases	Significant	KAB	2025-02-24
2	3	2025-01-24	JUG	Warnings when importing geometric training data	Insignificant	PME	2025-03-03
3	2	2025-01-28	FMB	Wrong mouse control for ellipses	Significant	FSC	2025-03-05
4	3	2025-01-28	JUB	Optical printouts distorted—rendering?	Insignificant	FSC	2025-03-07
5							
6							

ideally takes place after each increment or sprint (see also Chap. 4.1.3 on milestones). The Definition of Done (DoD) is verified. Only stories that fully meet the DoD criteria are delivered. During the sprint review, the shippable increment of the sprint is presented to the customer, the product owner, and possibly other key stakeholders and acceptance is confirmed or denied.

Projects following the sequential approach usually target "100% acceptance" at the end of the project. A "100% acceptance" must be planned much more extensively and requires at least the following points:

- Clear and measurable acceptance criteria
- The project results to be accepted (software, documentation, etc.)
- Provision of acceptance infrastructure and systems
- Designation of the personnel performing the acceptance task(s)
- Organization of appointments and meetings

100% project acceptance at the end increases the risk that incorrect implementations in project results will not be detected until very late, which delays the entire project acceptance. Among others, this has a negative impact on payment agreements, warranty claims and guarantee periods. For this reason, sequential projects are well advised to carry out interim acceptance procedures at milestones.

7.1.2   Contractual Acceptance

Although—or precisely because—there are no universal legal guidelines on how acceptance should be structured in detail, the customer and contractor of the project should already specify test and acceptance scenarios in the contract. The following topics should be considered:

- What does the contractor have to prepare (technically and organizationally) for acceptance by the client?
- What acceptance tests should exist and how will they be performed?
- Who performs which tests and when?
- What are the deviation categories (in Table 7.1 "Significant defect" and "Insignificant defect") and what do they mean?
- How is the acceptance documented (acceptance protocol)?
- When must the acceptance be repeated, what follows from this?

Depending on the form of the contract, various claims may arise as a result of any defects that may be present. In the case of work contracts, we speak in legal terms of "software contracts under the law on work contracts"—as opposed to contracts for service.

Under EU consumer law, remedies for defects and non-conformity typically focus on the performance of the supplied service or digital content, see Directive (EU) 2019/770 on digital content and services and Directive (EU) 2019/771 on the sale of goods: (EU 2019a, b).

The precise scope of remedies, however, depends on the Member State's national implementation. There is no single European civil code. Instead, we have country-specific laws like the German Civil Code ("Bürgerliches Gesetzbuch," BGB) or the French "Code Civil".[1] The EU directives mentioned above only set minimum rules for consumer contracts, which specify remedies for defects and lack of conformity such as repair, replacement, price reduction, or contract termination. Member States have transposed those rules into national law, so the parties (client and contractor) should cite and use the relevant national implementing law for their project contracts.

> **Example** In Germany, the project customer can in this case assert its so-called "defects liability"[2] in the event of deviation upon or after acceptance. In other words, the contractor must make improvements.

If subsequent performance fails and the defects are significant, the client may even withdraw from the contract for work and may claim damages. It is therefore not surprising that the question of what constitutes "significant defects" is a recurring one.

---

[1] Available at: https://www.legifrance.gouv.fr/codes/texte_lc/LEGITEXT000006070721/.
[2] See German Civil Code, §437, n. 1 (http://www.gesetze-im-internet.de/bgb/__437.html, accessed Sept. 19, 2025).

Attention Even several insignificant defects can in their entirety lead to a significant defect and thus give rise to claims for damages.

In the case of service contracts pursuant to German civil law BGB §611, there is usually no right of the customer to claim damages with respect to the software product, but only with respect to the service owed (e.g. if the promised working time was not performed).

7.2   Project Closing

"Project acceptance" refers exclusively to whether the owed project result, be it a software product or a service, is officially approved (i.e., "accepted"). However, there is more to the full closing of a project.

Every project should be officially closed beyond acceptance, regardless of whether a sequential or agile approach was chosen for project management. This can and should, especially in the case of longer projects—also be done in stages at the level of project phases or milestones. Therefore, the explanations here apply not only to project closing, but also to phase closings. The following activities are summarized under the term project or phase closing:

- The project manager must ensure that the project documentation is complete and up-to-date for the project closing phase, and that it can be found in an archive for later projects.
- All project participants reflect on the course of the project, e.g., in a project closing workshop, in the sense of a final review ("lessons learned"). The collaboration within the team and with external stakeholders of the project is also reflected. In the agile environment (e.g., Scrum), regular sprint retrospectives replace the one-shot lessons learned workshop. Suggestions for improvement so-called "impediment backlogs" are collected as lists of improvement, which are ideally implemented in the next sprint(s).
- The project manager evaluates the effectiveness and efficiency of the processes and identifies potential for improvement, preferably with the team. This is also part of the "lessons learned."
- The project manager undertakes an after-action review of the project risks (if necessary, also together with the team) in order to make these experiences useful for future projects.
- The project is post-calculated by the project manager. Post-calculation here means that the ACTUAL costs of the project are (or at least should be) finally determined. These are compared with the planned costs and the result is explained. In sequential projects this is usually done at the end of the project. Projects that follow Scrum review their efficiency more regularly when recomputing the team velocity during the sprint retrospective.

- The project manager ensures that the "lessons learned" results are archived and that they are available for future projects.
- The potential for improvement relating to the necessary readjustment of the selected project management framework is passed on to the company's central project management team as feedback for further process tailoring.
- The project manager and each team member complete the entries in the employee skills database.

Often, the minutes of the project closing workshop (or final review) constitute a final report. If no project closing workshop is held, the objectives achieved in the project should be evaluated by the project customer and the client and documented in a project closing report in a transparent way. The project closing is a valuable means of making project experiences usable for future projects, learning from mistakes, and thus gradually improving processes.

7.3   Required Soft Skills and Methods

Many studies report that projects that are not successfully completed, failed in the majority of the observed cases on the relationship level and in the area of "soft skills," see e.g., (Iriarte and Bayona Oré 2018; PMI 2022; Ochoa Pacheco et al. 2023; Avença et al. 2023). Therefore, a successful project manager should not only prepare project plans and estimate efforts and capacities, but should also be able to communicate and present ("sell") the project well, especially at the end, lead project participants to the result, and resolve technical as well as emotional conflicts.

The aforementioned "soft skills" and the use of appropriate methods by project management are particularly important during project acceptance and project closing. A successful project closing should have a lasting effect. Often, project customers are confronted with the situation that they no longer have direct "access" to important project members and that important know-how is "lost." At the same time, it is not uncommon for project closings to be direct starting points for new projects or follow-up projects.

It is therefore even more important that the project manager organizes the project acceptance and closing in such a way that, in addition to the content-related and technical retrospective of the project, there is also personal reflection by all project participants.

7.3.1   360-Degree Feedback

One instrument that has proven itself in practice is the 360-degree feedback system, also known as multisource feedback, see (Fleenor 2021). Although it was developed for the assessment of specialists and managers, it can be applied very well—usually in a leaner form—to all team members and other stakeholders in the

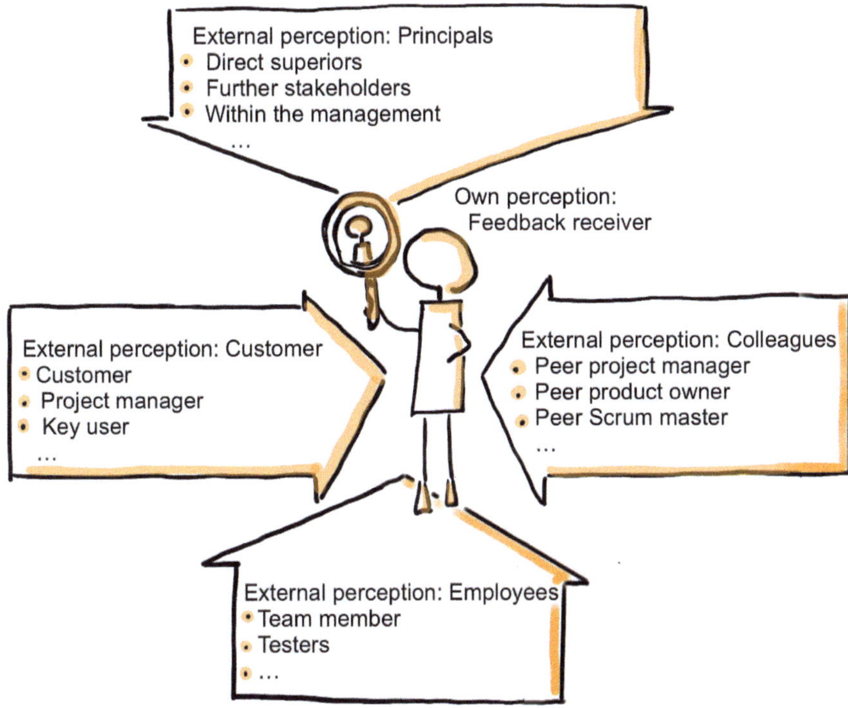

Fig. 7.1 360-degree feedback in projects

context of projects. The interested reader is referred to (Conger 2019) for suitable designs of multisource feedback arrangements.

The core of the 360-degree feedback system consists of broad feedback from all key stakeholders and the different hierarchies represented therein ("top," "bottom," "right," and "left," see Fig. 7.1) as well as roles (superiors, colleagues, customers, consultants, etc.). This creates a greater diversity of opinions, which in turn leads to more objectivity in the evaluation of the individual leadership and performance of the person being evaluated.

7.3.2 Self-assessment Versus External Assessment

To use the results (self-assessments and assessments by others) for personal and professional (further) development, a personal strengths/weaknesses profile (strengths/weaknesses matrix) can be created. In this matrix, the results of the assessment are assigned to the areas of "Actual weaknesses," "Hidden weaknesses," "Actual strengths," and "Supposed strengths." Fig. 7.2 shows this analysis schematically.

Fig. 7.2 Personal strengths/weaknesses profile based on 360-degree feedback

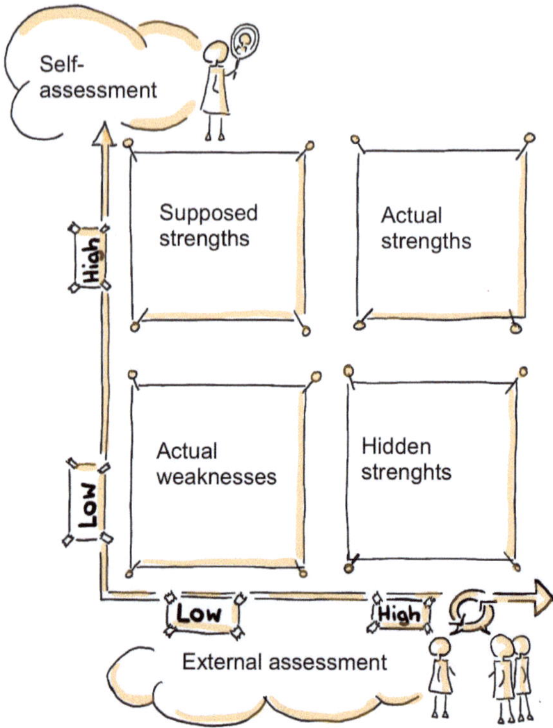

The personal strengths/weaknesses profile created can then be used beyond the project for short- and long-term development plans. In this way, skills and competencies acquired or deepened in the project can be made visible by means of entries in skills databases or other personnel development tools. This also applies to information on improvement potential. However, all of this personal information should be made available only to authorized users.

7.4 Summary

The project acceptance serves the formal acceptance of the system by the customer. The essential prerequisites for project acceptance are—depending on the project management framework selected—the successful completion of all tests planned prior to acceptance, the existence of acceptance criteria, and early and careful planning. Acceptance should be documented by an acceptance protocol, and identified deviations are summarized in a deviation list.

Project closing is a valuable means of making project experiences usable for future projects, learning from mistakes and thus gradually improving the processes in the software development project. The project closing typically includes at least:

- The completion of all project documents,
- A post-calculation and a post-evaluation of risks,
- An analysis and evaluation of the project work and actors,
- And an update of skill databases.

7.5   Exercises

1. What is the difference between project acceptance and project closing?
2. Explain the activities through which the goal project acceptance is pursued and achieved.
3. How does project acceptance take place in sequential and agile environments, respectively? Where are the differences?
4. What activities does the project closing include?
5. Which methods on the relationship level should be used meaningfully during project closing?
6. Explain what benefit will result from project closing.
7. Describe why project acceptance is closely linked to change management and project controlling.

References

(Avença et al. 2023): Avença, I., Domingues, L. & Carvalho, H., Project managers' soft skills influence in knowledge sharing. Procedia Computer Science, 219, pp.1705–1712. https://doi.org/10.1016/j.procs.2023.01.464. Available at: https://www.sciencedirect.com/science/article/pii/S1877050923004763

(Conger 2019): Conger, J. A. Harnessing the potential of 360 feedback in executive education programming. In A.H. Church, D.W. Bracken, J.W. Fleenor, & D.S. Rose (Eds.), The handbook of strategic 360 feedback (pp.343–351). Oxford University Press.

(EU 2019a): Directive (EU) 2019/770 — on certain aspects concerning contracts for the supply of digital content and digital services (EUR-Lex): https://eur-lex.europa.eu/eli/dir/2019/770/oj/eng

(EU 2019b): Directive (EU) 2019/771 — on certain aspects concerning contracts for the sale of goods (EUR-Lex): https://eur-lex.europa.eu/eli/dir/2019/771/oj/eng

(Fleenor 2021): Fleenor, J. W., What Can We Learn from Research on Multisource Feedback in Organizations? In: Student Feedback on Teaching in Schools (S. 221–236). Springer. https://doi.org/10.1007/978-3-030-75150-0_14

(Iriarte & Bayona Oré 2018): Iriarte, C. & Bayona Oré, S., Soft Skills for IT Project Success: A Systematic Literature Review. In: Mejia J., Muñoz M., Rocha Á., Quiñonez Y., Calvo-Manzano J. (eds) Trends and Applications in Software Engineering (CIMPS 2017). Advances in Intelligent Systems and Computing, vol. 688. Springer, Cham. https://doi.org/10.1007/978-3-319-69341-5_14.

(Ochoa Pacheco et al. 2023): Ochoa Pacheco, P., Coello-Montecel, D., Tello, M., Lasio, V. & Armijos, A.; How do project managers' competencies impact project success? A systematic literature review. PLOS ONE, 18(12): e0295417. https://doi.org/10.1371/journal.pone.0295417. Available at (open access): https://doi.org/10.1371/journal.pone.0295417

(PMI 2022): Project Management Institute. Pulse of the Profession® 2023: Power Skills, Redefining Project Success (14th ed.). PMI. Available at: https://www.pmi.org/-/media/pmi/documents/public/pdf/learning/thought-leadership/pmi-pulse-of-the-profession-2023-report.pdf

Quality Assurance

8

8.1 Quality Concerns Everyone—Quality Assurance as a Cross-Cutting Task

With software—even more than with hardware—quality cannot be tested into the product after it is built. Software products are far too complex. First, software usually offers many functions that do not necessarily have to be used in a predefined order. Second, it often runs on different platforms or operating systems. Third, it is not uncommon for software to be configured in a user-specific way. Each of these reasons in itself means that an all-encompassing test does not make economic sense or is simply not technically possible. For example, we cannot keep all smartphones in all languages with all operating system versions on the market in the test lab.

As always, when a full-fledged final manufacturing control (end-of-line-inspection) of is not possible, we must consider the manufacturing process instead. Just as natural beauty comes from within, good quality springs from a clean development process. But what do we mean by "good quality," and who evaluates the quality of a product?

Quite obviously, a product is not good enough if it cannot convince the customer. However, the reverse conclusion is only part of the truth. A product that excites the customer, but whose development drives the company to ruin, is also not "good" in the long run. The customer is an important stakeholder in the project, but not the only one. The expectations of the IT administrator, who is to install, operate, and, if necessary, update the software product, must also be met. Likewise, the development should take place within the given financial and time frame.

To be able to evaluate the quality of a product, we must first define the evaluation criteria, that is, the so-called quality objectives. In addition, quality assurance measures must be defined. By quality assurance, we mean the sum of all measures that are carried out during the entire duration of a project to ensure that the quality objectives are met. This also includes thinking about a clean software architecture before implementation. Every process that calls for a documented architecture created at an early stage contributes to quality assurance.

Thus, quality assurance has two aspects. On the one hand, it aims at ensuring that the product meets the requirements of the various stakeholders. On the other hand, it monitors the development or manufacturing process. We therefore distinguish between.

- Quality assurance for products and
- Quality assurance for processes.

In summary, we are dealing with a cross-cutting task that affects all project phases, all areas of activity, and thus all stakeholders of the project.

From a psychological perspective, it is important that all members of the project team have internalized this holistic concept of quality. Quality assurance should not be understood as a burdensome obligation, but as an intrinsic behavior. We perform quality assurance out of a desire to do a good job and to avert unnecessary project risks.

"Developers hate having to write documents." This sentence is, of course, a shameless generalization. Nonetheless, there is a grain of truth in it. Documentation is often considered to be an unpleasant, sometimes even burdensome task, especially if it is in a foreign language. For developers, the value of a detailed design document is not necessarily obvious. An often-heard comment in this context is, "Look at the source code. That's the best documentation." For the developer who has only been a member of the team for a few days, things are different. Anything that is suitable for giving him an overview and making it easier for him to get started is useful and therefore makes sense.

Documentation should be understood as self-protection. We write documents,

- To be able to go on vacation from time to time,
- To avoid constant interruptions because we must explain a module for which we were once responsible some time ago,
- To remind ourselves why we decided things the way we did (which unfortunately is not commented in the source code),
- And because it is required, for example by industry standards.

While the last reason is important, it should never be the main motivation. Therefore, convey to your team that they are writing the documents primarily for themselves and that this is an important contribution to quality assurance. Make sure that the content of the documents is useful. Pure post-documentation of the functions and parameters defined in the source code is not very helpful and can be generated automatically from the (well-commented) source code with little effort and suitable tool support.

Since we are already on the topic of tool support, we will take a brief excursus into AI support for system development. This area is rapidly making its way into the industry and will, of course, affect processes, organization, risks, and the overall quality of software development today and in the future: AI-agents are already being applied across various stages of software production, ranging from code generation to testing and project reporting. Exemplary tools include (Zheyuan Cui et al 2024):

- GitHub Copilot/Copilot X
- Amazon CodeWhisperer
- Replit Ghostwriter
- Tabnine
- Codeium
- Experimental multi-agent frameworks.

Example GitHub Copilot is an AI-powered coding assistant. It is directly integrated into the development environment of the programmers. GitHub Copilot can explain code, suggests code completions, functions, and comments directly as you type, thus speeding up development and the generation of automated unit tests. For more information, please refer to the website of the provider GitHub.

The effects are expected to be profound: the success rate of software projects could rise from today's roughly estimated 35%, while project selection, controlling, reporting, coding, and testing will significantly improve; at the same time, competence requirements for project managers and stakeholders are shifting (Nito-Rodriguez and Vargas 2023). The PMI Sweden report on AI and project management underlines that these changes will reshape not only the project processes but also the governance and skills landscape in software organizations (Nilsson 2024).

Example Recent research on autonomous AI agent for testing web applications shows that it is possible to measure the quality of AI generated output in a reliable, automated way (Chevrot 2025). This opens completely new possibilities for tool support that will considerably change the way testers work and the skills they require. Using tools like Lynqa® or Thunders will liberate testers from repetitive manual tasks.[1] In the future, they will require less programming skills, but more AI-related skills. The ISTQB® recently issued a new training scheme on "Testing with generative AI" (ISTQB 2025).

---

[1] For more information, refer to the websites of the providers: https://www.smartesting.com/ and https://www.thunders.ai/ (last accessed Oct 11th 2025).

8.2   The Quality Assurance Plan

Quality assurance (QA) should be planned, just like all other activities in the project. This applies to sequential project management frameworks as well as to agile ones. The short communication paths between the Scrum team and the product owner in agile projects may make some document reviews unnecessary—ultimately, they are also part of a higher-level quality assurance plan. After all, even in agile projects, it must be defined how quality is measured, which quality assurance measures are expected from whom and when, what work results are to be delivered, and what constraints exist.

8.2.1   Quality Assessment Criteria

Table 8.1 shows a listing of common quality assessment criteria. The right column contains a list of items that should be specified in the quality assurance plan.

8.2.2   Roles and Responsibilities

In addition, the plan contains statements about roles including the associated rights and duties. The most prominent role besides the quality manager is the tester, but even in this simple case the tasks may differ from project to project. Is there a separation between the test case author, whose job is to specify test cases, and tester who executes them? Is it planned to execute test cases in an automated way and if so, who implements the test scripts? Who will analyze the results and write deviation reports if necessary? As soon as several testers need to be coordinated, the project manager should also appoint a test manager.

Table 8.2 shows a list of common roles and a possible distribution of tasks.

We do not have the silver bullet for roles and task distribution in this book. Each project is different and has its own needs and framework. The project manager's task is to clearly specify what exactly is expected of whom.

Experience has shown that it is useful to separate roles from specific personnel assignments. The quality assurance plan can, but does not necessarily have to, name people. Especially in dynamic projects where the assignment of staff changes frequently, it is advisable to maintain only one document with concrete names and dates. This will usually be the project plan.

8.2.3   Methods and Measures

By "quality assurance methods," we mean specific procedures which help to improve or ensure the quality of the product to be developed on the one hand and of the development process on the other. If these methods are prescribed in the quality assurance plan, we speak of "measures."

Table 8.1 Common quality assessment criteria

Criterion	Meaning	To be specified in the quality assurance plan
Product was successfully verified	All tests were successfully performed and documented. The deviations found were either eliminated or assessed as "acceptable" and documented	– What tests should be performed? – How is the test execution to be documented? – According to which criteria are deviations evaluated? – How are deviations to be documented?
Documentation is complete and verified	All documents to be created are up to date and approved	– Which documents should be created? – What content is expected (document templates)? – How are the documents checked and released? – Where can I find the documents?
Successful validation of the product	The product was "put to the test" in a realistic environment and proven to be "usable"	– How should the validation be done? – Possible variants are beta testing by pilot customers or a formal validation of usability, e.g., in a usability lab
Conformity achieved	All other company-specific and/or externally specified (legal) requirements are met	– Which external specifications (e.g., standards, laws) and internal specifications (e.g., company guidelines) are to be applied? – How can/should the proof of conformity be provided?

Planning quality assurance means, among other things, thinking about methods and measures in advance and recording in the quality assurance plan. Usually, we distinguish between constructive, analytical, and organizational measures.

Constructive measures include all specifications regarding the process (e.g., model-based development, supplier selection procedures) or specifications of specific methods (e.g., a concrete modeling or programming language). Furthermore, this includes all prescribed architecture and design activities, which are, after all, aimed at "constructing" a high-quality product.

A very popular quality assurance approach in agile project management frameworks is called "Shift Left." "Left" refers to the left side of the V-model or, more generally, of the software development lifecycle (SDLC). Thus, shifting left means to start as soon as possible with testing activities—ideally already in the requirements elicitation phase. Depending on the project, different approaches are suitable:

Table 8.2 Examples of roles and tasks to be described in the quality assurance (QA) plan

Role	Tasks
Quality Manager	– Cross-project control of quality assurance – Definition of organization-wide guidelines (e.g., document templates, QA manual) – Verification of compliance with QA requirements – Supporting the project teams in the implementation of the specifications
Project Manager	– Creation of the project-specific quality assurance plan – This does not necessarily mean that the project manager writes the plan. He can delegate this task, but remains responsible for it – Verification of compliance with the QA plan – Provision of the resources required for the organizational measures – Definition and monitoring of process metrics – Evaluation of deviation reports – Training of the project staff
Test Manager	– Creation of the test concept – Detailed planning of all analytical measures – Control of the test execution – Preparation of documentation and reports – Evaluation of deviation reports
Test Case Author	– If necessary, selection of the test design procedure – Specification of the test cases – Review of requirements and design specifications
Test Automation Engineer (automated test execution)	– Conversion of test specifications into automated test scripts – Execution of automated test scripts – Evaluation and documentation of the results – Documentation of the analyzed deviations, if applicable
Tester (manual test execution	– Manual execution of the test cases – Documentation of the results – Documentation of observed deviations, if applicable

- In Test-Driven Development, developers start by writing the unit tests. Obviously, these tests fail (red), since there is nothing to test yet. In a second phase, they write the code of the component that is tested by the previously written unit tests. At a point in time, the tests pass (green), but that does not mean that the code is understandable and maintainable. Therefore, a third phase is dedicated to cleaning up the code (blue). For more info on TDD, please refer to (Beck 2002).
- In Behavior-Driven Development (BDD), a collaborative approach is used to determine the acceptance criteria of user stories by using exemplary scenarios (Nagy 2018). These scenarios are directly formulated as in a semi-formal language that may be easily translated into automated acceptance tests.
- Model-Based Testing (MBT) is an approach that uses graphical models or, to a lesser extend textual models, to describe test artifacts. MBT is not a shift-left approach per se, but it can (and should) be used as such. By drawing diagrams,

user stories are presented in context and become easier to understand. Ambiguities become apparent and discussions are stimulated. In other words, the models serve to validate the requirements. For a textbook on MBT, see (Kramer 2016).

All of these approaches can be applied equally well in agile and sequential frameworks together with a more detailed description of the concrete QA measures.

We distinguish analytical and organizational QA measures.

Analytical QA measures are aimed at checking the results of the work. This includes document reviews as well as manual or automated tests of the product. Analytical measures can also check the quality of a process or service. In this case, we tend to speak of metrics.

Organizational QA measures, as the name suggests, concern the organization, e.g., the composition of the project team, but also regular meetings or the provision of a suitable infrastructure. Another example is the choice of the project management framework (V-model, Scrum…).

The three categories influence each other. Thus, the project manager should ensure that suitable testers are available in the project team at an early stage. This is an organizational measure. "Suitable" testers are those who have a good knowledge of the specified analytical measures, i.e., training as an ISTQB® Certified Tester, for example (ISTQB 2024).

It proved to be best to have dedicated testers instead of assigning the task to a developer. On the one hand, developers should not test their own work, and on the other hand, not every developer is also a good tester, since testers require other soft skills. To put it bluntly, a "good tester" is a friend of clear specifications, which he insistently (but nevertheless diplomatically) demands and from which he does not deviate even under pressure. On the other hand, creativity regarding acceptance criteria is less popular in testing. However, it is precisely from the possibility of being creative that many developers draw their motivation.

8.2.4 Work Products

Typical work products listed in the quality assurance plan are all documents created as part of the quality assurance process for products. These include requirements documents, architecture and design specifications, and all test documents:

- Test plan,
- Test procedure specification ("test cases"),
- Test execution protocols,
- Anomaly reports, and
- Test summary report.

If the tests are automated, the quality assurance plan may in addition require that further proofs (e.g., log files) must be kept.

Documents are also created as work results in the context of quality assurance for processes and services. These can be completed checklists for supplier selection, results of supplier audits, or weekly management summaries with metrics and trend analyses.

8.2.5   Constraints

The most important constraints for quality assurance include applicable standards and procedures. Projects in safety–critical industries are subject to different requirements than projects e.g., in the telecommunications sector. In both cases, approvals or conformity statements must be obtained from independent testing bodies before the product can be sold on the market. For quality assurance, this means that:

1. The required evidence must be provided (usually documents) and
2. Certain rules may have to be followed in the development process.

For instance, the ISO 26262 standard (ISO 26262:2018) applicable in the automotive industry strongly recommends special test procedures for software. The responsible project manager is therefore well advised to stipulate these test procedures in the quality assurance plan.

The organization in which the project is carried out can also set constraints. This ranges from company-wide style guides or cross-project process policies to the use of maturity models, which we will discuss in Chap. 11.

8.2.6   Schedule, Resources, and Budget

Finally, the quality assurance plan contains what every plan should contain: Statements about deadlines, required resources and expected costs. In this context, we repeat our recommendation from above when we talked about roles. Experience has shown that it is convenient to separate milestones from specific deadlines and to maintain the former in the quality assurance plan, but the latter in the project plan.

8.3   Quality Assurance for Processes—How Well Do We Work?

There are numerous measures that are suitable for monitoring or ensuring the quality of processes. You should apply the ISO 9001 standard (ISO 9001:2015), which focuses on this topic. A new version of the ISO 9001 is currently under revision and is planned to be published in 2026. This standard lists minimum requirements for a quality management system that a manufacturer or service provider should fulfill in order to meet the basic expectations of customers and authorities. The core concepts of ISO 9001 include management responsibility, a process-oriented approach, and the principle of continuous process improvement. In a nutshell:

- Quality management is a task of the top management. Although the boss can delegate individual tasks, he or she remains responsible for ensuring that the entire company is committed to customer orientation, the pursuit of the highest quality and, associated with this, continuous improvement.
- Suitable processes ensure quality. Again, we must look at the "big picture." Quality can only be achieved if suppliers, service providers, management, and employees all pull together and all processes are coordinated.
- He who rests, rusts, or, to put it differently, what was good yesterday is not necessarily still good today. In a constantly changing environment, it is essential to keep a permanent eye on whether the existing processes are still suitable or whether they can be improved. Again, maturity models provide assistance.

With this in mind, quality assurance measures can be defined for processes. The quality assurance of processes is usually planned and carried out outside the project, but affects the project manager more or less directly in his daily work. Therefore, we present four measures in more detail here.

8.3.1   Milestone Reviews

Milestones are special points in time at which the project progress is evaluated internally between two phases of the development process or externally together with the customer. This evaluation takes the form of a so-called "milestone review." In this section, we describe the "classic" milestone reviews in the sequential environment. In the agile environment, every sprint review is a milestone review.

In principle, milestone reviews serve to monitor whether the processes defined for the project have been followed and whether the desired results have been achieved. In practice, stakeholders sit down and review (often using checklists) the work products produced. Have all the documents that were required for this milestone been created and released? Have all planned activities, such as purchasing components, been carried out? Are there any identifiable problems regarding the schedule, the cost plan or the expected quality?

The milestone review is an occasion to pause for a moment and take a bird's eye view of the project. It may be that new risks have been identified in the meantime that could jeopardize the success of the project. In this case, measures must be taken to control these risks. In rare cases, a milestone review may even lead to the cancelation of the project.

Milestone reviews are documented. Once they have been completed, the next project phase can begin. If project phases extend over a longer period, it makes sense to define intermediate milestones.

In agile project management frameworks, sprint reviews and retrospectives partially fulfill the function of milestone reviews, but higher-level milestone reviews are also important to ensure that the agile team gets feedback from external stakeholders, especially from quality management experts.

8.3.2　Metrics

Metrics are used to monitor data that can be used to make statements about quality. To ensure that this data is comparable, it is standardized. If 10 errors are found in a document, this measurement in itself has no significance. After all, it can be a document of a thousand pages. Only the statement "10 errors were found per hundred pages of document" enables us to make comparisons with other documents and draw conclusions.

We distinguish between progress, product, and process metrics. Recorded at a specific point in time, progress metrics enable us to make statements about the progress of the work. They are used less for controlling than for steering the process. An example of a progress metric is the number of requirements or backlog items implemented relative to their total number. It is a snapshot in time. If the metric is recorded regularly (e.g., daily), we get a trend. In agile frameworks, the burndown chart represents such a progress metric (see Fig. 8.1). The long line shows the cumulative remaining effort in hours according to the plan, the short line shows the current estimated remaining effort. The plan is not linear, as Easter holidays and team members' vacation days were considered.

Product metrics measure the quality of the product, while process metrics measure the quality of the process. An example of a product metric is the number of warranty cases in relation to the number of products sold. For software, the distinction is not as simple, as software quality is largely determined by the development process. The metric "errors found in the document per 100 pages" mentioned above can provide information about the quality of the document or about the effectiveness of the review process. It is important to check the comparability of the values. A new document will naturally contain more errors than the third revision.

A clear product metric is the number of defective features accepted at release relative to the total number of features. A clear process metric is the number of deviations in an audit per process group considered.

If you want to capture metrics, you should first define them carefully not every metric makes sense in every context. The number of changes per month provides information about the quality of the requirements in sequential project management frameworks. In agile frameworks, this metric has no significance whatsoever, since monthly changes are part of the plan.

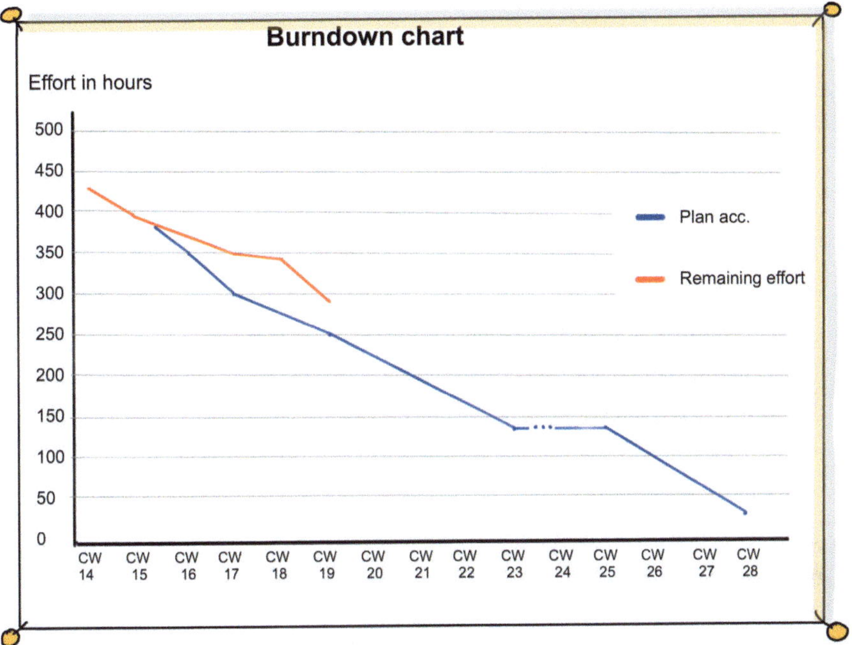

Fig. 8.1 Burndown Chart (progress metric)

While well-chosen metrics are an efficient way to get a quick overview, it is quite possible to steer a project in the wrong direction with poorly chosen metrics. This danger is especially true when rewards or punishments are tied to the metrics. If "finding bugs" becomes a problem, bugs will simply not be documented. But the reverse is also true: if finding errors leads to a bonus, any deviation, no matter how small, will be reported as an error. Both are understandable behaviors, but they are detrimental to the project in the long run.

8.3.3   Audits

Audits determine how well quality assurance processes fulfill their purpose and whether or where there is a need for improvements or corrections. Audits are not necessarily linked to a specific project, but can be triggered or made necessary by such a project.

We distinguish between internal and external audits. External audits are carried out either by the customer at our premises or by us at the premises of suppliers or service providers.

Each audit follows the scheme shown in Fig. 8.2.

Although the actual execution of an audit is only rarely the responsibility of the project manager, he will practically always be directly involved as a participant or

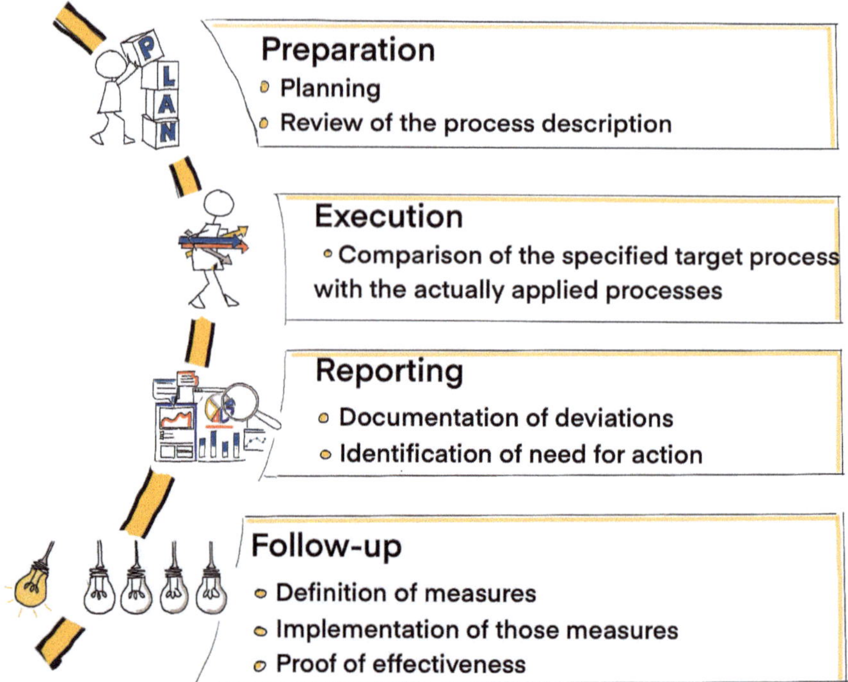

Fig. 8.2 Audit procedure

indirectly as a supplier of information. Apart from that, the project manager must communicate processes, methods, and tools to the project team and to monitor compliance and correct use. If he fails to do so, the result of the audit execution is directly affected.

8.3.4   Process Validation

Process validation is particularly common in safety–critical industries, where it is often mandatory. The basic idea is that a process should be tested before it is used for the first time. Process validation comprises three steps:

1. Targeted process design that creates the framework for a measurably high-performing process;
2. Process qualification, during which it is proven that the defined process really achieves the set objectives, and
3. Continuous monitoring, which ensures that no deterioration creeps in, even in daily operations.

The first point gears with "planning the quality assurance." Process design includes writing detailed work instructions and planning, conducting, and documenting training. The second point in the list above corresponds to the actual validation with acceptance criteria defined in advance. Process-supporting tools such as Application Lifecycle Management (ALM) systems or test tools are checked as part of the qualification process. The third point brings us back to metrics, with which the continuous performance of the process can be measured.

8.4 Quality Assurance for Products—How Good Are the Results?

Quality assurance for products is a topic in itself. Thanks to the activities of the International Software Testing Qualifications Board (ISTQB®), the profession of "software tester" now enjoys a certain recognition. The ISTQB® Certified Tester training program with its various levels and extension modules form a recognized body of knowledge (ISTQB 2024), the contents of which we cannot and do not wish to repeat in detail here. However, every software project manager should acquire basic knowledge in software testing and, for example, complete the ISTQB® Certified Tester Foundation Level or read a related text book such as (Forgács and Kovács 2021).

This section is therefore less about concrete roles, tasks, and methods of quality assurance for products. Instead, we focus on the significance of these and on the integration of quality assurance into the various project management frameworks.

8.4.1 Quality Assurance in Sequential Project Management Frameworks

In sequential project management frameworks, the roles between development and quality assurance are clearly separated. This is particularly obvious in the V-model with its various test levels (see Chap. 3).

Usually, the project manager appoints dedicated testers for integration, system, and acceptance testing, while it is quite common to have the developers perform the component tests. It is advisable not to formally appoint the developer as the tester of his own work, as there is a risk of a certain "operational blindness." In larger projects or organizations, there are often independent test teams ("test centers") headed by a test manager. Thus, the independence of testing from development is also underlined organizationally.

8.4.2 Quality Assurance in Agile Frameworks

In agile projects, the organization is somewhat different. Strictly speaking, the test levels from the V-Model do not exist in the same way, since the specifications on the left are set up differently in agile projects. In the syllabus of the ISTQB®️ Certified Tester "Agile Tester" you will therefore rather find the terms "unit test" (synonym for "component test"), "verification and validation tests for the feature" and, if necessary, a system test. The verification of the feature corresponds to the integration test against the acceptance criteria defined in the user story. Validation of the feature is more like an early acceptance test. System testing is useful when several larger components are assembled.

Unit or component tests count as a subtask of the implementation. Their successful execution is an integral part of the completion criteria of an iteration ("Definition of Done," in short: DoD). In addition, the verification and validation of the implemented features should take place within the same iteration. However, this can be difficult in practice. Due to the high rate of change in agile projects, as much testing as possible should be automated so that it can be repeated as regression tests in later iterations. However, test automation requires additional time. Therefore, it may well be that the feature test "lags behind" one or even several iterations. The system test is definitely performed in later iterations, since the system must first be assembled from several features.

Even in agile projects, the independence of the test should be maintained, which is a challenge for the project organization. In theory, Scrum does not provide for a "tester" role. However, even in agile projects developers may no longer "see the wood for the trees" and an independent test is advantageous. Agile literature speaks about the "3 amigos," a term that refers to product owner, developer, and tester, thus illustrating the importance of the latter, see for example (Cohn 2005).

Some projects run on two tracks and implement hybrid project management frameworks. On the one hand, their development is based on agile principles; while on the other hand, they stick with the sequential test levels. This situation is particularly common in safety–critical industries, where the regulatory requirements do not prescribe the V-model, but suggest it very strongly. In such structures, the project manager must take great care to ensure that the testers of all test levels are firmly integrated into the team and at least participate in the daily Scrums. Otherwise, a major advantage of the agile approach, namely the short communication channels, will be lost again.

8.5 When Something Goes Wrong—Dealing with Deviations

8.5.1 Product-Related Deviations

Both static and dynamic testing will reveal deviations. The opposite would be questionable, because then we would be proofreading documents and testing products without ever finding anything. We start by speaking neutrally of "deviations" because the assessment as "negative" or "positive" is not always obvious. Deviations can have different triggers, as shown schematically in Fig. 8.3. Only in a fraction of cases, the error is caused by an incorrect conversion of the requirements

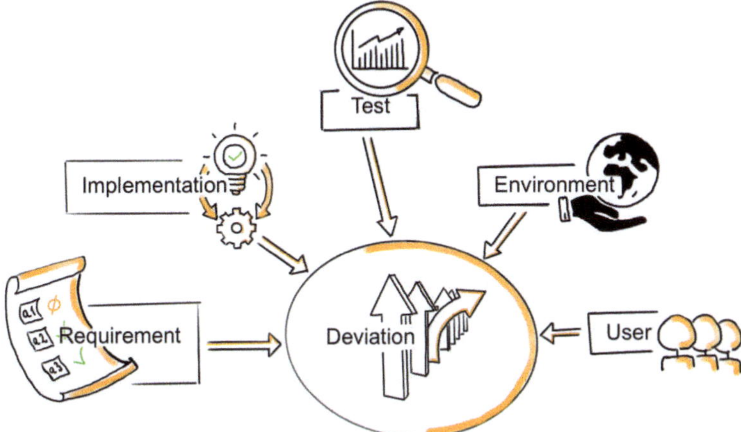

Fig. 8.3 Possible causes of a deviation found in the test

(to badly implemented software). Quite often, the error is already in the requirements or in the design. Test cases and especially automated test scripts can also be incorrectly specified or implemented. Finally, the test environment plays a role. Especially in hardware-related tests of embedded software, the test environment may be a disturbing factor that should not be underestimated.

Figure 8.3 shows a fifth cause: the famous "user error." Be cautious with this explanation! Of course, testers or even end users can also make mistakes. However, the root cause is quite often either a different understanding of the requirements or, in the case of the end user, a usability problem. So before dismissing a deviation as a "user error," it should be analyzed in detail.

> **Important** There are no "tester errors."

Psychology also plays a role: Testers want to be taken seriously. If they have fallen for misleading formulations in the requirements, that is bad enough. You should therefore be careful not to shift the blame to them.

Planning quality assurance for products also includes determining how the observed deviations are documented and followed up. Many companies use so-called defect or bug tracking systems in which the tester records the defect as a "defect," "issue," or "change request." The exact name of the record (which is basically, what it is), depends on the tool and differs from company to company.

The deviation should then first be analyzed and evaluated before a committee—the Change Control Board (CCB for short) already mentioned in Chap. 6—makes its decision regarding further actions. It is not a good idea to blindly try to correct all errors shortly before the final project deadline. Instead, the expected effort for correction and retesting, as well as the risk of endangering already functioning

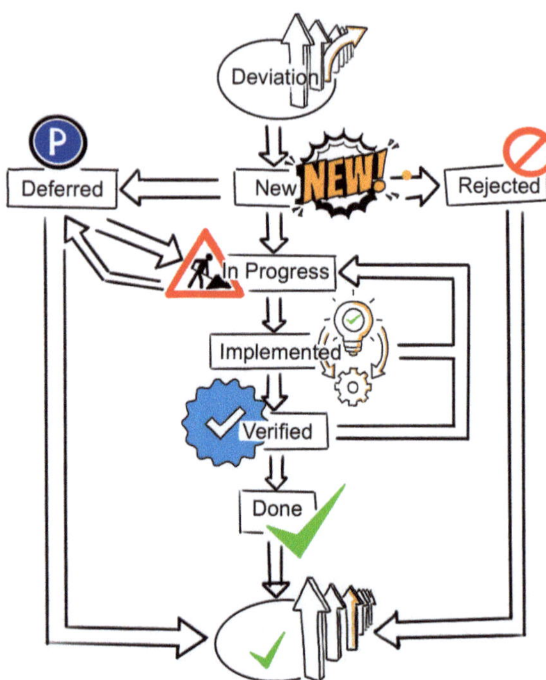

Fig. 8.4 Exemplary status model for the states of a deviation ("Defect")

functionality, should be weighed against the benefits of the correction. Perhaps there is some kind of "workaround," or the bug initially affects only a very small group of customers. In this case, the correction can possibly wait until the next product version.

If the CCB decides the fix, the decision should be documented for the deviation. The implementation and the various downstream checks should also be recorded in the database. Typically, the "defect" goes through a series of states, which in turn depend on the defect tracking software used. Figure 8.4 shows an example of such a status model.

The decision on whether and by when to perform the correction can have far-reaching consequences. Therefore, the project manager should not make it on his own. The closer the delivery of the final product, the higher the risk and possibly the expected costs, since regression tests may be required at all test levels. Conversely, errors that are still found during or shortly before acceptance testing are often extremely critical and require rapid fixes ("hotfix").

8.5.2   Process-Related Deviations

Even the most beautiful development process does not always go according to plan. Such deviations are readily found in the audit and can become quite unpleasant if the audit was carried out by the customer or an authority. It is therefore important to keep a watchful eye on the processes and to learn from mistakes. As a rule: Deviations should result in corrective and preventive measures. These measures are known as "Corrective Actions/Preventive Actions," short CAPAs.

Corrective actions ensure that the deviation does not have any negative consequences. If an immature software version is mistakenly installed on the final product during production, this will result in two corrective actions:

1. The manufactured product may not be shipped until this error is corrected.
2. The cause of the error must be eliminated, i.e., the production must receive the correct software version.

Preventive measures go one step further and get to the bottom of the causes of errors. How could this happen and what can we do to prevent it from happening again? Preventive measures are always steps in the continuous improvement process.

In fact, dealing with deviations is a popular entry point for auditors. For the audited organization it offers the possibility to prove how serious it is about quality control and how thoroughly it implements corrections.

8.6 Division of Labor in Practice

In practice, the organization's quality manager and the project manager often share the work. The former specifies general guidelines and processes and documents them in a QA manual that is valid throughout the company. This manual is supplemented by more detailed work instructions, which may also contain or specify concrete document templates.

The project manager adapts the general process specifications to project-specific needs and documents these deviations in the project's quality assurance plan. Depending on the size of the project, this QA plan can be a chapter of the project plan, part of a separate SW development plan or a stand-alone document.

In addition, the project manager plans the quality assurance for the product or delegates this work to a test manager. The resulting test plan is also a chapter of the project plan, part of a separate SW development plan or an independent document.

8.7 Summary

In this chapter, a core process of software project management was highlighted: quality assurance. In this context, it is important to understand that software quality originates from a "clean" development process and cannot be subsequently tested into the product.

The project manager must plan quality assurance, specifically for the product being developed. In this regard, sequential and agile frameworks differ fundamentally.

Quality assurance for processes is usually a task of the organization, but affects the project manager directly or indirectly, e.g., in the case of audits.

The less obvious tasks of the project manager include creating a basic understanding in the team of the importance of quality assurance processes, knowing and considering the soft skills required for the respective tasks, and generally maintaining motivation (e.g., with regard to documentation).

8.8   Exercises

1. Describe how a process-oriented approach benefits quality assurance.
2. Name the three essential contents of a quality assurance plan.
3. Explain two methods you can use to demonstrate quality assurance of processes.
4. Explain what special role the project manager has with regard to process quality assurance.
5. Agile projects also place demands on product quality. Explain the special agile features to ensure product quality.

References

(Beck 2002): Beck, K., Test Driven Development: By Example. Addison-Wesley Longman Publishing Co., Inc., USA. ISBN 978–0321146533

(Cohn 2005): Mike Cohn: Agile Estimating and Planning, Prentice Hall, 360 pages, 2005, ISBN 224 978–0131479418.

(Chevrot 2025): Chevrot A. et al, Are Autonomous Web Agents Good Testers? arXiv:2504.01495v1 [cs.SE] 2, April 2025, Available at: https://arxiv.org/abs/2504.01495

(Forgács & Kovács 2021): Forgács, I. & Kovács, A. Modern Software Testing Techniques: A Practical Guide for Developers and Testers. Apress. ISBN 978–1–4842–9893–0. https://doi.org/10.1007/978-1-4842-9893-0

(ISO 9001:2015): International Organization for Standardization, ISO 9001: Quality Management Systems – Requirements. Geneva: ISO. Available at: https://www.iso.org/standard/62085.html

(ISO 26262:2018): International Organization for Standardization, ISO 26262: Road Vehicles – Functional Safety. Geneva: ISO. Available at: https://www.iso.org/standard/68383.html

(ISTQB 2024) International Software Testing Qualifications Board (ISTQB). Certified Tester Foundation Level (CTFL) Version 4.0.1 Available at: https://istqb.org/wp-content/uploads/2024/11/ISTQB_CTFL_Syllabus_v4.0.1.pdf

(ISTQB 2025) International Software Testing Qualifications Board (ISTQB). Certified Tester – Testing with Generative AI (CT-GenAI) Version 1.0, Available at: https://istqb.org/wp-content/uploads/sdm-uploads/CT-GenAI-Syllabus-v1.0.pdf

(Kramer 2016): A. Kramer and B. Legeard. Model-Based Testing Essentials: Guide to the ISTQB Certified Model-Based Tester. John Wiley & Sons, Inc., Hoboken, NJ, USA, 2016. https://doi.org/10.1002/9781119130031

(Nagy 2018) Gaspar Nagy and Seb Rose. 2018. Discovery: Explore behaviour using examples (Volume 1) (1st. ed.). CreateSpace Independent Publishing Platform, North Charleston, SC, USA. ISBN 978–1–9835–9125–9

(Nilsson 2024): Marly Nilsson, Artificial Intelligence and Project Management. A global Chapter-Led Survey, Project Management Institute Sweden, Chapter Report, https://www.pmi.org/-/media/pmi/documents/public/pdf/artificial-intelligence/community-led-ai-and-project-management-report.pdf?rev=bca2428c1bbf4f6792f521a95333b4d.

(Nito-Rodriguez & Vargas 2023): Nito-Rodriguez, Vargas, How Generative AI Will Change Project Management. Harvard Business Review, July 2023.

(Zheyuan Cui et al. 2024): K. Zheyuan Cui, M. Demirer, S. Ja, An MIT Exploration of Generative AI: From Novel Chemicals to Opera. Massachusetts Institute of Technology, Schwarzman College of Computing, https://doi.org/10.21428/e4baedd9.3ad85f1c, https://mit-genai.pubpub.org/pub/v5iixksv/download/pdf.

Risk Management

9

9.1 Core Idea of the Risk Management Process

Risk management refers to all activities carried out to identify, assess, control, and track risks. But what is a risk, especially in the context of a project?

> **Hint** A risk is an uncertain event or condition that has a positive or negative effect on project objectives (Boehm 2014, p.107).

Risk management is far more present in our daily lives than we usually realize. Everyone who takes out insurance—i.e., every motorist, among others—engages in some form of risk management. However, we usually give little thought to potential losses and their likelihood of occurrence and severity, especially since many of these insurance policies are required by law. If we talk about a voluntary insurance, let's say a disability insurance, the situation is somewhat different. In this case, we think at least qualitatively about how likely occupational disability might be, what it means for our financial situation, and whether we are not paying more for the insurance in the long run than we can get out in the end.

Banks and insurance companies themselves conduct risk management on a completely different, much more quantitative level, see e. g. (Blatter et al. 2024). The same applies to product manufacturers in safety–critical industries. You could say that legislators are doing a rough estimate. In those areas where the probability or severity of a loss is rated so high that it could become economically relevant (e.g., an accident in a nuclear power plant or insufficient financial reserves at banks), the legislator "enforces" detailed risk management by the insurer, manufacturer, or operator.

© The Author(s), under exclusive license to Springer Nature Switzerland AG 2026
A. Johannsen et al., *Foundations for Software Project Management in Classic and Agile Environments*, https://doi.org/10.1007/978-3-032-16797-2_9

9.1.1   Risk Management as a Continuous, Iterative Process

Publicly listed companies in Europe and the US are required by law to conduct risk management at the organizational level—see (Ashby 2025) for more details. Risk management in the project is only partially required by law. Nevertheless, no project should simply "run blindly on it." A risk assessment based on gut feeling, as we usually do in our private lives, is insufficient for projects. Instead, every project manager should have a clear idea of the risks and possible countermeasures and document them. Given the growing digital share of today's products in all domains, software project risk management is a topic of increasing importance (Boehm 2014; Engemann and O'Connor 2021).

The Regulatory Landscape
In the EU, the evolving regulatory landscape currently encompasses the following regulations:

- NIS2 Directive (EU-NIS2 2022)
- CER Directive (EU-CER 2022)
- Digital Operational Resilience Act (EU-DORA 2022)
- Cyber Resilience Act (EU-CRA 2024), and the
- EU Artificial Intelligence Act (EU-AIA 2024).

All these regulations emphasize the necessity for large or even small and medium sized organizations to implement a systematic governance framework and a structured IT (project) management approach that ensures operational resilience, proactive risk control, and regulatory compliance, especially when they are part of critical infrastructures.

To operationalize these regulatory expectations, several international standards provide guidance that supports governance, structured risk assessment, and controlled change management throughout the project lifecycle. Examples are:

- ISO/IEC 27001—Information Security Management Systems (ISO 27001:2022),
- ISO/IEC 31000—Risk Management (ISO 31000:2018), and
- ISO/IEC 42001—AI Management Systems (ISO 42001:2023).

Addressing these evolving regulatory requirements, Johannsen et al. (2020) and Johannsen and Kant (2022) have proposed a competency-based IT-GRC approach[1] for small and medium sized organizations, which also entails professional risk management of all current and planned projects within the organization.

---

[1] GRC stands for "Governance, Risk, and Compliance." A competency-based IT-GRC approach focuses on building the specific IT-related skills and competencies required to manage these topics in a holistic way.

Types of Risks

In the contexts of projects, we distinguish between two types of risks:

- Product risks are risks to the environment, users, and third parties that emanate directly from the product. The nuclear power plant accident mentioned above is one of the product risks. Other products are also considered safety–critical: cars, pharmaceuticals, medical devices, airplanes, or trains. There is even more to consider than just the train and its brakes. The control system, for example, which controls signaling systems and switches, is particularly critical for rail traffic.

- Project risks are risks for the project, or—more broadly—for the company. Typical project risks are late deliveries, problems with technical feasibility, time delays, or cost explosion.

Both types of risk should be considered in risk management but can be dealt with in separate documents and with different levels of formalism. In principle, however, everything said in this chapter applies to both types of risk. In any case, the distinction is not always very clear. Defective brakes in a car are clearly a product risk, but the associated recall action quickly becomes a project risk as well.

This example also shows that the risk management process has a beginning, but only an end for discontinued products. Risks must be tracked continuously even after delivery. There are three main reasons for this:

1. If damage occurs during operation that was not considered in the risk analysis, it is obvious that the risk analysis must be revised. The damage does not even have to occur to us. We can also learn from the experience of our competitors.
2. Assumptions that went into the risk identification or assessment may turn out to be wrong in further development. The corresponding risks may therefore be much more probable or serious than originally assumed, necessitating a response at the project or organizational level.
3. The state of the art continues to develop. It is possible that other, better (and perhaps also financially more favorable) countermeasures will emerge in the future that should be used.

Risk management is therefore an ongoing process that iteratively passes through the activities of identification, assessment, control, and monitoring. Manufacturers of medical devices are required by law to revise their risk management files once a year for as long as the product in question is in use. By then, the actual development project has long since come to an end, but responsibility for risk management remains and passes to the successor project or product line.

9.1.2   Main Causes for Project Risks

While the causes of product risks are very product-specific and cannot be listed in general terms, several common causes can be identified for project risks. These include:

- **Unclear Requirements**

  If you do not know exactly what to implement, you basically cannot be successful at all. Almost inevitably, functionalities are not developed or are developed differently from what the customer or user wanted. If requirements are completely missing, it is not even possible to determine progress. In that case, the project is completely flying blind.

- **Unrealistic Targets in Terms of Deadlines and Costs**

  Schedules that are set too tightly jeopardize the success of the project right from the start. On the one hand, every obstacle automatically leads to problems. On the other hand, the motivation of the employees to give their best also decreases, since they know that the goal will not be achieved anyway. Project planning that assumes from the start that employees will work on weekends and never get sick is not only unrealistic, but also detrimental to the company in the long run.

- **Lack of Resources and/or Skills**

  Quite obviously, a project needs people with the necessary expertise. If these experts are missing, it becomes difficult for the project. However, the reality is often more complicated. The experts are available, their cooperation is promised, but in practice it turns out that they are far less available than originally planned. Experienced project managers know this and take the point into account in their risk analysis.

  Missing resources are not only limited to employees. If it turns out during the project that an oscilloscope is necessary for testing, which was not taken into account in the original planning, there is also a (in this case financial) loss.

- **Lack of expertise**

  Although this point is similar to the previous one, we wish to emphasize a particularly treacherous risk. If I am aware that knowledge is lacking in the project, I can remedy this by training or recruiting experts. But if I don't realize where the project is weak, I will also misjudge the related risks. Take usability as example. It is a science to developing <u>truly</u> usable user interfaces. However, the topic is often underestimated due to a lack of expertise.

- **Late and Frequent Changes**

  Along with unclear requirements, this is one of the most common causes of
  project risks, and the two points interact. Every change brings new risks. What
  is obvious for changes in the schedule (e.g., milestones brought forward at short
  notice) and budget cuts also applies to changes in functional scope. In this
  case, we must distinguish between sequential and agile project management
  frameworks.

9.1.3 Change-Related Risks

Changes always occur, regardless of the chosen project management framework.[2]
The main difference is how these changes are handled. In sequential frameworks,
we basically assume that changes should be the exception, i.e., the requirements
are basically stable. Each change is first recorded ("requested") and then analyzed.
Based on the so-called "impact analysis," the project manager can then assess
which risks are associated with the change and which effects the change will have.
In doing so, he should look at the change from two perspectives:

1. What happens when we implement the change? What effort does this mean?
   What might we have to test again? How high is the risk of affecting existing
   functionality?
2. What happens if we decide to do nothing? What are the consequences? What
   does it mean for the project/product if the functionality is missing, insufficient,
   or even incorrectly implemented?

In sequential project management frameworks, we therefore have a development process and a change process in parallel. In agile frameworks, there is no
such separation, since the entire development process is designed to allow for
changes. Changes resulting from unexpected risks are translated into new backlog items and will be dealt with in the upcoming sprints. Thus, the shorter the
iterations, the more "agile" a project can accommodate changes.

Although agile projects are much better adapted to changes, it is also true that
late and frequent changes can cause project risks. This is because it is by no means
certain that the "new idea" is compatible with the existing system architecture. It
is also possible that the change will affect measures that were implemented to mit-
igate other risks. Therefore, changes should be well analyzed and evaluated before
deciding to implement them. Moran (2014) proposes an explicit and systematic
approach to risk management in agile settings.

Regardless of the framework, project managers must have internalized this idea
of a risk-based approach. As great as the temptation may be to cut corners when

---

[2] In this section, we are essentially talking about changes in requirements.

the going gets tough, any "shortcut" in the change process can jeopardize the project.

9.2   Risk Management Activities

The term "risk" is defined as a combination of "probability of occurrence and severity of a loss." From this definition alone, the first activities of risk management can be derived:

1. Risks are identified.
2. Risks are assessed.

However, risk identification and assessment have not yet eliminated the risks. Therefore, two further activities follow:

3. Risks should be treated/controlled one way or another.
4. The development of risks and the implementation of planned countermeasures must be monitored.

In the following, we will take a closer look at these four activities.

9.2.1   Risk Identification—Do not Overlook Anything!

Every project manager should have a realistic idea of what could happen and what positive or negative impact the event could have on the project goals. For project risks, we talk about risk identification, while for product risks, we rather call it hazard or risk analysis. Risk identification or hazard analysis is initially non-evaluative. All events are collected that could possibly occur and have an influence on the project goals or could pose a risk to the environment, users, or third parties.

Risk identification is not an activity that the project manager can carry out alone in a quiet room. To really identify all relevant risks, he needs the support of his experts. For this reason, risk identification usually takes place as part of a workshop attended by selected project participants from all stakeholder groups. Of course, such workshops always lead to discussions that affect only some of those present. For this reason, it has proven useful to hold several workshops with different focal points in large projects. These focal points can be oriented to the product life cycle (overall system, software / hardware, production, maintenance, etc.) or relate to different subsystems (database, algorithms, hardware control, etc.). As a rule, such workshops should have 8 to maximum 12 participants, otherwise there is a risk of getting completely bogged down (Ashby 2025, S. 122).

According to the project management standard ISO 21502:2020 events with positive effects on project goals should also be identified. The standard distinguishes between "threats" and "opportunities." Identifying opportunities is particularly useful if both aspects (i.e., opportunities and risks) are evaluated financially, i.e., quantified in euros, dollars, or the like. In this case, the result is a realistic calculation that also takes "positive surprises" into account.

In software development projects, experience shows that the focus is usually on risks with a negative impact. As a rule, we give less thought to opportunities—after all, it is usually the case that something goes wrong. However, the project manager should be aware that this limited view can sometimes produce an overly pessimistic picture.

Methods of Risk Identification

We need a lively imagination to determine risk. Pessimists clearly have the advantage here. Many risk identification methods are therefore based on creativity techniques that we are also familiar with from requirements analysis—first and foremost the brainstorming or the brainstorming paradox which we looked at in Sect. 4.5.4. Interviews with stakeholders are also an effective means, since they have the necessary expertise and can better imagine situations in their daily work in which something could go wrong. All investigation methods follow the rules mentioned in the context of requirements analysis and differ only in their initial question.

Some companies develop checklists to assist and support risk identification. These checklists are based on the experience of past projects and should be revised regularly. Checklists may exist for project risks as well as for product risks. The ISO 14971 (ISO 14971:2019) standard "Medical devices—application of risk management to medical devices," which is quasi-mandatory in medical technology, even contains a list of possible hazards and another for possible causes in the appendix.

Table 9.1 shows typical causes of project risks in software development that can serve as the basis for a checklist.

A diagram technique for analyzing causes and their effects is the Ishikawa diagram (McDermott et al. 2022; Bauer 2024, pp. 94–97). Its form has also earned it the eloquent name "fishbone diagram," where the head corresponds to the problem to be analyzed—i.e., the ultimate effect. Cause categories are given on the main bones to facilitate and structure the search. Workshop participants identify and discuss each of the major and minor causes in the various categories. In addition to the categories shown in Fig. 9.1 presented categories, further categories such as "management" or "processes" can be defined in addition as required.[3]

A method related to the Ishikawa diagram is the fault tree analysis, in short FTA (Stoelinga 2025). Fault tree analysis is a top-down method. It identifies causes of a pre-identified hazard or project risk. These events are represented as rectangles (see Fig. 9.2). Successively, all events (= causes) are further decomposed until either the point is reached at which further decomposition is not possible or no

---

[3] The Ishikawa diagram is suitable for root cause analysis in any context. It is therefore also frequently used in quality management.

Table 9.1 Examples of causes of project risks in software development

Chapter of this book	Typical causes leading to project risks
Project initiation	– Unclear project goals – Incomplete, unclear, or unrealistic requirements – Uncertainty regarding technical feasibility (e.g., performance)
Project planning	– Lack of communication with the customer – requirements not agreed on (stakeholder conflicts) – Lack of risk assessment – Unrealistic estimates due to lack of availability of experts – Insufficient planning (Whiscy syndrome)[4] – Unrealistic targets, especially with regard to deadlines and costs
Implementing and controlling the project	– Insufficient availability of qualified employees (never promised / promised but not provided / provided but not available (e.g., due to illness) / withdrawn for other projects) – Frequent / late changes in requirements – Lack of experience with new technology – Missing SW architecture – Subcontracted supplies from subcontractors, service providers, other projects or from the customer – Postponements – Lack of feedback from the customer – Unplanned additional expenses, e.g., for internal audits
Project acceptance and closing	– Serious defects discovered late – Lack of acceptance by the customer (e.g., due to insufficient usability) – Cash flow or liquidity problems, e.g., due to different payment terms of the customer and suppliers

longer makes sense, because we are able to control it at that point. In the first case, we speak of elementary events. They are represented as ovals to distinguish them from the events that are not further decomposed (rhombuses) (see Fig. 9.2).

Another technique is the Fault Tree Analysis, in short: FTA. The FTA offers the possibility to show the interaction of several events. In the example from Fig. 9.1, a delay can be caused either by a late supply or by a delayed project. For the latter, however, two causes must come together: The late changes and the lack of impact analysis.

---

[4] The acronym Whiscy stands for "Why isn't Sam coding yet?" and describes the common mistake of already starting the implementation despite unclear specifications.

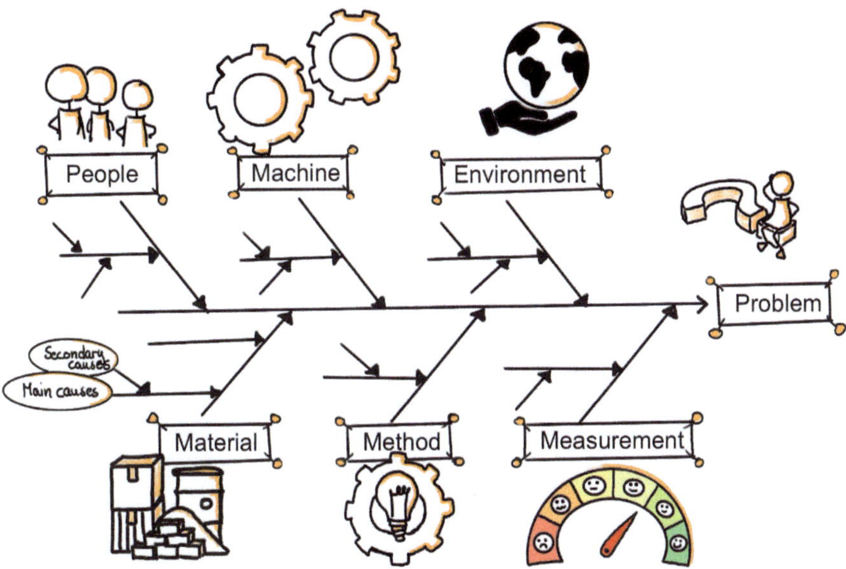

Fig. 9.1 Schematic representation of cause and effect in the Ishikawa diagram

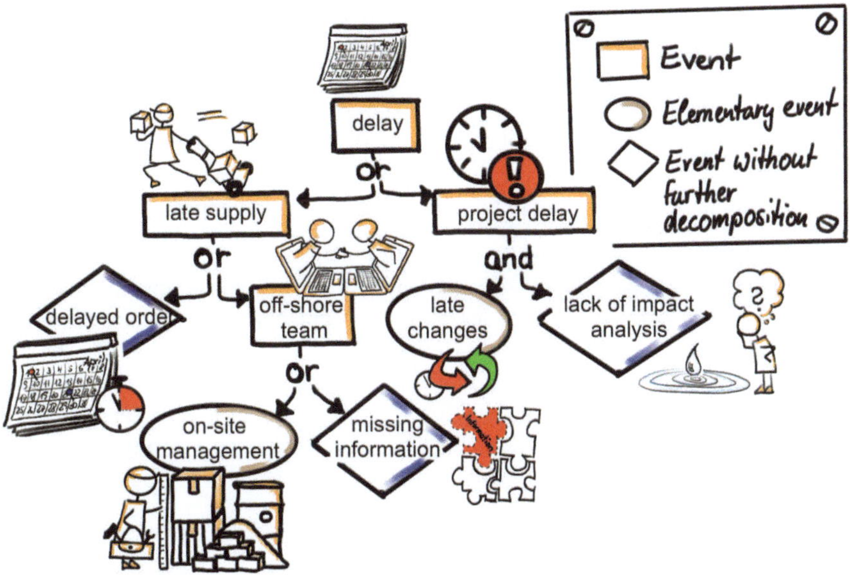

Fig. 9.2 Fault tree analysis (FTA)

Far more widespread than the FTA is the Failure Mode and Effects Analysis, in short: FMEA (Stamatis 2023). An FMEA is carried out in six steps:

1. Structure analysis
2. Function analysis
3. Failure analysis
4. Risk assessment
5. Definition of countermeasures
6. Reassessment considering the countermeasures

The structure analysis serves to delimit and structure the system under consideration. As part of the product risk analysis, the software is broken down into modules according to the architecture. For each of these modules, the second step then analyzes which functions this module offers and which interfaces exist. For a project risk analysis, it makes sense to break down the process into phases and to consider for each phase which essential activities belong to it.

In the third step, the persons involved in the FMEA consider what can go wrong in each case, what causes this could have and what effects are to be expected.

Strictly speaking, steps 4–6 no longer belong to risk identification, but already to risk assessment and risk control. Briefly explained: for each identified risk, the probability of occurrence and severity are assessed and countermeasures are defined. The risk is then re-evaluated, considering the countermeasures. At the end, a classification of the risk with and without measures is obtained.

The great advantage of FMEA is that it is a very structured method. Every function or every essential activity is considered. It is therefore rather unlikely that something will fall through the cracks. A disadvantage—especially compared to the fault tree analysis—is the strict mono-causality. Since it is a bottom-up method, it is not possible to map the interaction of several causes.

Approach and Success Factors

A very important success factor for risk identification is the involvement of suitable experts. When it comes to evaluating market acceptance, the software developer is usually not the best person to ask. Conversely, the end user will hardly be able to make statements about the causes of errors in the source code. Therefore, the risk analysis should be performed with different groups of people (project team, stakeholders external to the project such as members of the steering committee, independent experts, users, and many more).

Systematics also play a major role. What we have already said in connection with requirements analysis applies here, too. If stakeholders or use cases are overlooked, the risk analysis will also be incomplete. It is therefore extremely important to consider all project phases (for project risks) or the entire product life cycle (for product risks). The checklists already mentioned help enormously.

In general, risk management is an iterative process. This also means that there can be, and usually should be, more than one risk analysis during the project. It is a best practice to update the risk analysis again at each milestone. In addition, multiple risk analyses can be prepared, either for sub-projects or for sub-areas. Examples of sub-areas are:

- Design/Construction
- System development
- Hardware/Software development
- Production.

Another success factor is the integration of risk identification into the change process. We have already discussed how this can look in Sect. 9.1.

The result of the risk identification is a risk list. The list of project risks ideally contains at least four columns: Risk, causes, consequences, and triggers. By "trigger," we mean the symptoms or warning signs that announce the occurrence of the risk, a trigger for the project manager, who should then react immediately. For product risks, it is less common to list the trigger, as this column is not provided for in the FMEA. The risk list forms the basis for the next activities and will later be extended by further columns.

9.2.2 Risk Assessment—How Bad Can It Get?

Not all risks or hazards identified during risk identification are truly critical. To prioritize the identified risks, the probability of occurrence and severity of impact must first be assessed for each risk. This applies to both product and project risks.

Criteria for Evaluating the Probability
For project risks, the probability is usually documented qualitatively, e.g., in the form of levels such as low/medium/high, with each level corresponding to a probability interval. However, it has proven useful in practice to work with an even number of categories, since the persons assessing the risk must then determine whether they assume that the risk is more likely to occur or more likely not.[5] Table 9.2 shows a division of the probability intervals into four categories. Each

---

[5] The approach presented here is a middle ground between the purely qualitative assessment of risks and the quantitative approach taught in advanced project management courses.

Table 9.2 Categories for evaluating the probability of occurrence

Probability of occurrence	Meaning	Value
Unlikely	• Probability is less than 25% • The risk cannot be completely eliminated	1
Low	• Probability is 25% or more, but less than 50% • The risk is unlikely to materialize, but it is conceivable	4
Possible	• Probability is 50% or more, but less than 75% • It is likely that the risk will occur rather than not occur	7
Probable	• Probability is 75% or more • It is almost certain that the risk will occur	10

of these probability intervals is also assigned a value that allows us to prioritize the risks later.

The explanations of the intervals are important to ensure that all persons involved have the same understanding of the categories.

For product risks, the definition of probability categories may be more complex, as the number of products sold also plays a role. Even if it is possible to estimate the percentage probability of a braking system failing, the actual number of occurrences depends strongly on the number of cars sold and the number of braking operations within the lifetime of a car. In other words, the more cars with this braking system are sold and the more braking is done with it, the higher the probability that damage will occur, even if the braking system on its own fails only once in a million applications.

In some industries, it is customary to consider probability of occurrence and probability of detection separately for product risks. The total probability of occurrence is the product of the two individual probabilities. This distinction is also sometimes useful for project risks.

Criteria for Assessing the Impact

Just like the probability of occurrence, for each risk we need to assess its impact to prioritize the risk. The impacts are usually also documented qualitatively in levels (low/medium/high) and again, it is important to provide the evaluating persons with interpretation aids for the individual categories. Project risks essentially have three possible effects: The project goals can be impaired in terms of costs, deadlines, or product quality. Therefore, a categorization in the form of an impact matrix is useful. Table 9.3 shows an example of such an impact matrix. Please note: The categories and in particular the exact percentage values can vary from project to project.

In contrast to Tables 9.2 and 9.3 leaves open the possibility of further differentiation within the four categories, since the last column provides a range of values

Table 9.3 Impact assessment categories

Impact	...on budget	...on dates	...on quality	Value
Low	No or only minimal increases to be expected ($x \leq 5\%$ of the project budget)	No influence on end date	• Functionality only marginally limited; experienced users know how to manage on their own; • No safety–critical functions affected	1–2
Noticeable	Noticeable increases, but not jeopardizing the success of the project ($5\% < x \leq 15\%$)	Delivery date is at risk; however, deviation is within an acceptable range for the customer	• Functionality partially limited (e.g., lower performance), but main functions not affected; user can work around the problem with expert assistance; • No safety–critical functions affected	3–5
Serious	Increases that jeopardize the success of the project ($15\% < x \leq 30\%$)	Delivery date probably cannot be met; deviation may not be accepted by customers	• Functionality noticeably limited; product is only partially usable; • Safety–critical functions affected, but no severe damage possible	6–8
Catastrophic	Increases that also endanger other projects ($> 30\%$ of the project budget, e.g., contractual penalties)	Delivery date probably cannot be met; deviation is unacceptable for the customer	• Product is unusable; • Safety–critical functions affected; severe damage possible	9–10

for each category. A similar classification can also be introduced for the probabilities. Ultimately, each project manager must define for his project which criteria are to be used, unless these are already defined by company-wide guidelines.[6]

In the case of product risks, we usually speak of the "severity" of the potential damage. To be able to define meaningful assessment criteria, some preliminary considerations must first be made. In what range are we moving at all? What is the lowest (perceptible), what is the highest level of damage? For medical devices, this range can be anything from temporary impairment such as headache or mild nausea to serious injury or death, but not every medical device is potentially lethal. To provide a credible assessment, the scale must be adapted to the product in question.

Carrying Out the Evaluation and Prioritization

---

[6] Of course, it is also possible to evaluate probabilities directly, e.g., with 0.5 at 50% probability. However, the reduction to four categories simplifies the task and reduces the need for discussion.

Table 9.4 Example of a risk list (P = probability of occurrence, I = impact, RPN = Risk Priority Number)

ID	Risk	Causes	Effect	Trigger	P	I	RPN
1	Incorrect prioritization of the product backlog	Contact person of the customer is not available	Time is used incorrectly; important user stories may no longer be implemented	Backlog grooming takes place without customers	4	6	24
2	Continuous Integration Server not operational at start of implementation	Lack of expert knowledge	Integration must be done manually; automated tests cannot be triggered to the same extent	First night run (planned in CWxy) fails	4	5	20
3	Automated test provides false positive results	Incorrect implementation of the test scripts	Defects in the product remain undetected	Feedback from later test phases	7	8	56

It often makes sense to evaluate the identified risks anddefine countermeasuresduring a risk identification workshop. For this reason, risk workshops can sometimes last a day or more. The participants address each identified risk individually and evaluate its probability of occurrence as well as its impact. Naturally, lengthy discussions may ensue. These can be avoided by having each participant give their own assessment and then calculating the mean value. However, the result should be discussed again in the large group to give proponents of strongly differing opinions the opportunity to explain them.

The next step is purely mathematical. For each risk, the averaged values for probability and impact are multiplied to calculate the so-called risk priority number (RPN for short). Risks with a low probability of occurrence and harmless effects receive a small risk priority number, while those with high probabilities and serious effects receive a high-risk priority number. In projects that assess probability of detection in addition to probability of occurrence, the risk priority number is calculated as the product of probability of occurrence, probability of detection, and severity of impact.[7]

As the name suggests, the risk priority number is used for prioritization. The example in Table 9.4 shows three exemplary project risks. The risk priority number shows at a glance which risk requires special attention.

---

[7] The pure mathematical computation of the resulting RPN works well with the given in the examples (1, 3, 7 and 10) or, alternatively with power of 2 (1, 2, 4, 8, 16 etc.). Still, you should carefully consider the RPN, if your product is safety–critical. In this case, each combination of severity and probability of occurrence should be considered separately.

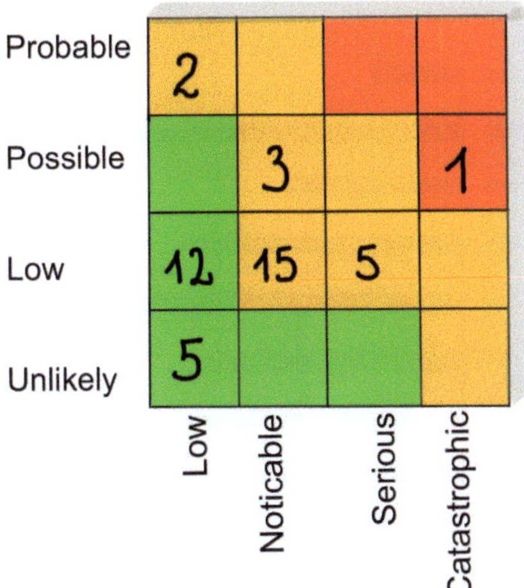

Fig. 9.3 Risk assessment matrix (the numbers quantify the number of risks with corresponding assessment and are purely fictitious in this example)

Usually, the risk list becomes rather long and confusing. To get a picture of the overall situation, the project manager should condense the information from the list. If only two evaluation criteria (probability and impact) are used, the presentation in the form of a risk evaluation matrix is suitable. If three evaluation criteria are used (probability of occurrence, probability of detection, and impact), the risk priority number must be used.

Figure 9.3 shows the condensed representation in the form of a risk assessment matrix. The number of risks whose assessment falls within this range is entered in the individual cells (12 risks were assessed with probability of occurrence "low" and impact "noticeable"). The differently colored areas indicate three different risk classes. For all risks in the green area, no further action is required (RPN < 10). Risks in the yellow area must be reduced as far as possible through action ($10 \leq$ RPN < 50). Risks in the red area are not acceptable a priori (RPN ≥ 50) and require separate treatment by management.[8]

Figure 9.4 shows an analogous representation for the risk priority number. Again, risk classes can be defined, which result in different procedures.

The assessment should be reviewed periodically in the project and updated (ideally at each project milestone).

The result of the risk assessment is the list of prioritized risks (see Table 9.4), as well as possibly an overall assessment of the risk level of the project relative to other projects or on a risk scale of the organization. A prerequisite for this,

---

[8] Note, that domain-specific standards for risk management such may define different rules. For example, ISO 14971:2018 does not allow to ignore any product risks for medical devices. There is no green area and all risks shall be reduced. The yellow area is, therefore, called "AFAP" which means "As Far As Possible."

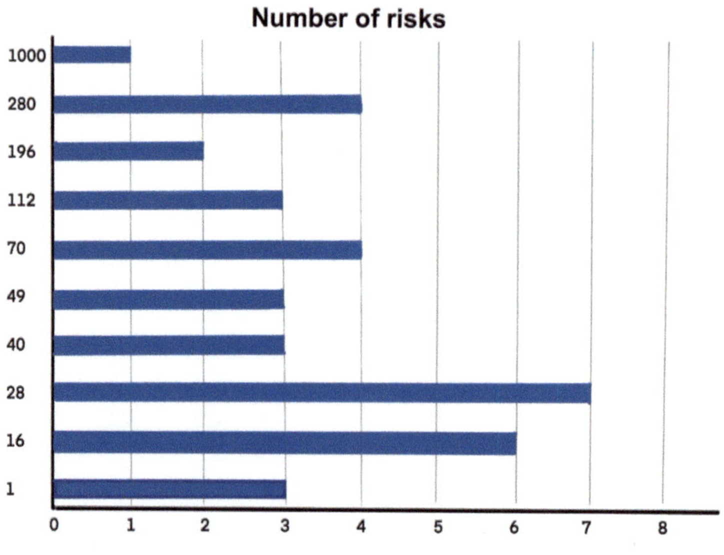

Fig. 9.4 Condensed presentation of risks with specific risk priority number

however, is that the organization collects historical data and provides appropriate guidance.

9.2.3 Risk Control—What Can We Do to Treat the Risks?

Once the risks have been identified and prioritized, the obvious next step is to define and implement countermeasures. The question "What can we do about it?" is already discussed in the risk workshop. The planned countermeasures are then documented in the risk action plan. In practice, this action plan is rarely a stand-alone document. Rather, the measures are documented as an additional column in the same risk list in which the assessment can be found.

An obvious and effective measure for risk control is to simply avoid risks. Instead of the risky approach, a better alternative (in terms of risk assessment) is chosen. Without remote access, for example, it also becomes more difficult for the hacker to penetrate a software system. Project risks can also be avoided, for example, through exclusions in the contract. If it is clear from the beginning that a certain functionality will not be part of the product to be delivered, there is no longer any risk that we may not be able to implement it. The risk is eliminated.

Unfortunately, you cannot simply avoid all risks. If we want to exclude all critical functions in the contract, the order will probably never be placed. Risk avoidance is therefore not always a viable path.

If the risk cannot be avoided, it may be possible to transfer it to another organization. Sometimes a supplier or subcontractor can be found who is willing to take over the critical part including the associated risk. Finally, not every risk is the same for all companies, as the assessment depends heavily on existing competencies and capacities. However, the project manager should be aware that engaging third parties carries other risks, as it is not 100% certain that the supplier or subcontractor will perform as promised in the contract. The original risk is therefore replaced by a new, hopefully lower risk.

However, most risks are neither completely avoided nor transferred, but mitigated in one way or another. Early measures either reduce the probability of occurrence, reduce the impact, or increase the probability of detection. Table 9.5 shows an extended risk list, which now also includes the countermeasures as well as an updated evaluation of the respective risk, taking the measures into account.

The re-evaluated risk priority number with countermeasures considered provides information on the remaining residual risk. Again, the results can be condensed and represented as risk assessment matrix or in a bar chart. Thus, we

Table 9.5 Risk list with measures and reassessment taking them into account (with *)

ID	Risk	Causes	...	P	I	RPN	Measure	$P*$	$I*$	RPN*
1	Incorrect prioritization of the product backlog	Contact person of the customer is not available	...	4	6	24	Contractually regulate participation	1	6	6
2	Continuous Integration Server (...) non-operational	Lack of expert knowledge	...	4	5	20	Plan staff for manual integration	4	3	12
3	Automated testing provides false positive results	Incorrect implementation of the test scripts	...	7	8	56	Provide for code reviews	4	8	32

have two versions of Figs. 9.3 or 9.4 in our projects: Once for risk evaluation before and once after implementation of the countermeasures.

Of course, there is always the possibility of simply taking risks. After all, it is not said that they will occur (if the probability of occurrence is 100%, we no longer speak of risks, since the incident has already occurred). If countermeasures are not possible or economically not reasonable, we can simply accept the risk. However, we should then protect ourselves against possible consequences. There are essentially two options:

- **Contingency plan**

  The contingency plan may include, for example, initially offering the product only to a specific market segment until full functionality is available.

- **The buffer**

  The project manager plans for an additional buffer in the form of time or money, or keeps a reserve of other resources (e.g., employees who can jump in or servers from other departments that may be used, if necessary).

We defined the countermeasures, but we are not yet done with them. After all, they still must be implemented and their effectiveness has to be checked. Therefore, the project manager should designate a person responsible for each measure and document this in writing. Depending on the project, the responsible person can be entered in another column of the risk list, in a separate action plan, or as the processor of a task in a project management tool.

9.2.4   Risk Monitoring—Always Stay Alert!

Risk management is an ongoing process. The project manager must remain permanently alert, as the situation can (and will) change every day. The further the project progresses, the more information is available. On the one hand, the uncertainty regarding the assessment of probability of occurrence and impact decreases. On the other hand, new risks crystallize that were not originally considered. These must also be evaluated and, if necessary, countermeasures taken. In addition, new options for measures may arise that should be considered.

The evaluation criteria themselves also belong under regular scrutiny, as they are based on assumptions that may prove to be incorrect. Every change request can potentially bring completely new aspects into play, e.g., if a previously uncritical product is suddenly to include safety–critical functionality.

The most important aspect of risk monitoring or "risk controlling," as it is called in ISO 21502:2020 standard, is the follow-up of the countermeasures. Were the provisions foreseen in the emergency plan made? Was the employee for manual integration (line 2 in Table 9.5) hired? If measures were implemented by the software itself, are they working as intended?

In practice, the project manager will update the risk list and the action plan on a regular basis, with the length of the intervals depending heavily on the type of project and its environment (once a week or at each sprint, but at least once a month). The project manager receives the necessary information for this from the respective assigned responsible persons.

Software tool support for project risk management will increasingly emerge not only in research but also in practice in the near future, for example, by means of decision support tools and AI-agents, see Mora et al. (2021) and Cox (2023) for further aspects.

Beyond project-internal risk tracking, the most important risks are also tracked at a higher management level. The condensed presentation as a matrix or bar chart provides an overview of the overall situation, but does not contain detailed information. Therefore, the regular project report should additionally include more detailed information on selected risks. In Sect. 9.2.3, we had defined corresponding rules depending on the risk class. In the absence of such a specification, the project manager should agree on a rule with the report recipients (e.g., the steering committee). One variant is to systematically report on the top 3 or top 10 risks. However, the rule should be applied in a meaningful way. If there is a risk of fire in four places, all four risks should be reported. Those who conceal or ignore risks are more likely to fail than their colleagues who look the problems in the eye.

An organization can learn from risks that have occurred for the future, e.g., by creating or expanding checklists for risk identification. In the final project review, the risk list should therefore be analyzed and risks with potential cross-project significance identified for the checklist.

9.3 **Required Soft Skills**

Risk management is one of the core tasks of the project manager and requires special technical and methodological knowledge. While it is helpful, it is not necessary for the project manager to be able to penetrate the issue to the smallest detail. It is much more important that he or she can conduct the numerous risk workshops. A lot of time and energy can be wasted if the group gets "lost." If in doubt, the project manager should take appropriate training or hire an external facilitator.

Facilitation skills have various aspects. For example, the facilitator must be able to adapt to different groups, understand and control the group dynamics and, if necessary, identify the causes of conflicts. Not every discussion that never ends stems from conflicting facts. Some participants participate little or not at all, although they have important contributions in mind. Other participants find fun in presenting themselves and tend to dominate the group. A good facilitator knows how to (repeatedly) focus the group on the goal, stimulate constructive discussions, and ultimately bring about a decision.

In this context, many of the visualization techniques already mentioned are helpful. The clearer the facilitator presents the facts, the easier it is for the group to stay focused. Risk workshops should be dynamic. Instead of poring over printed tables, the group should arm itself with cards and sticky notes and fill pin boards or regular walls. If they will not agree on the evaluation at all, let them vote using sticky dots. When nothing works anymore, a break helps.

Finally, the project manager must be able to clearly communicate risks and planned or taken measures. As already said, concealing or ignoring risks jeopardizes the success of the project.

9.4   Risk Management in Safety–Critical Domains

Structured risk management is mandatory in many contexts. For example, the standard ISO 9001 mentioned in Chap. 8 "Quality assurance," preaches a risk-based approach to quality assurance. Every manufacturer should think about risks and pay special attention to the critical points.

This idea is pursued in safety–critical domains with the concept of safety integrity levels (SIL for short). The term originates from a cross-industry standard on the subject of "functional safety," IEC 61508. The standard deals exclusively with product risks, i.e., potential hazards for the environment, users, or third parties. The basic idea is to classify the product or its functions into one of the following five levels depending on the risk: not safety–critical, SIL 1, SIL 2, SIL 3, SIL 4.

SIL 4 corresponds to the highest integrity level, SIL 1 to the lowest. Only functions that do not perform safety–critical tasks can be classified as "not safety–critical" and are usually designated "QM." "QM" stands for quality management and represents the minimum requirement for a clean development process for non-critical components.

Depending on the classification, the standard defines different failure limits for the safety–critical functions. For hardware, this results in rules for design and production. For software, we have rules regarding architecture and design as well as the development process. It is important to note that the standard does not prescribe any specific procedure, but rather, according to its own statement, provides a "risk-based conceptual framework and example procedures."

Projects in safety–critical industries are subject to stricter controls. Internal and external audits are the order of the day. All project participants are expected to strictly adhere to the process. Developers must demonstrably make certain considerations in advance, e.g., regarding architecture and design, and thoroughly document their work. The project manager is responsible for monitoring process compliance and planning the necessary resources. Documentation requires time and budget; reviews require at least one reviewer who must also be available. In addition, these projects require a high level of employee motivation, which project managers must encourage and maintain. We will discuss the topic of "motivation" in more detail in the next chapter.

9.5   Summary

Risk management is continuous, an iterative process that only ends for discontinued products. Risk management activities include risk identification, assessment, control, and monitoring.

A major cause of project risks is frequent and late changes. Sequential and agile project management frameworks deal with this very differently.

For both risk identification and risk assessment, there are proven methods and several success factors that the project manager should take to heart.

Typical countermeasures are avoidance, transfer, mitigation, or acceptance.

Risks and countermeasures should be documented and monitored. There are various, more or less condensed forms of presentation for this purpose.

Risk management requires similar soft skills from the project manager as requirements management.

There are normative requirements in safety–critical areas. In particular, functions are classified into so-called safety integrity levels (SIL), which must be handled differently in the development process.

9.6   Exercises

1. Explain whether risk management is a one-time process or an iterative process.
2. Name key risk management activities.
3. Name the main causes of risks and give an example that could occur in our case study.
4. Outline how to deal with change-related risks in sequential and agile frameworks.
5. Name methods and success factors to consider as part of a risk identification.
6. Explain different risk assessment methods using our case study.
7. Name the main possible types of countermeasures.
8. Name different methods for analyzing and documenting risks.
9. Describe the tasks of risk controlling and its importance for other project phases.
10. Name two important soft skills for project managers and their importance for risk management.
11. Describe the concept of safety integrity levels.

References

(Ashby 2025): Ashby, S., Fundamentals of Operational Risk Management: Understanding and Implementing Effective Tools, Policies and Frameworks. 2nd edn. London: Kogan Page. ISBN 978–1398622906.

(Bauer 2024): Bauer, P., A Comprehensive Project Management Guide. Management for Professionals. Springer, Cham. https://doi.org/10.1007/978-3-031-68252-0_5.

(Blatter et al. 2024): Blatter, A., Bradbury, S., Bruhn, P. & Ernst, D., Risk Management in Banks and Insurance Companies. Cham: Springer. https://doi.org/10.1007/978-3-031-42836-4

(Boehm 2014): Boehm, B. W., 'Software project risk and opportunity management', in Ruhe, G. and Wohlin, C. (eds.) Software Project Management in a Changing World. Berlin, Heidelberg: Springer, pp. 107–124. https://doi.org/10.1007/978-3-642-55035-5 5

(Cox 2023): Cox Jr, L.A., AI-ML for Decision and Risk Analysis: Challenges and Opportunities for Normative Decision Theory. Cham: Springer. ISBN 978–3–031–32013–2. https://doi.org/10.1007/978-3-031-32013-2

(Engemann & O'Connor 2021): Kurt J. Engemann & Rory V. O'Connor, Pro-ject Risk Management: Managing Software Development Risk, Walter de Gruyter GmbH, p 49–74. ISBN-13: 978–3110648232; ISBN-10: 3110648237.

(EU-AIA 2024): European Union. (2024) Regulation (EU) 2024/1689 of the Eu-ropean Parliament and of the Council of 13 June 2024 laying down harmonised rules on artificial intelligence (EU Artificial Intelligence Act). Available at: https://eur-lex.europa.eu/eli/reg/2024/1689/oj/eng

(EU-CER 2022): European Union. (2022) Directive (EU) 2022/2557 of the Euro-pean Parliament and of the Council of 14 December 2022 on the resilience of crit-ical entities and repealing Council Directive 2008/114/EC (CER Directive). Avail-able at: https://eur-lex.europa.eu/eli/dir/2022/2557/oj/eng

(EU-CRA 2024): European Union. (2024) Regulation (EU) 2024/2847 of the Eu-ropean Parlia-ment and of the Council of 23 October 2024 on horizontal cyberse-curity requirements for products with digital elements (Cyber Resilience Act). Available at: https://eur-lex.europa.eu/eli/reg/2024/2847/oj/eng

(EU-DORA 2022): European Union. (2022) Regulation (EU) 2022/2554 of the European Parlia-ment and of the Council of 14 December 2022 on digital opera-tional resilience for the financial sector (DORA). Available at: https://eur-lex.europa.eu/eli/reg/2022/2554/oj/eng

(EU-NIS2 2022): Directive (EU) 2022/2555 of the European Parliament and of the Council of 14 December 2022 on measures for a high common level of cyber-security across the Union (NIS2 Directive). Available at: https://digital-strategy.ec.europa.eu/en/policies/nis2-directive

(ISO 14971:2019): International Organization for Standardization (2019) Medical devices — Application of risk management to medical devices. ISO 14971:2019. Geneva: ISO. ISBN 978–9267111063. Available at: https://www.iso.org/standard/72704.html

(ISO 21502:2020): International Organization for Standardization (ISO). (2020) ISO 21502:2020 – Project, programme and portfolio management — Guidance on project management. Geneva: ISO.

(ISO 27001:2022): International Organization for Standardization/International Electrotechnical Commission (ISO/IEC). (2022) ISO/IEC 27001:2022 – Infor-mation security, cybersecurity and privacy protection — Information security management systems — Requirements. Avail-able at: https://www.iso.org/standard/27001

(ISO 31000:2018): International Organization for Standardization (ISO). (2018) ISO 31000:2018 – Risk management — Guidelines. Available at: https://www.iso.org/standard/65694.html

(ISO 42001:2023): ISO/IEC. (2023) ISO/IEC 42001:2023 – Artificial Intelligence Management Systems (AIMS). Available at: https://www.iso.org/standard/42001

(Johannsen et al 2020): Johannsen, A.; Kant, D.; Creutzburg, R.: Measuring IT security, compli-ance and digital sovereignty within small and medium-sized IT enterprises, in: IS&T Inter-national Symposium on Electronic Imaging 2020 Mobile Devices and Multimedia: Enabling Technologies, Algorithms, and Applications, San Francisco, January 2020. https://doi.org/10.2352/ISSN.2470-1173.2020.3.MOBMU-252

(Johannsen & Kant 2022): Johannsen, A. & Kant, K., IT-Governance-, Risiko- und Compliance-Management (IT-GRC) – Ein kompetenzorientierter Ansatz für KMU, in: Kristin Weber, Stefan Reinheimer (Eds.): Faktor Mensch (Edition HMD), Springer, Wiesbaden, 2022. Available at: https://doi.org/10.1007/978-3-658-34524-2_15

(McDermott et al. 2022): McDermott, O., Antony, J., Sony, M., Rosa, A., Hickey, M. & Grant, T.A., 'A study on Ishikawa's original basic tools of quality control in healthcare', The TQM Journal, 34(7), pp. 1770–1786. https://doi.org/10.1108/TQM-06-2022-0187.

(Mora et al. 2021): Mora, M., Wang, F., Phillips-Wren, G. and Gomez, M., The Role of DMSS Analytics Tools in Software Project Risk Management, In: Project Risk Management: Managing Software Development Risk (Engemann, K. and O'Connor, R., eds.), Walter de Gruyter GmbH, p 49–74. ISBN-13: 978-3110648232; ISBN-10: 3110648237.

(Moran 2014): Moran, A., Agile Risk Management. SpringerBriefs in Computer Science. Cham: Springer. ISBN-13: 978-3–319–05007–2; eBook ISBN: 978-3–319–05008–9. https://doi.org/10.1007/978-3-319-05008-9

(Stamatis 2023): Stamatis, D.H., Failure Mode and Effect Analysis. Milwaukee, WI: Quality Press. ISBN 978-0873899789.

(Stoelinga 2025): Stoelinga, M., Ruijters, E. & Krčál, P., Concise Guide to Fault Tree Analysis: Models, Methods and Algorithms. Cham: Birkhäuser / Springer. ISBN 978–3–031–78286–2.

Human Resource Management

10

10.1 Human Resource Management in the Organization

Qualified and motivated employees are crucial for the company's success.

Important This chapter applies to all project management frameworks.

Human resource management (hereafter abbreviated as "HR management") encompasses the management, control, leadership, development, and administration of the workforce, i.e., the employees of a company. While HR management is a critical overarching function within the company, it is also a vital aspect of project management. In fact, HR management serves as a key strategic partner of project management.

As discussed in Sect. 3.3.7 "Scrum and Agile Human Resource Management," adopting Scrum or other agile frameworks often leads to significant role changes and can even result in the complete transformation of certain areas or entire organizations, not just teams.

Agile methodologies necessitate a new approach to empowering project staff. For project management, this means that collaboration with the HR department must become more integrated and focused. HR personnel should be involved early in the process and familiarized with the new methodologies. Management should facilitate this collaboration by actively supporting the HR department's involvement.

© The Author(s), under exclusive license to Springer Nature Switzerland AG 2026
A. Johannsen et al., *Foundations for Software Project Management in Classic and Agile Environments*, https://doi.org/10.1007/978-3-032-16797-2_10

10.1.1 Targets and Policies

HR management in companies aims to balance organizational goals with employee needs to successfully produce and sell products and services. This challenge is intensified by a global context as shown in Fig. 10.1.

- **Technological Advancements**

New technologies require updated skills as job roles evolve or become obsolete.

> **Example** The company provides access to generative AI and organizes training sessions to ensure employees can efficiently utilize the new technology.

- **Demographic Changes**

On the one hand, an increasing number of older employees need careful management, training, and recognition. On the other hand, shifting employee values—from duty and diligence to meaningful work and flexibility—create diverse needs.

> **Example** The company organizes Yoga courses during lunch breaks to accommodate the needs of senior staff and promote their well-being.

- **Talent Shortages**

A limited supply of qualified young professionals means that older employees may not be adequately replaced upon retirement. This makes knowledge transfer and leadership of age-diverse teams crucial. Documenting expertise digitally ensures future accessibility.

> **Example** A project team establishes a centralized knowledge database to capture and share experiential knowledge, facilitating onboarding of new members.

- **Internationalization**

Different languages, cultures, working hours, and communication styles add complexity.

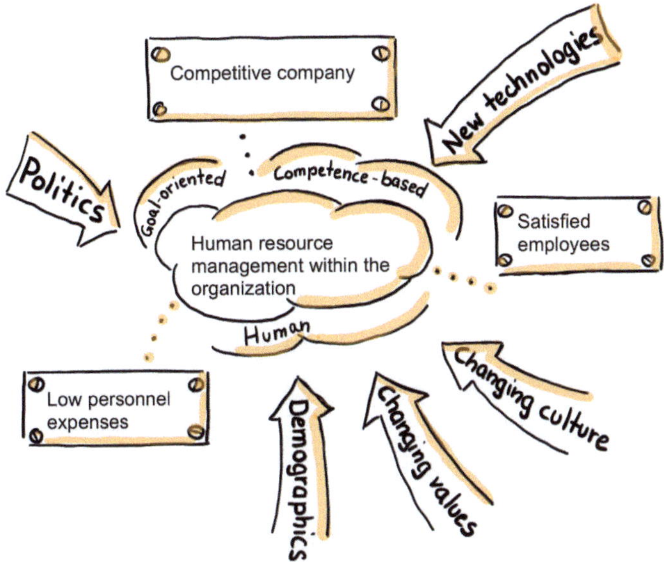

Fig. 10.1 Influencing factors, policies, and goals of HR management

Example A global organization offers intercultural communication training to enhance teamwork across borders.

Political and economic trends also affect HR management. To create a humane and authentic work environment, focus should shift from controlling employees to leading and developing them.

The key HR policies include:

- Competence-based personnel selection
- People-oriented[1] HR management
- Target-oriented personnel development.

The ultimate goal of HR management is employee satisfaction, low workforce costs, and an increase in the competitive strength of the company. Satisfied employees tend to be healthier, more productive, creative, and loyal, reducing personnel costs and boosting competitiveness. They are also valuable in attracting new talent, making these goals central to effective HR management.

---

[1] By "people-oriented," we mean successful human interaction and development within the company.

10.1.2 Key Players in HR Management in an Organization

Within an organization, several key stakeholders share responsibility for human resource management. Each has distinct roles and responsibilities, yet all work toward the common goal of ensuring that employee needs, organizational objectives, and legal requirements are aligned and harmonized.

C-level management includes all "chief executives." C-level leaders set the strategic direction for people management, ensuring that HR policies are consistent with the organization's vision and values. They model leadership standards and approve major HR initiatives.

The works council represents employees' collective interests and collaborates with management to ensure fair working conditions and compliance with labor laws.

Managers (including project managers) serve as the bridge between strategic HR objectives and day-to-day team operations, creating supportive conditions within their teams.

The HR departments manage the operational aspects of human resource management, from recruitment and onboarding to training, benefits, and employee development.

> **Example** The CEO approves a company-wide flexible work policy to promote employee well-being. The works council negotiates adjustments to working hours to improve work-life balance. As a result of the now flexible working hours, the team members no longer all work at the same time. This leads to increased conflicts in the team which are observed by the project manager facilitates. Following the manager's request, the HR department organizes a training program on effective feedback techniques.

10.1.3 Tasks of HR Management in the Company

HR management centers on aligning employees' skills, potential, and motivation with organizational goals. While recruitment is one important aspect, sustainable success is achieved by fostering engagement, professional development, and well-being across the employee lifecycle. HR management can be divided into six key domains:

1. **HR policy design** involves defining the organization's vision and strategic direction as an employer, including how it is perceived externally. This aspect is known as personnel marketing. Similar to product marketing, companies should participate in career fairs and establish a strong online employer brand.

2. **Human resource planning** focuses on aligning the number and qualification of employees with business needs. This includes demand forecasting, succession planning, transfers as well as defining job roles, time models, and compensation models.
3. **Staff deployment** ensures that employees are placed in roles that suit their strengths and interests, fostering optimal collaboration and working conditions. It is the responsibility of HR management to develop and enforce guidelines to prevent burnout and ensure a supportive work environment.
4. **Recruitment and onboarding** goes beyond hiring. It includes welcoming and integrating new employees through structured onboarding processes and internal career paths.
5. **Administrative HR functions** cover compliance, payroll, contracts, records, and data management. These ensure legal security and smooth operations.
6. **Human resource development** involves lifelong learning, training, and leadership development. It supports productivity and motivation, while helping employees grow in alignment with company needs.

> **Example** A mid-size fintech company wishes to introduce Artificial Intelligence into their products. However, six months after the announcement there is still no sign of a product. An external consultant identifies the need of a data scientist (HR planning). To be more attractive for global talents, the company introduces a "work-from-anywhere" policy and reflects this value in its social media presence (HR policy design).
>
> As a result, the new data scientist works fully remote. For better team cohesion and to improve future communication, the Scrum master organizes an on-site meeting of the entire team during the first week (Recruitment and Onboarding).
>
> Since the new employee had already expressed his interest in continuing research during the job interview, he is now participating in a research project alongside his main assignment (Staff deployment). To better know which effort was spend on which project, the HR department provides a digital time recording system (administrative HR functions). The results of the research project are regularly presented at community meetings so that colleagues can also develop their skills. (HR development).

Effective HR development is a strategic success factor, enhancing long-term employee loyalty by boosting job satisfaction, motivation, and productivity. In other words, satisfied employees are more engaged and perform better. Even in organizations without a formal HR department, project managers may take on many of these roles and should be familiar with them.

10.1.4   The Role of HR Management in the Company

HR management has an integrative function in the organization. It acts as a service provider within the company and links the following three management levels:

- Strategic management
- Tactical management
- Operational management.

Figure 10.2 shows the interaction of these three levels.

Strategic HR management is part of the overall corporate strategy. It is oriented toward the goals of the organization and sometimes conflicts with project goals. For example, it may be decided at the strategic level to reduce the number of employees and outsource parts of development, while the project is desperately seeking developers right now.

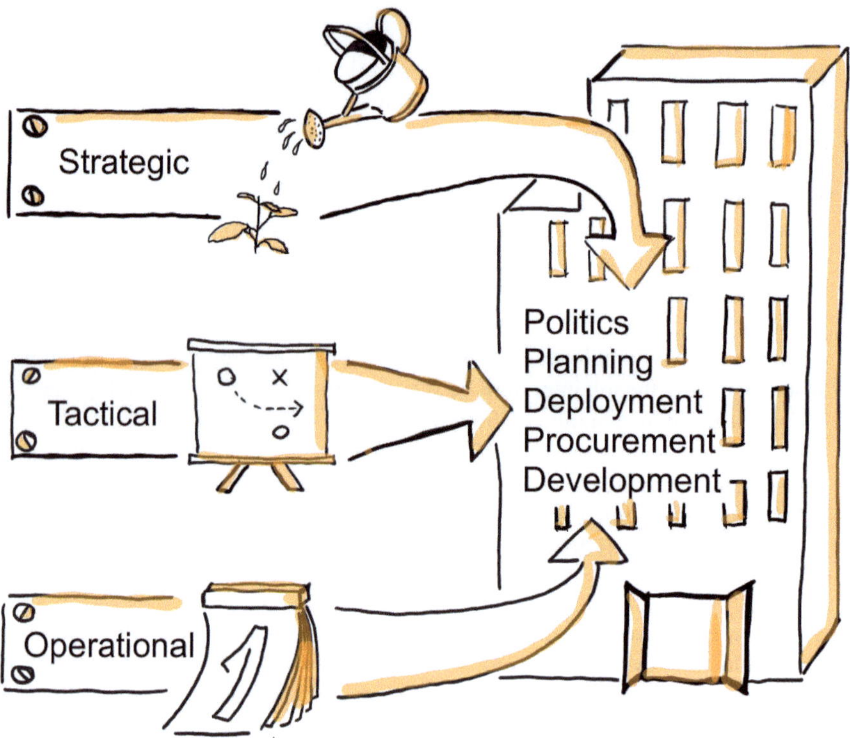

Fig. 10.2 Integrative function of HR management—interaction of the three levels

Tactical HR management forms the link (an interface) between the strategic and operational levels. While strategic HR management tends to focus on the employees of entire departments on a long-term time scale, operational HR management deals with individual employees and day-to-day business. Tactical HR management, on the other hand, typically focuses on groups of employees or workplaces and is usually oriented toward the medium term. Here, the organization of numerous areas, departments or groups is designed (e.g., optimal composition of certain team structures in international, mixed-age and virtual teams). Further development of individual employees across different departments is also part of tactical HR management (keyword "career plans").

Operational HR management deals with individual measures, e.g., the creation of skill profiles for employees or requirement profiles for specific positions. At this level, contracts are concluded, HR development measures are decided, training certificates are managed, and initial job interviews are conducted.

All three levels are closely interconnected (see Fig. 10.2). However, tactical HR management has the greatest significance for projects. It provides the answer to the following questions:

- How can individual teams/groups work efficiently, productively, and independently?
- How can the strengths of a group be optimally used to achieve the best possible results?

An increasing number of companies are breaking down their hierarchical structures and using forms of group/team work. This means that employees cooperate as experts in "cross-functional" teams, which has an impact on the management of these processes.

10.2 HR Management in the Project

Motivated project employees are no coincidence.

Projects rarely fail because of technological aspects, but usually because of problems of sociocultural nature. Consequently, in complex software projects, it is not so much the design, implementation or test methods used that are critical to success, but how people-related matters are handled. In other words, the most important success factor in the project are the people.

However, the way in which HR management is implemented in the project depends heavily on the organizational form of the project. In agile frameworks, the rigid decision-making processes and hierarchies of the classic organizational structure are increasingly moving into the background. Agility is understood as a dynamic and flexible adaptation to changing conditions, with changes that apply not only to software development processes, but to the entire company. "Working agile" means living lean and transparent processes in which self-organized and interdisciplinary teams participate, take responsibility, shape leadership, and thus achieve high flexibility and adaptation.

However, Scrum and other agile project management frameworks do not explicitly address the question of human resource management. The integration of agile approaches often represents a major challenge to the company's organization and human resources management.

10.2.1   Importance of HR Management in the Project

The HR department, line management department and project management do not always pull together. Apart from differing goals, there are often misunderstandings or ignorance that cause friction. Regulated processes for planning and selecting project employees prevent conflicts and reduce the need for coordination between the responsible departments in the organization and in the project. Such processes can, for example, use standardized skill profiles or require specific, recognized certificates.

In international projects or project teams with intercultural members, sociocultural and legal factors must also be taken into account. The idea behind this is to use social diversity constructively, but to do this you first have to know the differences and requirements. Therefore, every project manager who works with people from the far east, for example, should attend an appropriate intercultural training course.[2]

Example In order to weld the team together, a Hungarian employee had the nice idea of bringing along his goulash cannon and organizing a team meal. Unfortunately, we had not considered that the employee of Pakistani origin was not allowed to eat pork.

By the way, legal aspects do not only play a role in international teams. Especially in Germany, you should know and respect the rights of the works council, otherwise there may be considerable problems in the project.

10.2.2   HR Management as a Cross-Cutting Task

During a project, HR management emerges as a cross-cutting task across project phases on the one hand and various projects on the other. It consists of three core activities:

---

[2] Experience shows that cultural differences—both in subject matter and in expression—are so diverse that it is virtually impossible to be familiar with all possible variations. Time and again, we also encounter situations where gender role stereotypes, which may seem outdated from our perspective, resurface as a topic affecting team dynamics and collaboration.

- Selection of staff
- Staff leadership
- Know-how management.

Project management acts as an interface to the organization's HR management. As we will see in a moment, many of the tasks can only be performed in a targeted manner through close cooperation.

Staff Selection
The goal of staff selection is to place the "right people" in the "right place," "at the right time," and "in the right number." HR management in the project thus has the task of ensuring that planned and sufficiently qualified people are deployed in the required time. This also means providing replacements if employees drop out or, if necessary, hiring experts if required competencies are lacking.

Staff Leadership
Staff leadership means keeping both task-oriented and interpersonal aspects in focus and guiding, involving, and motivating team members with regard to the overall project goals.

Staff leadership is one of the most important tasks of HR management in the project and requires a high level of leadership and communication skills from the project manager.[3] This topic is so important that we will return to it later in connection with the success factors. Here is just one thing: Leadership competence is required throughout the entire duration of the project, and the greater the uncertainty of the project, the more so. Whenever changes are necessary, the project is confronted with challenges or the further course of action is unclear, the project team members need a firm foothold. The project manager can and must provide them with this foothold.

Apart from this, the project manager must be able to act as a leader in many other situations (e.g., with management, with customers, or other stakeholders). Project managers represent both the project and the company externally and must act confidently in the role of representative and adequate contact person.

Know-How Management
Know-how management means being able to uncover and use sound knowledge in the project. It is the task of the project manager to identify and link this knowledge and to enable its exchange. If knowledge gaps exist, the project manager should discover them and ensure that they are closed. Depending on the team size and the complexity of the tasks, project managers must decide whether the required knowledge should be distributed among specialists or whether each team member should operate as a generalist. Furthermore, they need to differentiate between tasks that

---

[3] Since we are talking about leadership and other people-related tasks at this point, we speak of the "project manager" and not 'project management." As already mentioned several times, this is the role that (especially in the agile environment) can be distributed among several people.

must absolutely be carried out—even in cases of absence, such as vacation or illness—and those that can be postponed or delegated without critical impact.

Systematic know-how management supports communication within the team and ensures that future projects can also benefit from the know-how gained (lessons learned).

Lessons learned should always be recorded in writing or visually. The biggest challenge here is to pass on the information sustainably. Wikis, knowledge databases, or AI tools can be very helpful.

10.2.3 HR Management Activities During the Project

As a cross-cutting discipline, HR management exerts influence throughout the entire duration of a project. Key HR management responsibilities in the course of a project include:

- **Staffing Analysis**—Continuously identifies and evaluates the competencies within the project team, providing structured feedback to inform individual, team, and organizational development.
- **Staffing and Recruitment**—Ensures that the defined personnel requirements are met cost-effectively, on schedule, and in line with project needs.
- **Personnel Assignment Management**—Aligns individual qualifications with specific project tasks to optimize performance and efficiency.
- **Personnel Change Management**—Manages changes in workforce composition, whether involving onboarding, role transitions, or redeployment, to maintain operational continuity.
- **Personnel Cost Management**—Plans, monitors, and controls HR-related expenditures to support financial precision and informed decision-making.
- **Personnel Development**—Designs and implements targeted training, promotion, and professional growth initiatives in alignment with both project goals and organizational strategy.
- **Staff Leadership**—Provides direction, fosters motivation, and maintains effective communication channels to ensure cohesive collaboration and engagement.

> **Example** Remember the example of the fintech company in Sect. 10.1.3 "Tasks of HR management in the company." When the external consultant arrived, he interviewed the Scrum master. The Scrum master reported that the team was highly interested in working with artificial intelligence, but that they were neither available nor specifically qualified (Staffing Analysis). The external consultant then organized a training for two junior team members (Personel Development). This slowed dans the teams velocity. When the newly hired data scientist arrived, the two team members switched to the other project (Staffing

and Recruitment). They were replaced by two senior developers (Personel Assignment Management). Although the project appeared to be more expensive at first glance, thorough monitoring revealed that the new team was more efficient and effective (Personel Cost Management). This was largely due to the Scrum master, who steered the team safely through this difficult phase thanks to his leadership skills (Staff Leadership).

10.2.4 Project Manager and HR Expert—Successful Cooperation

The project manager and the responsible expert from the line organization's HR department work together systematically.

A good example of this collaboration is staff selection. The ideal division of labor here looks as follows (see also Fig. 10.3):

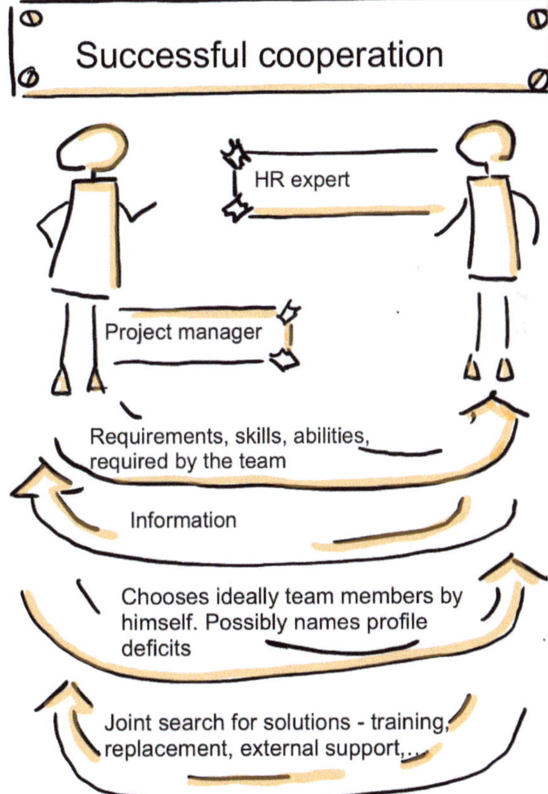

Fig. 10.3 Division of labor between project manager and HR expert

- The project manager formulates requirements, e.g., skills or abilities that his team needs for the task.
- The responsible HR department of the company organization provides the necessary information.
- Ideally, the project manager selects the personnel himself.
- The project manager names deficits if his requirement profile cannot be met.
- Both together (project manager and HR expert) look for solutions—training/replacement of the person, external support/freelancer.

Effective company-wide HR management does not stop after successful staffing and recruitment. The HR expert should regularly talk to both the employee and the project manager to obtain information about the project employees. This information helps to identify hidden competencies or weaknesses, as well as employees' development goals, so that it can be used effectively and properly documented.

10.2.5 Team Support by HR Management in Four Steps

You cannot just assemble a team from individuals and expect it to act like a unit right away. Teams must first form. One of the project manager's HR management tasks is therefore to accompany the team in the following four areas (Fig. 10.4):

Team Building
In this area, the team constitutes itself and forms its structures. The focus is on the start of the project, because it is decisive for the further course of the project. The more successful the start, the better the chances of building a high-performance team. For project managers, this means that they must put together their teams in a suitable way and determine the appropriate project organization.

Experienced leaders organize team development workshops at this stage, designed to foster mutual acquaintance, define individual roles within the team, and transparently articulate the shared project goal for all team members. In our case study, the project manager failed to address all of these aspects.

In agile frameworks, those tasks are distributed between the product owner, the Scrum Master and the team.

Team Management
Once the team is formed and the structures are clear, it is time to carry out the project work. The project manager deals with leading his team and steering it in the right direction. This phase requires a high level of soft skill of the project manager, but also on the part of the team. After all, they have to work together constructively.

Example In the case study, the project manager operated in isolation, coordinating individually with team members while acting as the sole point of contact and withholding critical information. As a result, the team lacked opportunities for collective exchange and was unable to collaborate constructively toward the project goal.

In agile project management frameworks, the responsibility for this is often less clear, as the team acts independently. To be successful, all must assume this leadership task. However, the Scrum master is guiding the team, not enforcing, but in an enabling manner.

Team Developing
As the name suggests, this phase is about further developing personnel and technical competencies of team members through training and education. Ideally, a continuous improvement process forms in the project (agile approaches integrate this into the retrospective). The project manager has the task of leading and further developing the team so that it has all the prerequisites to achieve high performance.

In summary, it is the project manager's responsibility to continuously assess whether each team member is provided with the individually appropriate conditions for effective work—be it through reviewing resource requirements, updating the staffing plan, ensuring effective internal communication, or addressing other key factors that contribute to successful collaboration.

In agile frameworks, the Scum Master helps the team to establish wikis, participate in guilds, or find other forms of skill development. Guilds are a guild is communities of practice across teams. In a Testing Guild, for example, test managers and testers from different teams come together to share knowledge, best practices, and drive innovation and improvements across the organization.

Team Closing
The final stage is often challenging for the project manager, involving project evaluation, team disbandment, and transferring employees to new roles. Recognizing individual performance and conducting formal appraisals are key tasks. Maintaining motivation is difficult since not everyone leaves simultaneously, but celebrating shared successes helps.

In sequential project management frameworks, team closing is driven by the project manager and sometimes embedded into a process which includes updating the employee profiles and lessons learned workshops. In agile frameworks, review and retrospective are performed after each sprint, but the HR aspects are often neglected. When an agile project ends, responsibility for the team members usually returns to the line manager. The scrum master will typically support team closing.

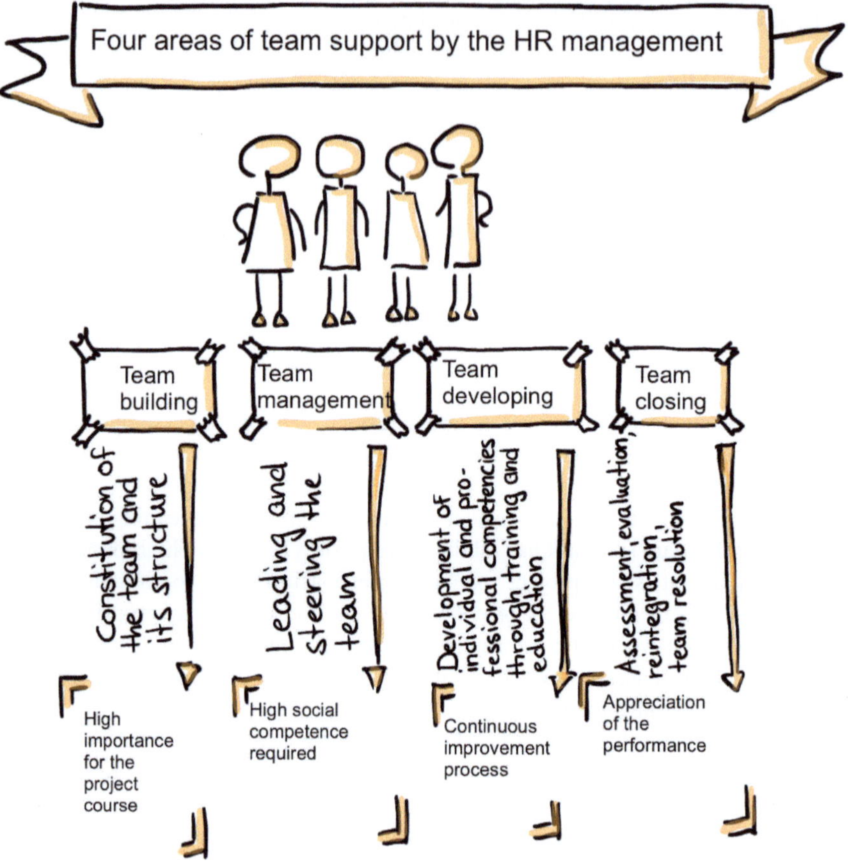

Fig. 10.4 Four areas of team support

Important Good project managers never "drop" their employees after the project has ended. Accompanying/motivating employees into new projects or even organizations are part of a complete project closing.

The project manager's goal is to boost team performance and project success by clearly defining roles, coordinating tasks, and ensuring effective communication and cooperation. Without this, misunderstandings and inefficiencies arise, as seen in the case study.

The project manager acts as a promoter and supporter of the team, responsible for fostering its performance throughout all project phases. The Tuckman team development model (the team clock, see Sect. 1.4.4) later provides valuable guidance for this process.

10.3   HR Management Done Right—What is Particularly Important

10.3.1 Success Factor "Social Competence"

Skillfully align your team and set your project management up for success!

Project teams are becoming more colorful, various and projects more global. "Virtual communication" has become the basis for collaboration in the future. This affects both small and large companies and both small and large projects. The goal is to overcome spatial, temporal, and cultural barriers and thus to bundle and efficiently utilize the competencies of the best subject matter experts. Project managers play a key role in this. They juggle the specific knowledge, skills, and competencies of their team members and steer the course of success to a large extent through their soft skills, communication, and leadership quality.

> **Definition** Social competence
> By social competence, we mean the availability (potential) and application (performance) of cognitive, emotional, and motor behaviors that lead to a long-term favorable balance of positive and negative consequences for the agent in specific social situations (Waters and Sroufe 1983).

Soft Skills

For decades, it has been well established that success or failure in organizations is determined not solely by financial indicators, but above all by the people who work within them—their attitudes, values, and belief systems. In the 7-S Model developed at the time by McKinsey consultants Tom Peters Jr and Robert Waterman (Peters and Waterman 1984), both "hard factors" (Strategy, Structure, Systems) and "soft factors" (Style, Staff, Skills, Shared Values) were identified for the first time as key elements that can elevate a company into the top tier of performance.

The term "soft" in this context refers to influencing factors that cannot be measured objectively, that is, variables that cannot be reliably quantified or recorded. These stand in contrast to the "hard factors," for which a broad array of objective performance metrics already exist. Today, these soft factors are largely encompassed by the concept of soft skills.

Soft skills are the ability to act effectively and appropriately in interpersonal situations. They comprise a wide range of abilities and personal qualities that are perceived subjectively and enable an individual to communicate successfully, collaborate with others, and resolve conflicts constructively.

Soft skills play a vital role not only in the workplace but also in social and private relationships. They are central to a person's ability to work productively with others and to build and sustain meaningful, cooperative relationships.

In summary, while social skills cannot be verified through objective criteria, they have a significant impact on the success of any project.

For a project manager, soft skills are one of the most essential prerequisites for assuming a leadership role. After all, leadership ultimately means enabling and guiding other people—in this case, the project team. At the same time, soft skills are also expected from each individual team member, since without them, successful teamwork—and thus high-performing teams—cannot be achieved. As a result, teamwork has become one of the most valued concepts in the field of human resource management.

Requirements for the Project Manager

This raises the question of which skills and competencies a project manager must possess to fulfill their role effectively. We distinguish between four categories:

1. **Behavioral Competence**

   Behavioral competence plays a fundamental role in any kind of work with people. Examples of behavioral competence in project management are reliability and assertiveness, but empathy, conflict solution skills, communication skills and openness are also part of it. Coaching as a behavioral competence enables a project manager to guide and develop team members, fostering growth, accountability, and collaborative performance.

2. **Methodological Skills**

   Knowledge of methods enables project managers to skillfully apply appropriate and target-oriented project management methods in their work. Some of these methods aim at dealing with people, i.e., the team or other stakeholders. These include, for example, facilitation and visualization techniques. Others aim more at the content-related project work (e.g., methods of requirements analysis).

3. **Expertise**

   Expertise enables project managers to orient themselves in the project material and, if necessary, to make specialist decisions. For example, it ensures that process planning not only aims at achieving the intended goal but also anticipates likely obstacles based on past experience. By fostering proactive action, this helps to avoid bottlenecks and enables a more efficient implementation of projects. Project managers without expertise also run the risk of not being accepted by the team.

4. **Industry Knowledge**

   In principle, the influence of domain knowledge is similar to the influence of expertise. Project managers with domain knowledge are better able to assess circumstances and react appropriately. In general, knowledge of the industry, whether of the project manager or of the project team members, has a positive influence on project activities.

Unlike in earlier times, soft skills have become an increasingly important criterion in personnel selection—not only for individuals in leadership positions, but also for high-performing team members. The ability to interact effectively, communicate constructively, and contribute to a collaborative working environment is now considered to be a key qualification in both management and team-based role (see Fig. 10.5). It plays a fundamental role because projects are social systems.

Requirements for the Team Members

Any project manager, no matter how competent, is in an unfavorable situation if his team does not have the necessary skills to make the project a success. In fact, the competencies of the individual project members influence the success of the project just as much as the personality of the project manager does. The project manager must therefore recognize the strengths and weaknesses to act accordingly.

Team members should be team players and flexible. They should be able to deal with complexity, show proactive initiative and be open-minded with respect to other cultures or new topics.

Four Essential Aspects of Social Competence

Figure 10.6 shows the four essential aspects that make up social competence.

Dealing with oneself sounds trite, but it's not. It's about pairing a high self-esteem with the ability to reflect on one's own attitudes and actions, to allow criticism and to learn from mistakes. This requires personal responsibility, self-discipline, self-confidence, self-observation, self-efficacy, all in all: good self-management. Only those who are at ease with themselves can also be at ease with others.

Dealing with other people starts with being polite. In our context, however, we would like to emphasize another aspect. It is important to show a genuine interest

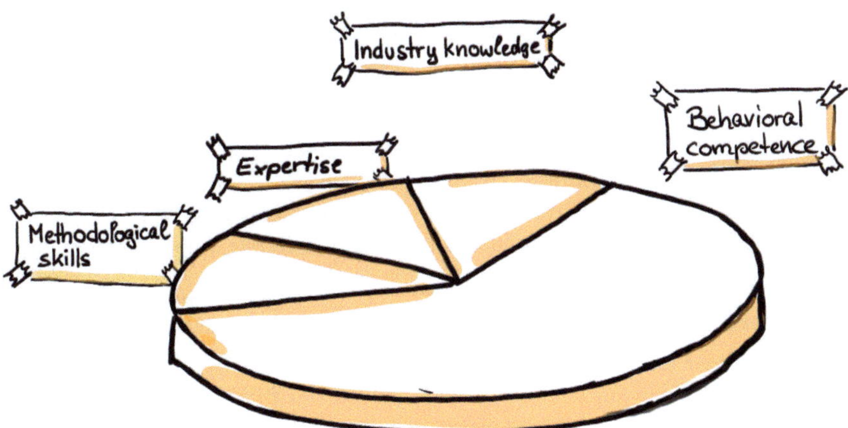

Fig. 10.5 Importance of behavioral competence

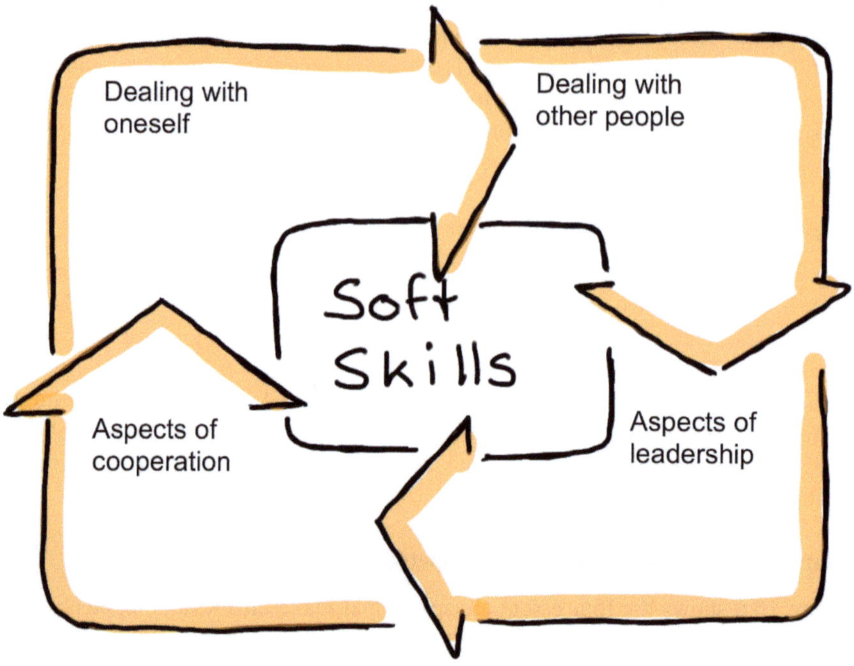

Fig. 10.6 Essential aspects of social competence

in the other person and not just to manage the "resource." The ability to perceive and understand others, to accept and respect different opinions and positions is a prerequisite for a healthy working atmosphere.

The following skills play an important role in dealing with people: recognition, respect, empathy, helpfulness, critical competence, perception, tolerance, respect, appreciation, communication, perspective-taking, inter- and intracultural competence, civil courage, knowledge of human nature, also the ability to "read between the lines"—in short, all skills aimed at understanding other people.

Aspects of cooperation include communication skills, teamwork skills, motivation skills, enthusiasm skills, and conflict management skills, as well as participation, collaboration, and networking skills.

The ability to motivate refers to both self-motivation and the motivation of others. Participation aims at letting others participate in one's own considerations, decisions, and, if necessary, activities.

Aspects of leadership are about being able to make decisions, give and take feedback, take responsibility, set an example. This requires a wide variety of skills, depending on the context: Flexibility, diligence, commitment, magnanimity, consistency, and so on.

Social competence cannot be learned completely from a book or with a computer. It is only trained and adopted in (inter)action with other people. However, this presupposes that the person concerned has the willingness and the desire to learn to work on himself. He or she must recognize his or her own, possibly obstructive behavior patterns and adopt new, more successful behavior patterns in their place. This is where training or coaching can help. Such training can only be effective if the person concerned has recognized the need himself.

10.3.2   Success Factor "Communication"

Communicate effectively in teams and projects and ensure project success!

Effective communication is a critical success factor in professional life. It enables the transfer of knowledge and supports productive collaboration. The clearer the communication processes, the more effective the outcomes.

In project work, communication plays a decisive role—especially in the implementation of requirements. The project manager is responsible for shaping communication processes and frequently faces situations that challenge their communication skills: agreements, negotiations, meetings, and presentations are all part of the daily routine.

Clearly established communication channels are essential. Projects that rely solely on e-mail or digital tools without personal exchange often start with a disadvantage. Even well-defined agreements and rules cannot fully prevent misunderstandings or conflicts. Ultimately, the human factor is what matters most.

A lack of communication can lead to problems, conflicts, and, in the worst case, project failure. In contrast, effective communication builds trust, facilitates knowledge-sharing, and strengthens collaboration.

Professional communication is:

- Clear, precise, and up to date;
- Characterized by appreciation and a shared language;
- Open to differing perspectives (also known as ambiguity tolerance).

Project managers need to know what to communicate, to whom, and how— and understand that communication always occurs within a specific context. A basic understanding of communication models and social dynamics makes this significantly easier. Importantly, communication skills are not only essential for project managers—every team member should have a solid foundational understanding of how communication functions within a collaborative environment.

Definition of Communication

Many still mistakenly believe that sending an e-mail guarantees the smooth transmission of information. However, in practice, it often becomes evident that merely sending messages does not always generate the expected response.

By sending a message, the sender exclusively ensures that the receiver receives the information. Communication takes place in one direction only. However, this act alone is not sufficient for a functioning communication process. Communication is complex and means the exchange of information between two or more people. It presupposes a process of understanding in which the information is received and understood. It is an elementary necessity of human existence and an important social bonding agent.

Communication works through speech, facial expressions, gestures through written exchanges, media, etc.... So there are several channels of communication:

- Analogue, whereby the communication can be informal as well as formal
- Digital, where communication is pictorial/visual, acoustic, or written.

You Can't not Communicate!

The crux of the matter is: you cannot NOT communicate. Communication is always verbal and non-verbal at the same time (see also (Watzlawick et al. 1967)). Every behavior of people has a communicative character, even if it is only a turning away or a silence. For the project manager, this means:

- Everything that the project manager says or does not say and does or does not do is communication and has corresponding effects.
- Statements made by the project manager are perceived against the background of his role as a leader.

In the worst case, the communication of the project manager leads to misunderstandings, confusion, and ultimately to demotivation of the employees. Therefore, the project manager should also consciously exercise his role as a leader when communicating. This means he or she should:

- Conduct conversations mindfully and purposefully so that connection (commonality, orientation) occurs;
- In problematic team discussions, focus on the common goal and possibly establish new rules of procedure instead of looking for causes or the culprit;
- Prefer to formulate his thoughts diplomatically and even more so as long as he does not really know and can assess the people and situations;
- Give praise and recognition on a regular basis;
- Show appreciation;
- Express criticism in a constructive manner and fosters a culture that values learning from mistakes.

All these points are part of the daily management tasks of a project manager.

In a conversation, it is not only what one says that is important, but also how one says it. The WHAT corresponds to the content (subject level) and is transmitted through our words (language). The HOW stands for the relationship that arises in communication. This relationship level becomes clear through tone of voice, gestures, pitch of voice, emphasis, facial expressions, and the whole body. As the great mime Marcel Marceau once said: "Gestures are thoughts made visible."

Consequently, we talk about verbal and non-verbal communication. These two aspects are in constant interaction with each other. The relationship level forms a foundation for the communication process and thus supports the exchange on the subject level.

To communicate successfully, pay attention to non-verbal signals as well. Be aware of the overall impression of your counterpart. Perceive the person you are talking to, the entire situation and the way you experience this situation. Here, a distinction is made between external and internal perception, meaning we differentiate between objective observation and subjective evaluation. How we perceive or understand a conversation or what is being said largely depends on our own expectations, fears, biases, experiences, and so forth. Consequently, the sender of information can never be entirely certain that the message has been understood exactly as intended. To ensure clarity in cases of doubt, understanding must be verified through the technique of "active listening." Active listening involves checking whether your impression aligns with the other person's perception by asking appropriate questions or by paraphrasing what you have understood.

However, pay attention to the verbal signals as well. Ask yourself the following questions:

- Is there real communication, or is the conversation reduced to sending out information?
- Is the effect checked or does everyone just assume that the other person has already understood?
- What really gets through?

Again, use questions to check your impression and provide feedback to your interlocutor.

Every project manager as a communication participant should know (i.e., perceive) which signals he sends through his behavior, how the context affects him, and what he achieves through his communication. Only then, he can prevent misunderstandings or conflicts instead of being the cause himself.

Human communication is rarely unambiguous. Conversations are conducted by people and are therefore never free of personal parts and messages. Seen in this light, our dilemma with communication is quite natural. This makes it even more important for project managers to formulate their statements consciously in order to reduce the risk of escalating situations in the project. The following types of statements are absolutely taboo:

- Interpret, add to, judge, and evaluate (e.g., "I think this solution is very good and the other one is just bad"),

- Generalize and suggest a rule instead of giving a concrete example (e.g., "You're always late."),
- Judging the partner and giving them a classifying "label" (e.g., "You are a chaotic person."),
- Block the discussion with general statements (e.g., "You'll see how it goes."),
- Mind reading (e.g., "I know exactly what you mean, I don't need to hear it."),
- Making insinuations ("You certainly didn't prepare."),
- Exposing the partner (e.g., "So, did your little secret have you back in its grip?"),
- Exaggerating and multiplying hidden negative sentiments/feelings with supposedly factual statements (e.g., "That was a hundred times sure it couldn't work in this context."),
- Send non-verbal/paraverbal messages that contradict objectivity (e.g., roll eyes, shrug shoulders, seek affirming eye contact with others, slap forehead, etc.).

Messages of this kind are mostly perceived unconsciously and also answered unconsciously. However, their effect is devastating.

Project managers can also counteract the communication dilemma by taking into account the communication needs of their interlocutors. Not all team members have the same preferences. Some prefer to listen, others would rather see pictures or be able to "touch" something. By using different types of communication, the project managers can better involve the participants. For example, in a meeting, they can ensure that the content is not only discussed but also continuously visualized.

When project managers are really professional, they not only deliver a "slide battle" on the beamer, but also have flipcharts, pin boards, workshop cards etc., in their repertoire. These enliven the meeting and make it accessible and interesting for everyone. Today, communication in projects often takes place digitally across various media. As a result, the portfolio of available digital tools for collaboration expands in tandem with the increasing demands placed on the communication skills of the participants involved in the conversation. The point is that all participants feel addressed and thus motivated to participate. To do this, project managers must take into account the context and consider the specific communication situation. By asking questions, they can check how what was "said" was received. After all, they are the ones who wants to be understood and who have a strong interest in ensuring that the team also communicates successfully with each other. Project managers are therefore also responsible for ensuring that the information reaches its intended recipients.

Special Features of Digital Communication

The increasingly favored digital communication in its various forms (conference systems, chats, e-mails, concept boards, etc.) often presents team members with additional technical and personal difficulties. On the one hand, not all team members are equally proficient with the various media, meaning that not all intended communicative functions are used by everyone. This results in unequal access to information and exchanges among team members. Additionally, personal and individual attitudes toward using digital media may vary. For instance, older generations, despite having a general affinity for virtual communication channels, may still exhibit resistance when it comes to adopting new interactive tools or utilizing AI technologies—such as for drafting requests or summarizing meeting outcomes. The reduction of non-verbal communication options in virtual spaces may not only lead to misunderstandings but also create uncertainties in project-specific and personal communication.

An experienced project manager is aware of the limitations of virtual communication and chooses the appropriate medium for team discussions based on the occasion and objective. Therefore, personal conversations or conflict discussions should preferably be conducted in person.

How Our Perception Influences Communication

People are unique beings and have quite subjective and selective perceptions that provide a lot of room for interpretation. This room for maneuver makes it difficult to communicate clearly.

Our perception works (quite simply explained) as follows (see Fig. 10.7):

- We perceive the information that confirms already set opinion. All deviating information is sorted out.
- We also reinterpret the divergent information we have received until it fits into the picture we already have.
- We continue to reinterpret and adjust already filtered information until it confirms the known idea.
- We unconsciously fill in missing information with imagined content derived from our own personal experiences and prior knowledge.

Human perception is subjective. It is oriented to the individually given previous experiences, values, interests, and needs. This is the lens through which we interpret and describe the world.

> **Important** Objectivity is therefore an illusion![4]

What does this mean in concrete terms for project communication?

- Misunderstandings in the project arise when clear statements are missing and the messages expressed are ambiguous. "You understand what you want" with the result that participants may behave incorrectly in terms of the project.
- Different opinions and ideas will always exist in the project. Fighting against them means "tilting at windmills" and is accordingly nonsensical. What is decisive is how we deal with these opinions and what emerges from them.

---

[4] If you want to learn more about it, you should study works of constructivism.

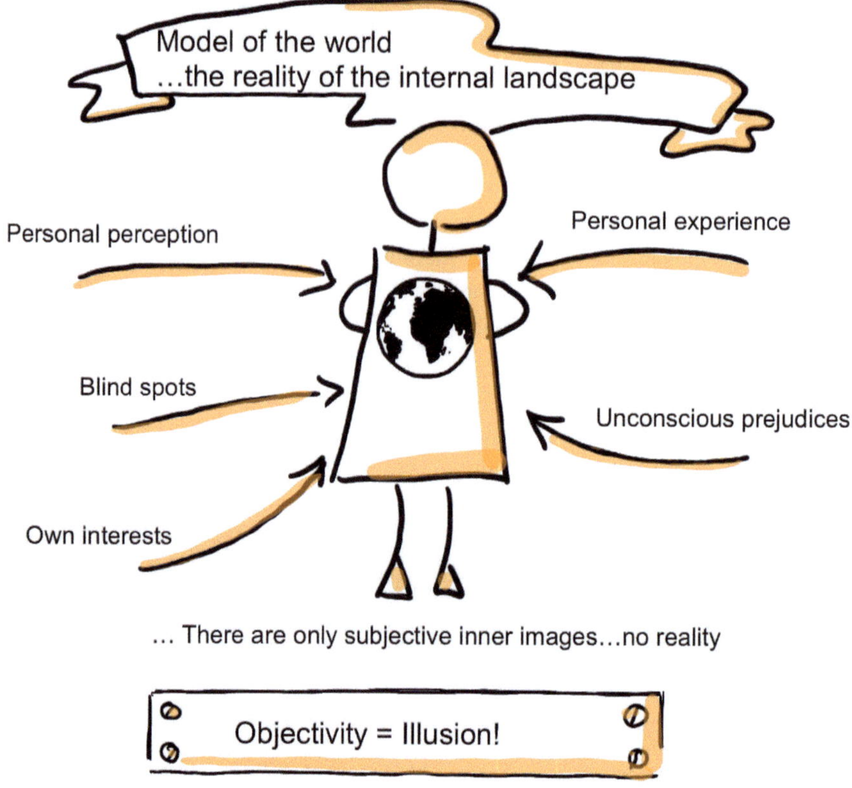

Fig. 10.7 Model of the world—our perception

- Discussions about which opinion is right and who is right are unproductive. Every point of view is justified. It is more helpful to ask questions about needs, interests, goals, desires (i.e., about what connects).
- Be careful with evaluative terms, such as "objective," "right," or "wrong"! Instead, use terms such as "different," "according to my experience," or "as far as generally known."

Especially when a team is newly assembled and the members do not yet know each other, but are already to work together, the team members must be given the opportunity to adjust their perceptions and "world models" to the project. This takes time, but prevents misunderstandings and conflicts in the further course of the project.

10.3.3 Success Factor "Motivation"

Burn for what you do! Awaken enthusiasm and desire for team performance!

Without motivation, there is no drive for one's own actions. For the project manager, therefore, the question arises: "How can I best motivate my team members?" or "Is it even possible?"

Motivation Versus Demotivation
To be able to answer this question, we should first understand the term "motivation." "Motivation" refers to the inner driving force and willingness of a person to act in a certain way. Motivation presupposes that the person moves in an environment that is characterized by reliability, credibility, predictability, and goodwill and in which he or she is socially integrated.

Our behavior is the result of physical and psychological needs on the one hand and external influences on the other. It is largely influenced by unconscious thought processes. We humans have many needs, which are usually difficult to separate from each other. We feel physical and social needs at the same time, whereby social needs are further subdivided into professional and private needs. Some needs we can suppress, but none of them we can really "turn off." We are always and everywhere, i.e., in every situation, guided by them.

Consequently, not only the current events relevant to the project affect our behavior in the project, but also the previous, present and the expected future events—regardless of whether they are relevant to the project or not.

The motives that guide each of us most strongly in our daily lives are also guiding motives in project work.

Each team member chooses an approach that best meets his or her personal needs. This can be goal-oriented for or competing with the project goals. That is why it is extremely important to create good framework conditions in the project. They are the prerequisite for covering the physical and social needs and creating space for growth and self-realization of the team members. Only then will everyone be satisfied and willing to do something.

Example Too abstract? Here are two examples that illustrate how individual motivation works:

1. A new employee feels comfortable and at ease within the team, as everyone is working toward a shared goal, each member has a clear understanding of their roles and responsibilities, processes are continuously reviewed and aligned, and the professional as well as personal exchange among colleagues is characterized by mutual respect and appreciation.

2. The project manager feels proud, having been appointed solely by senior management as the project lead for two teams. He is highly motivated, as this appointment represents a significant step forward in his career.

However, the goals set must be realistic and achievable, otherwise demotivation will quickly set in.

Demotivation is a blockage (restriction) or loss of drive and willingness to act. Demotivated feeling and acting limits the form, direction, strength, and duration of the individual's commitment to organizational goals or roles. Demotivated action not only causes "non-doing" or lower willingness to perform, but also points to commitment in an undesirable direction (Ng et al. 2004).

The new employee described in the example above would not remain motivated for long if he lacked a clear understanding of the project goal and his role within it, or if he received neither feedback nor essential information necessary for his work. Few things are as damaging to a project as employee demotivation. Therefore, the project manager must do everything possible to keep motivation high.

Intrinsic and Extrinsic Motivation

"You can't motivate employees. They have to be it by themselves." We hear this phrase over and over again. In fact, it is true that only intrinsic motivation is effective. However, this does not mean that the project manager has no influence on the motivation of his employees.

If a person is intrinsically motivated, even performing an action has a motivating effect because the action is perceived and felt as exciting, interesting, valuable, and enriching.

Intrinsically motivated employees get involved out of curiosity, because they enjoy their work, because they want to be the best, or because their job allows them to act out their spontaneity. This form of "intrinsic motivation" has a long-term, sustainable effect. Their needs include: success, recognition, interesting work content, more responsibility, growth, joy, and fun.

Extrinsic motivation acts from the outside. A person performs his action to achieve positive consequences (e.g., bonus/reward) and to avoid negative consequences (e.g., punishment, disadvantages). The action is a means or instrument to achieve or prevent a particular end. It is less interesting than the end associated with it. Extrinsically motivated employees engage in action to obtain, for example, better pay, a promotion, or better working conditions.

The needs of an extrinsically motivated person include: security, stability, freedom from fear, friendship, belonging (Fig. 10.8).

In fact, intrinsic motivation is preferable to extrinsic motivation. However, this does not at all mean that the project manager can do nothing to motivate his employees. On the contrary, doing nothing has an extremely demotivating effect.

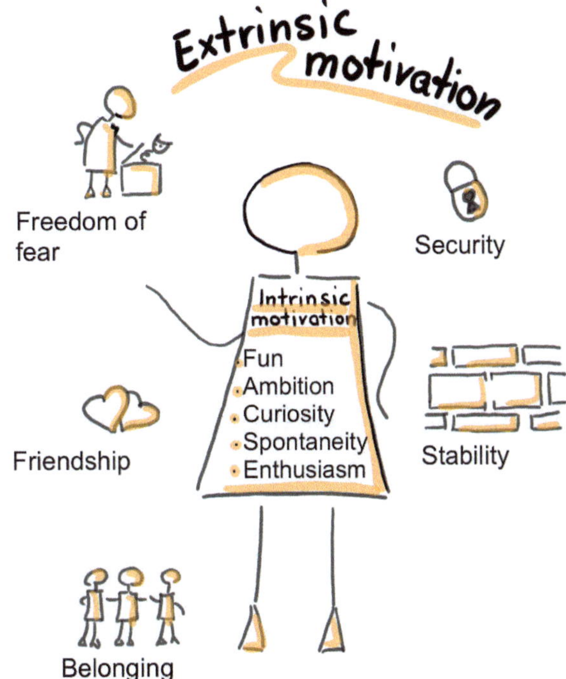

Fig. 10.8 Intrinsic and extrinsic motivation

The Project Manager as Motivator

> The main task of a project manager is to keep the team motivated.

The project manager significantly influences the motivation and commitment of the project team, both positively and negatively, through their attitude, behavior, and leadership style. Lack of communication, unreliability, or poor integration leads to decreased motivation, which manifests as delays, quality deficits, and performance drops. Often, difficulties arise from organizational structures or processes. Project managers must recognize their role as motivators rather than solely focusing on task execution.

While a project manager cannot motivate someone who lacks intrinsic motivation, they can stimulate positive impulses and prevent demotivation. This requires identifying and maintaining motivating and demotivating factors. Understanding the mechanisms of human motivation is essential.

Four brain systems play a crucial role in motivation:

- **The Reward System** is activated by recognition and appreciation, for example when a project manager publicly praises a team member's contribution, boosting their motivation.

- **The Emotional System** regulates feelings through neurotransmitters such as dopamine (drive), opioids (joy), and oxytocin (bonding). For example, shared team successes trigger dopamine release and strengthen team cohesion.
- **The Memory System** shapes expectations based on past experiences, such as whether promises have been kept. For example, if prior commitments were broken, team members may be skeptical about new assurances.
- **The Decision-Making System** integrates values and information to guide decisions, for example, when a project manager fairly assigns tasks based on team values and individual skills.

Sustainable motivation is achieved only when the project manager employs measures that engage all four of these systems effectively.

The Appreciation as the Most Important Motivating Factor

Research shows that recognition, appreciation, and social connectedness are essential drivers of human motivation and significantly enhance engagement and performance in collaborative work (Visser and Arnold 2022; Vo et al. 2022).

In other words, feeling valued and recognized by others strongly boosts motivation and commitment, making social appreciation a key factor for success in team and project work. The most important motivating factors are appreciation coupled with praise and recognition.

Appreciation is a positive basic attitude toward other people and has nothing at all to do with a performance, a result or a desired behavior. It should be a matter of course in the way we deal with others. Unconditional appreciation is an existential need of all people. Those who can recognize and understand different value concepts can live and promote cooperation much better.

The project manager should identify how much appreciation exists in the project and where it can be expanded.

Example When analyzing the case study, we observe that project team members are not provided with documented requirements or a clearly articulated goal. Team members have not had the chance to get to know one another, roles are not clearly defined, and responsibilities are not transparently allocated. This lack of communication and interaction around objectives and processes also reveals something deeper: a lack of appreciation toward both the team as a collective and the individuals within it.

An appreciative project culture is built on a foundation of welcoming new members, creating engaging and inclusive participation formats, setting shared goals, coordinating processes, giving constructive feedback, and embracing a healthy error culture.

Praise and Recognition refer to special behavior or outstanding performance. Project managers should not only use this generously and promptly when there are outstanding performances, but they should also ensure that their criteria for praise are transparent, reliable, and independent of the person. Otherwise, the employee will perceive the expressed praise merely as a formality.

Praise and recognition alone are not enough to keep project members motivated and committed to the project. Motivation always requires appreciation as a basis. "He does not give a damn about me as a person" is one of the worst messages a project manager can convey. Of course, no one says it so directly in the project, but non-verbal communication can be very treacherous. So as a project manager, make sure you perceive people as such, know their needs, and act accordingly.

10.3.4 Success Factor "Leadership"

> Those who lead by vocation have people who are happy to follow them.

There are no standard recipes for good leadership behavior. Every project manager must develop his own leadership model. Otherwise, they will never appear authentic.

The problem often lies simply in the fact that project managers do not automatically live out their organizationally defined position as a leadership role. As a result, they are not perceived as leaders.

Leadership is generally the effort to influence others purposefully. It can be technical/content-related, strategic, personal, and situational. In project management, leadership is intended to have a guiding and controlling effect on the actions or behavior of project team members to achieve project goals. Particularly in agile environments, leadership should be situational, servant-oriented, and empowering. Agile leaders should adapt to complex and dynamic project situations. A practical, flexible, and people-centered approach is key.

Leading project teams is not fundamentally different from leading departments in a company. However, leadership in a project can become very complex. Leadership roles can either be organizationally defined or arise without any formal authority from the structure and size of a project. For example, a department head may have the authority to give directives, while a software project manager may have only partial or no authority at all. The general leadership principles provide a solid foundation in projects on which every project manager can build. We will explore these leadership principles in more detail in the following sections.

Important Leadership is above all the avoidance of demotivation and means creating development opportunities for employees (according to Wong 2018).

Aspects of Successful Project Leadership

How do you envision an ideal leader? The answers can vary widely, but the following descriptions are often mentioned:

Ideal project managers…

- Are authentic—their words and actions align, making them appear credible and "real,"
- Serve as a role model—they demonstrate what they expect from others,
- Offer as much freedom and decision-making space as possible while also setting clearly defined boundaries,
- Provide direction—they explain the framework within which team members can exercise their autonomy,
- Set realistic goals,
- Know the way,
- Communicate effectively,
- Are able to communicate goals and visions,
- Take time and get involved,
- Identify mistakes or misconduct promptly and address them,
- And much more…

However, there is no universal rule for good leadership behavior. Instead, a project manager is expected to understand, analyze, and respond to the specific situation by applying the necessary and appropriate leadership approach. This is why we talk about situational leadership, which requires a high degree of soft skills.

Successful leaders, and thus project managers who want to lead successfully in the project, should know and consider the aspects of leadership in Table 10.1.

Adaptive Leadership

Leadership is a two-way process. In a figurative sense, the shepherd also has to adapt his leadership style to the flock and the respective situation. Sometimes he has to get the flock across the road quickly; sometimes he has to carry an injured sheep home. Accordingly, the "project manager" should have a repertoire of different leadership styles (see Agarwal 2023, p. 132).

- **Authoritarian Leadership Style**

  This leadership style is also referred to as autocratic leadership. The project manager decides on the processes and content himself. The team members receive precise individual instructions. The result is controlled in detail.

  The authoritarian leadership style appeals to employees who are far away from taking responsibility and prefer clear instructions. In the event of a crisis, decisions can be made and implemented quickly without much questioning. However, there is hardly any room for feedback, shared responsibility, and creativity.

Table 10.1 Aspects of leadership, see (Agarwal 2023), (Troger 2022) and (Hagemann 2023)

Aspects of leadership	Explanation
Leading with vision	The vision gives meaning to the project. It should be comprehensible and inspiring so that it spurs on, motivates and carries away the project team members. The project manager should communicate the vision and occasionally recall it
Leading through structure	The structure gives the project a foothold. The project manager specifies goals and framework conditions. He makes decisions and ensures that decisions are adhered to In agile projectmanagementframeworks, structure is created through roles and time-boxing
Leading through communication	Communication is the heartbeat of the project. In agile approaches like Scrum, daily meetings and regular feedback loops are established practices that make communication an integral part of the process. The project manager must ensure that communication is effective. This includes persuading people in an appreciative manner, resolving conflicts and giving feedback. A good dose of humor is often helpful
Leading by designing the environment as a maker	Project managers have creative freedom and should make use of it. In general, the project manager shapes the project culture. In a fault-tolerant culture, mistakes are seen as an opportunity for improvement ("learning from mistakes"). In a learning culture, the project manager creates a learning-friendly environment (training programs, wiki etc.) Project managers can also shape organization-wide. They can maintain networks and thus, for example, obtain support for the project through the "short way." If the framework conditions are unclear, the project manager can actively make assumptions, which he then represents in higher level committees

(continued)

Table 10.1 (continued)

Aspects of leadership	Explanation
Leading as a role model	As a role model, the project manager can exemplify enthusiasm and integrity. The prerequisite for this is that he is authentic (one also speaks of "being congruent"). His decisions should be sustainable, the environment he provides meaningful. The project work should be effective and interesting As already mentioned, Scrum Masters should act as servant leaders which means that they lead trust, respect, and influence rather than through hierarchy, power, or control. In this environment, it is essential to exemplify respect, trust, and a sense of responsibility
Leading with appreciation	Appreciation is the be-all and end-all of motivation. Appreciative project managers provide individual leadership impulses per employee, so that they feel respected and psychologically safe. They can listen and take their counterparts seriously. A very simple but effective form of appreciation is to let the other person finish
Leading with a positive attitude	Project managers with a positive attitude assume that their team will get the job done. The basic attitude alone creates teams with self-responsibility and confidence, which muster the necessary energy and creative power on their own

For example, there may be situations in which a time-critical decision must be made on a particular issue due to various circumstances, yet no consensus can be reached within the team—because there are numerous well-founded arguments both for and against the matter. In such a case, it may be necessary for the project manager to make an authoritative decision, a so-called "final word," in order to maintain momentum and prevent the project from stalling.

However, in an agile environment, an authoritarian leadership style is generally counterproductive—if only because it risks undermining the intrinsic motivation of the team members. Agile teams thrive on self-responsibility, transparency, and collaborative decision-making. An authoritarian intervention can jeopardize the atmosphere of trust and ownership that is essential for agile collaboration.

- **Cooperative or Participative Leadership Style**

  This style is defined by participation, delegation, result-oriented control, transparency, and a strong emphasis on individual responsibility. Often referred to as "team-oriented leadership," it involves team members in decisions, content development, and processes. The guiding principle is cooperate, engage in dialogue, and show appreciation.

The cooperative leadership style requires excellent communication skills, facilitation expertise, trust in the team's capabilities, conflict resolution abilities, and the capacity for self-restraint.

Example In an agile project, backlog prioritization is done collaboratively by the team. The project manager facilitates the discussion but refrains from making unilateral decisions. In our case study, the exact opposite had occurred: there was no communication, no coordination processes, and consequently a lack of orientation and growing demotivation among team members.

- **Democratic Leadership Style**

This leadership approach encourages discussions and group decisions regarding both content and processes. The project manager contributes ideas but ultimately defers the decision-making to the team. Personal and professional preferences of team members are acknowledged and actively integrated into the collaboration.

The democratic leadership style requires patience, decisiveness in consensus-based environments, empathy, ability to recognize diversity, and openness to alternative perspectives.

Example In a user experience (UX) design project, the team jointly decides on usability testing methods, with everyone contributing to the process—resulting in high-quality outcomes, albeit with a slower pace.

- **Situational Leadership Style**

This flexible leadership approach allows the project manager to adapt their style depending on the situation, project phase, team maturity, or the individuals involved. It is based on the belief that leadership should be context-specific rather than guided by a universal formula.

The situational leadership style requires strong analytical thinking, adaptability, high self-awareness, understanding of human behavior, and the ability to make decisions under uncertainty.

Example In a crisis, such as a supplier delay, the project leader may act in a directive manner. During the project kick-off, however, a participative, facilitative approach might be more appropriate.

- **Authentic Leadership Style**

This leadership style is rooted in acting in alignment with personal values such as respect, openness, trust, and tolerance. A project manager who is aware of and guided by their core values—and whose actions reflect these values—demonstrates coherent and reliable leadership behavior. This consistency makes them predictable and trustworthy in the eyes of their team, fostering stability and confidence throughout the project.

The authentic leadership style requires strong value orientation, personal integrity, self-awareness, emotional intelligence, consistency in behavior, and the ability to serve as a role model.

Note: The authentic leadership style does not stand independently of the others but rather influences and shapes how each of the other leadership styles is practiced in real-life situations.

Example A project manager who is transparent about mistakes and takes responsibility strengthens the team's trust, even in challenging project phases.

10.4   Working in a Team

The ability to work in a team, social skills and a high level of leadership competence—soft skills make all the difference.

A team is a group of people who work together, depend on each other, and are jointly responsible for achieving project goals. For each individual this means:

- To network with other team members,
- To be able to respond to other ideas,
- To approve of other interests and successes.

If a team is to deliver top performance, it needs the appropriate resources. These include professional qualifications, appropriate technical equipment, but also cultural and social factors such as team spirit, a sense of community, a culture of openness, appreciation, and tolerance that allows mistakes and learns from them through lessons learned. Equally important are the willingness of team members to assume responsibility, the personal positive attitude of each individual, a common understanding of the project, and a common language.

In fact, the team development process always runs simultaneously on two levels: the factual level, which is about the set task, and the so-called interaction level, which is about the social interaction. Unfortunately, in practice, teams are often defined only by the factual level.

A team always needs a certain lead time and shared experience before the collaboration is beneficial. It must grow together first.[5] Experienced project managers know this. They have the challenging task of accompanying the team, developing it to its best performance, and finding a balance between team and individual work.

The higher the autonomy of a team, the more likely it is that this team will achieve best performance. A prerequisite for this is the participation of the individual team members. A high level of participation suggests a high level of intrinsic motivation, which is positive.

10.4.1 Classic Versus Agile Teams

Chapter 3 was about project management frameworks and how the processes and methods of software development differ in sequential and agile environments. In this paragraph, we take a closer look at teamwork and the prerequisites that lead to successful collaboration in classic and agile teams.

Especially in companies where both models are in use or even combined (hybrid models in Sect. 3.4), project staff should understand both approaches. In this way, prejudices can be reduced and the potential for conflict can be lowered, since misunderstandings are less likely to occur.

The "Classic" Project Manager and His Team
In classic teams, there is a clear distribution of roles and tasks. Each phase has its experts: requirements engineer, SW architect, developer, tester, and many others. Team resources are allocated according to plan for the entire duration of the project.

The project manager is responsible for the overall project and the team leadership. When decisions have to be made, he should consult his or her team—but ultimately he makes the individual decisions himself and bears responsibility for them. The project team is given clear guidelines on how the project should proceed. The project manager coordinates the individual activities and "pulls all the strings." His focus is on coordination. He coordinates the project assignment and project planning with the steering committee and monitors deadlines, costs, quality, and target achievement. If necessary, he procures suitable resources.

---

[5] Surprisingly, it is teams working under high pressure that form high cohesion. Cohesion is good, but not sufficient for project success. After all, the team can also coalesce in its rejection of the project goals.

Agile Teams and Their Scrum Master

Agile teams are established as cross-functional groups. Each of them brings their competencies to the common task and contributes to improving the quality of the product. The whole team is responsible for the quality of the solution. Decisions are made jointly and self-imposed tasks are implemented together. The hierarchy of instructions is eliminated. As a result, the team develops a high degree of self-organization and dynamism.

Accordingly, the focus of project management in the agile environment also differs from that in the sequential environment. For the Scrum master, the focus is less on tight management by directive and more on operational team leadership. In concrete terms, this means that project management consists of,

- Facilitating planning meetings, reviews and retrospectives,
- Supporting the team building process during release planning and initial iterations,
- Ensuring that the defined processes are adhered to,
- Ensuring that all team members are optimally capable of working (e.g., have computers with sufficient memory).

The Scrum master provides orientation. He is responsible for the productivity of his team, ensures that the team members are able to work, and organizes the collaboration. He also removes obstacles that can prevent the team from working. He applies Scrum methods and ensures that the agile principles are adhered to.

The separation between the roles "Project Manager" and "Scrum master" is fluid. The project manager can be a Scrum master, but does not have to be. The Scrum master takes over some of the tasks that belong to the area of the classic project manager, but not all of them either (see Chap. 3). Another part is transferred to the product owner.

Commonalities of Both Approaches

However, there are also several tasks that are identical in both environments. As soon as things get complicated or difficulties arise, it is the task of the project manager (or the person who has taken on the respective subtask) to solve the problems together with the team. This also applies to conflicts within the team.

During the actual implementation of the project, the situational management style is used. To do justice to his task, the project manager therefore needs a feeling for the given situation in order to be able to choose the appropriate behavior in each case. In this way, he can accompany the team in its work and develop it to a good performance.

10.4.2 Methods and Tools for Successful Team Leadership

Successful team leadership is not a matter of luck, but a result that is influenced, among other things, by the methodological competence of the project manager or

Scrum master. Those who take on project management tasks should be familiar with:

- Project management tools,
- Communications techniques,
- Facilitation techniques,
- Creativity techniques,
- Conflict and problem-solving techniques,
- Presentation techniques,
- Leadership techniques, and
- Self-management techniques.

This toolbox of supporting methods should also be known to the team. In this way, the team members can consciously and competently participate in the entire group process and independently solve their tasks with commitment.

> **Example** Presentation techniques are required in many situations. Project managers must present the project status to the steering committee. Product owners present user stories to the developers. Scrum masters have to present impediments and their solution to upper management. Developers may present architectural choices to key stakeholders.

The classic or agile approaches often require different, methodical approaches and tools with regard to team management. The virtual Scrum board which is used in the agile environment may not be a suitable project management tool in the sequential environment.

Basically, many parallels can be drawn. For example, the project manager must be able to "feel" the role he or she should take in a given situation (e.g., facilitator, presenter, leader, mediator, or simply interlocutor).

Successful Meetings Require Facilitation

Facilitation means more than just colorful cards…

Facilitators have the central responsibility of guiding the flow of an event in a focused, structured, and results-oriented manner without taking a position on the content. Their primary tasks include:

- **Creating Orientation and Structure**

  Successful meetings require at first a clear goals (already in the invitation), so that people can prepare themselves. The facilitator clearly communicates the goals, agenda, and ground rules again at the outset and ensures that the process follows a logical and goal-oriented structure.

- **Guiding the Process and Maintaining Oversight**

  They keep the group focused (if necessary), manage time effectively, and steer the discussion through coherent stages to ensure progress.

- **Engaging All Participants and Encouraging Involvement**

  The facilitators fosters active participation from all group members, ensures a respectful atmosphere, and creates space for diverse viewpoints.

- **Supporting Communication and Visualizing Content**

  They ask targeted questions, summarize key points, clarify misunderstandings, bridge differing perspectives, and visualize input and intermediate results in an accessible way.

- **Securing Outcomes and Establishing Accountability**

  The facilitator clearly summarizes the results achieved, ensures transparent documentation, and helps define concrete next steps with shared commitment.

> **Important** Facilitation is a service to the group process.

The facilitator creates the conditions in which others can think, work, discuss, and make decisions effectively. This requires a supportive atmosphere, openness on the part of the participants, taking the roles in the group into account, accompanying visualizations, and—most importantly—a neutral and unbiased stance from the facilitator (Fig. 10.9).

In everyday project work, maintaining the required neutral stance presents a significant challenge. In practice, it is common for the roles of project management and facilitate to become blurred, as the project manager often possesses subject matter expertise or personal interests they wish to contribute. However, by doing so, they risk losing their neutrality, potentially compromising the quality of both the process and its outcomes.

For the project manager, this means that if they intend to contribute content-wise while acting as a facilitator, they should always clearly distinguish when they are guiding the process impartially and when they are expressing their views as a member of the team or in their leadership capacity. In many cases, especially with complex or sensitive topics where the project manager wants to participate substantively, external facilitators are brought in to preserve neutrality. Scrum Masters typically do not face these issues, as their role is defined strictly as process facilitators and they often do not bring in detailed technical expertise.

The facilitation process is governed by fundamental rules of conversation, facilitation, and organization that help ensure meetings are productive, respectful, and goal-oriented:

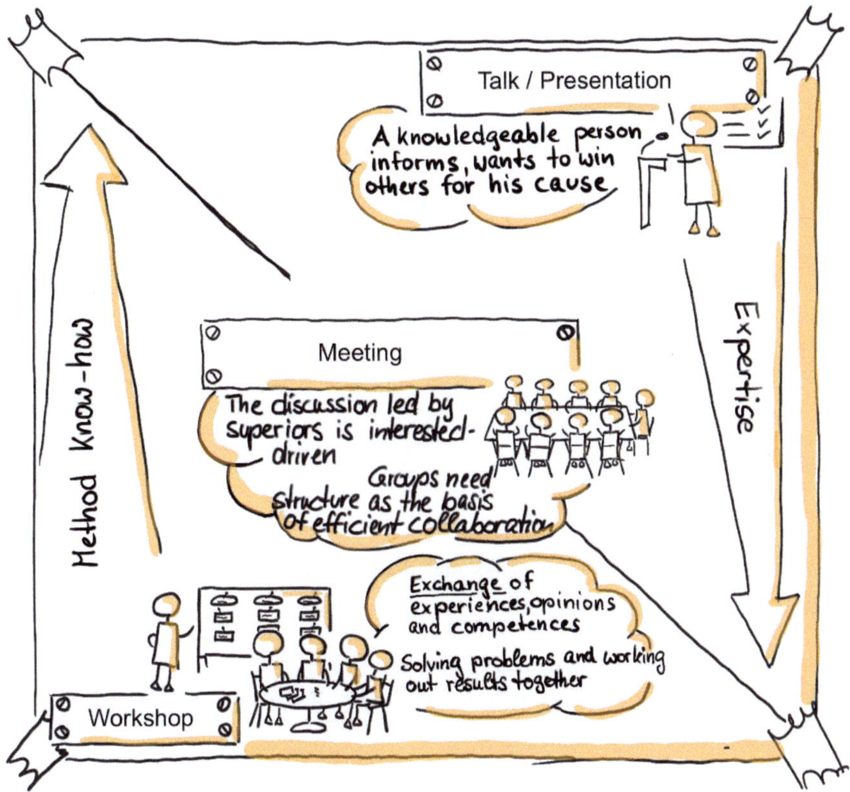

Fig. 10.9 Requirements for workshops, meetings and presentations

- Punctual start and finish: Meetings begin on time and conclude at the scheduled end to respect everyone's time.
- Clear agenda: A well-defined objective and structured agenda promote focus and targeted discussions.
- Active participation and attentiveness: All participants engage actively, listen attentively, and contribute meaningfully.
- Openness and respect: Ideas are shared without prejudice, and dismissive or derogatory remarks are prohibited.
- Separation of critique and idea generation: Criticism is constructive and kept separate from brainstorming to foster creativity.
- Result orientation: Discussions aim at solutions and decisions to achieve concrete outcomes.
- Clear roles: The facilitator ensures structure, manages time, and keeps the process on track.
- Visualization: Key points, results, and action items are made visible to enhance transparency.

Fig. 10.10 The facilitation cycle and possible uses of facilitation methods

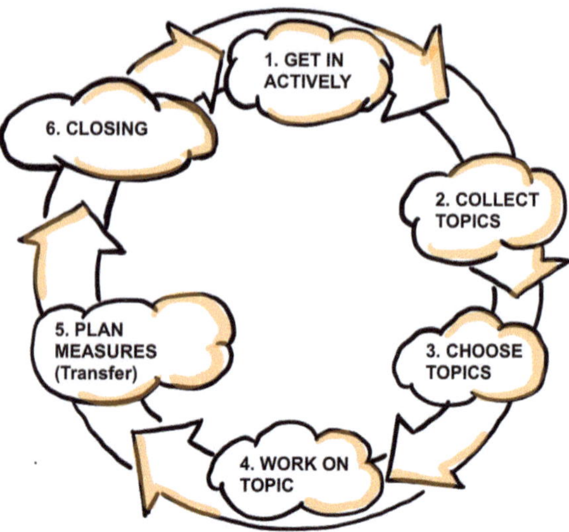

- Commitment: Agreed-upon tasks and decisions are documented and followed up consistently.

The actual execution follows the cycle shown in Fig. 10.10.

After each meeting, the facilitator should save the results in a protocol, which can also be a photo protocol.

> **Example** AI tools for creation of meeting minutes
>
> Today, there are already numerous AI-enhanced tools to automatically produce records or meeting protocols just from recording the audio stream of the meeting. As examples, we refer to two practical articles that describe specific AI tools for creating meeting minutes: (Schultz 2024; Rashidi 2024). However, be aware that AI can make mistakes. Check the protocol and make sure that all important decisions are listed. If necessary, shorten the protocol.

10.4.3 HR Management in the Future: AI Tools and Skills

The progressive integration of artificial intelligence (AI) will fundamentally and sustainably transform all areas of HR management, including talent development, and consequently influence project management processes. In fact, recruitment is already partly driven by AI, especially the publication of job postings and selection of candidates. In a near future, it is probable that all HR activities will be augmented with AI—see (Tursunbayeva 2024) for more details.

The way we develop project-specific competencies is also changing. Traditionally, people followed educational pathways, such as university degrees, long-term training programs, or standardized courses. Today, micro-credentials and interdisciplinary learning formats have become more prominent. Micro-credentials are small, focused certifications obtained through short online courses or specialized workshops. Interdisciplinary learning formats combine knowledge from multiple fields, making courses more lively, more hands-on, and—as a consequence—more interesting to the trainees.

Last, but not least, the processes within the projects themselves are also becoming increasingly AI-driven. This leads to a reduction of certain responsibilities traditionally held by project managers and project teams, while simultaneously creating new tasks and roles. However, using AI-based tools does not reduce the accountability of the project manager. You should take AI governance seriously, since it is required by regulations such as the EU AI Act.

Example It is already possible to create project dashboards using generative AI, which replace the progress reports previously created "by hand." To implement these dashboards, the project manager needs knowledge of prompt engineering techniques. Possibly, the organization will even hire a data scientist whose role is to ensure input data of good quality.

The so-called "future skills" include:

- Digital literacy—being able to use AI-based tools efficiently and effectively
- Critical thinking—being able to work with AI without relying blindly on it
- Collaboration—managing teams with AI-driven copilots as "digital colleagues"
- Ethical awareness—making responsible decisions in AI-driven projects

These skills are becoming an essential component of the competency framework required for the successful implementation of projects.

10.4.4 Team Clock According to Tuckman

All teams—whether operating in traditional or agile environments—undergo a natural developmental process characterized by distinct phases. To effectively guide a team through these stages, project managers should be familiar with Bruce Tuckman's model of team development (Tuckman 1965), which outlines five key phases: Forming, Storming, Norming, Performing, and Adjourning.

According to Tuckman's "team clock" (Fig. 10.11) teams begin by getting to know each other (Forming), then move through a phase of tension and role clarification (Storming), followed by the establishment of shared norms and

Fig. 10.11 Team clock
according to Tuckman

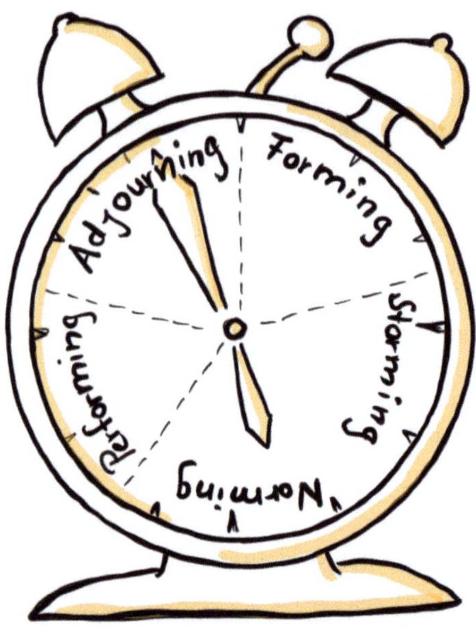

collaboration (Norming). Only after these steps can a team reach peak performance (Performing). Eventually, the team disbands (Adjourning)—a phase often overlooked, yet emotionally significant.

When teams skip the storming phase, unresolved conflicts remain hidden, preventing genuine collaboration. Similarly, changes such as new members or shifting tasks disrupt team cohesion and reset the "team clock," impacting performance.

Tuckman's model shows that conflict is a natural and necessary part of team development. Avoiding it hampers progress; addressing it constructively is essential. Project managers must adapt their leadership style to each phase—recognizing where the team stands is key to guiding them effectively.

Forming—Orientation Phase

In this initial stage, the team comes together, and members begin to get acquainted with one another. There is still a sense of uncertainty, and initial roles, expectations, and rules are tentatively negotiated. The project manager is responsible for assembling the team, clarifying roles and responsibilities, and establishing a transparent framework for collaboration. He or she communicates goals, expectations, and project structures, lays the groundwork for trust, and organizes a collective kick-off meeting. Furthermore, the project manager ensures that clear communication channels are in place from the outset.

Storming—Conflict/Frustration/Power Struggle Phase

In this phase, differing opinions, personal interests, and working styles become apparent. Conflicts may arise, and power struggles or tensions can develop as the team struggles to align on common goals and methods. The project manager plays a crucial role by identifying emerging conflicts early, addressing them openly, encouraging discussions of controversial topics, and fostering a constructive atmosphere for resolution. He facilitates dialogue between divergent viewpoints, mediates discussions, and strengthens the team's willingness to engage in respectful debate. At the same time, he ensures that decision-making processes are transparent and helps each team member find their place and contribution within the project structure.

Norming—Decision/Organization Phase

During the Norming phase, the team begins to establish shared norms, values, and behavioral standards. Trust and cohesion grow, and collaboration becomes more structured and constructive. The project manager actively supports the formation of these common frameworks and ensures adherence to the defined processes. He cultivates team spirit and encourages self-responsible behavior. In addition, he recognizes and makes successes visible, promotes mutual appreciation, and fosters an open and supportive communication culture within the team.

Performing—Production/Performance Phase

At this stage, the team operates with high efficiency, autonomy, and alignment toward shared objectives. Roles and responsibilities are clearly defined, and collaboration flows smoothly. The project manager now primarily assumes the role of a coach and enabler. He creates space for high performance and innovation, ensures the quality of results, and oversees optimal use of resources. Simultaneously, he supports the team in its ongoing development and growth and encourages the use and strengthening of individual talents.

Scrum is designed to help teams reach this performing phase as quickly as possible. A key principle is maintaining "stable teams," as any personnel changes can set the team back into the forming phase.

Adjourning—Farewell/Resolution Phase

This final phase marks the disbanding or transformation of the team, usually upon project completion or organizational restructuring. The project manager orchestrates a structured project closure—through formats such as "lessons learned" workshops and comprehensive project documentation. He acknowledges the team's achievements, facilitates a respectful and appreciative farewell, and supports team members in transitioning to new roles. Additionally, he encourages collective reflection on both the team's accomplishments and its internal dynamics.

Example During a four-day online training course, e.g., on ASQF® CPPM, the group of training participants goes through all five phases of the team clock. The adjourning phase is particularly striking. All questions have been answered, the feedback forms have been filled out, and yet no one hangs up. Trivialities are exchanged to delay the moment of parting.

10.4.5 Team Roles According to M. Belbin

In addition to understanding team development and its various phases, a project manager should also be familiar with the concept of team roles. Team members do not simply act as individuals; they assume specific roles within their team.

Responsibilities and authority are associated with a role. In a Scrum team, "everyone (…) bears responsibility for the success of product development. One assumes this responsibility voluntarily." (Meyer 2014, p. 80). Thus, a role should not to be confused with a position, which is more closely tied to formal responsibilities within the organization. Roles can be categorized as follows:

- **Active Roles**: These reflect what a person aspires to be, such as the efficient worker, the innovator, the achiever, the artist, or the mediator.
- **Passive Roles**: These are often assigned by others, such as the judge, expert, diplomat, sounding board, or the group clown.
- **Formal Roles**: These are officially designated positions, such as department manager, project manager, or team leader.
- **Informal Roles**: These develop over time through collaboration and are recognized by all team members, such as the behind-the-scenes influence, timekeeper, or facilitator.
- **Biographical Roles**: These relate to personal background or experience, such as senior advisors.

Belbin's team role theory explores the various roles individuals assume within a team setting (Belbin 1981). It offers insights into how teams function, how members can recognize and understand their own roles, and how individual strengths can be harnessed while compensating for weaknesses. This model provides valuable perspectives on team dynamics and enables project managers to identify and address role ambiguities or conflicts effectively. It is based on the observation that people complement one another through their diverse characteristics, expertise, and skills, thereby enhancing the team's overall performance.

He identified nine distinct roles within a team, each characterized by unique behavioral patterns, personality traits, and key attributes. Figure 10.12 illustrates these nine roles, which Belbin categorized into three main orientations. Belbin's research suggests that most people are adept at performing two or three of these roles effectively.

According to the Belbin model, several key insights can be drawn for effective teamwork:

Fig. 10.12 Team roles according to Belbin

- **Absence of a Role**: The absence of a specific team role can weaken the team, as a lack of particular competencies cannot simply be compensated for by another role.
- **Role Overlap**: When multiple individuals occupy the same role (e.g., several Shapers or Innovators), it can lead to predictable disruptions and significant potential for conflict.
- **Role Imbalance**: A team with an overabundance of Innovators may struggle to produce a completed result.
- **Team Composition**: A team consisting only of Makers and Innovators may appear impressive but is likely to underperform compared to a team with a well-balanced distribution of roles.
- **Team Size**: Effective teams can be formed with as few as four individuals.

Belbin's team role theory provides project managers with a practical framework to understand team dynamics and align tasks with individual strengths. By recognizing formal, informal, and emergent roles, managers can balance responsibilities, reduce friction, and enhance collaboration. This approach helps address role overlaps early and leverage complementary skills. For example, in a digital platform project, two members both act as "Plants," generating ideas but leaving execution gaps. Introducing a "Completer" (also called "Finisher") ensures balanced progress while maintaining creativity.

However, the optimal composition of team members alone is not sufficient. A positive working environment characterized by mutual respect is equally crucial for effective teamwork. Additionally, well-functioning processes, such as effective communication, are essential for the team's success.

The model does have its limitations. For instance, it overlooks factors like the "chemistry" between team members and the significance of team processes such as communication, coordination, leadership, and interface management. Despite these shortcomings, the model remains valuable for understanding team dynamics.

10.4.6 Roles of the Project Manager

In Chap. 1, we discussed the role-related tasks of project management. Since projects are social systems, the soft skills the project manager are essential. Table 10.2 provides a summary of the skills a project manager needs to effectively handle the tasks associated with each specific role.

Table 10.2 Project manager roles that need soft skills

Role	Task	Suitability/Ability
Coordinator	Clarify goals, distribute work/ tasks, organize processes, coordinate with others	Obliging and consistent (tenacious), diplomatic rather than dominant
Facilitator	Let everyone have their say, make stakeholders out of those affected, recognize and solve problems in communication, summarize, record intermediate results, pay attention to time limits, reflect	Visualize, be neutral - hold back with own opinion, keep the red thread, proceed in a structured way, have methodological competence, control creative processes
Consultant	Clarify relationship problems between team members, technical and methodological issues	Mastering conversation management techniques (e.g., active listening, questioning techniques, formulating I-messages), changing perspectives, pointing out alternatives
Conflict Manager	Resolve role conflicts	Self-confident, open-minded, reflective, aware of own impact
Representative	Represent team interests (project interests) to others	Self-confident, open-minded, reflective, aware of own impact
Negotiator	Negotiate resources (time, money, equipment) with the organization	Realistic, master negotiation strategies
Presenter/Speaker	Present results and successes of the team to the outside world	Visualize, speak and argue - have rhetorical competence, be self-aware of
Coach	Support team members in developing their potential and resolving challenges	Offer consistent backup, encourage, empathize, give personal feedback, nurture trust

10.5 Summary

In this chapter, we provided an overview of "human resource management" and defined key terms essential for understanding the topic. The main points include:

- **Importance of HR Management**: Effective HR management is crucial for successful project management. It is important to differentiate between company-wide HR management and project-specific HR management, which operates on three levels: strategic, operational, and tactical.

- **Project Manager's Tasks**: The responsibilities of a project manager vary depending on the project phase and methodology (sequential or agile). These responsibilities encompass team support in areas such as team building, team management, team development, and team closure.

- **Social Competence/Soft Skills**: Soft skills are critical success factors and a fundamental requirement for a management position. Communication and social skills are intricately linked, with communication being vital for effectively implementing project requirements.

- **Communication Dynamics**: Everything a project manager says or does, or fails to say or do, constitutes communication and has consequential effects. People have subjective and selective perceptions, which can lead to varied interpretations, complicating clear communication.

- **Impact on Motivation**: A project manager's leadership can significantly influence the motivation and commitment of team members, both positively and negatively. Key motivating factors include appreciation, praise, and recognition.

- **Leadership Style**: There is no one-size-fits-all approach to leadership. Each project manager must develop their own leadership style to be perceived as authentic and effective.

- **Team Development Stages**: Teams go through predictable stages of development, as described by Tuckman's model. The roles and tasks of the project manager vary depending on the team's current phase.

- **Team Roles**: According to Meredith Belbin's theory, there are nine distinct team roles that should be represented in any project.

In conclusion, it is essential to be passionate about your work. Foster enthusiasm and a strong desire for team performance, and lead by example. This approach will create the ideal conditions for your team's success.

10.6   Exercises

1. What is the ultimate goal of human resource management in an organization?
2. List the key players of human resource management in an organization.
3. Name the six domains of HR management tasks and discuss one of them in more detail.
4. Explain the role of tactical HR management in contrast to strategic and operational HR management.
5. Name the three core activities of HR management as cross-cutting task.
6. Name three main HR activities of a project manager that are probably required during project planning.
7. Explain the interaction between company-wide and project-related human resources management.
8. Name the four phases of team support.
9. Describe what tasks the project manager performs within the different phases of team support. What is the importance of this for the project?
10. Name core competencies that a project manager should have in any case.
11. Using our case study, describe why the project manager's soft skills are important to project success or failure.
12. Which social skills of team members influence are important to project success or failure.
13. Name the four essential aspects that make up social competence.
14. Explain why communication is inherently difficult.
15. Name and describe the positive and negative effects of verbal and non-verbal communication.
16. What basic rules should a project manager observe when expressing criticism?
17. Define motivation and demotivation.
18. Explain the difference between intrinsic and extrinsic motivation and how you can influence it as a project manager.
19. Using our case study, describe where recognition and appreciation could serve as a motivating factor.
20. Explain the difference between appreciation and praise.
21. Explain why leadership is important for project success and name core aspects of leadership.
22. Explain the difference between participative, situational, and authentic leadership styles
23. Explain why it is important as a leader to be self-aware.
24. Describe how project management differs in sequential and agile project management frameworks.
25. Use the case study to explain why method and tool skills are a critical factor for team leadership.
26. Provide an example of a situation, in which a project manager needs presentation techniques.
27. Explain why it is important that the facilitator of a meeting keeps a neutral attitude.

28. Outline Tuckman's team clock, explaining his approach.
29. Depending on the team development phase, name possible actions of the project manager.
30. Explain what roles are assumed by the team members according to M. Belbin.
31. Outline the different competencies and tasks of the project manager depending on the role he/she assumes in the project.

References

(Agarwal 2023): U. A. Agarwal, K. Jain, V. Anantatmula, S. Shankar: Managing People in Projects for High Performance, Springer Nature, 2023

(Meyer 2014): Meyer, B., Agile!: The Good, the Hype and the Ugly. Berlin, Heidelberg: Springer, https://doi.org/10.1007/978-3-319-05155-0

(Belbin 1981): Belbin, R. M., Management Teams: Why They Succeed or Fail. London: Heinemann. ISBN 978-0434901265

(Hagemann 2023): Hagemann, M., A Leadership Paradigm Shift to 'Eclectic Leadership. Springer Gabler. https://doi.org/10.1007/978-3-658-41578-5

(Ng et al. 2004): Ng, S. T., Skitmore, R. M., Lam, K. C. & Poon, A. W. C. (2004) 'Demotivating factors influencing the productivity of civil engineering projects', International Journal of Project Management, 22(2), pp. 139–146. https://doi.org/10.1016/S0263-7863(03)00061-9

(Peters & Waterman 1984): Thomas J. Peters, Robert H. Waterman, In Search of Excellence: Lessons from America's Best-run Companies, Collins Business Essentials, ISBN 978-0063380028.

(Rashidi 2024): Rashidi, S., How To Use AI To Make You Faster And Better At Your Job, Forbes, 4 October. Available at: https://www.forbes.com/sites/solrashidi/2024/10/04/ai-tools-that-can-make-you-faster-and-better-at-your-job/

(Schultz 2024): Schultz, B., 8 AI meeting assistants to consider in 2025, TechTarget Search Unified Communications, 30 December. Available at: https://www.techtarget.com/searchunifiedcommunications/tip/AI-meeting-assistants-to-consider

(Troger 2022): Troger, H., Resetting Human Resource Management. Springer. https://doi.org/10.1007/978-3-031-06166-0

(Tuckman 1965): Bruce W. Tuckman: Developmental Sequence in Small Groups. Psychological Bulletin, 63(6), 384–399. https://doi.org/10.1037/h0022100

(Tursunbayeva 2024): Aizhan Tursunbayeva, Augmenting Human Resource Management with Artificial Intelligence: Towards an Inclusive, Sustainable, and Responsible Future, 2024, https://doi.org/10.1007/978-3-031-75266-7

(Visser & Arnold 2022): Max Visser, Thomas C. Arnold, Recognition and Work in the Platform Economy: a Normative Reconstruction, Philosophy of Management (2022) 21:31–45, Springer, https://doi.org/10.1007/s40926-021-00172-2

(Vo et al. 2022): Vo, T.T.D.; Tuliao, K.V.; Chen, C.-W. Work Motivation: The Roles of Individual Needs and Social Conditions. Behav. Sci. 2022, 12, 49, https://doi.org/10.3390/bs12020049

(Waters & Sroufe 1983): E. Waters; L.A. Sroufe, Social Competence as a Developmental Construct, Developmental Review, 3(1), 79–97.

(Watzlawick, Beavin & Jackson 1967): Watzlawick, P., Beavin, J. H. & Jackson, D. D. Pragmatics of Human Communication: A Study of Interactional Patterns, Pathologies, and Paradoxes. New York: W. W. Norton & Company. ISBN 978-0-393-31006-3.

(Wong 2018): Zachary Wong: The Eight Essential People Skills for Project Management: Solving the Most Common People Problems for Team Leaders, 256 pages, ISBN-13 978-1523097937

Maturity Models 11

First: Now it's getting a bit more technical again. This last content chapter is about maturity models. Maturity models describe the state of the art that has been established for the qualitative development of systems and are used to assess processes and their quality in a specific project. They also provide guidance on what an organization could improve, how and where. Basically, it is a collection of best practices, combined with a rating scale, which should enable an assessment of projects that is as objective as possible (i.e., independent of the individual organization).

There is a whole series of different maturity models with names that are sometimes reminiscent of science fiction movies: CMMI®, SPICE, OPM3®, and many more. Each of these models has a special focus. We will discuss CMMI® and SPICE in more detail in a moment, but we will clearly focus on SPICE, since this standard is worldwide used.

Warning Do not confuse the maturity models described here with the process models and frameworks introduced in Chap. 3 for mastering individual software projects. The maturity models described in this chapter follow another tradition inspired by the general idea of process improvement—especially software process improvement (SPI)—for entire organizations, leaving behind the boundaries of a single software project.

Maturity models are the central vehicle and benchmark for long-term and systematic software process improvements designed to improve the performance and maturity of the entire organization's processes as a whole and measured against international standards such as CMMI, ISO/IEC 330xx, or ISO 9000.

OPM3 stands for "Organizational Project Management Maturity Model." It is propagated by the Project Management Institute (PMI®) and, as the name suggests, focuses on the topic of project management. It is used primarily—and almost

A. Johannsen et al., *Foundations for Software Project Management in Classic and Agile Environments*, https://doi.org/10.1007/978-3-032-16797-2_11

exclusively—in US-based or large international conglomerates (Maylor & Turner 2022).[1]

11.1   The Basic Principle of Maturity Models

Most maturity models are similar in their basic principle. First of all, the area to be assessed is divided into categories, which we will call "process groups".[2] For example, all processes around software development can be grouped into a process group called "engineering processes."

For each of these process groups, the model provides us with a list of associated processes that belong to it, and for each of these processes, in turn, the respective "practices." Under these practices, one must imagine relatively generic instructions on how the process can be implemented. In other words, the maturity model specifies which activities are included in the respective process and, to some extent, which work results are to be produced.

The practices provide the basis for an assessment, because when an assessor analyzes the processes in a real project, he naturally expects to find the very application of these practices. However, since no one wants to prescribe exactly how organizations should name their documents or which method they should use to perform their risk analysis, the practices are inevitably rather general. They are therefore not necessarily proven procedures in the sense of "best practices," but rather generic or base practices. For example, in the SPICE maturity model, the "Management" process group states (simplified), "Create a project schedule. Assign resources to activities, arrange activities in a sequence, and determine when to perform them." Recommendation such as "Do not use spreadsheets for this task, if you can avoid it," are looked for in vain in maturity models. SPICE and CMMI assess compliance with practices based on the evidence required. The maturity models do not provide methods of how this is to be done.

Maturity models are very valuable. The compilation of the individual practices alone already contains a great deal of experience, and not just that of a single company, but the cumulative experience of all the players involved in the creation of the maturity model. It is therefore certainly a good recommendation to follow this guidance. The result of a process can only get better as a result. Maturity models therefore draw their right to exist from three essential points:

---

[1] Not a maturity model in the true sense of the word, but nevertheless highly interesting for project managers is SFIA, the Skills Framework for the Information Age. It is about the evaluation of soft skill competencies in the IT industry. SFIA is unfortunately far too little known and goes beyond the scope of this book. If you are interested, you can find out more about it on the SFIA Foundation's website: https://www.sfia-online.org/en.

[2] The term "process group" does not really apply to OPM3. OPM3 mentions the domains "project management," "program management," and "portfolio management." However, the basic idea is identical.

1. They offer assistance to anyone who needs to redefine processes. No one has to reinvent the wheel.
2. They enable projects or organizations to identify weaknesses or potential for improvement. If a project lacks evidence such as an activity schedule or sprint planning, there is definitely potential for improvement.
3. Assessment reports can be used as objective evidence when the quality of a process is questioned.

The last point brings us to the implementation of the assessment. In Chap. 8, in connection with quality assurance for processes, we have already discussed audits. In the case of maturity models, we speak of "assessments".[3] The main difference is that assessments do not provide a "hop or top" rating, i.e., they do not end in a "pass" or "fail" like audits. Instead, an evaluation of the various process areas takes place. This means that individual processes can reach a certain level, while others do not. This allows the strengths and weaknesses in individual areas to be identified in a targeted manner.

The process of an assessment is very similar to that of audits. The individual processes are measured against the practices defined in the maturity model, which form the guide through the assessment, so to speak.

Assessments serve to judge the quality of the processes. For this reason, every maturity model contains a maturity dimension in addition to the process dimension already described. This defines the "grading system" and thus forms the yardstick against which each activity in the process is measured. The SPICE maturity model already mentioned defines six capability levels from 0 to 5 (see Fig. 11.1). Level 5 is the best rating an organization can achieve. Of course, each maturity model has its own benchmark. Assessors learn this in their training.

11.2 Historical Development

The history of maturity models began in the second half of last century. In 1989, Watts Humpfrey (1989) from the famous Software Engineering Institute (SEI) came up with the good idea of collecting best practices in software development and making them available to everyone. This resulted in the first maturity model for software development, the Capability Maturity Model CMM.

Due to the increasing complexity of software, people realized that software development projects might require a little more care and systematics than previously thought if one did not want to blow a lot of money. Accordingly, CMM was gratefully taken up; in particular by the US Department of Defense, which had also financed the development of the model.

---

[3] In CMMI, assessments are officially called "appraisals." However, for the sake of simplicity, we will stick to the SPICE terminology.

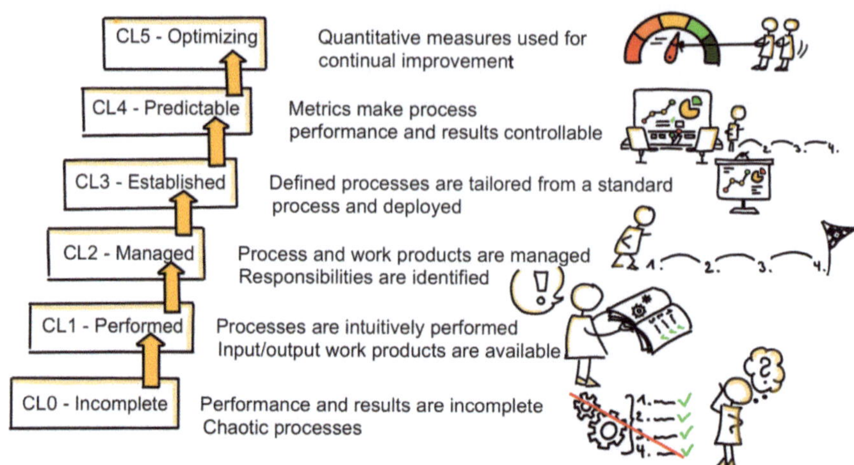

Fig. 11.1 Capability levels (CL) from ISO/IEC 330xx (SPICE)

CMM quickly became very successful. This led to the development of further maturity models for other areas. About 10 years later, things had become so confusing that CMMI was brought into being. CMMI stands for "Capability Maturity Model Integration." Again, the U.S. Department of Defense together with the Software Engineering Institute (SEI) were the main players. CMMI is now in use worldwide, and the latest version is from 2023 (ISACA 2023). Strictly speaking, it is not one but three models covering different disciplines (hence the "I" for "integration"):

- CMMI for Development (short: CMMI-DEV) deals with product development (be it hardware, software, or systems);
- CMMI for Services (CMMI-SVC for short) addresses the topic of "services" and
- CMMI for acquisition (short: CMMI-ACQ) deals with the purchase of hardware, software, or systems.

In 1993, after things became increasingly confusing, two well-known standardization bodies, the International Organization for Standardization (ISO) and the International Electrotechnical Commission (IEC), came together to jointly define rules on what such models used for quantitative assessments should actually look like. Behind this was the desire to define assessment scales that were as comparable as possible.

The working group was called SPICE—an acronym for "Software Process Improvement and Capability determination".[4]

SPICE was only the project name. The result of the project was ISO/IEC 15504 (even though SPICE is still often used as a synonym). Today, ISO/IEC 330xx describes internationally the SPICE standard and is more widespread than CMMI. The extent of adoption, however, strongly depends on the industry, region, and regulatory requirements. Moreover, the two models have largely converged. CMMI fulfills the requirements of ISO/IEC 330xx and there are only a few differences in content. If a project passes a maturity level in CMMI, it can be assumed that it will also reach the corresponding level in SPICE. Ultimately, the same practices have proven themselves worldwide.

11.3   A Few Details About CMMI

CMMI distinguishes between two forms of representation: Staged representation and continuous representation.

The level representation determines the maturity level of the organization as a whole. It is a kind of "overall grade," but does not allow any statement about selective strengths in sub-areas. This is provided by the continuous representation, which reflects the capability level of individual process areas and specifically shows the strengths and weaknesses in individual areas.

The rating scale for CMMI has a total of five maturity levels:

- **Level 1—Initial**

  If practices are implemented at all, it is due to the initiative of individual project staff and is not a credit to the organization.

- **Level 2—Managed**

  The processes are carried out, but they can look different from project to project. Either there are no uniform specifications, or they are not observed.

- **Level 3—Defined**

  The process has been established throughout the organization. In addition, there is the possibility of process tailoring and initial evaluations of lessons learned.

- **Level 4—Quantitatively Managed**

  The process is predictable and monitored with metrics.

---

[4] Originally, SPICE stood for "Software Process Improvement and Capability Evaluation." Unfortunately, "evaluation" in French has a very judgmental connotation. It's not about "pass or fail," but about determining a position with regard to improvements. But the acronym was too nice to give up—so the meaning was changed.

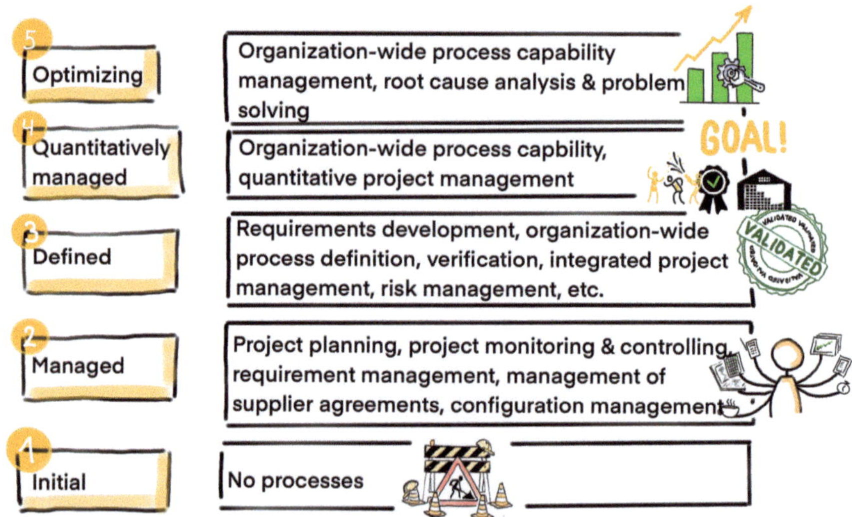

Fig. 11.2 Assignment of the process groups to the CMMI levels

- **Level 5—Optimizing**

  The processes are continuously improved.

CMMI defines specific and generic objectives and practices per process area. While generic goals and practices are general, i.e., valid for all process areas, specific goals and practices clearly refer to the respective process area. Generic practices are, e.g., (simplified stated): "Perform the specific practices," "Plan the processes," and "Provide resources." Specific practices for the process area "Project Planning" are, e.g., "Define the project scope" (referring to the WBS), "Estimate effort and costs" and "Identify project risks".[5]

By the way, it depends on the targeted maturity level which process groups have to be considered at all. Figure 11.2 shows the assignment of some process groups to the maturity levels, with the groups relevant for project management highlighted in bold.

CMMI has been developed further in recent years and v3.0 was released in 2023. For more detail, go to the CMMI Institute (https://cmmiinstitute.com), which is now part of ISACA (Information Systems Audit and Control Association) for the latest developments concerning CMMI (ISACA 2023).

---

[5] It would go beyond the scope of this book to list all practices relevant to project management. Anyone who wants or needs to specifically use CMMI in their project should attend a more in-depth training course on the subject.

11.4 Further Details on ISO/IEC 330xx (SPICE)

Project evaluations based on ISO/IEC 330xx usually prefer the continuous representation form. After all, it is less about an "overall score" than about identifying potential for improvement. The basic structure is also somewhat different from CMMI. While CMMI links the process areas to maturity levels, ISO/IEC 330xx allows you to freely compile the process areas to be considered. This makes the standard particularly suitable for organizations that do not want to put everything to the test right away, but only see a need for improvement in certain areas (e.g., in software development). The disadvantage of the lack of assignment is that SPICE does not suggest an order for improvements.

Figure 11.3 once again shows the capability levels, from ISO/IEC 330xx (ISO 33001:2015; Ayed 2018, p. 23; ISO 33020:2019). Each level is assigned so-called process attributes, for which generic practices and work results are defined in turn. In the assessment, the degree of fulfillment of these process attributes is evaluated according to a four-level scale:

- N: 0–15% = not achieved
- P: 16–50% = partially achieved
- L: 51–85% = mostly achieved
- F: 86–100% = completely achieved

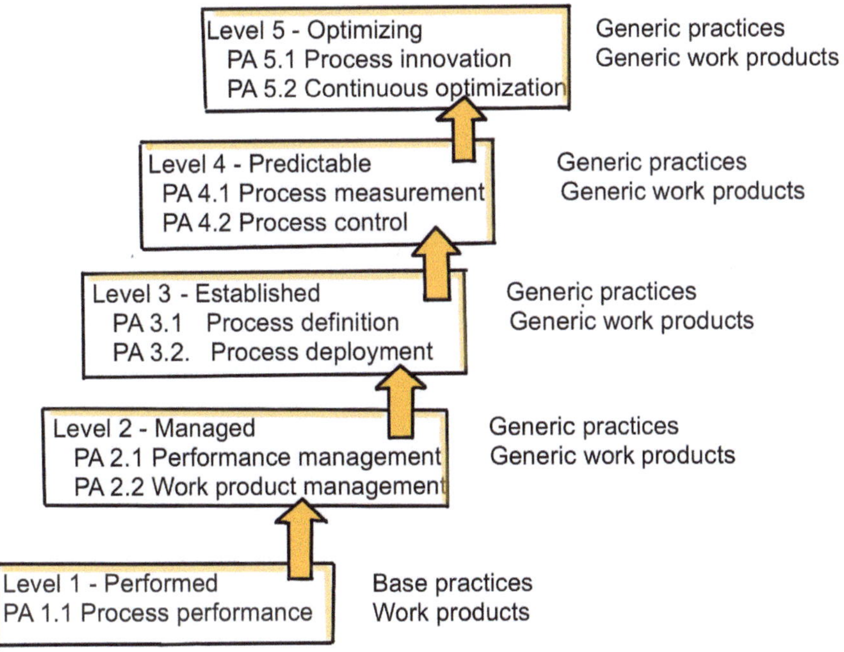

Fig. 11.3 Assignment of process attributes to capability levels in ISO/IEC 330xx

If the process attributes of a level result in a "Largely," the tested level of the process is considered to be passed. However, only when all process attributes of a maturity level have been assessed with "F" is the transition to the next level possible.

As already mentioned, the whole SPICE project was started to make assessments comparable. Accordingly, ISO/IEC 330xx actually only contains requirements for the models, not the models themselves. The standard distinguishes between the Process Reference Model (PRM) and the Process Assessment Model (PAM).

PRM and PAM always belong together. The PRM describes the processes to be implemented (process group, process name, goal, results).

The Process Assessment Model (PAM) always refers to the PRM and describes the required generic and base practices and process attributes. It thus provides the basis for assessing the maturity level, which is why it is also called the Process Assessment Model. ISO/IEC 330xx contains an exemplary PAM, which is described in ISO 33060 to ISO 33079. Anyone performing an assessment according to ISO/IEC 330xx therefore refers to these sources.

The separation of requirements for the model and the model itself used makes it possible to define domain-specific maturity models. This is also eagerly used in practice. The derived maturity models are then called Automotive SPICE®, SPICE4SPACE, Medical SPICE or TestSPICE, to name just a few examples.[6]

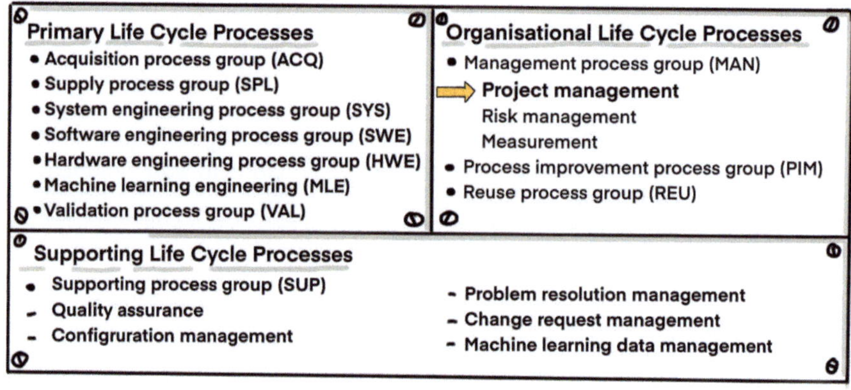

Fig. 11.4 Overview of the process groups in Automotive SPICE® based on ISO/IEC 330xx

---

[6] Unfortunately, there are many, partly competing maturity models. Automotive SPICE® is most common, it is used in 51 countries and there are more than 7500 assessors (VDA QMC 2023). In addition to Medical SPICE, there is also MediSPICE, and in addition to TestSpice, there is also TMMI®, which is based on CMMI. In practice, it depends on the respective context which of the models achieves the highest degree of diffusion.

Table 11.1 Mapping of base practices from Automotive SPICE® to the ASQF® CPPM syllabus

ISO/IEC 33xx (base practices)	Textbook chapter
MAN.3 BP1: Define the scope of work	4—Project initiation
MAN.3 BP2: Define project life cycle	3—Projectmanagement frameworks in SW development
MAN.3 BP3: Evaluate feasibility of the project	4—Project initiation
MAN.3 BP4: Define and monitor work packages	5—Projectplanning
MAN.3 BP5: Define and monitor project estimates and resources	5—Projectplanning
MAN.3 BP6: Define and monitor required skills, knowledge and experience	10—HR management
MAN.3 BP7: Define and monitor project interfaces and agreed commitments	5—Projectplanning
MAN.3 BP8: Identify and monitor project schedule	5—Projectplanning 6—Project implementing and controlling
MAN.3 BP9: Ensure consistency	5—Projectplanning 6—Project implementing and controlling
MAN.3 BP10: Review and report progress of the project	6—Project implementing and controlling 7—Projectacceptance and closing

Figure 11.4 shows an overview of the process groups as defined in Automotive SPICE®, that is specifically based on ISO/IEC 33002 (ISO 33002:2015) and ISO/IEC 33004 (ISO 33004:2015). Project management belongs to the organizational processes.

Presenting SPICE in further detail would go beyond the scope of this book. The interested reader is referred to (Hoermann et al. 2022). Therefore, only this much: The 10 base practices that the standard provides for the MAN.3 project management process group are all covered in this textbook, as Table 11.1 shows.

11.5 Maturity Models and Agile—A Contradiction?

Admittedly, practically all maturity models were developed having sequential project management frameworks in mind. This is simply because Agile was not yet a topic at that time.

In fact, maturity models in no way contradict Agile. After all, they only describe **WHAT is** to be done, not **HOW**. The former can be considered independently of the project management framework and thus can be evaluated. The second depends on the project management framework, but plays no role from the perspective of maturity assessment. On the contrary, if we look at the Scrum framework, we will see how many of the practices of the project management processes required by the maturity models are already delivered "free of charge" here.

11.6   Summary

In this last content chapter, the concept of maturity models was introduced. Maturity models can serve as a basis for assessing development processes and as a guide for process improvement.

The two best-known maturity models in the context of software development are CMMI® and ISO/IEC 330xx (SPICE).

11.7   Exercises

1. Name the different maturity models which may serve in project management.
2. Describe the underlying principle of all maturity models.
3. Using a self-selected example, explain the principle of different maturity levels.

References

(Ayed 2018): Ayed, H., Guiding Agile Methods Customization: the AMQuICk Framework. PhD thesis. Namur: Université de Namur. ISBN 978-2-39029-023-0. Available at: https://doi.org/10.5281/zenodo.1475150

(Hoermann et al. 2022): Hoermann, Klaus; Pepe, Guiseppe; Wall, Dan; Zhang, Yanhua: The guide for Automotive SPICE® Interpretation. Kugler Maag CIE GmbH, 2022.

(Humpfrey 1989): Humphrey WS, Managing the software process. Addison-Wesley, Reading, MA.

(ISACA 2023): CMMI V3.0 – Capability Maturity Model Integration. 1st edn. Schaumburg, IL: ISACA. Available at: https://cmmiinstitute.com/products/cmmi/content-release

(ISO 33001:2015): ISO/IEC 33001:2015(E) – Information technology – Process assessment – Concepts and terminology. 1st edn. Geneva: ISO. Available at: https://www.iso.org/standard/54175.html

(ISO 33002:2015): ISO/IEC 33002:2015(E) – Information technology – Process assessment – Requirements for performing process assessment. International Organization for Standardization. Available at: https://www.iso.org/standard/54176.html

(ISO 33004:2015): ISO/IEC 33004:2015(E) – Information technology – Process assessment – Requirements for process reference, process assessment and maturity models. International Organization for Standardization. Available at: https://www.iso.org/standard/54178.html

(ISO 33020:2019): ISO/IEC 33020:2019(E) – Information technology – Process assessment – Process measurement framework for assessment of process capability. International Organization for Standardization. Available at: https://www.iso.org/standard/78526.html

(Maylor & Turner 2022): Maylor, H. & Turner, N., Project Management (5th ed.). Pearson. ISBN: 978-1-292-08843-3.

(VDA QMC 2023): VDA Quality Management Center, Automotive SPICE® Process Assessment Model and Process Reference Model Version 4.0. Edited by the VDA QMC Working Group 13. Available at: https://vda-qmc.de/wp-content/uploads/2023/12/Automotive-SPICE-PAM-v40.pdf

Summary 12

12.1   The Most Important Facts in Short

Why do we need software project management? Computer science is a young discipline compared to engineering. In addition, software sometimes has completely different characteristics than physical engineering products such as buildings, machines. This results in special requirements for software development.

Introduction: Given the still high failure rates of IT projects, the importance of project management has increased significantly today compared to the past. Modern approaches such as agile frameworks ensure that the industry continues to develop positively. This book summarizes the basics of modern software project management. Apart from the theory, the book also reflects the authors' years of practical experience in this field.

Chapter 1: To ensure the most uniform terminology possible, we first introduced the most important terms and concepts of project management. We used the international standard on "Project Management," ISO 21502:2020, as a basis.

The diverse requirements for the competence of a project manager were also a topic. Since most projects do not fail because of technical difficulties but because of interpersonal aspects, the "soft" factors, also called "soft skills", were a recurring theme throughout the book.

Chapters 2–4: Next, the book covered the four basic organizational forms of project management. In addition to the organizational structure, the project process organization was presented. This refers to the sum of the software development processes planned for a project, as well as the information flows between the individual task managers and the project committees.

Chapter 3 described the most common project management frameworks of today' software projects. A distinction was made between two fundamentally different worlds: sequential project management frameworks on the one hand and agile frameworks on the other hand.

Chapter 4 dealt with what is known as project initiation, i.e., the beginning of any project. Both the technical task involved in initiating the project and the interpersonal activities and methods are crucial, as a project usually ends as well—or as chaotically—as it began. Therefore, every effort should be made to set up a project as precisely and structured as possible.

Chapter 5 and 6: From Chap. 5 onwards, the focus was on the core of a project manager's daily work—starting with project planning (Chap. 5) and later, in Chap. 6, focusing on the management and control of projects. In the process, the sequential and agile approaches were systematically compared.

In the sequential environment, planning is usually done at a relatively early stage. The "classic" project manager works with milestone planning and work breakdown structure from which he or she analytically derives the effort planning, the detailed activity schedule, and the detailed cost planning. This initial planning must then be achieved as a fixed goal during project implementing—often "at any price."

In the agile environment, planning is also done, probably even more, but iteratively, at the beginning of each iteration repeatedly, constantly updating the first version of the iteration and release planning, making it (hopefully) more realistic.

The management and control of projects also differs significantly depending on the environment. In the sequential environment, projects are controlled at activity level, while in the agile environment they are controlled based on tasks and with the help of transparency and inspection, e.g., by means of daily stand-up meetings and burndown charts. The decisive difference is that in a sequential project management framework, changes are seen as a disruptive factor. They tend to be undesirable and are handled via change management. In agile frameworks, changes are seen as normal, are basically welcome, and can be incorporated and controlled in future iterations at any time.

Chapters 7–9: Project acceptance and closing are basically similar in both worlds, but they happen at different points in time. In the agile environment, milestone and project acceptance generally take place at the end of each iteration (i.e., incrementally over the entire project duration). In sequential project management frameworks, final acceptance usually occurs at the end of the project, with milestone acceptances serving as interim approvals along the way.

Quality assurance (Chap. 8) and risk management (Chap. 9) are not one-time events, but two essential, parallel processes in every software development project. They should, therefore, already be prepared in detail during project initiation and in the project planning phase and should be carried out accordingly in later phases.

Chapter 10: In Chap. 10, things got human. Here, the focus was on the outstanding importance of various success factors of HR management for project success. The role of classic project management has changed drastically from sequential to agile environments. Whereas in the classic picture the project manager as a person still played the leading and decisive role, pulling all the strings and generally bearing responsibility, in the agile environment the role of "project management" tends to be depersonalized and rests on all shoulders of the project team.

Whoever takes on project management tasks should be aware of his or her impact. Topics such as social competence, communication, motivation, and leadership are therefore extremely important. Facilitation in particular is always important (regardless of the project management framework) in the project. The chapter also provided insight into typical team development processes and team roles.

Chapter 11: At the end of the book, we took a brief look beyond the actual project business and looked at the importance of maturity models on the organizational level. These provide the basis for assessing the software development process within the organization and thus serve as a starting point for continuous process improvements—which extend far beyond the lifetime of a single project.

12.2   Outlook

This book is an introduction to the topic "software project management." Therefore, some topics that are more or less closely related to project management in companies could not be covered. These include the topics of multi-project management and governance.[1] In this section, we do not want to "catch up" on these topics, but instead venture a brief outlook on a trend in software project management that is relevant in agile environments.

Let us have a look on current trends around agile frameworks. What is happening in this environment? What is currently being discussed?

12.2.1   Design Thinking

Design thinking, which shows strong similarities to agile paradigms, is one of the approaches that has been increasingly discussed recently. Design thinking was first developed by (Kelley 2005; and Brown 2008), and later promoted in practice by Hasso Plattner—among other things, by founding the "d-school"—and further expanded in research (Plattner et al. 2013). It is a user-centered approach to product and service development that is intended to lead to problem solving and the development of new ideas and products, and is built on three equally important fundamental principles. These principles are:

---

[1] Loosely translated: control/regulation (in this case of project management processes).

1. Interdisciplinary teams.
2. Freedom to think and act.
3. Highly iterative design process.

Design thinking is not so much a single method, but rather a combination of fundamental attitudes. That is why it is also referred to as an "approach." The basic idea is to bring people from different disciplines together in an environment that promotes creativity and to let them work as freely as possible.

One premise of design thinking is that product innovation always takes place at the intersection of desirability (user), feasibility (project resources and economic efficiency (management). This is strongly reminiscent of the general conflict of goals in project management—the triangle of deadlines, costs, and functional scope.

The procedure for a product and service development project according to the design thinking approach is shown in Fig. 12.1.

The six phases can be roughly divided into three areas: At the beginning, we have the exploratory and creative approach to the inexplicable, challenging or seemingly unsolvable, followed by conjectures, many attempts, and deductions. In the end, we have a converging process toward crystallizing and optimizing solutions.

The focus of the first phase ("**Understanding**") is the design challenge. It is the "assignment" for the development team to find the right questions and understand the design problem.

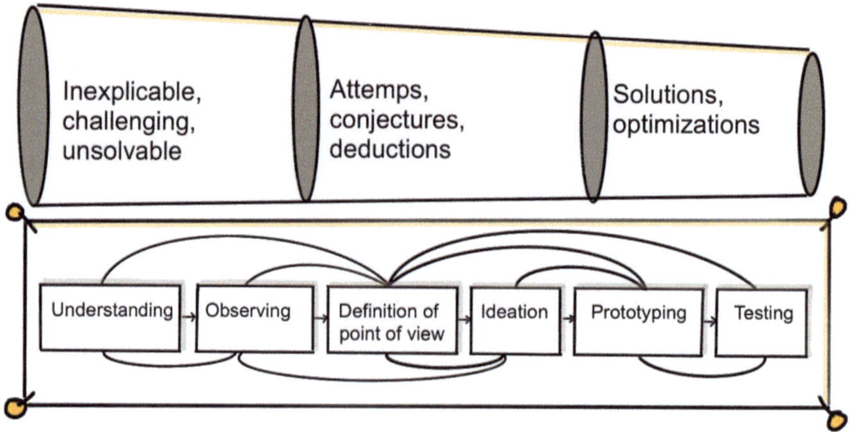

Fig. 12.1 Phases of the design thinking process, based on (Plattner et al. 2013)

Example In our case study, the right design challenge would be: How can basic graphics functionalities for cockpits and displays in vehicles be made available to development engineers seamlessly?

Based on this, the team creates a suitable project plan for the task, and tries to research relevant knowledge to become "ad hoc experts" on the challenge as soon as possible.

In the second phase ("**Observing**"), the team tries to dive as deeply as possible into the role of the user and learn as much as possible about the task and the problem. Observations, user interviews or trial and error are part of this phase of "Observing."

In the third, (now converging) phase of "**Definition of point of view**," the task is to look through and prioritize the vast amounts of information and knowledge. The condensation of information into viewpoints corresponds to the procedure from classic product design. This is where the name "Design Thinking" comes from. However, other methods are used, in particular personas, stakeholder maps and customer journey maps.

In the fourth phase ("**Ideation**"), the team is finally allowed to formulate solutions to the problem, which usually takes the form of several brainstorming sessions.

The fifth phase ("**Prototyping**") involves initial testing of ideas using first rough and improvised prototypes, which can be sketches, mockups, stories, videos, or even just storytelling. The principle here is: The less effort that went into the prototype, the more honest the feedback will be!

In the sixth phase ("**Testing**"), the emphasis remains on rapid, iterative feedback and testing of the prototypes, and merging of the results.

Due to the similarities between design thinking on the one hand and agile product development approaches on the other, some companies are currently combining the strengths of design thinking as a method for the creative identification of innovations with agile project management approaches in the implementation of these innovations. Design thinking today evolved from a trend to an established approach for innovative, industrial design.

12.2.2 Other Trends

This textbook cannot cover all the topics and trends in modern software project management, but we will briefly highlight a few of them as a short outlook:

- Remote project management will continue to increase in importance, including support for digital nomads as well as special problems of global virtual project teams.
- AI in software project management will spread to all areas, spanning from routine task support (e.g., status reports, time tracking, documentation), to

advanced AI-services for predictive analytics to identify risks early, and estimate schedules more realistically, or select and recruit suitable staff.

- Regulation and data protection (e.g., EU AI Act, GDPR, other national data protection laws) will more deeply influence how projects are planned, data collected and tools selected.
- In general, ethics and sustainable software project management will play an increased role, not only because of the widespread use of AI-tools.
- The trend from project to Product (Portfolio) management and optimization of the overall lifecycle of software will remain in its significance.
- Software security will further come to the forefront within the projects. Approaches such as DevSecOps will become the norm: security is not an add-on, but integrated into CI/CD pipelines, development cycles, etc.

We would like to conclude with citing Lawrence Peters, who wrote an insightful and thought-provoking chapter on myths of project management (Peters 2023, p. 108):

> It has been shown that the management of software projects is where we can obtain the highest leverage [...] and the greatest return on investment if only we turn our attention to it.

This aligns perfectly with the authors' own experience and underlines the lasting importance of human interaction and soft skills—a pattern that, in our view, will continue to prevail even in the forthcoming, technology-driven era of AI in software project management. We hope that this book contributes to raising the level of project management training and, in doing so, helps to further improve the success rates of projects in our field.

References

(Brown 2008): Brown, T., Design Thinking, in: Harvard Business Review, 86th ed. (2008), June, pp. 84–92.

(ISO 21502:2020): International Organization for Standardization (ISO), ISO 21502:2020(E) – 292 Project, programme and portfolio management — Guidance on project management. Geneva: 293 ISO.

(Kelley 2005): Kelley, Tom, The Ten Faces of Innovation: IDEO's Strategies for Defeating the Devil's Advocate and Driving Creativity Throughout Your Organization, Crown Business Publishers.

(Peters 2023): Peters, L., Software Project Management Myths. In V. Gupta, L. Rubalcaba, C. Gupta & T. Hanne (Eds.), Sustainability in Software Engineering and Business Information Management: Proceedings of the Conference SSEBIM 2022 (pp. 98–110). Springer. https://doi.org/10.1007/978-3-031-32436-9

(Plattner, Meinel & Weinberg 2013): Plattner, H., Meinel, C., & Weinberg, U. Design Thinking: Understand – Improve – Apply. Berlin: Springer Vieweg. ISBN 978–3–642–26638–6.

Sample Solutions

For each question, the tables below refer to the respective pages in the book where the content required for the solution can be found.

Chapter 1—Introduction

Number	Task/question		Solution on page
1	Explain what factors usually cause projects to fail	Common factors include: • Lack of technical skills, especially insufficient knowledge of requirements management • Communication problems and leadership weaknesses, e.g., unclear decision-making authority • Process-related deficiencies	1 (Sect. 1.1)
2	Name and describe three key terms defined by ISO 21500	**• Project** Consists of a unique set of processes that include goal-oriented, coordinated and controlled operations with start and completion dates to create deliverables **• Project management** Is the application of methods, tools, techniques and competences in a project **• Project lifecycle** Covers the period from the start of the project to its end and is divided by milestones	3 (Sect. 1.2)

(continued)

A. Johannsen et al., *Foundations for Software Project Management in Classic and Agile Environments*, https://doi.org/10.1007/978-3-032-16797-2

(continued)

Number	Task/question		Solution on page
3	Name the seventeen management practices according to ISO 21502:2020	The seventeen project management topic groups are planning, benefits, scope, resources, schedule, cost, risk, issues, change control, quality, stakeholders, communications, organizational & societal change, reporting, information, procurement, and lessons learned	9 (Table 1.1)
4	Describe the relationship that exists between the integrated project management practices "Managing Delivery" and "Controlling"	Control processes are used to monitor and control the execution of the project. This includes the control • whether deliveries take place at milestones as planned and • the quality of the deliverables	11 (Table 1. 2)
5	Name five core project management tasks	Core tasks include: • Management of the project team • Milestone planning • Maintaining contact with customers and conducting negotiations • Selection of methods and tools • Definition and monitoring of reporting	12 (Sect. 1.3.3)
6	Explain why a project manager should have entrepreneurial skills	Project activities and contracts often affect the entire company or have an impact on the entire company—in the form of benefits, but also of risks	13 (Sect. 1.3.4)

Chapter 2—Project Organization

Number	Task/Question		Solution on page
1	Please explain the difference between structural and process organization within projects	• Organizational structure describes the distribution of responsibilities and roles within the project • Process organization describes the work organization within the project, in particular processes and interfaces	17 (Sect. 2. 1)
2	Please describe, which organizational model is nearest to the example project in this book—at the beginning of the project	Since there is no separate project department and the project manager with the authority to issue directives also acts as the superior, it is probably a case of project execution within the parent organization	25 (example)
3	Is the structural project organization chosen in the example project suitable for the project? What advantages and disadvantages do you see?	It was advantageous that no additional project organization had to be set up, as the project was executed within the parent organization Overall, however, the organizational form was rather unsuitable because: • predefined communication standards, planning, quality assurance and controlling were missing (and were not established as part of the project), • the exchange within the project and with the project environment was insufficient	25 (example)
4	Which structural project organization would you choose for the further course of the project? Please explain your choice!	The project should change to Scrum—not least to strengthen communication. In the case study, a Scrum master from another department was brought in to relieve the original project manager. The matrix organization was the ideal solution. On the one hand, the project was too small for a pure project organization and, on the other, the assignment of team members to the project was clear and unambiguous. The disadvantage of the matrix organization, that team members have (too) many supervisors with authority to issue instructions in several simultaneous projects, was therefore not a problem	41 (Sect. 2.2.3)
5	Please explain two of the essential tasks of process organization within a project	• definition of the interfaces to the outside world • organization of the infrastructure	26
6	Why is it reasonable to define communication standards as part of process organization within projects?	Standards should exist, especially for communication with external stakeholders, in order to avoid friction losses	27

(continued)

(continued)

Number	Task/Question		Solution on page
7	Please name three important project committees, and describe the typical information and decision paths, using two events of your choice. In these scenarios, the project manager picks up information in one committee, presents it in another committee, and the decision made there on the topic is communicated back to the first committee	Important project committees: • team meetings • project management meeting • steering committee Possible scenario: Absence of an important project employee: • Team meeting reveals major risk for individual project • In the project management meeting it becomes apparent that employee is involved in several projects— > cross-project problem. Thus an escalation to the steering committee is necessary • The steering committee decides to seek external support	45 (Sect. 2.3.3)

Chapter 3—Project Management Frameworks in SW Development

Number	Task/question		Solution on page
1	What are the main differences between sequential and agile frameworks?	• Sequential project management frameworks are predominantly document-driven, agile frameworks are predominantly product-driven • Sequential project management frameworks divide projects into phases that are processed sequentially, agile frameworks structure projects into short iterations with completion in each case • Sequential project management frameworks usually only actively involve the customer/end user in late phases, agile frameworks are characterized by constant involvement of the customer/end user in all phases	32 (division into phases) 36 (iterative approach)
2	What weaknesses do sequential project management frameworks have? How are these circumvented in agile frameworks?	Possible weaknesses of sequential project management frameworks: • User requirements may be insufficiently implemented due to late feedback. This risk is minimized in agile frameworks through the consistent involvement of the user • Late delivery of usable software. This is mitigated in agile frameworks by iterative delivery of results • Late changes to requirements result in high expenses. Due to the iterative approach, agile frameworks offer the possibility of incorporating new requirements promptly in the next iteration, which is significantly less time-consuming	50 (late feedback) 55 (clarification through interim results)

(continued)

(continued)

Number	Task/question		Solution on page
3	Name and explain two advantages and disadvantages each of sequential and agile project management frameworks	Two advantages of sequential project management frameworks: • Reducing complexity by separating subtasks into phases • Focus on external and hierarchical control options Two disadvantages of sequential project management frameworks: • User feedback usually only after (partial) delivery • High planning effort Two advantages of agile frameworks: • Relatively short development times until the first version • Relatively good consideration of changing requirements Two disadvantages of agile frameworks: • Availability of the customer/user necessary • No focus on analyses and documentation at project start	56 (Sect. 3.1.3)
4	What requirements should be met for the use of an incremental approach?	Prerequisites for the use of incremental approaches: • Self-directed reporting within defined roles • Availability of the customer guaranteed • Hierarchical project monitoring can be dispensed with	56 (Table 3.1, column "Suitability range"))
5	Assign the following models to the sequential or agile project management frameworks: Scrum, waterfall model, V-model, Kanban, eXtreme Programming	Agile: • Scrum • Kanban • eXtreme programming Sequential: • Waterfall model • V-model	50 (Sect. 3.1.1—Waterfall Model, , V-Model) 54 (Sect. 3.1.2—Kanban, eXtreme Programming, Scrum)
6	What are criteria that should guide process tailoring of a project management framework for a given company and project?	Criteria to be considered are: • industry conditions • competitive situation • corporate mentality • willingness to take risks • market conditions • development potential	57 (Sect. 3.2)
7	Explain why "process tailoring" should be done in every project	• Standard processes should be aligned with the respective process environment • Environmental factors, internal as well as project specifics should be considered in the project processes in order to be able to achieve optimal work results	39 (Sect. 3.2)
8	Name and explain three guiding principles of agile system development	• Quick feedback, especially on product development • Acceptance of change: changes in requirements are welcome • Open communication between all project participants on all topics	59 (Sect. 3.3.1)
9	In addition to agile guiding principles, agile frameworks also provide typical elements. Name these	Typical elements include: • User Stories • Iterations (called sprints in Scrum) • Planning game	63 (Sprints) 70 (User Stories) 67 (planning game) Summary on page 85 (Scrum elements)

(continued)

(continued)

Number	Task/question		Solution on page
10	Briefly explain the basic ideas of agile system development according to Scrum!	Scrum follows three basic ideas: • **Transparency** Is ensured through regular review of interim results and clear definition of when work packages are ready (DoD) • **Inspection** Is ensured by regular reviews of project and product progress • **(Continuous) adaptation** Is ensured by sprint planning, Daily Scrum, review and retrospective	43 (Sect. 3.3.2) and 47 (Fig. 3.6 and accompanying text)
11	Which three essential roles does Scrum define? Describe the tasks and rights of a role of your choice!	Scrum knows the roles Product owner, Scrum master and Developer • **Product owner** This person represents the customer, is responsible for setting the development goals, managing the project budget, and defining and prioritizing the elements in the product backlog, and is a central point of contact for the team	61 (Sect. 3.3.3)
12	Outline the Scrum process and name four core events of Scrum	Initially and constantly: Creation/adjustment of the product backlog, determination of the basic architecture as well as the basic requirements The entire system is developed in iterations Scrum specifies the following four evens within a sprint: 1. **Sprint planning** Sprint planning I, sprint planning II: Breakdown into tasks and creation of the sprint backlog 2. **Daily Scrum** 15-min meeting of the developer team and the Scrum master 3. **Sprint review** Evaluation of the product 4. **Sprint retrospective** Evaluation of the general project process	67 (Sect. 3.3.5)
13	Name and explain the tasks and outcomes of the "Sprint Planning I and II"	• Determination of the backlog elements that will be processed in the following sprint • Effort planning and work distribution of the individual elements Results: Sprint backlog and sprint goals	49 (Sect. 3.3.5)
14	What are the benefits of running a "Daily Scrum"?	• Each project member knows the current state of the work of all team members • Disruptive factors can be identified at an early stage	48 (Sect. 3.3.4), 50 (Sect. 3.3.5)
15	Name and explain the tasks and outcomes of the "Sprint Review"	• Presentation of the newly developed sprint results to the product owner by the developers • Obtain feedback from the product owner/ customer Results: Sprint backlog review list, new requirements for product backlog if necessary	49 (Sect. 3.3.4), 51 (Sect. 3.3.5)

Chapter 4—Project Initiation

Number	Task/question		Solution on page
1	Explain the importance of project initiation	Project initiation is not a single event, but an important project phase that sets the stage for the project by clarifying opportunities and risks, requirements, rights and obligations of stakeholders, project management frameworks, and resources for the project	69 (Sect. 4.1)
2	Name and explain three key project initiating activities	• Opportunities and risks must be systematically identified and weighed up • Information required to begin implementation, e.g., project objectives, must be obtained • Contractual issues need to be clarified, e.g., the project management framework and the required resources	89 (Sect. 4.1)
3	Explain why negotiation, facilitation, and communication skills are required during project initiation	Project initiation is characterized by negotiations within and outside the company For success, it is important, on the one hand, to include the different aspects of all stakeholders in clarifying open points, e.g., facilitation of workshops, and, on the other hand, to document the results and communicate them in all directions	102 (Sect. 4.5)
4	Name and explain three aspects that should be covered as part of the project definition	• Defining the project motivation: This refers to the business reasons, i.e., why the project should be undertaken • The project objectives should be quantified in terms of the required costs, times, and qualities • Recording the most important stakeholders of the project, e.g., the customer, experts or steering committee members	96 (Sect. 4.2)
5	Explain why it should be contractually regulated how to deal with subcontractors or freelancer	In order for the various parties involved in a project to work together successfully, the exact manner of cooperation must be binding and, as a rule, also contractually regulated. Subcontractors and also external personnel need clarity about their rights and duties, about decision-making processes and escalation paths	98 (Sect. 4.3)

(continued)

(continued)

Number	Task/question		Solution on page
6	Which aspects should be contractually fixed in any case? How could you contractually anchor these aspects in agile frameworks?	A clear definition of the client's wishes and the contractor's obligations must be recorded. In the case of a sequential approach, this can be done in the form of requirements specifications and functional specifications In agile projects, this can be done by contractually defining the following points: • Coordination of the procedure • Definition of communication channels and forms • Dealing with changes and deviations	80-81 Specifically the paragraph on rights and duties
7	Explain possible consequences resulting from an unsystematic requirements analysis	A good requirements analysis is extremely important for project success. Poor requirements analysis can result in significant additional costs, for example due to trouble-shooting activities. In addition, requirements are an important basis for measuring the project's progress	100 (Sect. 4.4)

Chapter 5—Project Planning

Number	Task/question		Solution on page
1	Name and explain three key project planning activities	• **Milestone planning** Milestones are defined and planned as important path markers in the course of the project • **Creating the work breakdown structure** All deliverables of the project are identified, structured and defined • **Activity scheduling** All identified and estimated activities of the project are arranged over time	93 (Milestone planning) 99 (Work breakdown structure) 103 (effort estimate) 116 (cost estimate) 117 (activity scheduling) 146 (cost planning) 147 (project plan)
2	Explain what aspects and relationships are represented within milestone schedules	The milestone plan shows the main milestones (e.g., start of project implementation, agreed requirements, agreed system architecture, start of implementation, etc.) as well as supporting, internal milestones, if applicable	113 (Sect. 5.3)

(continued)

(continued)

Number	Task/question		Solution on page
3	Outline a work breakdown structure for our case study	The WBS for our case study contains the main delivery object of the project, i.e., the graphics platform to be developed, in the uppermost node. These include the delivery objects of the most important project areas, i.e., in our case the system design ("system"), the hardware connection component, the graphics engine, the graphics library and also the project and quality management. Below are then arranged delivery objects of the work packages	5.4.2 (Fig. 5.4)
4	Using a self-selected example, explain what non-functional delivery objects are	Example "Project management": It is a non-functional delivery object, since the project management does not create (its own) functionalities for the software product to be delivered, but is necessary for the coordination of software product creation	99 (Sect. 5.4.1)
5	Explain how the work breakdown structure could be referenced in subsequent planning activities	The work breakdown structure is of great importance for further planning activities because it provides the basic input for further estimates, in particular for the expected effort and the necessary HR requirements	118 (Sect. 5.4) 117 (activity scheduling) 104-105 (determination of HR requirements)
6	Explain the difference between effort and cost estimates. What is the connection between the two?	• Effort estimate determines the time required for the realization of the individual work packages • Cost estimate determines the expected costs and is largely based on the effort estimate	104-105 (Sect. 5.5)
7	Using a self-selected example, explain when the use of size estimation is appropriate	• For projects of a certain size, if an effort estimate has to be provided at short notice for a large number of work packages, e.g., for preparing a quotation • If experience values from previous projects are available	124 (Sect. 5.5.2)
8	Explain under what circumstances expert estimates are used	• If people are available who can quantify the effort well based on experience, and it is a known subject matter or technology • Expert estimates are the tool of choice for agile frameworks	specifically 107 (limits)

(continued)

(continued)

Number	Task/question		Solution on page
9	Name the different methods of expert estimation and explain one	• Delphi method • Informal expert estimate • Planning poker (in agile environment) • Three-point estimate The Delphi method proceeds in four steps: 1. Presentation of the activities by a facilitator 2. Anonymous estimation of the experts 3. Evaluating results by the facilitator 4. Estimation vote by the facilitator and expert	126 (Sect. 5.5.3)
10	A key principle for successful expert estimation is to obtain multiple opinions. Name other rules for successful expert estimation	• Estimating the smallest possible activities • Estimation by the subsequent processor • Estimation based on experience, i.e., employees should be given time to gain experience and to be able to reflect on the estimation quality	127 (rules)
11	Explain the methodology of analogy estimation and under what circumstances it should be used	Analogy estimates are based on historical data. Historical data can be used to draw analogies and thus determine expected expenses. The historical data must be reliable	130 (Sect. 5.5.4)
12	Name the different types of analogy estimates	• Multiplier method • Percentage method	111 (multiplier method) 112 (percentage method)
13	One of the advanced estimation methods is called COCOMO II model. Name another advanced estimation method	Function point analysis	114 (Function Point Analysis)
14	Explain what impact estimates have on project costing. What challenge arises in this context?	In software projects, there is one main cost factor: personnel expenses. Accordingly, the estimation of effort is important, for which suitable methods and experts should be chosen and sufficient time should be planned	135 (Sect. 5.6)

(continued)

(continued)

Number	Task/question		Solution on page
15	Name and explain benefits of using an activity schedule	• The activity schedule is the basis for progress monitoring • Dependencies of work packages and deadlines become transparent • Presentation of the critical path of activities and work packages	91 (basis for project controlling) 121 (calculation of dates) 124 (determination of the critical path)
16	Explain the concept of the critical path	The critical path is the sequence of activities in the activity schedule that determines the earliest possible completion date for a project or phase. If an activity on the critical path is delayed, milestones are at risk	124 (Sect. 5.7.3)
17	Name different types of workforce planning	Workforce planning can be more informal or formal, depending on the project. Possible are, for example: • Gantt chart in sequential environment • Scrum board in the agile environment	145 (Sect. 5.8)
18	Explain the relationship that exists between project planning and milestone planning and project control	Project planning and milestone planning must be coordinated with each other and they are the basis for project control. Any deviations identified during project controlling require a revision of the plan If the end or milestone dates in the project plan are not correct after the initial activity scheduling, the milestone and project planning must be optimized accordingly. Project controlling may also require replanning due to deviations in the actual values. In the agile environment, therefore, an iterative planning approach is used from the outset	137 (Sect. 5.7.1)

(continued)

(continued)

Number	Task/question		Solution on page
19	What are the basic rules for successful activity scheduling? Describe one of them in more detail	• Compatibility with the WBS is necessary • Unambiguous description of the activities is necessary • The framework conditions must be documented • Activities should be of the shortest possible duration • Easy adaptability of the planning should be given by suitable tool support • If possible, plan an activity with only one employee (if three employees share an activity, the project manager may be missing important information)	117 (Activities with short duration) 121 (matching tool support) 5.7.2 (Fig. 5.11, one activity per employee)
20	Explain what specifics need to be considered in activity scheduling in sequential project management frameworks	Sequential activity scheduling takes place in advance and often for the entire course of the project. Problems here are: • Changes must be expected from the outset • It is not possible to predict whether high costs will arise from unplannable events	120 (Sect. 5.7.2)
21	Explain what specifics need to be considered in activity scheduling in agile project management frameworks	In contrast to sequential project management frameworks, in the agile environment there is no detailed activity scheduling as upfront planning for the entire project. Instead, planning takes place at the following two levels: • Rough planning (release planning) • Detailed planning (sprint planning I and II)	122 (Sect. 5.7.2)
22	Explain how cost planning differs in different project management frameworks	• **Sequential environment** Time-related cost plan for the entire project • **Agile environment** Focus on residual budget for remaining activities	145 (Sect. 5.8)
23	Name content that you define as part of a project plan	• Work breakdown structure • Milestone plan • Communication plan • Software quality assurance plan • Risk planning	147 (Sect. 5.10)

Chapter 6—Implementing and Controlling a Project

Number	Task/question		Solution on page
1	Explain the consequences of poor project controlling	Without controlling, little or nothing is known about the true state of a project. It can therefore not be controlled. In particular: • The status of the project is unclear • Deviations from the original planning cannot be identified • There is no knowledge of whether and when replanning, and new planning will be necessary	151 (Sect. 6.1) Without controlling, the project is "flying blind" and cannot be managed Without controlling, the project is "flying blind" and cannot be managed
2	Name the essential components of project controlling and describe one of these components	• Determination of the project status • Determination of the plan deviation • Initiation of appropriate countermeasures in case of unacceptable deviation • Reports The determination of the project status is made in reports with the following content: • Progress compared to plan • Condensed information for stakeholders • Problems encountered	151 (Sect. 6.1)
3	How can the survey of project progress be put on a reliable basis?	For this purpose, a reporting and information system is required in which the key parameters are recorded and documented at an appropriate frequency A culture based on trust and transparency is important	153 (Sects. 6.3.1 and 6.3.2)
4	Outline how you might collect progress data in each of sequential and agile projects	In sequential projects: • Regular recording of start as well as end of an activity • For larger and critical activities, also estimation of the remaining effort by the employee (despite associated risks) In agile projects: • Daily (informal) recording of progress • (formal) update of the project status on the task board	152 (Sect. 6.2)

(continued)

(continued)

Number	Task/question		Solution on page
5	One possible form of reporting is the so-called traffic light system. Name other forms	• Formal status reports • Sprint Review • Top 3 of progress • Top 3 risks	158 (Sect. 6.3.3)
6	Explain why the use of regular progress reports is useful	Stakeholders and employees need good news With condensed information in regular progress reports, stakeholders can be efficiently updated in their own language	161 (Sect. 6.4.1 and specifically the definition of the term "status report").")
7	Explain what benefits target group-oriented meetings have	By selecting the participants in a targeted manner, an efficient meeting with a shorter duration can be realized	147-148 (Sect. 6.4.2)
8	What points do you consider to make a meeting effective and efficient?	Careful planning of the participants, designation of the topics, preparation of the agenda, determining the duration, paying attention to punctuality, involving all participants, making decisions and clearly assigning responsibilities for tasks	148-149 (Sect. 6.4.2)
9	Explain why milestone trend analysis is appropriate for time-oriented progress monitoring	The MTA is low effort and very informative. The graphical representation gives a quick overview, monitoring of the deadlines is easy	166 (Sect. 6.5.1) The MTA is low effort and very informative
10	Explain how the release burndown chart visualizes project progress	The Release Burndown Chart shows the amount of remaining work over time and helps identify trends or deviations in the team's velocity and delivery pace	171 (Sect. 6.5.3) See Fig. 3.11 in Sect. 3.3.6 for an example
11	Describe the impact of changes in sequential and agile projects and how you will deal with them	In sequential project management frameworks, changes are always variations from the initially defined requirements and, depending on the status of the project, are associated with additional effort in the form of renewed analysis, rescheduling and rework In the agile approach, changes are treated like requirements. Urgent changes can be processed in the next sprint	155-160 (Sects. 6.6.1-6.6.2)

(continued)

(continued)

Number	Task/question		Solution on page
12	Name two levels of change management in sequential project management frameworks	Changes that alter the scope of the project are handled at an organizationally usually higher level (CCB) Changes without impact on the project scope are handled by the project team together with the project manager	156 (Sect. 6.6.1)
13	Name change management activities that typically occur in sequential project management frameworks	• Capture and categorization of the change • Analysis, evaluation and, if necessary, decision, prioritization • Determination of the impact and scheduling of the change • Accompany and support the change • Follow-up of the change • Updating the project plan	172 (Sect. 6.6.1)
14	Explain the specifics that arise for change management in agile frameworks	Agile frameworks do not distinguish between user stories resulting from requirements and those resulting from changes. Therefore, there is no additional effort for planning, since the changes can be processed in the course of the next sprints	177 (Sect. 6.6.2)

Chapter 7—Project Acceptance and Closing

Number	Task / Question		Solution on page
1	What is the difference between project acceptance and project closing?	Project acceptance serves as formal acceptance of the project results by the project customer, whereas project closing, which is downstream of project acceptance, is intended to evaluate and record the internal project processes and the knowledge gained	163-167 (Sects. 7.1 and 7.2)
2	Explain the activities through which the goal in project acceptance is pursued and achieved	The goal of formal acceptance by the client requires the definition and early planning of acceptance activities, acceptance criteria, and possibly other measures	164-165 (Sect. 7.1)

(continued)

(continued)

Number	Task / Question		Solution on page
3	How does project acceptance take place in sequential and agile environments respectively? Where are the differences?	Sequential: • The acceptance usually takes place completely at the end of the project • The approval of requirements implementation often provides extensive lists of deviations Agile: • Acceptances typically occur after each increment • Unfulfilled requirements will be considered in a timely manner	182 (Sect. 7.1.1)
4	What activities does the project closing include?	Completion and archiving of project documentation, collection of lessons learned, post-calculation, evaluation of project processes, follow-up of project risks, updating of skills database	184 (Sect. 7.2)
5	Which methods on the relationship level should be used meaningfully during project closing?	The project manager should be able to "sell" the project to stakeholders as well as possible, resolve emotional conflicts if necessary, and use social assessment methods such as 360-degree analysis to conduct an analysis of self-perception and perception by others	186 (Sect. 7.3)
6	Explain what benefit will result from project closing	Project closing activities allow potential process and product improvements to be specifically analyzed and made available for the future. Without project closing, these improvements are rather left to chance	167 (Retrospective/ "Lessons Learned")")
7	Describe why project acceptance is closely linked to change management and project controlling	Project acceptance may require extensive activities if a large number of deficiencies are noted that need to be planned for, corrected, and post-controlled as part of the established change procedure	164 (Sect. 7.1)

Chapter 8—Quality Assurance

Number	Task/question		Solution on page
1	Describe how a process-oriented approach benefits quality assurance	• Quality is ensured by suitable development processes • Qualitative deficiencies in these processes affect the overall product	191 (Sect. 8. 1)
2	Name three essential contents of a quality assurance plan	Essential elements include • Quality assessment criteria to be applied • Roles and responsibilities • General conditions, e.g., schedule and budget	193 (Sect. 8. 2)
3	Explain two methods you can use to demonstrate quality assurance of processes	Methods include • **Milestone reviews** Comparison of target and actual status per milestone • **Audits** Verification of the quality of process performance	198 (Sect. 8. 3)
4	Explain what special role the project manager has with regard to process quality assurance	The project manager deploys processes, methods and tools and monitors compliance and correct use	174 (teach mindset)
5	Agile projects also place demands on product quality. Explain the specifics of ensuring this	Tests are integrated into each iteration and are part of the "Definition of Done"(DoD)	185-186 (Sect. 8.4.2)

Chapter 9—Risk Management

Number	Task/question		Solution on page
1	Explain whether risk management is a one-time process or an iterative process	Iterative process, because changes are almost always necessary in the course of the project and, among other reasons, each change can bring new risks	194 (Sect. 9.1.1)
2	Name key risk management activities	Key activities include: • Risk identification • Risk assessment • Risk control • Risk monitoring	214 (Sect. 9.2)
3	Name the main causes of risk and give an example that could occur in our case study	Possible causes include: • Unclear requirements • Lack of resources/skills • Lack of expertise • Unrealistic demands regarding deadlines and costs Relation to the case study: • Lack of documentation of requirements complicates risk identification and assessment	196-197 (Sect. 9.1.2)
4	Outline how to deal with change-related risks in sequential and agile project management frameworks	• **Sequential** Analysis of the impact of risks associated with a change as part of change management • **Agile** Entire development process is designed for changes	197 (Sect. 9.1.3)
5	Name methods and success factors to consider as part of a risk identification	Promising methods include: • Involving experts • Brainstorming sessions • Checklists Success factors: • Systematic approach, involvement of experts, integration in the change process	199-203 (Sect. 9.2.1)

(continued)

(continued)

Number	Task/question		Solution on page
6	Explain different risk assessment methods using our case study	• Determination of the probability of occurrence and impact of each individual risk on the basis of assigned criteria that are as clear as possible • Creation of a list of prioritized risks Explanation by example: Initial risks were first identified in a workshop (e.g., the risk "Continuous integration server not operational at the beginning") and then assessed by jointly estimating the probabilities impacts and entering them in a risk list. Three categories (low, medium, severe) of impact on the project's time and cost objectives were established as the clearest possible criteria for impact. Risk priority numbers were then determined by multiplying the values for probability and impact, resulting in an initial risk list	219 (Sect. 9.2.2)—in particular Table 9.4
7	Name the main possible types of countermeasures	• Avoidance • Transfer • Mitigation • Acceptance	225 (Sect. 9.2.3)
8	Name different methods for analyzing and documenting risks	Possible methods include: • Ishikawa diagram • Fault tree analysis (FTA) • Risk assessment matrix • Risk lists	215 (Sect. 9.2.1) Figure 9.1: Ishikawa diagram Figure 9.2: FTA Figure 9.3: risk assessment matrix and above all Tables 9.4 and 9.5 (risk list

(continued)

(continued)

Number	Task/question		Solution on page
9	Describe the tasks of risk control and its importance for other project phases	• Assessment of probabilities of occurrence and impact are to be considered periodically • New risks that arise during the course of the project must be identified and assessed periodically Significance for other phases: • All defined measures are to be followed up	227 (Sect. 9.2.4)
10	Name two important soft skills for project managers and their importance for risk management	• Facilitation skills to lead risk workshops • Communication skills to proactively communicate risks and measures	228 (Sect. 9.3)
11	Describe the concept of safety integrity levels	• The functions of a product are classified into one of the levels of safety criticality (according to IEC 61,508) depending on the risk • Different SIL levels (1–4) describe different integrity levels, with SIL 1 representing the lowest hazard and SIL 4 the highest	229 (Sect. 9.4)

Chapter 10—Human Resource Management

Number	Task/question		Solution on page
1	What is the ultimate goal of human resource management in an organization?	The ultimate goal of HR management is employee satisfaction, low workforce costs and an increase in the competitive strength of the company	234 (Sect. 10.1.1)
2	List the key players of human resource management in an organization	Key players are • C-level management • Works council • Managers including project managers • Operating departments of HR management	236 (Sect. 10.1.2)

(continued)

(continued)

Number	Task/question		Solution on page
3	Name the six domains of HR management tasks and discuss one of them in more detail	The six domains are: • HR Policy Design • Human resource planning • Staff deployment • Recruitment and Onboarding • Administrative HR functions • HR development Human resource planning ensures that workforce capacity and skills match organizational objectives	243 (Sect. 10.1.3)
4	Explain the role of tactical HR management in contrast to strategic and operational HR management	Tactical HR management is oriented toward groups of jobs (e.g., career plans). It forms the link between the strategic level (which is part of the overall corporate strategy) and the operational level (which deals with individual measures)	238 (Sect. 10.1.4)
5	Name the three core activities of HR management as cross-cutting task	The project manager is responsible for the following areas as part of the project's human resources management: • Selection of staff • Staff leadership • Know-how management	241 (Sect. 10.1.2)
6	Name three main HR activities of a project manager that are probably required during project planning	• Staffing analysis—understand, which competencies are required in to which extent • Personnel Assignment Management—align the individual expertise of the team members with the specific project tasks • Personnel Cost Management—plan the expected personnel-related costs	243 (Sect. 10.2.3)
7	Explain the interaction between company-wide and project-related human resources management	The typical division of labor is as follows: • The project manager formulates the staffing needs • The responsible HR expert provides the necessary information • Ideally, the project manager selects the team members • The project manager names deficits if his requirement profile cannot be met • Project manager and HR expert search together for solutions	243 (Sect. 10.2.4)
8	Name the four phases of team support	The team support is divided into the four phases: • Team building • Team management • Team developing • Team closing	245 (Sect. 10.2.5)

(continued)

(continued)

Number	Task/question		Solution on page
9	Describe what tasks the project manager performs within the different phases of team support. What is the importance of this for the project?	• During team building, the project manager assembles his team and determines appropriate team structures. These activities at the start of the project are crucial for the course of the project • In team managing, the project manager estimates staffing needs, creates the staffing schedule, and manages his team during project execution. This leads to constructive cooperation • For a high project performance, the further development (team development) of the project members is essential. The project manager must recognize deficits and reduce them through appropriate training and education In team closing, the project manager is responsible for the project evaluation, assesses the employees and dissolves the team. This leads to sustained motivation	245 (Sect. 10.2.5)
10	Name core competencies that a project manager should have in any case	Requirements that a project manager should meet include: • Behavioral competence • Methodological skills • Expertise • Industry knowledge	247 (Sect. 10.3.1) Figure 10.5 and accompanying text
11	Using our case study, describe why the project manager's soft skills are important to project success or failure	Our example project was in danger of failing not because of a lack of technical knowledge, but primarily because of a lack of communication and leadership of the team by the project manager. After switching to Scrum as a framework and the associated significant increase in project communication (daily standup meetings, etc.) as well as intensification of leadership, the project was completed quickly	247 (Sect. 10.3)—There was a particular lack of communication (10.3.2) and motivation (10.3.3)
12	Which social skills of team members influence are important to project success or failure	The social competence of the individual team members influence the project success just as strongly as the personality of the project manager Team members should be team players and flexible. They should be able to deal with complexity, show proactive initiative and be open-minded with respect to other cultures or new topics	247 (Sect. 10.3.1) Sub-section "Requirements for the team members "

(continued)

(continued)

Number	Task/question		Solution on page
13	Name the four essential aspects that make up social competence	The four aspects that describe social competence include: • Dealing with oneself • Dealing with other people • Aspects of cooperation • Aspects of leadership	247 (Sect. 10.3.1)
14	Explain why communication is inherently difficult	Communication involves both sending and receiving messages, and misunderstandings can occur at either stage. Even small variations in language, tone, or non-verbal signals can cause misinterpretations, especially when communication crosses cultural or technological boundaries	252 (Sect. 10.3.2)
15	Name and describe the positive and negative effects of verbal and non-verbal communication	Human perception and thus communication and its interpretation are always subjective (e.g., "What was said and how?", "How was it gestured?"). This creates a communication dilemma The project manager can counteract this dilemma by recognizing the verbal and nonverbal communication needs of the team members and adapting his own communication accordingly to the situation	252 (Sect. 10.3.2)
16	What basic rules should a project manager observe when expressing criticism?	Even when expressing criticism, a project manager should always be respectful and show appreciation. Conduct the conversation mindfully and focus on solutions. "Finger-pointing" does help anybody. Express your thoughts diplomatically rather than sharply and recognize achievements	252 (Sect. 10.3.2) Sub-section "You can't not communicate!"
17	Define motivation and demotivation	The term motivation refers to the inner driving force and willingness of a person to act in a certain way Demotivation is a loss of this willingness to act	257 (Sect. 10.3.3)

(continued)

(continued)

Number	Task/question		Solution on page
18	Explain the difference between intrinsic and extrinsic motivation and how you can influence it as a project manager	• Extrinsic motivation works from the outside. A person acts to achieve positive consequences and avoid punishment or disadvantages. The project manager can support this, for example, through higher pay or promotion • Intrinsic motivation is a form of self-motivation that works through needs such as success, recognition, interest, responsibility, growth, joy, and fun Impact: • Project manager can set impulses as a role model • Project manager can maintain existing motivation, avoid demotivation Essential motivating factors are: Appreciation, recognition and praise	257 (Sect. 10.3.3) Sub-section "Intrinsic and extrinsic motivation"
19	Using our case study, describe where recognition and appreciation could serve as a motivating factor	The very fact that the team is given responsibility during the transition to Scrum as a process model conveys a certain appreciation. In addition, the project manager would have had the opportunity beforehand to strengthen the flow of information, to actively support reliability in the cooperation and integration of all team members, and to promote decisiveness. However, these factors were only intensified by the newly appointed product owner and Scrum master	257 (Sect. 10.3.3) Sub-section "The project manager as motivator"
20	Explain the difference between appreciation and praise	Praise and appreciation refer to special behavior or outstanding performance, whereas appreciation is a positive basic attitude toward a person	257 (Sect. 10.3.3) Sub-section "The appreciation as the most important motivating factor"
21	Explain, why leadership is important for project success and name core aspects of leadership	Leadership means purposefully guiding teams to achieve shared goals. It provides orientation and has a strong influence on team motivation Core aspects of leadership are: • Vision • Structure • Communication • Environment Design • Role Modeling • Appreciation • Positive Attitude	261 (Sect. 10.3.4)

(continued)

(continued)

Number	Task/question		Solution on page
22	Explain the difference between participative, situational, and authentic leadership styles	Leaders that apply the participative leadership style actively involve team members in decision-making processes—as opposed to the autocratic style (completely authoritarian) and the democratic style The situational leadership style is adaptive. The way, the project manager acts, depends on the specific situation. It may be participative or democratic in one situation and autocratic in another Leaders that apply the authentic leadership style acts with transparency, consistency, and self-awareness, building trust through honesty and integrity	261 (Sect. 10.3.4) Sub-section "Adaptive leadership"
23	Explain, why it is important as a leader to be self-aware	Leadership is a mutual process requiring versatility and continuous development. There are no universal solutions. Therefore, project managers should regularly reflects their actions and decisions, as well as their own feelings and the reactions of others they observed	261 (Sect. 10.3.4) Sub-section "Adaptive leadership"
24	Describe how project management differs in sequential and agile project management frameworks	In sequential project management frameworks the project manager's focus lies on coordination, responsibility for the overall project and team leadership. In Agile frameworks, the roles and responsibilities are shared between the project manager (if present), the Scrum master and sometimes even the product owner. Also, the focus lies on operational team management	266 (Sect. 10.4.1)

(continued)

(continued)

Number	Task/question		Solution on page
25	Use the case study to explain why method and tool skills are a critical factor for team leadership	The project manager needs method/tool skills especially in the following areas: **• Project management tools** In the project, the team lacked transparency regarding central project documents **• Communication techniques** These could have resolved the communication bottlenecks **• Facilitation, presentation and creativity techniques** With their help, meetings (including distributed ones) could have been conducted more efficiently and effectively **• Presentation, leadership, conflict, and problem-solving techniques** Using these techniques, motivation and the feeling of togetherness could have been significantly strengthened **• Self-management techniques** With these, the project manager could have reduced the double burden of being a line manager and a project manager	268 (Sect. 10.4.2) The transition to agile made facilitation even more important
25	Provide an example of a situation, in which a project manager needs presentation techniques	• Project managers have to present the project status to the steering committee • Product owners have to present user stories to the developers • Scrum masters have to present impediments and how to solve them to upper management • Developers have to present architectural choices to key stakeholders	268 (Sect. 10.4.2)
26	Explain, why it is important that the facilitator of a meeting keeps a neutral attitude	Only facilitators with neutral attitude will be able to engaging all participants and encourage involvement	268 (Sect. 10.4.2) Sub-section "Successful meetings require facilitation"
27	What happens to meetings that lack facilitation?	Good facilitation during the meeting re-focusses the group discussion on the goal (if necessary), fosters the creativity of the participants and makes the resulting ideas accessible to all. If the meeting lacks this facilitations, it may happen that there are endless discussions between two "opponents" while the rest stares at the ceiling	268 (Sect. 10.4.2) Sub-section "Successful meetings require facilitation"

(continued)

(continued)

Number	Task/question		Solution on page
28	Outline Tuckman's team clock, explaining his approach	Tuckman's team clock model makes it possible to identify group dynamics in the team and to understand and reflect on group developments. According to the model, each group goes through five phases of team development: • Forming • Storming • Norming • Performing • Adjourning	273 (Sect. 10.4.4)
29	Depending on the team building phase, name possible actions of the project manager	• **Forming phase** Project manager acts as host, creating a feel-good and welcoming atmosphere • **Storming phase** Project manager acts as catalyst, mediator and driver, creates an open and trusting climate, handles conflicts and directs focus to project goals • **Norming phase** Project manager uses the participative management style, allows the project team to act autonomously, accompanies the team as a partner and is guaranteeing valid and functioning rules • **Performing phase** Project manager focuses on targets, supports the team and acts as an advisor for further development • **Adjourning phase** As a coach and mentor, the project manager accompanies the team and enables mutual feedback	273 (Sect. 10.4.4)
30	Explain what roles are assigned to team members according to M. Belbin	Each team member takes at least one of nine roles. These roles can be divided into the three main orientations • Knowledge-oriented, • People-oriented, and • Action-oriented An ideal team should cover all three main orientations	275 (Sect. 10.4.5)

(continued)

(continued)

Number	Task/question		Solution on page
31	Outline the different competencies and tasks of the project manager depending on the role he/she assumes in the project	• **Coordinator** Coordinate goals and tasks in a binding and consistent manner • **Facilitator** Act in a neutral and structured manner, summarize the results • **Consultant** Clarify relationship problems, technical and methodological issues, show alternatives • **Conflict Manager** Analyze and resolve role conflicts with confidence and open-mindedness • **Representative** Represent team interests to the outside world in a self-confident and reflective manner • **Negotiator** Negotiate resources competently and realistically • **Presenter/Speaker** • Visualize and present results and successes • **Coach** Support team members	277 (Sect. 10.4.6)

Chapter 11—Maturity Models

Number	Task/question		Solution on page
1	Name the different maturity models which may serve in project management	Possible maturity models include: • CMMI • ISO/ IEC 330xx (SPICE)	288 (Sect. 11.3) 290 (Sect. 11.4)
2	Describe the underlying principle of all maturity models	Maturity models measure process quality according to the following principle: • Grouping of processes into process groups • Definition of base practices for the implementation of the processes • Application of practices and documentation • Evaluation of the processes within the assessment framework based on the required evidence	285 (Sect. 11.1)

(continued)

(continued)

Number	Task/question		Solution on page
3	Using a self-selected example, explain the principle of different maturity levels	Process "Risk analysis" from the case study: • Initially, no risk analyses were carried out by the project management. Thus, the process can only be assessed with the lowest level, e.g., "CL0—incomplete" • If we introduce a standardized process for risk analysis and implement in it, for example, that an adjusted risk report is submitted at the beginning of each month, we can assume level "CL2—controlled"	285 (Fig. 11.1 and accompanying text)

Glossary

This glossary contains only the terms required by the ASQF® CPPM syllabus (ASQF CPPM 2025).

Activity

Identified component of work within a schedule that is required to be undertaken to complete a project.

Source: ISO 21500:2012(E).

At the lowest level, the WBS defines the work packages from which the activities are derived, which must be estimated and planned out in detail. As the smallest unit, the planned activities later form the basis for project control.

Source: ASQF CPPM 2025 (EN).

Burndown Chart

A Burndown Chart visualizes the amount of remaining work over time and helps identify trends or deviations in the team's velocity and delivery pace.

Source: ASQF CPPM 2025 (EN).

Change Control Board (CCB)

Change control body that decides or rejects changes and documents the decision made.

Source: ASQF CPPM 2025 (EN).

Change Request

A documentation that defines a proposed alteration to a project.

Source: ISO 21502:2020(E).

Critical Path

Sequence of activities that determine the earliest possible completion date for a project or phase.

Source: ISO 21502:2020(E).

Deliverable

Unique and verifiable element that is required to be produced by a project.

A. Johannsen et al., *Foundations for Software Project Management in Classic and Agile Environments*, https://doi.org/10.1007/978-3-032-16797-2

Source: ISO 21502:2020(E).

Milestone

A milestone is an event of special significance in project management.
Source: ASQF CPPM 2025 (EN).

Milestone Trend Analysis (MTA)

The milestone trend analysis (MTA) is used to provide a graphical overview of project progress based on milestones in the project status report.
Source: ASQF CPPM 2025(EN).

Process

A process consists of a series of interrelated procedures.

Software development process refers to the set of activities performed to create a software system. Input data are stakeholder requirements, output data are the created software system as well as further achievements of the project team. Project management processes determine how the activities selected for the project are managed and controlled.
Source: ISO 21500:2012(E).

Process Tailoring

Process tailoring is the adaptation of project management frameworks to company and project specifics in order to ensure the most suitable project processes possible.
Source: ASQF CPPM 2025 (EN).

Product Backlog

A list of backlog items representing the requirements of the software or solution to be developed within the project.
Source: Schwaber and Sutherland (2020).

Project

A project is a temporary endeavor to achieve one or more defined objectives. Projects are temporary and focus on retaining or adding value or capability, for a sponsoring organization, stakeholder, or customer.
Source: ISO 21502:2020(E).

Project Definition

Single overarching document, that describes the objectives and the management approach of a project, and thus serves as orientation for all stakeholders involved.
Source: ASQF CPPM 2025 (EN).

Project Life Cycle

A project life cycle is a defined set of phases from the start to the end of a project. The phases are separated by decision points (milestones), which may differ depending on the organizational environment.

Source: ISO 21502:2020(E).

Project Management

Project Management can be defined as coordinated activities to direct and control the accomplishment of agreed objectives. Project management integrates practices to direct, initiate, plan, monitor, control and close the project, manage the resources assigned to the project, and motivate those individuals involved in the project to achieve the project's objectives.

Source: ISO 21502:2020(E).

Project Management Framework

Project management frameworks compile methods and elements of software development including project management into processes and project phases of a standardized project flow in order to achieve the often challenging project goals as efficiently and effectively as possible.

Source: ASQF CPPM 2025(EN).

A project management framework shapes methods and elements of software development including project management toward a delivery approach consisting of processes or project phases as a standardized project flow, in order to achieve the often challenging project goals as efficiently and effectively as possible. Project management frameworks serve as *delivery approaches* and can be sequential, predictive, iterative, incremental, adaptive, or hybrid approaches.

Source: ISO 21502:2020(E).

Project Organization

The project organization is a temporary structure that defines roles, responsibilities and authorities in the project. Individuals are assigned by names to specific roles in the project organization.

Source: ISO 21502:2020(E).

The project organization enables the cooperation in the project with regard to responsibilities, tasks and rights of the persons involved. The task of the project organization is to manage both the static aspects (organizational structure) and the dynamic aspects (process organization) of the project. A good project organization ensures short decision-making paths and clear responsibilities.

Source: ASQF CPPM 2025(EN).

Project Phase

Projects can be divided into project phases. The number and names of a project's phases depend upon the type of project being undertaken, desired governance, and the anticipated risk. The phases can reflect the delivery approach or project management framework being taken, and should have a defined start and end, as well as specific milestones that relate to the decisions, key deliverables, outputs, or outcomes.

Source: ISO 21502:2020(E).

Pull System

In a "pull" system, the processing of tasks is a collective team responsibility. Tasks enter an iteration without being pre-assigned and are then "pulled" by individual team members when they are ready to work on them. Agile project management frameworks are generally "pull" systems.
Source: ASQF CPPM 2025(EN).

Push System

In a push system employees are assigned to activities during planning at the beginning of the project. Sequential project management frameworks are push systems.
Source: ASQF CPPM 2025(EN).

Social Competence
By social competence we mean the availability (potential) and application (performance) of cognitive, emotional, and motor behaviors that lead to a long-term favorable balance of positive and negative consequences for the agent in specific social situations.
Source: Waters and Sroufe (1983).

Sprint

According to Scrum, products are developed in iterations, so-called Sprints.
Source: Schwaber and Sutherland (2020).

Stakeholder

Person, group, or organization that has interests in, or can affect, be affected by, or perceive itself to be affected by, any aspect of a project
Source: ISO 21502:2020(E).

Status Report

Formal status reports address external stakeholders in order to obtain optimally condensed information in their language and vocabulary.
Source: ASQF CPPM 2025.

Story Points

A relative unit of measure used by the development team to estimate the effort needed to complete a product backlog item, typically a user story.
Source: Cohn (2005, p. 36).

Task

Activities in agile frameworks that are derived by the team from the user stories at the beginning of an iteration.
Source: ASQF CPPM 2025(EN).

User Story

User stories are typically used in agile frameworks for the specification of requirements by the later users of the system.
Source: ASQF CPPM 2025(EN).

Work Breakdown Structure (WBS)

Decomposition of the defined scope of a project or program into progressively lower levels consisting of elements of work.
Source: ISO 21502:2020(E)
The work breakdown structure (WBS) is used to create a picture of a project based on its deliverables. The purpose of the work breakdown structure is to identify all deliverables and prevent components and work packages from being overlooked.
Source: ASQF CPPM 2025(EN).

Work Package

Group of activities that have a defined scope, deliverable, timescale, and cost.
Source: ISO 21502:2020(E).

References

(Agarwal 2023): U. A. Agarwal, K. Jain, V. Anantatmula, S. Shankar: Managing People in Projects for High Performance, Springer Nature, 2023.

(Agile Alliance 2001): Manifesto for Agile Software Development. Available at: https://agilemanifesto.org/ (Accessed: 10 September 2025).

(Alt et al. 2021): R. Alt, G. Auth, und C. Kögler, Continuous innovation with DevOps: IT management in the age of digitalization and software-defined business, SpringerBriefs in Information Systems, Cham, Switzerland, 2021. https://doi.org/10.1007/978-3-030-72705-5

(Amber 2012): Ambler, S. W., Disciplined Agile Delivery: A Practitioner's Guide to Agile Software Delivery. IBM Press. ISBN: 978-0132819405.

(Ashby 2025): Ashby, S., Fundamentals of Operational Risk Management: Understanding and Implementing Effective Tools, Policies and Frameworks. 2nd edn. London: Kogan Page. ISBN 978-1398622906.

(ASQF CPPM 2025): Project Management Foundations, Syllabus (EN), ASQF® Certified Professional for Project Management (2025) - Foundation Level, Version 3.0, 2025.

(Avença et al. 2023): Avença, I., Domingues, L. & Carvalho, H., Project managers' soft skills influence in knowledge sharing. Procedia Computer Science, 219, pp.1705–1712. https://doi.org/10.1016/j.procs.2023.01.464. Available at: https://www.sciencedirect.com/science/article/pii/S1877050923004763

(Ayed 2018): Ayed, H., Guiding Agile Methods Customization: the AMQuICk Framework. PhD thesis. Namur: Université de Namur. ISBN 978-2-39029-023-0. Available at: https://doi.org/10.5281/zenodo.1475150

(Bauer 2024): Bauer, P. A Comprehensive Project Management Guide: Quality Management, Integrated Six-Sigma and Change Management Compilation. Management for Professionals series. Cham: Springer. https://doi.org/10.1007/978-3-031-68252-0

(Beck 2000): Kent Beck: Extreme Programming Explained – Embrace Change – 1. edition, Amsterdam, Addison-Wesley Longman, ISBN 978-0201616415.

(Beck 2002): Beck, K., Test Driven Development: By Example. Addison-Wesley Longman Publishing Co., Inc., USA. ISBN 978-0321146533.

(Belbin 1981): Belbin, R. M., Management Teams: Why They Succeed or Fail. London: Heinemann. ISBN 978-0434901265.

(Blatter et al. 2024): Blatter, A., Bradbury, S., Bruhn, P. & Ernst, D., Risk Management in Banks and Insurance Companies. Cham: Springer. https://doi.org/10.1007/978-3-031-42836-4

(Boehm 1979): Boehm, B. W. (1979), Guidelines for Verifying and Validating Software Requirements and Design Specifications, in P. A. Samet, ed., 'Euro IFIP 79', North Holland, pp. 711–719.

(Boehm 2014): Boehm, B. W., 'Software project risk and opportunity management', in Ruhe, G. and Wohlin, C. (eds.) Software Project Management in a Changing World. Berlin, Heidelberg: Springer, pp. 107–124. https://doi.org/10.1007/978-3-642-55035-5 5.

(Boem et al. 2000): Boehm, B.W., Abts, C., Brown, A. W., Chulani, S., Clark, B.K., Horowitz, E., Madachy, R., Reifer, D.J. & Steece, B. (2000) *Software Cost Estimation with COCOMO*

© The Editor(s) (if applicable) and The Author(s), under exclusive license to Springer Nature Switzerland AG 2026

A. Johannsen et al., *Foundations for Software Project Management in Classic and Agile Environments*, https://doi.org/10.1007/978-3-032-16797-2

II (with CD-ROM). Upper Saddle River, NJ: Prentice Hall. ISBN: 0-13-026692-2. https://doi.org/10.5555/557000

(Brown 2008): Brown, T., Design Thinking, in: Harvard Business Review, 86th ed. (2008), June, pp. 84–92.

(Bundesverwaltungsamt 2023): PMflex-Projektmanagement-Leitfaden. Bundesverwaltungsamt. Available at: https://www.bva.bund.de/SharedDocs/Downloads/DE/Behoerden/Beratung/GrossPM/PMflex/PMflex-Projektmanagement-Leitfaden.pdf

(Cai et al. 2023): Cai, X., Hall, N.G., Wang, S. & Zhang, F. (2023). Cooperation and contract design in project management with outsourcing. Journal of Systems Science and Systems Engineering, 32(1), 34–70. https://doi.org/10.1007/s11518-023-5548-x

(Chevrot 2025): Chevrot A. et al, Are Autonomous Web Agents Good Testers?, arXiv:2504.01495v1 [cs.SE] 2, April 2025, Available at: https://arxiv.org/abs/2504.01495

(Cohn 2005): Mike Cohn: Agile Estimating and Planning, Prentice Hall, 360 pages, 2005, ISBN 978-0131479418.

(Conger 2019): Conger, J. A.. Harnessing the potential of 360 feedback in executive education programming. In A.H. Church, D.W. Bracken, J.W. Fleenor, & D.S. Rose (Eds.), The handbook of strategic 360 feedback (pp.343–351). OxfordUniversityPress.

(CPRE 2024): International Requirements Engineering Board, IREB® Certified Professional for Requirements Engineering – Foundation Level, V 3.2.0, February 2024, https://www.ireb.org/en/cpre/foundation/

(Deming 1982): Deming, W. E., Out of the Crisis. MIT Press.

(Digital.ai 2022): 15th State of Agile Report. Digital.ai, Lexington, MA. Available at: https://digital.ai/resource-center/analyst-reports/state-of-agile-report

(Digital.ai 2024): 17th State of Agile Report. Digital.ai, Lexington, MA. Available at: https://digital.ai/resource-center/analyst-reports/state-of-agile-report

(Dijkstra 1972): Dijkstra, E. W. The Humble Programmer [Turing Award Lecture]. In EWD 340. Available at: https://www.cs.utexas.edu/~EWD/transcriptions/EWD03xx/EWD340.html

(Dittmann & Dirbanis 2024): Dittmann, K. & Dirbanis, K. Project Management (IPMA®): Study Guide for Level D and Basic Certificate (GPM), 2nd edn. Haufe München. https://doi.org/10.34157/978-3-648-16629-1

(EU 2019a): Directive (EU) 2019/770 — on certain aspects concerning contracts for the supply of digital content and digital services (EUR-Lex): https://eur-lex.europa.eu/eli/dir/2019/770/oj/eng

(EU 2019b): Directive (EU) 2019/771 — on certain aspects concerning contracts for the sale of goods (EUR-Lex): https://eur-lex.europa.eu/eli/dir/2019/771/oj/eng

(European Commission 2021): PM²-Agile Guide v 3.0.1. Luxembourg: Publications Office of the European Union. Available at: https://op.europa.eu/en/publication-detail/-/publication/ed85debf-decc-11eb-895a-01aa75ed71a1

(European Commission 2024): PM² Project Management Guide 3.1. Publications Office of the European Union. Available at: https://op.europa.eu/en/publication-detail/-/publication/ed85debf-decc-11eb-895a-01aa75ed71a1

(EU-AIA 2024): European Union. (2024) Regulation (EU) 2024/1689 of the Eu-ropean Parliament and of the Council of 13 June 2024 laying down harmonised rules on artificial intelligence (EU Artificial Intelligence Act). Available at: https://eur-lex.europa.eu/eli/reg/2024/1689/oj/eng

(EU-CER 2022): European Union. (2022) Directive (EU) 2022/2557 of the Euro-pean Parliament and of the Council of 14 December 2022 on the resilience of crit-ical entities and repealing Council Directive 2008/114/EC (CER Directive). Avail-able at: https://eur-lex.europa.eu/eli/dir/2022/2557/oj/eng

(EU-CRA 2024): European Union. (2024) Regulation (EU) 2024/2847 of the Eu-ropean Parlia-ment and of the Council of 23 October 2024 on horizontal cyberse-curity requirements for products with digital elements (Cyber Resilience Act). Available at: https://eur-lex.europa.eu/eli/reg/2024/2847/oj/eng

(EU-DORA 2022): European Union. (2022) Regulation (EU) 2022/2554 of the European Parliament and of the Council of 14 December 2022 on digital opera-tional resilience for the financial sector (DORA). Available at: https://eur-lex.europa.eu/eli/reg/2022/2554/oj/eng

(EU-NIS2 2022): Directive (EU) 2022/2555 of the European Parliament and of the Council of 14 December 2022 on measures for a high common level of cyber-security across the Union (NIS2 Directive). Available at: https://digital-strategy.ec.europa.eu/en/policies/nis2-directive

(Feng et al. 2023): Feng, K.J.K., Liao, Q.V., Borenstein, J., Li, J. & Liu, Y. (2023) Understanding Collaborative Practices and Tools of UX Professionals. In: Proceedings of the 2023 CHI Conference on Human Factors in Computing Systems (CHI '23). New York: ACM, pp. 1–16. https://doi.org/10.1145/3544548.3581273 (dl.acm.org).

(Fleenor 2021): Fleenor, J. W., What Can We Learn from Research on Multisource Feedback in Organizations? In: Student Feedback on Teaching in Schools (S. 221–236). Springer. https://doi.org/10.1007/978-3-030-75150-0_14

(Forgács & Kovács 2021): Forgács, I. & Kovács, A. Modern Software Testing Techniques: A Practical Guide for Developers and Testers. Apress. ISBN 978-1-4842-9893-0. https://doi.org/10.1007/978-1-4842-9893-0

(Google 2006): Schwaber, K., Talk on Scrum, in: Google TechTalk, Sept. 5, 2006, https://www.youtube.com/watch?v=_47VWIvOKH8, accessed 03.10.2025.

(Habib, Graziotin & Wagner 2025): Habib, M.K., Graziotin, D. & Wagner, S. (2025) ReqBrain: Task-Specific Instruction Tuning of LLMs for AI-Assisted Requirements Generation. arXiv preprint arXiv:2505.17632. Available at: https://arxiv.org/abs/2505.17632

(Hagemann 2023): Hagemann, M., A Leadership Paradigm Shift to 'Eclectic Leadership. Springer Gabler. https://doi.org/10.1007/978-3-658-41578-5

(Hamid 1988): Abdel-Hamid, T.K.,'Understanding the "90% syndrome" in software project management: A simulation-based case study', Journal of Systems and Software, 8(4), pp. 319–330. https://doi.org/10.1016/0164-1212(88)90015-5

(Hoermann et al. 2022): Hoermann, Klaus; Pepe, Guiseppe; Wall, Dan; Zhang, Yanhua: The guide for Automotive SPICE® Interpretation. Kugler Maag CIE GmbH, 2022.

(Humpfrey 1989): Humphrey WS, Managing the software process. Addison-Wesley, Reading, MA.

(Iriarte & Bayona Oré 2018): Iriarte, C. & Bayona Oré, S., Soft Skills for IT Project Success: A Systematic Literature Review. In: Mejia J., Muñoz M., Rocha Á., Quiñonez Y., Calvo-Manzano J. (eds) Trends and Applications in Software Engineering (CIMPS 2017). Advances in Intelligent Systems and Computing, vol. 688. Springer, Cham. https://doi.org/10.1007/978-3-319-69341-5_14

(ISACA 2023): CMMI V3.0 – Capability Maturity Model Integration. 1st edn. Schaumburg, IL: ISACA. Available at: https://cmmiinstitute.com/products/cmmi/content-release

(ISO 14971:2019): International Organization for Standardization (2019) Medical devices — Application of risk management to medical devices. ISO 14971:2019. Geneva: ISO. ISBN 978-9267111063. Available at: https://www.iso.org/standard/72704.html

(ISO 21500:2012): International Organization for Standardization (ISO), ISO 21500:2012(E) – Guidance on project management. Geneva: ISO.

(ISO 21502:2020): International Organization for Standardization (ISO), ISO 21502:2020(E) – Project, programme and portfolio management — Guidance on project management. Geneva: ISO.

(ISO 21511:2018): ISO 21511:2018(E) – Work breakdown structures for project and programme management. International Organization for Standardization. Available at: https://www.iso.org/standard/71028.html

(ISO 25000:2014): ISO/IEC 25000:2014 – Systems and software engineering - Systems and software Quality Requirements and Evaluation (SQuaRE) - Guide to SQuaRE. Available at: https://www.iso.org/standard/64764.html

(ISO 26262:2018): International Organization for Standardization, ISO 26262: Road Vehicles – Functional Safety. Geneva: ISO. Available at: https://www.iso.org/standard/68383.html

(ISO 27001:2022): International Organization for Standardization/International Electrotechnical Commission (ISO/IEC). (2022) ISO/IEC 27001:2022 – Infor-mation security, cybersecurity and privacy protection — Information security management systems — Requirements. Available at: https://www.iso.org/standard/27001

(ISO 29148:2018): ISO/IEC/IEEE 29148:2018 – Systems and software engineering — Life cycle processes — Requirements engineering. Available at: https://www.iso.org/standard/72089.html

(ISO 31000:2018): International Organization for Standardization (ISO). (2018) ISO 31000:2018 – Risk management — Guidelines. Available at: https://www.iso.org/standard/65694.html

(ISO 33001:2015): ISO/IEC 33001:2015(E) – Information technology – Process assessment – Concepts and terminology. 1st edn. Geneva: ISO. Available at: https://www.iso.org/standard/54175.html

(ISO 33002:2015): ISO/IEC 33002:2015(E) – Information technology – Process assessment – Requirements for performing process assessment. International Organization for Standardization. Available at: https://www.iso.org/standard/54176.html

(ISO 33004:2015): ISO/IEC 33004:2015(E) – Information technology – Process assessment – Requirements for process reference, process assessment and maturity models. International Organization for Standardization. Available at: https://www.iso.org/standard/54178.html

(ISO 33020:2019): ISO/IEC 33020:2019(E) – Information technology – Process assessment – Process measurement framework for assessment of process capability. International Organization for Standardization. Available at: https://www.iso.org/standard/78526.html

(ISO 42001:2023): ISO/IEC. (2023) ISO/IEC 42001:2023 – Artificial Intelligence Management Systems (AIMS). Available at: https://www.iso.org/standard/42001

(ISO 9001:2015): International Organization for Standardization, ISO 9001: Quality Management Systems – Requirements. Geneva: ISO. Available at: https://www.iso.org/standard/62085.html

(ISTQB 2024) International Software Testing Qualifications Board (ISTQB). Certified Tester Foundation Level Syllabus (CTFL) Version 4.0.1, Available at: https://istqb.org/wp-content/uploads/2024/11/ISTQB_CTFL_Syllabus_v4.0.1.pdf

(ISTQB 2025) International Software Testing Qualifications Board (ISTQB). Certified Tester – Testing with Generative AI (CT-GenAI) Version 1.0, Available at: https://istqb.org/wp-content/uploads/sdm-uploads/CT-GenAI-Syllabus-v1.0.pdf

(Jacobson 1999): Jacobson I, Booch G, Rumbaugh J.: The Unified Software Development Process. Reading, MA: Addison-Wesley.

(Johannsen et al 2020): Johannsen, A.; Kant, D.; Creutzburg, R.: Measuring IT security, compliance and digital sovereignty within small and medium-sized IT enterprises, in: IS&T International Symposium on Electronic Imaging 2020 Mobile Devices and Multimedia: Enabling Technologies, Algorithms, and Applications, San Francisco, January 2020. https://doi.org/10.2352/ISSN.2470-1173.2020.3.MOBMU-252

(Johannsen & Kant 2022): Johannsen, A. & Kant, K., IT-Governance-, Risiko- und Compliance-Management (IT-GRC) – Ein kompetenzorientierter Ansatz für KMU, in: Kristin Weber, Stefan Reinheimer (Eds.): Faktor Mensch (Edition HMD), Springer, Wiesbaden, 2022. Available at: https://doi.org/10.1007/978-3-658-34524-2_15

(Kelley 2005): Kelley, Tom, The Ten Faces of Innovation: IDEO's Strategies for Defeating the Devil's Advocate and Driving Creativity Throughout Your Organization, Crown Business Publishers.

(Kersten 2018): Mik Kersten: Project to Product: How to Survive and Thrive in the Age of Digital Disruption with the Flow Framework, IT Revolution, 2018, ISBN: 978-1942788393.

(Klünder et al. 2019) Klünder, J., Hebig, R., Tell, P., Kuhrmann, M. et al.: Catching up with method and process practice: An industry-informed baseline for researchers, in Proceedings of the ICSE-SEIP2019. Montréal, Canada, IEEE Computer Society Press, pp.255–264. https://doi.org/10.1109/ICSE-SEIP.2019.00036

(Knaster & Leffinwell 2020): Richard Knaster and Dean Leffingwell. SAFe 5.0 Distilled: Achieving Business Agility with the Scaled Agile Framework. Addison-Wesley, Boston, MA, USA,2020.

(KPMG 2022): Agile Transformation Survey 2022. KPMG International. Available at: https://home.kpmg/xx/en/home/insights/2022/11/global-agile-survey.html

(Kramer 2016): A. Kramer and B. Legeard. Model-Based Testing Essentials: Guide to the ISTQB Certified Model-Based Tester. John Wiley & Sons, Inc., Hoboken, NJ, USA, 2016. https://doi.org/10.1002/9781119130031

Kruchten, P. (2004). Scaling Down Large Projects to Meet the Agile "Sweet Spot". The Rational Edge, IBM developerWorks.

(Larman & Vodde 2017): Larman, C. & Vodde, B. Large-Scale Scrum: More with LeSS. 3. ed. Boston: Addison-Wesley Professional. ISBN 978-0-321-98571-0.

(Maximini 20218): Maximini, D. The Scrum Culture: Introducing Agile Methods in Organizations. 2nd edn. Springer International Publishing, Cham. ISBN 978-3-319-73841-3. https://doi.org/10.1007/978-3-319-73842-0

(Maylor & Turner 2022): Maylor, H. & Turner, N., Project Management (5th ed.). Pearson. ISBN: 978-1-292-08843-3.

(Meyer 2022): Meyer, B.: Handbook of Requirements and Business Analysis. Cham: Springer. https://doi.org/10.1007/978-3-031-06739-6. eText ISBN 978-3-031-06739-6.

(Mora et al. 2021): Mora, M., Wang, F., Phillips-Wren, G. and Gomez, M., The Role of DMSS Analytics Tools in Software Project Risk Management, In: Project Risk Management: Managing Software Development Risk (Engemann, K. and O'Connor, R., eds.), Walter de Gruyter GmbH, p 49–74. ISBN-13: 978-3110648232; ISBN-10: 3110648237.

(Moran 2014): Moran, A., Agile Risk Management. SpringerBriefs in Computer Science. Cham: Springer. ISBN-13: 978-3-319-05007-2; eBook ISBN: 978-3-319-05008-9. https://doi.org/10.1007/978-3-319-05008-9

(Mroz 2018): Mroz, J. et al., Do We Really Need Another Meeting? The Science of Workplace Meetings. Current Directions in Psychological Science. 27. 096372141877630. https://doi.org/10.1177/0963721418776307. Available at: https://www.researchgate.net/publication/328399884_Do_We_Really_Need_Another_Meeting_The_Science_of_Workplace_Meetings

(Nagy 2018) Gaspar Nagy and Seb Rose. 2018. Discovery: Explore behaviour using examples (Volume 1) (1st. ed.). CreateSpace Independent Publishing Platform, North Charleston, SC, USA. ISBN 978-1-9835-9125-9.

(Ng et al. 2004): Ng, S. T., Skitmore, R. M., Lam, K. C. & Poon, A. W. C. (2004) 'Demotivating factors influencing the productivity of civil engineering projects', International Journal of Project Management, 22(2), pp. 139–146. https://doi.org/10.1016/S0263-7863(03)00061-9

(Nilsson 2024): Marly Nilsson, Artificial Intelligence and Project Management. A global Chapter-Led Survey, Project Management Institute Sweden, Chapter Report, https://www.pmi.org/-/media/pmi/documents/public/pdf/artificial-intelligence/community-led-ai-and-project-management-report.pdf?rev=bca2428c1bbf4f6792f521a95333b4d

(Nito-Rodriguez & Vargas 2023): Nito-Rodriguez, Vargas, How Generative AI Will Change Project Management. Harvard Business Review, July 2023.

(Olson 2024): Olson, D. L. Project Management Tools. AI for Risks series. Singapore: Springer. https://doi.org/10.1007/978-981-97-1720-0

(Ochoa Pacheco et al. 2023): Ochoa Pacheco, P., Coello-Montecel, D., Tello, M., Lasio, V. & Armijos, A.; How do project managers' competencies impact project success? A systematic literature review. PLOS ONE, 18(12): e0295417. https://doi.org/10.1371/journal.pone.0295417. Available at (open access) 10.1371/journal.pone.0295417.

(O'Regan 2025): G. O'Regan: Guide to Software Project Management. Undergraduate Topics in Computer Science. Cham: Springer Nature. https://doi.org/10.1007/978-3-031-80578-3

(Parabol 2024). Agile and Scrum Statistics 2024. Parabol Inc. Available at: https://www.parabol.co/resources/agile-statistics

(Patton 2014): Patton, J. User Story Mapping: Discover the Whole Story, Build the Right Product. Sebastopol, CA: O'Reilly Media.

(Peters 2023): Peters, L., Software Project Management Myths. In V. Gupta, L. Rubalcaba, C. Gupta & T. Hanne (Eds.), Sustainability in Software Engineering and Business Information

Management: Proceedings of the Conference SSEBIM 2022 (pp. 98–110). Springer. https://doi.org/10.1007/978-3-031-32436-9

(Peters & Waterman 1984): Thomas J. Peters, Robert H. Waterman, In Search of Excellence: Lessons from America's Best-run Companies, Collins Business Essentials, ISBN 978-0063380028.

(Pichler 2010): Pichler, R., Agile Product Management with Scrum: Creating Products that Customers Love. Upper Saddle River, NJ: Addison-Wesley.

(Plattner, Meinel & Weinberg 2013): Plattner, H., Meinel, C., & Weinberg, U. Design Thinking: Understand – Improve – Apply. Berlin: Springer Vieweg. ISBN 978-3-642-26638-6.

(PMI 2022): Project Management Institute. Pulse of the Profession® 2023: Power Skills, Redefining Project Success (14th ed.). PMI. Available at: https://www.pmi.org/-/media/pmi/documents/public/pdf/learning/thought-leadership/pmi-pulse-of-the-profession-2023-report.pdf

(PMI 2025): Project Management Institute Pulse of the Profession 2025: Amplifying Impact in the Age of AI. PMI, Newtown Square, PA. Available at: https://www.pmi.org/learning/thought-leadership/pulse

(PRINCE2 2004): Office of Government Commerce, Managing Successful Projects with PRINCE2, (2004).

(Rankovic et al. 2024): Rankovic, N., Ranković, D., Ivanovic, M. & Lazić, L. (2024) Recent Advances in Artificial Intelligence in Cost Estimation in Project Management. Cham: Springer Nature. Artificial Intelligence-Enhanced Software and Systems Engineering, Vol. 6. https://doi.org/10.1007/978-3-031-76572-8

(Rashidi 2024): Rashidi, S., How To Use AI To Make You Faster And Better At Your Job, Forbes, 4 October. Available at: https://www.forbes.com/sites/solrashidi/2024/10/04/ai-tools-that-can-make-you-faster-and-better-at-your-job/

(Royce 1970): Winston D. Royce: Managing the Development of Large Software Systems, in Proc. IEEE, WESCON, 1970, www.cs.umd.edu/

(Scaled Agile 2025): SAFe® Explained: Succeeding with Lean and Agile at Scale. Scaled Agile, Inc., https://scaledagile.com/

(Schultz 2024): Schultz, B., 8 AI meeting assistants to consider in 2025, TechTarget Search Unified Communications, 30 December. Available at: https://www.techtarget.com/searchunifiedcommunications/tip/AI-meeting-assistants-to-consider

(Schwaber 1995) Schwaber, K., The Scrum Development Process. In: Proceedings of the 1995 OOPSLA Conference.

(Schwaber & Beedle 2002) Schwaber, K., Beedle, M., Agile software development with Scrum, Upper Saddle River, NJ, Prentice Hall, 2002.

(Schwaber & Sutherland 2020): K. Schwaber, J. Sutherland: The Scrum Guide: The definitive guide to Scrum: The rules of the game, (U.S. English ed.). https://scrumguides.org/scrum-guide.html

(SFIA8 2021): SFIA 8 Framework Reference, Skills Framework for the Information Age, Version 8, 2021. Available at: https://sfia-online.org/en/sfia-8

(Shastri et al. 2021): Y. Shastri, R. Hoda, R. Amor, Spearheading agile: the role of the scrum master in agile projects, in: Empirical Software Engineering (2021) 26: 3, p. 2–31, https://doi.org/10.1007/s10664-020-09899-4

(Standish 1996): Standish Group International, CHAOS: A Recipe for Success. West Yarmouth, MA: Standish Group International.

(Sutherland 2014): Jeff Sutherland: Scrum: The Art of Doing Twice the Work in Half the Time, 256 pages, ISBN-13 978-1847941107

(Sutherland 2022): Sutherland, J. The Scrum@Scale Guide: The Definitive Guide to the Scrum@Scale Framework, Version 2.1, Scrum Inc. Available at: https://www.scrumatscale.com/scrum-at-scale-guide-online/

(TechReport 2022): Scrum Usage Statistics 2022. TechReport, Business Workplace Research. Available at: https://techreport.com/statistics/business-workplace/scrum-usage-statistics

(Trendowicz & Jeffery 2014): Trendowicz, A. and Jeffery, R., Software Project Effort Estimation: Foundations and Best Practice, Guidelines for Success. Berlin: Springer. https://doi.org/10.1007/978-3-319-03629-8

(Troger 2022): Troger, H., Resetting Human Resource Management. Springer. https://doi.org/10.1007/978-3-031-06166-0

(Tuckman 1965): Bruce W. Tuckman: Developmental Sequence in Small Groups. Psychological Bulletin, 63(6), 384–399. https://doi.org/10.1037/h0022100

(Tursunbayeva 2024): Aizhan Tursunbayeva, Augmenting Human Resource Management with Artificial Intelligence: Towards an Inclusive, Sustainable, and Responsible Future, 2024, https://doi.org/10.1007/978-3-031-75266-7

(Uludağ 2022): Uludağ, Ö., Empirical Analysis of the Adoption of Large-Scale Agile Development Methods. PhD Dissertation, Technical University of Munich (TUM).

(Ulusoy & Hazir 2021): Ulusoy, G. & Hazır, Ö. (2021). An Introduction to Project Modeling and Planning. Springer Nature. https://doi.org/10.1007/978-3-030-61423-2

(Vanhoucke, 2014) Vanhoucke, M., Integrated Project Management and Control: First Comes the Theory, then the Practice. Berlin, Heidelberg: Springer. https://doi.org/10.1007/978-3-319-04331-9

(VDA QMC 2023): VDA Quality Management Center, Automotive SPICE® Process Assessment Model and Process Reference Model Version 4.0. Edited by the VDA QMC Working Group 13. Available at: https://vda-qmc.de/wp-content/uploads/2023/12/Automotive-SPICE-PAM-v40.pdf

(Visser & Arnold 2022): Max Visser, Thomas C. Arnold, Recognition and Work in the Platform Economy: a Normative Reconstruction, Philosophy of Management (2022) 21:31–45, Springer, https://doi.org/10.1007/s40926-021-00172-2

(Vo et al. 2022): Vo, T.T.D.; Tuliao, K.V.; Chen, C.-W. Work Motivation: The Roles of Individual Needs and Social Conditions. Behav. Sci. 2022, 12, 49, https://doi.org/10.3390/bs12020049

(Waters & Sroufe 1983): E. Waters; L.A. Sroufe, Social Competence as a Developmental Construct, Developmental Review, 3(1), 79–97.

(Watzlawick, Beavin & Jackson 1967): Watzlawick, P., Beavin, J. H. & Jackson, D. D. Pragmatics of Human Communication: A Study of Interactional Patterns, Pathologies, and Paradoxes. New York: W. W. Norton & Company. ISBN 978-0-393-31006-3.

(Weit 2024): Weit e. V., V-Modell XT: System development standard for IT projects, Release 2.4. Bonn: Weit e. V. (released May 2024).

(Wong 2018): Zachary Wong: The Eight Essential People Skills for Project Management: Solving the Most Common People Problems for Team Leaders, 256 pages, ISBN-13 978-1523097937.

(Wysocki 2019): Robert K. Wysocki: Effective Project Management: Traditional, Agile, Extreme, Hybrid, 656 pages, ISBN-13 978-1119562801.

(Yin et al. 2021): Likang Yin, Zhuangzhi Chen, Qi Xuan, and Vladimir Filkov: Sustainability Forecasting for Apache Incubator Projects, In: Proceedings of the 29th ACM Joint European Software Engineering Conference and Symposium on the Foundations of Software Engineering (ESEC/FSE '21), ACM, New York, USA, https://doi.org/10.1145/3468264.3468563

(Zheyuan Cui et al. 2024): K. Zheyuan Cui, M. Demirer, S. Ja, An MIT Exploration of Generative AI: From Novel Chemicals to Opera. Massachusetts Institute of Technology, Schwarzman College of Computing, https://doi.org/10.21428/e4baedd9.3ad85f1c, https://mit-genai.pubpub.org/pub/v5iixksv/download/pdf

Index

© The Editor(s) (if applicable) and The Author(s), under exclusive license to Springer Nature Switzerland AG 2026

A. Johannsen et al., *Foundations for Software Project Management in Classic and Agile Environments*, https://doi.org/10.1007/978-3-032-16797-2